73953

DATE DUE

PRAIRIE FIRE

The 1885 North-West Rebellion

Bob Beal & Rod Macleod

PRAIRIE FIRE

The 1885 North-West Rebellion

Hurtig Publishers
Edmonton

Hurtig Publishers Ltd.
10560–105 Street
Edmonton, Alberta
Canada   T5H 2W7

Canadian Cataloguing in Publication Data

Beal, Bob, 1949–
  Prairie fire

Includes index.
Bibliography: p. 362
ISBN 0-88830-262-2

1. Riel Rebellion, 1885. I. Macleod, R.C., 1940–
II. Title.
FC3215.B42 1984   971.05′4   C84-091286-2
F1060.9.B42 1984

Grateful acknowledgement is made for the assistance of the Riel Project Office of the University of Alberta in giving the authors proofs of *The Collected Writings of Louis Riel/Les Ecrits Complets de Louis Riel*, to be published in five volumes by the University of Alberta Press, 1985.

Editor: Nancy Marcotte
Design: David Shaw & Associates Ltd.
Composition: Attic Typesetting Inc.
Manufacturer: T.H. Best Printing Co. Ltd.

Edited, designed, typeset, printed, and bound in Canada for Hurtig Publishers Ltd.

Contents

Preface

The North-West Rebellion of 1885 cannot be said to have been neglected by historians. There are dozens of books and articles in print, many of them very good indeed. We undertook the project in the belief that the definitive history of the rebellion, whatever that elusive concept might mean, had yet to be written. Since the last full-scale history of the rebellion, Desmond Morton's *The Last War Drum*, appeared eleven years ago, a number of important documents bearing on the rebellion have appeared in various archives. Some important sources, particularly the newspapers, were not given sufficient attention by many previous writers. Historians depend on many people in their work, especially archivists. We would like to thank the many archivists who assisted us cheerfully and efficiently at the following repositories: Archives of Ontario, Toronto; Glenbow-Alberta Institute, Calgary; Hudson's Bay Company Archives, Winnipeg; Metropolitan Toronto Library; Montana Historical Society, Helena; Oregon Province Archives, Society of Jesus, Spokane; Provincial Archives of Alberta, Edmonton; Provincial Archives of Manitoba, Winnipeg; Public Archives of Canada, Ottawa; and Saskatchewan Archives Board, Regina.

Claude Rocan of the Riel Project, University of Alberta, very kindly let us make use of a copy of the definitive edition of Riel's writings before they were published. The History Department, University of Alberta, provided a base for the writing of the book as well as many patient and helpful friends to discuss it with. Olive Dickason, Des Brown, John Foster, Doug Owram, Paul Voisey, Burton Smith, David Mills, and Brian Beaven were all subjected to discussion of the manuscript from time to time. Jim Robb of the Faculty of Law, University of Alberta, provided valuable advice on some of the legal issues involved in the trials of the rebels. The Historic Sites officials at Battleford and Batoche were most helpful during a tour of the battle sites. Where practical, we have used modern phonetic spellings of Cree names and where appropriate the English translations. Anne Anderson helped us in that task. This book was written on a Franklin 1000 computer; our special thanks to Phil King for his technical expertise. Zoltan Pinter and the staff at MICR Microsystems were very helpful in reproducing hundreds of pages of microfilmed documents. Artist Rick Pape helped with the newspaper illustrations. Lillian Wonders drew the maps. Nancy Marcotte was a very efficient and helpful editor whose work made this a better book. Our families—Joanna and Christopher; Elaine, Laura and Daphne—were patient and supportive.

Research for the book would not have been possible without the assistance of a Canada Council Explorations grant.

Maps

PART ONE

Waiting for a Spark

CHAPTER ONE

The Métis and Red River

The cold spring of 1885 was the last time that Canadians took up arms and fought other Canadians in an effort to overthrow the duly-constituted government of the country. The rebellion that broke out that year on the banks of the Saskatchewan River bore a strong resemblance to the prairie fires that the early settlers of the region came to know and fear. These conflagrations could be caused by lightning strikes or other acts of God, but as often as not they resulted from human negligence or were deliberately set. The native population used fires as a tool in hunting and game management. Settlers sometimes set fires to rid their lands of unwanted weeds and stubble and make spring cultivation easier. When the railroad came, sparks from the engines frequently started fires along the tracks. Regardless of how they started, prairie fires were terrifying in their intensity and very difficult to stop once they had taken hold. After a brief but destructive rampage, they would stop as quickly as they had arisen.

So it was with the rebellion of 1885. Its causes are to be found partly in carelessness and incompetence, partly in deliberate acts that were the equivalent of setting a match to dry grass, and partly in plain bad luck. The rebellion blazed up quickly and to some degree unexpectedly, although many experienced observers in the North-West Territories had been saying for months that conditions were ripe and only a spark was needed to set off the blaze. The rebellion swept through the central portions of the Territories before being snuffed out with dramatic suddenness at the battle of Batoche. The intensity of the uprising was offset to a considerable degree by its briefness. The rebellion left no real legacy of bitterness in the West, although its repercussions in national politics were profound. The rebellion was essentially an incident in the occupation of the North-West Territories by white settlers and the imposition of their institutions of government on the indigenous population. A little more flexibility, generosity, and attention to the special problems of the region on the part of those who were administering the territory would have prevented the bloodshed that occurred.

One of the more widespread popular notions about the rebellion is that it was almost entirely a Métis affair, planned and fought by the mixed-blood population with some rather half-hearted participation by a few Indians. This misconception is natural enough because the leader of the rebellion, Louis Riel, was a Métis, and his personality was so compelling that attention has tended to focus on him and his people to the exclusion of the other participants. The way things worked out, also, it was the Métis who did most of the fighting on the rebel side. But if the events leading up to the rebellion are examined, a different picture emerges. The Indians, and to a lesser degree the white settlers, were inextricably involved in the outbreak. No rebellion would have occurred in 1885 if these two groups had not been seriously alienated by a distant and uncaring government. When it came to the crunch, most of the whites and Indians were not quite ready to join Riel and the Métis in 1885, but they were close enough to lead Riel to believe that he could count on active support from some and at least neutrality from the rest. The rebellion cannot be understood without an examination of the predicament of each component of the population.

None of this is to deny the central role of Louis Riel or the importance of his people. Riel was one of those truly charismatic leaders who so often come from the peripheries of the societies they influence: Hitler was Austrian, not German; Napoleon Bonaparte was a Corsican but became leader of the French; Alexander the Great came from Macedonia but conquered the world as leader of the Greeks. Louis Riel, whose personality dominated the Canadian political scene periodically from 1870 to 1885, falls into this category. Born into an obscure group of people in a remote corner of British North America, always poor and occasionally mad, he nevertheless fascinated almost everyone who met him and many thousands who never saw him, whether they hailed him as a prophet and saviour of his people or despised him as a hypocrite and rebel. The fascination has continued to the present day. Indeed it would be fair to say that no other Canadian figure has attracted such consistent attention over the years. Histories, plays, and even an opera have been written about his life, not to mention a dozen or so biographies and assorted movies and television programs. Hanged for treason, he has become a popular hero both in French Canada and the West. Two provincial capitals have statues of him and over the years there have been several campaigns attempting to persuade the federal government to pardon him.

Part of Riel's magnetic appeal came from the fact that he was highly intelligent, even brilliant. The quality of his mind had been noted very early by the priests who ran the schools in the isolated community at Red River where he grew up. Young Louis was chosen to be the first Métis sent to Canada to be trained for the priesthood. After some initial difficulties there he proved an excellent student, his failure to complete the course being due to emotional rather than intellectual problems. Although he did not receive a diploma, his years in Montreal left him with an impressive grasp of law, politics, and foreign relations.[1]

Riel's sense of humour was well-developed, although it ran heavily to puns. He could not resist them, even in times of intense stress. On March 19, 1885, Riel and his followers seized the church of St. Antoine de Padoue at Batoche, a fateful and irreversible move. The resident priest, Father Moulin, tried to resist and said, "I protest your touching the church." Riel replied, "Look at him, he is a Protestant."[2] Puns are not much to the modern taste but in the nineteenth century they were much more popular and respectable. In the midst of the rebellion the Winnipeg *Times* published an extensive collection of puns on Riel's name gleaned from American newspapers under the headline RIEL FUNNY. The general impression Riel made on people was summed up by a priest who knew him well in the last year of his life and described him as "affable, polite, pleasant and a charitable man"[3] as long as religion and politics did not enter the conversation.

Riel came from an intensely pious family and grew up to be a deeply religious man. Father Alexis André, the stern and austere Oblate priest who led the Church's opposition to Riel in the spring of 1885 and who was appalled by Riel's heresies, confessed a reluctant admiration for the depth of his piety. Riel's diaries from the final year of his life reveal a man obsessed by religion. He saw every event, even the most mundane, as significant in terms of his unique beliefs. In his persona as "prophet of the new world," which became increasingly dominant in 1885, Riel liked to speak in dark, ambiguous phrases. On March 18, 1885, when Dr. John Willoughby tried to find out Riel's intentions, he would reply only that it would be well in the immediate future for a man to have lived a good life. Those who openly disagreed with him on religious topics, even close friends, risked provoking outbursts of rage. Political arguments, which to Riel were virtually indistinguishable from religious questions, brought equally violent responses. When his cousin Charles Nolin disagreed with him shortly after the rebellion began, Riel wanted to execute him and had to be restrained by his council.

The people who produced this passionate and contradictory man had emerged in the area known as Rupert's Land in the late eighteenth century. They were, of course, the racially mixed descendants of marriages (known as *mariages à la façon du pays*) between fur traders and native women. But racial mixing alone does not produce a new people. At first there is an overwhelming tendency for the offspring to assimilate totally to the society of one parent or the other. It has sometimes been said that the Métis appeared nine months after the first white man set foot ashore in North America, but the truth is that the process took about a century and required a distinctive set of social and economic circumstances. The right circumstances existed for long enough only in the area that was to become Western Canada and a few small adjacent parts of the United States, and it was only in the Canadian West that the Métis existed as a self-conscious and culturally distinct people.

The fur trade was the single most important force in shaping the new people. For more than two centuries the fur trade was the only form of commercial activity in the gigantic tract of territory that ran from Hudson Bay west to the Pacific and from the 49th Parallel north to the Arctic Ocean. From 1821 to 1870 the fur trade was a legal monopoly of the Hudson's Bay Company. By the beginning of the nineteenth century the mixed-blood descendants of fur traders and Indian women had carved out a distinctive niche for themselves in the economic life of the trade and were on the way to becoming a separate people. They had taken over the bulk of the semi-autonomous service functions necessary for the successful operation of the trade, manning the boat brigades that brought supplies to the inland posts and returned the furs to salt water and hunting the buffalo to make the pemmican that fueled the whole enormous transportation network.

This is not to say that there were no mixed bloods who hunted and trapped with the Indian bands and spoke mainly Cree. There were many of these, but in every sense except the biological, they were Indians. There were also a few mixed bloods who had been sent to school in England or Canada and were employed by the fur companies as traders. They too, although they undoubtedly encountered more resistance and prejudice than those who assimilated to the native culture, were essentially Europeans with slightly darker skins. Those in the middle who followed the buffalo hunt and who spoke both French and Cree were the forerunners of the Métis, the beginnings of the "New Nation" that was starting to emerge at the end of the eighteenth century. By 1816 they were sufficiently conscious of their collective identity to become involved in the so-called Seven Oaks Massacre. This was an incident that took place June 19, 1816, in which the Métis attacked the newly founded settlement at Red River that had been established by Lord Selkirk and the Hudson's Bay Company. The Governor of the settlement, Robert Semple, and twenty-one of the settlers were killed, as well as one Métis. The Métis saw the incident as an effort to defend their territory against encroachment by outsiders.

Paradoxically, Lord Selkirk's settlement at Red River, which at first seemed to threaten the Métis, quickly became one of the most significant factors in the development of their identity. In 1821, only five years after Seven Oaks, the British government imposed a merger which brought an end to the bitter rivalry between the Hudson's Bay Company and the North-West Company. The end of competition meant drastically reduced manpower requirements in the fur trade and created an immediate unemployment crisis among the Métis. The existence of the Red River settlement helped to cushion the blow and make possible the transition to a new way of life. In 1818, the Roman Catholic Church had established at Red River a mission which from the start concentrated its efforts on the Métis. The church encouraged the Métis to take up land at Red River, and subsistence agriculture gradually emerged as a supplement to the buffalo hunt.

But despite the efforts of the church and the economic pressures created by the monopoly of the Hudson's Bay Company, the annual buffalo hunt remained the most important fact of Métis life. These hunts were organized with military precision and involved the whole Métis community. In June 1840 an enormous cavalcade consisting of 1210 two-wheeled Red River carts, 620 hunters, 650 women, 360 children, 1058 horses, 586 oxen, and 542 dogs left Red River. They stopped at Pembina, just south of the 49th Parallel, where they chose the leaders of the hunt and reaffirmed the rules that would govern the conduct of all who went along. In 1840 the senior of the ten captains chosen was Jean-Baptiste Wilkie, a man who would later become the father-in-law of the greatest of all Métis hunters, Gabriel Dumont. Alexander Ross, the first historian of Red River, went along on the 1840 hunt and has left a detailed description of how it was organized.

Each captain had ten soldiers under his orders; in much the same way that policemen are subject to the magistrate. Ten guides are likewise appointed; and here we may remark that people in a rude state of society, unable either to read or write, are generally partial to the number ten. Their duties were to guide the camp, each in his turn—that is day about—during the expedition. The camp flag belongs to the guide of the day; he is therefore standard-bearer in virtue of his office.

The hoisting of the flag every morning is the signal for raising camp. Half an hour is the full time allowed to prepare for the march; but if anyone is sick, or their animals have strayed, notice is sent to the guide, who halts till all is made right. From the time the flag is hoisted, however, till the hour of camping arrives, it is never taken down. The flag taken down is the signal for encamping. While it is up, the guide is the chief of the expedition. Captains are subject to him, and the soldiers of the day are his messengers: he commands all. The moment the flag is lowered, his functions cease and the captain's and soldier's duties commence. They point out the order of the camp, and every cart, as it arrives, moves to its appointed place. The business usually occupies about the same time as raising camp in the morning; for everything moves with the regularity of clock-work.

Before leaving Pembina, a council of the chief hunters ratified the traditional rules for the hunt, which did not vary from year to year:

1. No buffalo to be run on the Sabbath day.
2. No party to fork off, lag behind, or go before, without permission.
3. No person or party to run buffalo before the general order.
4. Every captain with his men, in turn, to patrol the camp, and keep guard.
5. For the first trespass against these laws, the offender to have his saddle and bridle cut up.
6. For the second offence, the coat to be taken off the offender's back and be cut up.
7. For the third offence, the offender to be flogged.

8. Any person convicted of theft, even to the value of a sinew, to be brought to the middle of the camp, the crier to call out his or her name three times, adding the word "Thief" at each time.

The hunt, as Ross described it, was a lively, jovial affair but the carefree atmosphere could not hide the fact that many of the Métis were desperately poor after a hard winter.

The state of the families in the camp revealed to me the true state of things: that one half of them were generally starving. Some I did see with a little tea, and cups and saucers too—rather fragile ware for such a mode of life—but with a few exceptions of this kind, the rest disclosed nothing but scenes of misery and want: some had a few pounds of flour; others, less fortunate, a little wheat and barley, which they singed, and were glad to eat in that state. Others, again, had no earthly thing but what chance put in their way—a pheasant, a crow, or a squirrel; and when they failed they had to go to bed supperless, or satisfy the pangs of hunger with a few wild roots, which I saw the children devour in a raw state! A plains hunter's life is truly a dog's life—feast or famine.

It was almost three weeks before the hunt of 1840 reached the buffalo, after having travelled four hundred kilometres. When the herd was finally located, more than four hundred hunters lined up waiting for the order from Captain Wilkie to spur their horses forward and begin firing. "Those who have seen a squadron of horse dash into battle may imagine the scene, which we have no skill to depict. The earth seemed to tremble when the horses started; but when the animals fled, it was like the shock of an earthquake. The air was darkened; the firing rapid at first, soon became more and more faint, and at last died away in the distance. Two hours and all was over; but several hours more elapsed before the result was known, or the hunters reassembled."[4] They had killed twenty-five hundred buffalo.

Two months after the expedition started, after more hunts and a brush with the Sioux, the hunters were back home at Red River. In his description, Ross bemoans the waste that had occurred during the hunt. Some animals were abandoned untouched after they were killed. Many other carcasses were used only for the tongue or some other choice morsel. Young females were preferred but it wasn't always easy to pick them out in the mad excitement of the chase. The wastefulness and the selective killing of breeding stock had already begun to make an impact on the numbers of the buffalo by 1840. The hunters had to travel farther every year to find the herds, and there was increasing competition and tension with the Sioux.

The community the hunters returned to every August at the junction of the Red and the Assiniboine was tiny and isolated yet highly complex. In addition to

16

the Métis, who were the most numerous group, there were a substantial number of English-speaking Protestants of mixed blood. These people were sometimes called English Métis, sometimes referred to as "country-born," but whatever the label, they were a distinct group who lived in their own section of the community and interacted relatively little with their French-speaking counterparts. The descendants of the original Selkirk settlers retained their cohesiveness as a major component of Red River society. A smaller but wealthier and more influential group were the retired Hudson's Bay Company servants and their families. The smallest significant group consisted of a few French Canadian families who had been recruited by the Roman Catholic Church and settled on the east bank of the Red River along a small tributary called the Seine.

The Métis were set apart from the other groups by their semi-nomadic way of life. William F. Butler in his book *The Great Lone Land* characterized them as "gay, idle, dissipated, unreliable, and ungrateful, in a measure brave, hasty to form conclusions and quick to act upon them, possessing extraordinary powers of endurance and capable of undergoing immense fatigue, yet scarcely ever to be depended on in critical moments, and ignorant, having a very deep-rooted distaste to any fixed employment, opposed to the Indian, yet widely separated from the white man—altogether a race presenting, I fear, a hopeless prospect to those who would attempt to frame, from such materials, a future nationality."[5]

This was the point of view of an outsider who had only observed the Métis for a few months and whose attitude may have been coloured by a run-in with Riel in 1870. Alexander Ross, who spent most of his life at Red River, had a more balanced assessment.

> The half-breeds are by no means ill-disposed people—on the contrary, they possess many good qualities; while enjoying a sort of licentious freedom, they are generous, warm-hearted and brave, and left to themselves, quiet and orderly. They are, unhappily, as unsteady as the wind in all their habits, fickle in their dispositions, credulous in their faith and clannish in their affections. . . .
>
> These people are all politicians, but of a peculiar creed, favouring a barbarous state of society and self-will; for they cordially detest all the laws and restraints of civilized life, believing all men were born to be free. In their own estimation they are all great men, and wonderfully wise; and so long as they wander about on these wild and lawless expeditions, they will never become a thoroughly civilized people, nor orderly subject in a civilized community. Feeling their own strength, from being constantly armed, and free from control, they despise all others; but above all they are marvellously tenacious of their own original habits. They cherish freedom as they cherish life.[6]

The Métis retained few of the customs of their native ancestors. They did not have anything like a Cree Thirst Dance (sometimes mistakenly called the Sun Dance) in which the young men submitted themselves to torture by putting wooden pegs through the flesh of their chests as a test of manhood. The Métis did not develop a warrior society. Although they engaged in warfare with various Indian bands who regarded them as usurping their hunting grounds, their wars tended to be purely defensive. Stealing enemy horses was not the essential mark of status for the Métis that it was for the Indians. Christianity was almost universal among the Métis and their social organization was much closer to that of the white community than the Indian.

They did take one custom directly from the Plains Indians because it was necessary to cope with the precarious life of a plains nomad. Those who were fortunate in the hunt (or later in business) were expected to share the wealth. Generosity was an essential attribute of great leadership among the Métis as it was a mark of great chieftainship among the Indians. John Kerr, an Ontarian who lived among the Métis on the plains in the 1870s, once came across an Indian who had been gambling with Gabriel Dumont and had lost almost everything he owned. When Kerr stumbled on the man's teepee in the woods, he was sick and the family near starvation. Kerr told the Indian's story to Gabriel, who went to the rescue with a sled loaded with provisions and medicine. Gabriel didn't expect to be repaid; it was simply his duty as a Métis leader to take care of the hungry and sick.[7] Individual saving and frugality, which were seen as virtues by the whites, appeared very different to the Métis.

Although it appeared stable to the point of somnolence, Red River had its internal strains and tensions. The economy of the settlement was always precarious and even in good years depended heavily on the buffalo hunts to feed the population. The spread of American settlement into Minnesota brought American fur traders into direct contact with Red River and threatened the trading monopoly of the Hudson's Bay Company. The company responded by attempting to use its governing powers over Rupert's Land to enforce its monopoly. The result was an explosion which exposed the underlying tensions and divisions in the community.

A system of courts had existed at Red River since the 1830s, mainly to settle local disputes over land and property and deal with petty crime. The authority of the court, however, rested entirely on community consensus since no effective enforcement agency existed to back up its rulings. Thus when a Métis named Guillaume Sayer was charged in 1849 with violating the company's monopoly, no one dared arrest him. The company persisted with the prosecution and on the trial day the court was surrounded by an armed and angry crowd of Métis led by Louis Riel, a member of the French Canadian community and owner of a mill on the Seine. In the face of this threat the court sensibly declined to sentence Sayer and the monopoly of the company was effectively broken. The power of the company was waning but it would be another generation before it disappeared altogether.

Far to the east, a small group of individuals in Toronto had begun to assert Canadian claims to a territory that most of their countrymen, in the unlikely event that they thought of it at all, thought of as a frozen wasteland. This movement was part of the revolution that took place in the 1850s in attitudes towards the Interior Great Plains region of North America. For a variety of reasons, what had been perceived as desert was suddenly considered to be potentially rich agricultural land. Geographers were discovering that the climate of the interior was less severe than had been believed. The railway almost magically promised to make impossibly remote areas accessible. The Hudson's Bay Company, whose trading monopoly was due to be reviewed by the British Parliament in 1859, vigorously denied that any of its vast territories could support agriculture. To investigate the situation, both the British and Canadian governments sent scientific expeditions to the Prairies, the British under Captain John Palliser in 1857, the Canadian under Henry Youle Hind in 1858. Helping to fuel this new interest in Rupert's Land was a fear on the part of both Britain and Canada that the territory was in danger of being swallowed up by the rapidly expanding frontier of settlement in the United States. The Americans had simply moved in and taken over Texas and California in this manner. Even more recently Oregon, which had once been the exclusive domain of the Hudson's Bay Company, had passed from British control under threats of war by the United States.

The outbreak of the American Civil War in 1861 temporarily eased these anxieties, but the end of that conflict in 1865 brought them back with greater force than ever. Political difficulties that in the 1850s had prevented Canada from pursuing its claims to the territory had been resolved by Confederation in 1867. The colony of British Columbia on the west coast appeared ready and willing to join if the fate of the intervening territory could be settled. Serious negotiations for the transfer of the Hudson's Bay Company territories to Canada began almost as soon as the new federal government was organized. By the spring of 1869 agreement had been reached. Canada would buy out the Hudson's Bay Company for £300,000 sterling and one-twentieth of the land between the 49th Parallel and the North Saskatchewan River. The Company would surrender its rights to the British government, which would transfer them to Canada on December 1, 1869.

The major flaw in this arrangement was that neither side had bothered to consult the inhabitants of Red River. While most of its population would have preferred it to remain a separate British colony once the company gave up its responsibilities, there was no deeply rooted hostility to a Canadian takeover, in spite of the unpopularity of the small group of aggressive Canadian annexationists who had moved into the settlement in the 1860s. Some credible reassurances from the British government, the Hudson's Bay Company, or the Canadian government that the rights and property of the inhabitants would be respected, and some minimal consultation with community leaders, would have prevented trouble; but there was no consultation and the promises to respect local rights came too late to be believed.

Because the Métis were the largest group at Red River and had the most vigorous tradition of direct action in defence of their interests, it was scarcely surprising that they took the lead in resisting the Canadian takeover and demanding guarantees of their rights. What was more unexpected was the emergence as Métis leader of twenty-five-year-old Louis Riel, son of the Louis Riel who had organized the Métis during the Sayer trial in 1849. Riel eventually became the leader of the whole Red River community.

Riel returned to Red River in 1868 after a decade away from his homeland. Most of that time had been spent at a Jesuit college in Montreal where Riel had done well as a student but had withdrawn a few months before graduation due to an emotional crisis engendered by an unhappy love affair. After articling for a short time in a law office and failing to convince his prospective father-in-law that he was worthy of his daughter, Riel left the city and headed west, spending some time in Minnesota before arriving back at Red River.

Young Louis followed with great interest the mounting tension in the Red River community over the impending transfer of territory. Resentment and anxiety were rife among all the long-term inhabitants, especially the Métis. Why should the Hudson's Bay Company get £300,000 and the people of Red River nothing? What was going to happen to their language and religion under Canadian rule? What would become of their long, narrow river-lot farms under the new square survey system? All these questions came to a head in August 1869 when the Canadian government sent in a survey party under the leadership of J. S. Dennis. Encouraged by a young priest, Father J. N. Ritchot, Riel began to speak out in public against the surveys. By September Riel had persuaded his people to elect two representatives from each parish to a Métis "National Committee," of which he acted as secretary.

The committee made plans to halt the takeover but took no action until the survey crew neared land which was actually occupied. On October 11, when the crew attempted to run a line across the farm of André Nault, Riel and a few others from the National Committee barred the way. Word had arrived by this time that William McDougall had been chosen as the first Lieutenant Governor of the territory and was on his way from Canada to take over. The Métis decided to put into effect their plan to bar him from the territory until Ottawa was prepared to negotiate satisfactory guarantees. On November 2, 1869, armed men turned back McDougall's party at the American border, and Riel and his followers seized Fort Garry from the Hudson's Bay Company. Possession of Fort Garry gave the Métis effective military control of Red River until late the following spring, the earliest time that Canadian troops could reach the territory.

Louis Riel in 1879 in Montana. Five years later he would be again leading the Canadian Métis. [Glenbow-Alberta Institute]

The only serious challenges to Riel's leadership came from within the settlement. The English-speaking section of the community was disturbed by Riel's tactics and the small group of Canadians under the leadership of their most prominent figure, Dr. John Christian Schultz, was actively organizing itself to counter the Métis ascendancy. It was essential to consolidate his political base at once and Riel set about doing so in very impressive fashion. At a series of meetings through the month of November, Riel did his utmost to convince the English that a provisional government chosen by the entire community was the best way to approach negotiations with Canada. He encountered stubborn opposition because the English side of the community, as well as a few of the Métis, believed that creating a provisional government amounted to an act of rebellion.

Lieutenant Governor McDougall broke the stalemate with a hasty and foolish action. Assuming that the transfer of the territory to Canada would take place on December 1 as planned, he issued a proclamation announcing that Hudson's Bay Company rule was at an end. At the same time he appointed J. S. Dennis "Lieutenant and Conservator of the Peace" and empowered him to recruit and arm a body of men to impose the authority of the Canadian government. The most obvious source of recruits for Dennis was among the Canadian settlers, about fifty of whom had barricaded themselves in Dr. Schultz's house. Riel had no choice but to confront the situation directly if he wished to remain in control. He and his men surrounded the house, arrested the Canadians, and marched them off to cells in Fort Garry. A few days later news arrived that gave a semblance of legality to Riel's actions. The transfer of the territory had not taken place after all but had been postponed indefinitely at the request of the Canadian government. Hudson's Bay Company authority had ended and since there was no effective Canadian authority to replace it, a provisional government was a virtual necessity. The provisional government was proclaimed December 10 and Riel became president just over two weeks later. Dennis and McDougall retreated ignominiously to Canada.

By the time Riel proclaimed his provisional government, Prime Minister John A. Macdonald had already decided that he had no choice but to negotiate. Just before Christmas the first two Canadian delegates, Grand Vicar Jean-Baptiste Thibault and Colonel Charles de Salaberry, arrived at Red River. They brought with them promises of an amnesty and assurances of good will on the part of the Canadian government. On January 5 the third Canadian representative, Donald A. Smith of the Hudson's Bay Company, made his appearance. He alone had authority to negotiate.

Smith spent two weeks sounding out the situation and attempting to wean influential Métis away from their allegiance to Riel. He then proposed a mass meeting of the entire Red River community to hear him explain the Canadian position. On January 19 more than a thousand people gathered in temperatures

22

of thirty-three degrees below zero Celsius at Fort Garry to hear Smith, who had so many documents to read that the meeting had to be continued the following day. At Riel's suggestion it was decided that twenty English and twenty French delegates should be elected to meet with Smith and decide on the basis for a settlement. Elections were held and the forty met and managed to agree on a "List of Rights," although debate was often heated to the point of violence. The list would be sent to Ottawa in the keeping of three delegates from Red River. In the meantime Riel and his provisional government were confirmed in control. Everyone relaxed and Riel sent many of his Métis "soldiers" home.

But there were those in the settlement who were not party to the agreement that legitimized the provisional government. The Canadian prisoners remained in jail, except for Dr. Schultz and a few other leading spirits who had broken out. The escapees had made their way to the outlying areas of the settlement, most of them, although not Schultz, going to Portage la Prairie. Plans were made to march to Fort Garry and release the remaining prisoners. The plotters were so slow in getting organized that by the time they got to Fort Garry, Riel had already set the prisoners free. When they discovered what had happened, the Portage group turned for home but were almost immediately surrounded and arrested by Riel's men. The situation was tense and confused and it is not surprising that the intentions of a group of armed men so close to the headquarters of the provisional government should be misread. The leader of the group, Charles A. Boulton, was tried by court-martial and sentenced to be shot on February 17.

After hearing pleas from a number of people, including Donald Smith, Riel backed down and agreed to spare Boulton's life. He traded clemency for stronger support for the provisional government from Smith and the leaders of the English parishes. The incident strengthened Riel's hand to the point that the two most prominent Canadian leaders, Dr. Schultz and Charles Mair, despaired of overthrowing the provisional government and secretly left Red River for Ontario. Their departure left the remaining prisoners under the dubious leadership of Thomas Scott. Born and raised in Northern Ireland, Scott had immigrated to Ontario, where he had lived for seven years before coming to Red River to work on the road that was under construction to the Lakehead. Scott was a large, physically strong man, bigoted, quick-tempered, and violent. In the summer of 1869 he had been fined for assaulting his employer.

After his second capture Scott refused to accept his status as a prisoner. He assaulted and verbally abused his guards at every opportunity. Interpreting Riel's clemency in Boulton's case as timidity, Scott dared the Métis to shoot him. After two weeks of listening to Scott, his guards decided they would be happy to oblige. They told Riel that if something were not done, they would take matters into their own hands. On March 3 Scott was tried in the same manner as Boulton and sentenced to be shot. This time Riel refused to listen to any pleas for mercy

and Scott was executed by firing squad the following day. The shooting of Scott was Riel's single important error in the whole episode. Scott's death provided Schultz and Mair with the symbol they needed to arouse the people of Ontario. Scott had been a member of the immensely influential Orange Order, and it was easy to portray him as a martyr to the French Catholics who were trying to deny Protestant Ontario its rightful heritage. Feelings were running so high that in April, when the Red River delegates arrived in Ottawa, they were arrested and jailed for a short time. They were quickly released by the government, and in spite of the mounting furore in Ontario, Parliament quickly passed the Manitoba Act, which embodied the "List of Rights."

Ottawa did not even balk at accepting the demand for the immediate creation of a new province. Smith had indicated that this demand was unacceptable to Ottawa and after lengthy debate the provisional government had dropped it. Riel unilaterally put it back in before the delegates went East. The other main features of the Manitoba Act were guarantees of protection for the French language and denominational schools and, in addition to the confirmation of all existing land claims, the setting aside of 1.4 million acres of land for the Métis and their children.

The main street of the village of Batoche where the Saskatchewan Métis would make their headquarters after the Red River resistance. This photograph was taken shortly after the 1885 rebellion. On the right is Xavier (Batoche) Letendre's store. Next door is Philippe Garnot's stopping house. [Saskatchewan Archives Board]

Ottawa's concession to the outrage in Ontario over the Scott execution was to send a military expedition to Red River in the summer of 1870. The British government contributed a commander, Colonel Garnet Joseph Wolseley, and a regiment of troops, the 60th Rifles. Two Canadian Militia battalions, one from Quebec and one from Ontario, completed the little force, which totalled just over a thousand men. A new Lieutenant Governor, Adams G. Archibald, was sent out separately to emphasize the fact that this was not a military conquest of Red River. Riel remained in charge of the provisional government at Fort Garry until the troops were almost in sight on August 24. Then, giving in at the last moment to rumours that he would be arrested or murdered, he fled into hiding.

Riel was to remain a fugitive for the next five years. He and two others were exempted from the general amnesty granted to all those who had participated in the resistance. In and out of hiding in Canada and across the border in Minnesota, he was three times elected to the House of Commons. On the third occasion, in 1874, when he attempted to take his seat, the government was finally forced to deal with the situation. After long and bitter debate, the House voted to deprive Riel of his seat and exiled him to the United States for a period of five years. At this point the strain and exhaustion of living in hiding caught up with Riel. His friends were forced to commit him to an insane asylum.

Some of Riel's people stayed in Manitoba and adapted to the rapidly changing conditions after 1870. The majority were not yet ready to abandon the excitement of the buffalo hunt for the steady and secure, but tedious, life of the farm. The land-scrip issued by the government to each family could as easily be exchanged for cash as for land and most of it found its way into the hands of white speculators. Several locations in the vast region west of Manitoba offered the Métis better access to the dwindling herds of buffalo and freedom from the noisy and aggressive settlers from Ontario. A large temporary settlement sprang up on Buffalo Lake while a more permanent community began to coalesce under the auspices of the Oblate priests. The new focus of Métis life centred around the place where the Carlton Trail, the main route between Winnipeg and Edmonton, crossed the South Saskatchewan River. A Métis trader named Xavier Letendre *dit* Batoche established himself there, a few miles upstream from the church headquarters at St. Laurent, and the place quickly became known as Batoche's Crossing or simply Batoche.

CHAPTER TWO

Settlers and Government

While most of Ottawa's attention was focused on the Indians in the North-West Territories in the decade and a half after 1870, the government had not lost sight of its primary goal: to fill the Prairies with white settlers. Furthermore the Canadian government wanted to control every detail of the settlement process from the centre. Strong government institutions would be established in the West before most of the settlers got there and there would be little local autonomy for the foreseeable future. This administrative philosophy was based in about equal measure on the innate Canadian longing for order and the very practical consideration that local conflicts in the North-West could not be allowed to escalate into a ruinously-expensive Indian war. The American example was, as always, much on the minds of Canadian legislators. The Americans encouraged local autonomy and rapid movement to statehood in their western territories and what Canadians saw in that process was a lack of federal government control leading to anarchy and to bloody and expensive warfare with the Indians. As far as Canadians were concerned, there was a direct connection between the American commitment to local autonomy and the fact that the United States government was spending twenty million dollars a year fighting the Plains Indians by 1870. That was a million more than the total Canadian budget.

In the early 1870s the Lieutenant Governor of the North-West Territories was a virtual dictator. He had a small advisory council, also appointed by Ottawa, but even had the council been disposed to oppose the Lieutenant Governor, there was little they could do since he alone controlled government spending. In 1873 the government took steps to provide the Lieutenant Governor with powerful administrative backing. First a new department, the Department of the Interior, was created specifically to manage the vast new empire in the West. It was given control over Indian Affairs, the survey, mining, crown lands, and homestead regulations—just about everything that really mattered in the region. At the same time the North-West Mounted Police were established and were given extraordinary powers to ensure that Ottawa's policies were carried out. The fundamental policy of tight central control over the Territories and the machinery to make the policy effective was the work of the Conservative government of John A. Macdonald. His Liberal opponents, in theory, favoured more local autonomy. When in office from 1874 to 1878, however, they showed little interest in making basic changes in the administration of the North-West Territories. The fledgling Mounted Police, after momentary hesitation by the incoming Liberal Prime Minister, Alexander Mackenzie, were allowed to continue recruiting and organizing in Ontario, and it was Prime Minister Mackenzie who ordered them west in the spring of 1874. The following year the Liberal government passed a North-West Territories Act which, while it made provision for the election of members to the Territorial Council at some future date, imposed conditions that meant that the first elections could not be held for six years. It would be twenty years before the Territories achieved responsible government and thirty before new provinces were created. There was no provision in the 1875 Act for representation of the North-West Territories in the Senate or the House of Commons.

On the positive side, the Liberals did give the North-West its own Lieutenant Governor and capital. Up to 1875 the Lieutenant Governor of Manitoba had also been Lieutenant Governor of the Territories and the government was physically located in Winnipeg. In 1876 the capital was moved to Swan River, then to Battleford in August of 1877. Battleford was a sensible choice since it was on the Carlton Trail and the river route to Edmonton as well as on the line of the projected Pacific railway.

The first Liberal appointees to the Territorial government showed little sensitivity to western concerns. David Laird, who was appointed Lieutenant Governor in 1877, was honest and hard-working but he was a newspaper editor from Prince Edward Island with little administrative experience and even less interest in the affairs of the North-West Territories. His first council consisted of the two magistrates newly appointed for the Territories and the Commissioner of the Mounted Police, James F. Macleod. The failure to appoint even one Métis to the council was such a glaring omission that even Laird could see at once the problems that might arise. At his urging, Ottawa appointed to the council Pascal Breland, an aging Métis who was untainted by any connection with the Manitoba resistance of 1869-70.

While the Territorial government was located in the North Saskatchewan Valley after 1875, most of the North-West Mounted Police had been sent to the far southwest corner of the Territories to combat the sale of liquor by American traders to the Blackfoot, Bloods, and Piegans. So great were the distances, so tentative the communications in this early period, that the Mounted Police were virtually a separate government. In addition to policing the border country, they collected customs duties, carried the mail, took the census, acted as Indian agents, and generally carried out whatever administrative duties needed to be done. In theory the Lieutenant Governor had the power to decide, in consultation with the Commissioner, on the disposition of the Mounted Police. In practice this almost never happened until both the government and the Mounted Police headquarters were moved to Regina in 1883.

David Laird's term as Lieutenant Governor was quiet and undistinguished, in part at least because the rush of settlement to the Prairies that Laird's appointment had been intended to cope with did not happen. When Macdonald and the Conservatives returned to power in 1878, they were inclined to regard the separation of the Territorial government from that of Manitoba as an expensive mistake. The possibility of returning the government to Winnipeg was hinted at but brought such an outraged reaction from the settlers that Macdonald backed down. The stiff, upright, Liberal David Laird was definitely not Macdonald's kind of man, and he naturally chose a more congenial individual to replace him when his term expired in 1881. The Prime Minister's choice was Edgar Dewdney, a civil engineer and surveyor who was born and raised in England but had immigrated to British Columbia as a young man. Dewdney had been a member of the British Columbia legislature before the colony joined Canada in 1871. In the new province's first federal election, Dewdney won a seat as a supporter of the architect of British Columbia's union with Canada, John A. Macdonald.

Macdonald was a hero in British Columbia at first because he had relieved the province of its crushing debt load and had promised to build a railway to the Pacific immediately. As the railway project dissolved in scandal Macdonald became far less popular on the West Coast but Dewdney's loyalty was unshaken; he would remain the Old Chieftain's man as long as he lived. His fidelity was rewarded in 1879 when he was made Indian Commissioner for the North-West Territories, an office he retained on becoming Lieutenant Governor two years later. Dewdney was a tall, bulky man with wavy hair and jutting, mutton-chop

Lieutenant Governor Edgar Dewdney, his wife and his ever-present dogs at their Regina home. O.B. Buell took this photograph in 1885. [Glenbow-Alberta Institute]

whiskers. His face would have been imposing and even fierce were it not for the eyes, which were mild and kindly. The eyes reflected the inner man. Childless, he lavished affection on half a dozen dogs of all sizes and shapes. As an administrator, Dewdney's strengths were organization, hard work, and loyalty. His weaknesses were his undisguised partisanship, which drove Liberals in the west into frenzies of vituperation; an unfortunate proclivity to use his office for personal gain; and an unwillingness to confront his superiors, especially Macdonald, with hard facts. When Dewdney left office in 1886, his political foes were not prepared to forgive and forget. Frank Oliver commented in the Edmonton *Bulletin*, "His appointment was a calamity, his administration a crime, its results a disaster and his retirement his most acceptable act."[1]

It was certainly not a disadvantage to have a man with Dewdney's experience as a surveyor in charge of the administration of the North-West Territories in this period. The survey of the Prairies was by far the largest single government activity during Dewdney's years in office and it created some of the knottiest political problems. The survey was an essential precursor to the arrival of the vast numbers of homesteaders the government planned to attract to the region. The survey was a technological undertaking on a heroic scale, of the kind that appealed enormously to the Victorian imagination. The whole gigantic area would be surveyed in a single continuous operation, the largest area on earth to be so treated. The same craving for order that lay behind the structure of the Territorial government found intense satisfaction in this scheme to ensnare more than six hundred thousand square kilometres in an invisible, seamless net.

The work had begun even before the Hudson's Bay Company possessions had passed into Canadian hands and it proceeded rapidly thereafter. As soon as enough land had been subdivided in Manitoba to satisfy the immediate requirements of incoming settlers, the surveyors moved west to locate the five principle north-south lines, known as meridians, and the major east-west base lines with their complex corrections for the curvature of the earth's surface. This work was completed by the end of the decade and the surveyors were ready to begin placing the iron stakes that marked the corners of each square mile of land.

The Canadian government had adopted a modified form of the American square-lot survey system. The basic unit was the township of thirty-six sections, each 640 acres or one square mile in area. It was a marvellously simple and logical system. Any of the millions of quarter sections could be located exactly and unambiguously with a few numbers and letters. In the first four years Dewdney was in office, over fifty million acres of land were made ready for occupation.

Ottawa decided at the start that most of the agricultural lands of the Prairies would be available free to homesteaders. Any man over the age of eighteen could come to the North-West Territories, select an unoccupied quarter section, and claim it simply by making an entry at a government land office. The regulations varied in detail from time to time but essentially the homesteader had to occupy the land for three years, bring a percentage of it under cultivation, and make improvements of a specified value. When these conditions had been met, the settler had only to pay a ten-dollar registration fee and the land was his. He was also entitled to buy an adjoining quarter section at a low fixed price. Some of the unoccupied land was withheld from the system. The Hudson's Bay Company had received one-twentieth of the land south of the North Saskatchewan River as part of the price for the transfer of Rupert's Land to Canada. The Canadian Pacific Railway was given twenty-five million acres and two sections in every township were set aside as school lands. In most of the Territories this meant that all the odd-numbered sections in each township were railway lands, except for Sections 11 and 29, which were set aside as school lands. Section 8 and three-quarters of Section 26 were Hudson's Bay Company lands.

Only a few minor flaws marred the majestic symmetry of the survey. Indian reserves had to be carved out and provision had to be made for those few whites and Métis who had settled before the survey began. The holdings of the early arrivals naturally did not conform to the precise geometry of the survey. The Métis had marked out their traditional long, narrow river lots and whites often followed suit. Anyone who had been in residence before 1870, however, was entitled to a special survey which located the boundaries of his property as they were, without reference to the square system. Those who had taken up land between 1870 and the subdivision of the land were legally entitled to no special consideration, but the surveyors were instructed to try to fit in their claims as well as they could. In most cases the claims could be fitted into the new system in a way that satisfied both parties. Disputes over the ownership of individual parcels of land were almost unknown, except where changes in government policy required the eviction of squatters from lands granted to railways or colonization companies. With the conspicuous exception of the case of the Métis at St. Laurent, the survey was a success.

The return to office of the Macdonald government in 1878 with a commitment to build the Pacific railway speeded up the flow of immigration. Most of the settlers headed for the North Saskatchewan valley, where the railway was expected to run. Proximity to the line was not a mere convenience; it meant the difference between marginal subsistence and prosperity. The 1881 census showed the bulk of the non-native population of the Territories along the river, with Prince Albert being by far the largest population centre. The great majority of these earliest settlers were from Ontario; the vast waves of European and American immigrants would not appear for another generation. As a group the settlers were vocal, articulate, and very conscious of their rights as Canadians. Their cultural baggage included a strong taste for the ferociously partisan politics of nineteenth-century Canada. Like all emigrants, their principal motivation was the hope and expectation of a better life in their new home.

Homesteading on the Prairies, especially in the first few years, was usually a hard, often a desperate, struggle for survival. The settlers did not need the extra difficulties imposed by the vagaries of government policy. When their homesteads inevitably turned out to be something less than earthly paradises, they did not have to look far to find the source of their troubles.

Until 1883, however, most of the settlers in both Manitoba and the North-West Territories were able to hang on to their hopes. The new Canadian Pacific Railway company that Macdonald had conjured into existence began pushing track west from Winnipeg with enormous energy. One immediate result was a spectacular boom in land. Most of the speculation and investment was in urban, or at least potentially urban, land but the price of farm land was also pulled up to artificially high levels. The hardships of the homestead seemed to be paying off very quickly in the form of large capital gains. The weather was generally cooperative in those years, producing bumper crops that exceeded even the rhetoric of the boosters. The settlers in the North Saskatchewan valley were worried when the CPR announced its decision to move the main line two hundred miles to the south but they were certainly not despondent. Even if the railway did not come to its senses about the location of the main line, the agricultural potential of the area and the location of the capital at Battleford would surely mean the construction of a branch line to the major centres.

At the end of 1881 the first ominous sign appeared. The government announced that the railway would not go to the capital, the capital would come to the railway. A spot on the prairie hitherto known as Pile of Bones was hastily renamed Regina and designated as the new government centre. A few months later the land boom suddenly collapsed, wiping out millions in paper profits overnight. In 1883 the frosts came early and seriously damaged about a quarter of the wheat crop. The CPR main line was being constructed across the prairies with unprecedented speed but the farmers were already discovering that their interests and those of the railway were not necessarily identical. The rapid construction of the main line ate up money at such a rate that there was none left over to build the branch lines, sidings, platforms, and grain elevators that would make the line usable. The CPR's insatiable appetite for capital and its monopoly position in the West meant that freight rates were set at very high levels, so high that farmers found they needed bumper crops just to get by. The poor crop of 1883 combined with falling prices threatened many with bankruptcy.

With their dreams being shattered, the settlers began to take a harder look at the policies and practices of the government. They did not like what they saw. The Department of the Interior was inordinately slow in processing homestead documents. It often took two or three years between the time a settler fulfilled his obligations and the awarding of title. In the meantime the farmer found it almost impossible to sell, lease, or borrow money on the land. At the behest of the CPR, the government changed the homestead regulations to remove all the land for a mile on each side of the main line from entry and then moved to evict a number of settlers who were already in residence within this so-called "mile belt."

Large land companies were able to buy up huge tracts at low prices. Very few of these land companies in fact made money, but that was not the popular impression. In the area south and west of Calgary, homesteaders were excluded altogether while immense grazing leases were handed out to wealthy friends of the government like Senator Matthew Cochrane, whose Cochrane Ranch spread over two hundred thousand acres. The single action that seemed to best symbolize the arrogance and corruption of the government was Dewdney's location of the government buildings at Regina. The CPR had naturally placed its station at Regina on one of its own sections of land. This was the practice the railway followed all the way from Winnipeg to Vancouver so that it could subdivide the land around the stations into building lots and sell them at high prices. In most cases the choice of the location of the station automatically meant that was where the town centre would be, but in Regina the Lieutenant Governor was in a position to challenge the CPR. The railway put its station on Section 24. Section 26, two miles away, was Hudson's Bay Company land that Dewdney and a group of friends had purchased as soon as they found out where the railway station was to be. It was here that Dewdney placed the government buildings and the North-West Mounted Police headquarters. The CPR subdivided its land and made money; Dewdney and friends did likewise; but the public was left with an extremely inconvenient layout for the capital. The Regina situation was a perfect metaphor for the plight of the settler: caught between a remote government that rewarded only a favoured few and a giant corporation apparently intent on squeezing every possible dime out of those who depended on it.

There were other, less pressing, grievances. The tariff structure meant that farmers in the West could not import American farm machinery without paying high duties. Few homesteaders could afford much in the way of machinery in any case, but the very existence of tariff protection for bloated eastern manufacturers irritated them. When the tariff was actually raised from twenty-five to thirty-five per cent in 1883, irritation became outrage. Ottawa had decreed that liquor would be unavailable in the North-West Territories except by permit granted by the Lieutenant Governor. These measures, which made the settlers feel like second class citizens, were imposed by Ottawa, and the settlers were not even represented there. As the population of the Territories increased, the settlers' sense of injustice found expression in the Territorial Council and in the pages of the newspapers that were appearing in the larger towns. The trouble was that criticism from both these sources could be dismissed by Macdonald's government as mere Liberal partisanship, since the most vocal critics of government policy in both the press and the Territorial Council were Liberals. What the settlers needed was a strong independent voice.

In the spring of 1883, groups calling themselves Settlers' Rights Associations began to appear in Manitoba and the North-West Territories. The Qu'Appelle Settlers' Rights Association, one of the earliest to be formed, passed a series of resolutions in March 1883 calling for: representation in parliament, land law reform, laws "for the benefit of the settler, and not in the interest of rich corporations and needy officials," honesty and integrity in appointed officials, and government assistance for immigrants.[2] In October the Territorial Council, now with a majority of elected members, sent off to Ottawa a list of sixteen resolutions that supported the settlers' demands and criticized Ottawa's policies. With the crops, such as they were, harvested in the fall of 1883, the farmers had more time on their hands and the tempo of protest quickened. In November a Manitoba Rights League was formed and called for an end to the CPR monopoly, removal of all duties on farm machinery, transfer of the administration of crown lands to the province, and construction of a railway to Hudson Bay. The Manitoba Rights League and the various independent local groups were absorbed in December into a new body, the Manitoba and Northwest Farmers' Union. Just before Christmas a large and enthusiastic meeting in Winnipeg's Albert Hall set up a central executive and provided for local branches throughout the West.

The delegates to the Union's organizational meeting spent four days discussing their grievances at great length. They decided to send a delegation to Ottawa at once to present to the government a "Bill of Rights" drawn up at the meeting. This was far too mild an action for some of the farmers. The *Manitoba Free Press* had published a number of letters in the fall calling on Manitoba to secede from Confederation. While emphasizing the legitimacy of the farmers' grievances, the paper had done its best to discourage talk of secession. At the convention the separatist sentiment reappeared. A motion was introduced calling for the repeal of the British North America Act and the formation of "a new confederacy of the North-West Provinces and British Columbia."[3] The motion was defeated but not before a lengthy discussion revealed that many delegates were angry enough to consider such a move if other measures failed. Interestingly, the delegates explored in some detail the idea that the sale of Rupert's Land to Canada by the Hudson's Bay Company was invalid because it had been done without the consent of the inhabitants of the territory.

The Farmers' Union delegation to Ottawa had little success. The only point the government was prepared to concede was to restore homesteading in the "mile belt." The delegation returned to report their rejection and letters advocating separatism began to appear in the columns of the newspapers again. But though support for the Farmers' Union was growing, as a vehicle of protest it had serious weaknesses, which the Macdonald government proceeded to exploit. Government strategy was to identify the Union with the Liberal party, something that proved easy to do despite its professions of non-partisanship. For one thing the Liberal newspapers in the West, especially the *Manitoba Free*

Press, could not resist the temptation to use the farmers' agitation as a stick to beat the Tories. The *Free Press* also had a tendency to try to steer the debate in the direction of those issues, like the tariff, that fitted its editor's own ideological predilections, at the expense of more locally important matters.

Some Manitoba politicians also saw an opportunity in the Farmers' Union. Party politics, although not yet visible in Manitoba at the provincial level, flourished federally. A provincial politician might have ties to the Liberal party, for example, and work for its candidates during federal elections. But that same individual would not identify himself as a Liberal in his capacity as a member of the provincial legislature. There was a tacit agreement to avoid party labels and concentrate on presenting a united front in an effort to rewrite the conditions of the province's entry into confederation. The "better terms" agitation had made very little headway and Manitobans were becoming increasingly irritated. Partly for this reason and partly because it had been in power long enough to make mistakes and enemies which left it vulnerable, the government of John Norquay was in trouble. For a group of Norquay's opponents in the legislature led by Thomas Greenway, the opening offered by the agrarian discontent was too tempting to be ignored. Greenway and his supporters in the early months of 1884 became more and more openly Liberal and at the same time identified themselves closely with the Farmers' Union and its demands. The farmers had paid little attention to the Manitoba government so far and Greenway attempted to make political capital by blaming Norquay for not doing enough to influence the federal government.

In March the Farmers' Union met again in Winnipeg to discuss the rejection of the "Bill of Rights." The meeting revealed that tempers had not cooled over the winter; in fact the level of militancy was higher than ever. Leadership passed from the moderates who had sponsored the delegation to Ottawa to the hard-liners who advocated secession. The delegates promptly passed a resolution opposing further immigration to the West until grievances were redressed. The March meeting proved to be the high point in the organization's brief existence. The resolution denouncing immigration was, on reflection, too heretical for any but the most embittered. The secessionist talk was making people uneasy and many Conservatives began dropping out because of the growing identification with the Liberal party. The Tory press, recognizing its opening, moved in for the kill. By the time the farmers had finished their seeding in the spring of 1884, the Union had ceased to be a viable force.

The easy victory over the Farmers' Union did nothing to eliminate the very real grievances of the settlers. Worse still, it left Macdonald and the government in Ottawa with a number of dangerous illusions. Macdonald came away from the episode believing that western discontent did not amount to much when it could be dissipated with such elementary political manoeuvring. The protests, he believed, had no real foundation. They were the work of land speculators and

Liberals and could safely be ignored. The other crucially important consequence of the rise and fall of the Farmers' Union was the change it brought about in the attitudes of the settlers. The agitation created a mood that was very receptive to the return of Louis Riel. The experience changed the settlers' perception of Riel from the man who murdered Thomas Scott to the man who had successfully wrung important concessions from Ottawa. Riel himself could scarcely believe the difference. When he visited Manitoba in the summer of 1883 his presence provoked a few letters demanding that he be lynched for the murder of Scott. The press treated him with mild hostility and faint contempt. A year later, as he pointed out in a letter to his brother, the same people were enthusiastically applauding his speeches and calling him a hero. The impact of the change on Riel's self-confidence and sense of mission was profound. To make any headway he needed at least the neutrality of the whites and the Farmers' Union controversy seemed to make that possible.

CHAPTER THREE

Agitation:
The Métis at the South Branch

Gabriel: the bravest, proudest, most respected man in the North-West. There was no need to use his last name. To many of his people, the Plains Métis, he ranked just a little lower than the archangel. Gabriel Dumont was a frontiersman's frontiersman, the stuff of legends. He was the best shot in the North-West, the best rider, the best gambler among a people who gambled for days on end, the best buffalo hunter, the greatest leader. He was a good canoeist and swimmer, unusual talents on the Plains, and a better-than-average billiards player. He owned the fastest horses in a society that loved horse-racing. He was fluent in French and several Indian languages but never bothered to learn much English. He was a shrewd trader and businessman. To his friends he was the most gracious, most generous person in the North-West; to his enemies he was a dangerous foe. When John Kerr arrived in the North-West in 1872 to take up a short career as buffalo hunter and adventurer, Gabriel took the young man under his wing. "I grew to know and respect the redoubtable Gabriel—chief outstanding figure of the plains. To me he was kindness itself. He adopted me into his family, and never called me by the name bestowed upon me by the rest of his band, namely le Petit Canada, (Petit referred to my age, for I had height) but invariably addressed me as *mon frère*, while his family and relatives called me son, nephew, cousin, and so forth, and I spoke to them in similar terms. Dumont has been painted in lurid colours as a savage, brutal man. He was anything but that, kindly and generous."[1]

Gabriel Dumont was born in 1837, the third child of Isidore Dumont and Louise Laframboise. He was named for his uncle, a flamboyant, violent, hard-drinking man who had gained a reputation as a buffalo hunter and native leader. Gabriel's father was the son of a French Canadian voyageur who worked for the Hudson's Bay Company and a Sarcee woman. His mother was a member of a prominent Red River Métis family. Isidore had spent much of his life in the Saskatchewan country and after trying farming for a short time at St. Boniface, Manitoba, he moved back west with his family in 1840 to settle near Fort Pitt on the North Saskatchewan River near the present Alberta-Saskatchewan border. Before he moved back, Isidore was a member of the last great Red River buffalo hunt and three-year-old Gabriel probably accompanied him. Isidore had come

Gabriel Dumont, photographed at Fort Benton, Montana, in the summer of 1885.
[Montana Historical Society]

back to Manitoba by 1848, living with the buffalo hunters on White Horse Plains just west of Red River. From that headquarters in 1851, the Dumont family accompanied into the United States the buffalo hunt that ended in the Battle of Grand Couteau. Young Gabriel was one of the defenders as the Métis hunters held off a large Sioux war party. Only one Métis and probably only slightly more than twenty Indians died in the battle, but the Métis would consider it their greatest victory, establishing how well their defensive tactics of fighting from a circle of wagons ringed by rifle pits worked. The family was back west by 1858, and there Gabriel married Madelaine Wilkie, beginning a relationship that would be the envy of their friends. The couple were both very fond of children but they had none of their own. A few years after their marriage, the Dumonts adopted a daughter. In 1862, the twenty-five-year-old Gabriel was elected leader of the Saskatchewan buffalo hunt, a position he never relinquished. By this time he had moved to the area between the North and South Saskatchewan rivers east of the Hudson's Bay Company post of Fort Carlton, where Métis settlement would mushroom.

It was the area known as the South Branch of the Saskatchewan, south of Prince Albert, that was the spiritual and political centre for the Plains Métis. About 1790, the Hudson's Bay Company and its rival North-West Company built posts there on the banks of the South Saskatchewan River. Just to the west on the North Saskatchewan was the Hudson's Bay Company's Fort Carlton. Shortly after the South Branch posts were built, Louis Letendre was born in the vicinity, the son of Métis trader and interpreter Jean-Baptiste Letendre, nicknamed Batoche. That nickname would be passed on to the son, then to the grandson, Xavier Letendre. In 1872, Xavier Letendre *dit* Batoche built a trading post and established a ferry on the Carlton Trail, the main route between Winnipeg and Edmonton, in the middle of the collection of Métis communities known as the South Branch. In 1878 Letendre sold his ferry, which competed with Gabriel Dumont's about fifteen kilometres south, to fellow merchant Alex Fisher, but the little community retained the name Batoche's Crossing after its leading citizen.

After the only partial success of their Manitoba agitation and with the buffalo having disappeared from the eastern plains, in the early 1870s many of the Red River Métis moved west. Some went to more settled communities but some also joined the buffalo hunters who made the South Branch their centre of operations. In 1871, Oblate priest Father Alexis André founded a mission at St. Laurent, one of the Métis South Branch communities a few kilometres north of what became Batoche's Crossing. (It was not until 1884, after much effort by a committee headed by Batoche and Gabriel, that St. Antoine de Padoue, the church at the crossing, was built.) By 1871, the South Branch communities boasted a population of 322. Almost all the men listed "hunter" as their occupation in the census of the communities that year. On the last day of 1871, the leading members of the South Branch wintering communities, including Louis Letendre and Isidore Dumont, met at the St. Laurent mission.

What the Métis hunters must do, meeting chairman and Hudson's Bay Company Factor Lawrence Clarke told them, was

> decide whether they would continue to lead the lives of semi-savages without any fixed Residence, but like the Indians of the prairies change their habitations and abodes from year to year, to follow the excentric [sic] wanderings of the Buffalo. Content to eke out a precarious living from the muzzle of the Gun. Content to isolate themselves from all the benefits to be derived from a civilized community, to cut themselves off from all the duties and consolations of their Religion and debar their children from receiving that education, without which they could never hope to rise in the world but must remain for ever the slaves and helots of their more intelligent fellow citizens.[2]

Clarke continued for some time in a similar vein, warning the Métis about the consequences of the imminent disappearance of the buffalo if they did not make provision for a new way of living. Clarke laid it on a bit thick but the Métis agreed with the substance of what he said. They resolved to form a permanent community in the St. Laurent neighbourhood and become farmers. Isidore Dumont, Gabriel's father, told the meeting that "he could remember when vast herds of Buffalo covered the prairies from the foot of the Rocky Mountains to Fort Garry. Now they were only to be found in the Saskatchewan, and as the country got peopled, the Buffalo would disappear. He was an old man and could tell the young people that the decision they had come to was good, they must do like other white men, cultivate the ground or they must live and die like Indians." Louis Letendre *dit* Batoche agreed. "The Country is opening up to the stranger and the Métis must show his white blood and not be crushed in the struggle for existence."[3]

Father André, who was secretary of the meeting, was delighted with the Métis' resolve. "Your childrens [sic] children will bless this day, and keep it as a perpetual feast, to commemorate the happy epoch when their fathers raised them from the slough of ignorance and placed within their reach the blessed influences of a Religious education, training them to something more noble vastly more beneficial than the sitting on a horse or shooting a Buffalo."[4] Clarke was just as pleased. He wrote Hudson's Bay Company Chief Commissioner Donald Smith that the new Métis colony would provide the company with a stable source of freighters. The Métis would compete among themselves for that employment, not only enabling the company to reduce wages to a minimum but also to cut expenses by reducing the amount of equipment and the number of full-time transport employees.[5]

The South Branch Métis rushed headlong into their first dispute with the

Canadian government over their claims to a land settlement. On January 17, 1872, Lawrence Clarke, on behalf of the Métis, wrote Adams Archibald, Lieutenant Governor of Manitoba and the North-West Territories. Clarke asked if the government had any objection to the Métis claiming a large reserve on which to build a colony near Fort Carlton. The Métis also wanted to know "what steps they should adopt to secure to themselves the right to prohibit people of other nationalities from settling in the lands occupied by them, without the consent of the Community."[6] Clarke estimated that by the next autumn such a colony would have a population of fifteen hundred.

The scheme to establish a large exclusively-Métis colony had been suggested by the priests and Archibald replied before he even received the Métis' letter. The Roman Catholic Bishop of St. Albert, Vital-Justin Grandin, had been discussing a similar proposal with Archibald and with Hudson's Bay Company Edmonton Factor William Christie. In a letter to Christie early in January 1872, Archibald said it was out of the question that the Métis would be considered any different from any other settlers. "The only Half breed Claim is that which is created by the Act of Manitoba and that is confined to this Province." He dismissed Grandin's own proposal, for a Métis reserve of about two hundred and twenty-five kilometres by thirty kilometres, as "absurdity. No Government and no Government officer could entertain such a proposition."[7]

The Métis of the South Branch may not have known about Archibald's strong objections to their plans. In any case, in May 1872 the committee the Métis had established for the purpose selected a site for their colony. It would be on both sides of the South Saskatchewan River from the community of St. Louis in the north to Gabriel Dumont's homestead in the south, a distance of about forty-five kilometres. It would extend at least ten kilometres west to include the community of Duck Lake.[8] When the buffalo hunters settled down, they expected to take river-lot farms, as had been done in Manitoba. These would have a river frontage of about two hundred metres and extend back from the river for a little more than three kilometres. Behind each lot traditionally was another three-kilometre hay privilege. In effect, what the South Branch Métis did was carve out a section of land about equivalent to a large Indian reserve, straddling both the country's main road, the Carlton Trail, and the main water route, the South Saskatchewan River. They believed they were entitled to such an arrangement because of the settlement their cousins received in the Manitoba Act. Getting the government to agree was a difficult matter. The discussions during the next few years were generally held through intermediaries and neither side was very sure what the other's position actually was.

The Canadian government's own plans were radically opposed to the Métis proposals. The 1871 decision to divide the North-West using a sophisticated version of the American square-lot system looked nice on paper but it bore no relationship to any pattern of settlement that had already developed. The

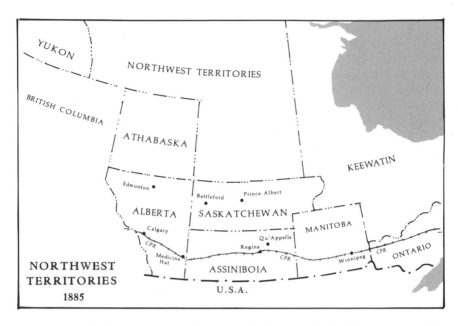

government had to make some allowances in its plan for Indian reserves, old settlers, and squatters. By the time the Plains Métis began thinking about settling down, and long before most of them actually began to lay claim to specific farming lands, the government had decided how settlement ought to proceed. As well, the government homesteading rules presumed that the land would be used for continuous farming and residence. Many of the Métis would be only part-time farmers, supplementing their income with hunting and freighting. If the Métis were not granted a form of aboriginal rights and if they could not be considered old settlers or squatters prior to the survey, there was no way their plans for a colony at the South Branch could be put into practice.

In December 1873 the wintering Métis again met at the St. Laurent mission. By this time, many of them were serious about settling down and were ready to claim farming lands. Encouraged by Father André, the Métis took their colony scheme one step further by establishing a government and laws for it. The meeting unanimously elected Gabriel Dumont the first president of the South Branch community, assisted by eight councillors. The organization and laws were closely modelled on the old buffalo hunt rules, regulating such things as lighting fires on the prairie, breach of promises to marry, horse theft, and free passage on ferries for people going to church on Sunday. The laws also granted the council the right to levy taxes. Father André and the Métis were pleased with their efforts. "This little bit of legislation produced the happiest results and seemed like the true dawn of civilization," Father André wrote.[9]

But the Métis were careful not to appear to want to usurp the powers of the

Canadian government. They only formed their own government and made their own laws, they declared, in the absence of any other authority in the country. When Canada enforced a legal system in the North-West, they would dismantle their government.

In February 1874 the community of the South Branch met again, this time to apportion land within their colony. They decided that each head of a family had a right to a river lot in the settlement. For each son more than twenty years old, he could take one additional lot.

Dumont's government operated without interference until it tried to enforce its laws. On the spring buffalo hunt in 1875, a group of South Branch Métis ran some buffalo ahead of the main party, a clear violation of the rules. The council applied their laws and punished the offenders, who went to Fort Carlton and loudly complained to Factor Lawrence Clarke. According to Father André, the company had had deep misgivings about the South Branch government and Clarke seized the opportunity to write Lieutenant Governor Alexander Morris that "the Métis of Carlton, along with the Indians, were in open revolt against the authority of the Canadian government, they had already established a provisional government."[10]

Clarke's alarming letter described events that sounded ominously similar to the Red River troubles. The *Manitoba Free Press* wildly exaggerated Clarke's already overblown description of the situation. Its headlines read: "Another stand against Canadian government authority in the North-West; a Provisional Government at Carlton; M. Louis Riel again to the front; 10,000 Crees on the warpath; Fort Carlton in possession of the Rebels; a number of Mounted Police killed."[11] That was all nonsense, but the authorities were sufficiently concerned to send a detachment of NWMP under Commissioner George French to the South Branch. French reported that the complaints were trivial, that, in Father André's words, "the intentions of the alleged revolutionaries were as pacific as they were reasonable. Furthermore our good Métis, wanting to show their peaceful intention, even consented at their general assembly to give back the fines imposed on the malcontents." That was the end of the South Branch government. "The humble legislature of the St. Laurent colony, having no longer the right to punish delinquents, naturally lost all its sanction and died while just out of its cradle."[12]

By 1878, Xavier Letendre *dit* Batoche, the proprieter of one of the largest trading establishments in the North-West, was already the wealthiest man in the area and was building and furnishing the large house he would brag was the finest west of Winnipeg. The community was also prospering. The first issue of the North-West's first newspaper, the *Saskatchewan Herald*, noted in August 1878:

A large and very flourishing settlement is being made on the north bank of the South Branch of the Saskatchewan, ten miles below St. Laurent Mission.

43

Many of the settlers are of the old families of Manitoba, while a few are from Ontario. The land is of the very finest quality, with an abundance of good wood and water. This settlement is bound to prosper, as most of those taking up land are practical men of ample means, who begin by taking in plenty of young stock, pigs, poultry, farming implements, etc. It is commonly spoken of as "South Branch."[13]

In all the early proposals and programs of the South Branch Métis, there was no mention of any claim to rights based on their relationship with the Indians. Influenced initially by the priests and the Hudson's Bay Company, the South Branch Métis claimed privileges they thought ought to be accorded old settlers in the country, white or half-breed, or privileges based on the Manitoba Act settlement. But Métis in other communities quickly seized the precedent of the Indian treaties as a way of coming to a settlement.

A few days before Treaty No. 4, the Qu'Appelle Treaty, was signed in 1874, the Métis in the Qu'Appelle area composed a petition to the government. It was vaguely worded and made no specific mention of the amount of land they thought the Métis were due, except that they ought to be allowed to keep "the lands which they have taken, or which they may take, along the River Qu'Appelle." But they asked the government "to remember them in the various arrangements that the Government may make with the Indians." The Qu'Appelle petition also asked the government to preserve Métis hunting and fishing rights in their territory. It was signed by about thirty men, including Alex Fisher and Moïse Ouellette, who would become prominent members of the South Branch community. At the signing of the treaty with the Blackfoot-speaking peoples in 1877, half-breeds of that area petitioned the new North-West Territories Lieutenant Governor David Laird to help them settle as farmers, as the government had promised to assist the Indians. In late 1878, the half-breeds in the Cypress Hills area submitted a lengthy petition based almost solely on their position as aboriginal people, demanding the same hunting and land rights as the Indians. It was by far the largest petition the government would receive from half-breeds in the North-West, signed by about two hundred and seventy-five people. The Cypress Hills half-breeds said it was impossible for them to live in white communities and they asked for an Indian-style reserve "perpetual and inalienable, upon which they can establish themselves in a permanent manner, and fix their families, to the exclusion of all whites."[14]

As the South Branch Métis pressed on the government their demands for a land settlement, they studiously avoided mentioning their kinship with the Indians. They regarded their 1871 request for a large settlement on the South Branch not as a demand for an Indian-style reserve but as a request for a colony more in the manner that white organizations would later be granted tracts of land in the North-West. In February 1878, the South Branch Métis met again to draw up a new petition to the government. Under the chairmanship of Gabriel Dumont, and with merchant Alex Fisher as secretary, the Métis asked for a French-speaking magistrate, two Métis members of the North-West Territories Council, and help to begin farming and schools. But the most important part of the representation concerned land. The Métis said "it is of the most urgent necessity that the Government should cause to be surveyed, with the least possible delay, the lands occupied and cultivated by the half-breeds or old residents of the country, and that patents therefor be granted to them." They also asked for land grants as had been awarded under the Manitoba Act.[15]

In a reply to that petition, Minister of the Interior David Mills avoided the question of a half-breed land grant. He did assure the Métis that the surveys of already-settled homesteads would proceed as quickly as the government found money to do the job and that it was possible that one of the appointed members of the Territorial Council might be of French Canadian descent. But he emphasized his view that the Métis were just another "class of white settlers" so there would be no assistance for farming such as had been given the Indians, despite Lieutenant Governor Laird's strong support for that particular Métis proposal. Dumont's 1878 petition was quickly followed by a strongly-worded appeal from many of the settlers in the Prince Albert district pleading for quick river-lot surveys and land grants for half-breeds and old settlers in the manner of the Manitoba settlement. In 1880, half-breeds in the Edmonton district added their voices to the plea for a land grant like that contained in the Manitoba Act, and the next year the Qu'Appelle half-breeds made a similar demand.[16]

The government had, in fact, acted quickly on the two major points of all these petitions: an immediate river-lot survey and a half-breed land grant. But the government took only the first steps. After the initial gestures, the solution of the problems seemed to fall by the wayside. It is likely that no one bothered to tell the North-West half-breeds what the government was doing or planned to do.

Surveys in the area began shortly after Dumont sent his petition. The surveyors were under strict instructions to vary the survey according to the needs of those who had already settled and at Prince Albert in the summer of 1878 they drew a river-lot survey. They moved south and began to survey the South Branch according to the already-established river lots, just as the Métis wanted. But it was late in the season when the surveyors began and they only finished about one-fifth of the area that year. The next summer, for reasons that were neither explained at the time nor are obvious from the documents that remain, the rest of the South Branch was surveyed on the square-lot principle.

The South Branch Métis then began to demand that their communities be resurveyed to conform to the river-lot system they had adopted. The government steadfastly refused to spend the money on another survey and most Métis stubbornly continued to carve river lots out of land that had already been

Gabriel Dumont's homestead on the east side of the South Saskatchewan River, south of Batoche. It was here that Dumont ran his ferry. [Toronto *Mail*, May 29, 1885]

surveyed into square lots. There was a solution that the government suggested. By a process of subdividing the square lots, the Métis could create *de facto* river lots. The scheme made perfect sense to a surveyor but it is unlikely that anyone properly explained it to the grumbling Métis. Even if they had, it is unlikely the Métis would have been satisfied. They wanted the government to recognize their rights to river lots, not suggest loopholes they could find in the land laws. As well, if they had themselves redrawn the square lots into river lots, there would be no surveyor's stakes to settle disputes between neighbours. To add to their problems, there was an unaccountable delay in opening the government's land office at Prince Albert and in producing the map of the river-lot survey so that even those Métis whose homesteads were included in the river-lot survey could not make legal claim to it until the map was available in 1884.

In 1878, the Ottawa government recognized the aboriginal land rights of the North-West Métis in a vaguely-worded amendment to the Dominion Lands Act authorizing the federal cabinet "to satisfy any claims existing in connection with the extinguishment of the Indian title, preferred by half-breeds resident in the North-West Territories outside the limits of Manitoba, on the fifteenth day of July, one thousand eight hundred and seventy by granting land to such persons, to such extent and on such terms and conditions, as may be deemed expedient."[17] Politicians would look for ways of putting that into effect. But for the next few years nothing concrete was done, certainly nothing that was obvious to the South Branch Métis.

Rumours that the government intended to abolish the North-West Territories Council sparked a new round of meetings on the South Branch in early 1880. A petition protesting the rumoured changes was drawn up but one Métis settler, Abraham Montour, refused to sign even though he agreed with its sentiment. He told the meeting that "several other petitions had already been forwarded to Ottawa setting forth the rights and certain wants of the Half-breed element throughout the Territories, and the action of the Government was still to be learned. He feared the present petition would receive similar treatment.''[18]

In September 1882 Gabriel Dumont's name again headed a petition to Ottawa, addressed to John A. Macdonald, then Minister of the Interior as well as Prime Minister. It complained about the land regulations, then said:

> Having so long held this country as its masters and so often defended it against the Indians at the price of our blood, we consider it not asking too much to request that the Government allow us to occupy our lands in peace, and that exception be made to its regulations, by making to the half-breeds of the North-West free grants of land. We also pray that you would direct that the lots be surveyed along the river ten chains [about 200 metres] in width by two miles [3.2 kilometres] in depth, this mode of division being the long established usage of the country. This would render it more easy for us to know the limits of our several lots.[19]

A short time later, residents of the St. Louis area, at the northern limit of the South Branch communities, sent a similar appeal.

At the beginning of 1884, the government seemed on the verge of settling the problem of the South Branch river lots. Dominion Lands Inspector William Pearce arrived in January to investigate the problem. Then, prodded by a strong plea from Oblate Father Valentin Végréville, the government told Pearce that he had the power to resurvey the South Branch into river lots. It did not exactly order him to make the resurvey but simply suggested he could do it if that was what the Métis wanted. Pearce replied bluntly that he didn't have time to resurvey the square blocks into river lots and there was no other surveyor readily available who had the expertise to do the work. He said the Métis demands could be met on paper by subdividing the existing lots to form river lots. But, Pearce told his employers, the Métis would have nothing to do with that scheme. In the first place, they wanted surveyor's stakes marking the limits of their property, something that could only be provided by a resurvey. And they were not willing to try to understand the complex process of subdivision. When he tried to explain the subdivision scheme to them, the Métis, in Pearce's words, replied: "That is plain enough to you as a surveyor, but it is Greek to us; those parties are bona fide settlers, as such have or will acquire title, and if they wish their land laid off in a certain way, why should the government object? In fact, it is the duty of the government to survey it as requested."[20]

Pearce went on to make two sensible suggestions. Either the government spend the money to get a river-lot resurvey properly done or, cheaper, make a rough survey for entry on the subdivision principle at the same time as giving the Métis the boundary stakes they wanted. Pearce went on with his investigations as the government did nothing about his recommendations.

In the spring of 1884, a dozen years after they first resolved to form the colony at the South Branch, the Métis appeared to have accomplished nothing. It is clear that the South Branch Métis and the priests who advised them misunderstood the government's land regulations and the compromises that might have been worked out. But it is also clear that the Métis felt that it was not their responsibility to understand the government and its motives. They thought things ought to be the other way around. In the Métis' minds, it was up to the government to make rules that acknowledged their rights and coincided with their demands.

At best, the government seemed to ignore the Métis. At worst, with most of their settlement surveyed in square lots diametrically opposed to their wishes, the government appeared to be gradually denying their demands. All the eloquent pleas from Father André and the other priests seemed to have fallen on deaf ears. The support of David Macdowall, the representative of their district on the North-West Council, appeared to have done little good. Gabriel Dumont was a great leader of the buffalo hunt but he had obviously no success dealing with the Canadian government. Their other main political spokesman, Charles Nolin, had similarly failed even though his status as a former Conservative cabinet minister in Manitoba should have given him some clout with Ottawa. On the South Branch, it was obvious the Métis would have to do something that shocked the government and awakened its officials from their seeming lethargy.

CHAPTER FOUR

Indians and Treaties

News of the sale of the Hudson's Bay Company territory to Canada in 1869 spread quickly west over the moccasin telegraph. The Indians of the North-West Territories, the vast tract of land between the western boundary of the newly-created Manitoba and the Rocky Mountains, were even more fundamentally opposed to the sale than the Red River Métis were and they were less prepared for it.

The Indians of the plains were firmly convinced that the land belonged to them, not to the Queen or the Hudson's Bay Company or Canada. They thought the company maintained its posts in their country at the pleasure of the Indians. In the Indian view, the company owned no land and certainly no one had the right to survey land around the company's posts and sell it.

In 1871 Sweetgrass, the leading chief of the River People, one of the main branches of the Plains Cree, wrote Manitoba and North-West Territories Lieutenant Governor Adams Archibald: "We heard our lands were sold and we did not like it; we don't want to sell our lands; it is our property, and no one has a right to sell them."[1]

The Indians realized they must come to terms with the whites, both on the question of land ownership and to insure their economic future. By 1871 the buffalo, which provided the Plains Indians with food, clothing, and shelter, were already disappearing. The Indians were also the victims of epidemics of diseases that were previously unknown to them. It was obvious to the Indians that fewer buffalo and increased disease at the same time as the arrival of growing numbers of white men was no coincidence.

When he transmitted the message of Sweetgrass and other chiefs to Lieutenant Governor Archibald, William Christie, Chief Factor of the Hudson's Bay Company's Saskatchewan District, warned that the Indians must be dealt with soon.

> Had I not complied with the demands of the Indians—giving them some little presents—and otherwise satisfied them, I have no doubt that they would have proceeded to acts of violence, and once that had commenced, there would have been the beginning of an Indian war, which it is difficult to say when it would have ended. The buffalo will soon be exterminated, and when starvation comes, these Plain Indian tribes will fall back on the Hudson's Bay

Forts and settlement for relief and assistance. If not complied with, or no steps taken to make some provision for them, they will most assuredly help themselves; and there being no force or any law up there to protect the settlers, they must either quietly submit to be pillaged, or lose their lives in the defence of their families and property, against such fearful odds that will leave no hope for their side.[2]

The Plains Cree were by far the largest single group of people in the Canadian West in 1871, with a population estimated by explorer William F. Butler at seven thousand. They lived and hunted buffalo over a wide area of the Canadian plains, from Fort Ellice in the east at the junction of the Qu'Appelle and Assiniboine Rivers near the present Manitoba-Saskatchewan border, to just west of Edmonton House. Their territory extended from the north side of the North Saskatchewan River to the international border in present-day Saskatchewan and to the Red Deer River in what is now Alberta. In the southernmost portion of the Cree territory were some bands of Plains Stoney, an Indian people often called the Assiniboine. There were also some bands of Sioux who had fled the United States after the Minnesota massacres of 1862. From the Qu'Appelle area east through Manitoba were Plains Saulteaux, who shared a similar history with the Cree.

Southwest of the Cree, in what is now southern Alberta, lived their traditional enemies, the Blackfoot-speaking peoples, who ranged well into the United States. In this group, Butler estimated in 1871, were four thousand Blackfoot, two thousand Blood, and three thousand Piegan.[3]

The few whites in the country were scattered mainly along the Saskatchewan River. The majority of them were employees of the Hudson's Bay Company and most of the rest clustered around the company's posts. Edmonton House, as Methodist missionary John McDougall described it, "was the metropolis of the whole western country. It was only twelve hundred miles from a railroad, and some thousand miles from a telegraph office, and there was no regular mail communication."[4] In 1871, thirty-eight people were permanent residents at Edmonton. The largest settlement in the North-West was actually clustered around the Roman Catholic mission at St. Albert, a short distance north of Edmonton. About nine hundred Métis lived there, Butler estimated, before the smallpox epidemic of 1870 claimed three hundred and twenty of them.[5]

The people who became the Plains Cree had migrated from northern Ontario as the fur trade expanded in the eighteenth century. They had a close relationship with the Hudson's Bay Company and were considered friendly to the whites, unlike the Blackfoot-speaking peoples, whom they pushed to the southwest as they moved on to the plains. All the Hudson's Bay Company posts in the North-West were in Cree country. There were few furs to trade in Blackfoot territory; hence the company's relationship with its inhabitants was limited and wary.

Chief Big Bear. One of the tragedies of the rebellion was that white men overestimated Big Bear's hostility toward the settlers. [Public Archives of Canada]

The Plains Cree grouped themselves into several large divisions based on the areas where they tended to live and trade. Within the divisions were small bands, numbering usually about a hundred people, each headed by a chief. The only requirement for band membership was living and working with the band. Chiefs held their positions as long as they could control a personal following. An unsuccessful chief would find his band dwindling as members deserted for bands led by more popular chiefs. An unusually successful chief might find his band growing to as many as a thousand members. Sometimes the major divisions recognized an individual chief as their leading spokesman. In 1871 Sweetgrass, who called himself "chief of the country," was the leading chief of the River People division, who lived along the North Saskatchewan River. Big Bear was the leading chief of the Prairie People, themselves a large branch of the River People, which included the Cree bands most committed to the plains.[6]

The Hudson's Bay Company would often encourage chiefs who were a little more friendly and acquiescent than others by giving them larger presents at trading time and by appearing to give more consideration to their advice, creating political problems between these "company chiefs" and those who wanted to pursue a more independent course. That was a policy the Canadian government would adopt and formalize as part of its efforts to get treaties signed and the Cree settled onto reserves. There was an informal hierarchy among Cree chiefs but unlike the Blackfoot-speaking peoples, who had formed a loose confederacy, the Cree bands found it difficult to plan concerted action.

The whites had had little trouble with the Cree but when Butler visited the North-West in 1870 and 1871, he noticed what he believed was a dangerous change of attitude in the Indians. The buffalo were visibly diminishing, the pattern of white settlement was beginning to restrict the Cree movements, and the smallpox epidemic of 1870 had taken a terrible toll in the North-West. Butler estimated that twelve hundred people had died, not including Blackfoot-speaking people. He reported to Lieutenant Governor Archibald: "Hitherto it may be said that the Crees have looked upon the white man as their friend, but latterly indications have not been wanting to foreshadow a change in this respect—a change which I have found many causes to account for, and which, if the Saskatchewan remains in its present condition, must, I fear, deepen into more positive enmity."[7] One of the factors in the Cree discontent, Butler found, was news of the Red River insurrection.

Many of these events have been magnified and distorted—evil-disposed persons have not been wanting to spread abroad among the natives the idea of the downfall of the Company, and the threatened immigration of settlers to occupy the hunting-grounds and drive the Indian from the land. All these rumors, some of them vague and wild in the extreme, have found ready credence by camp-fires and in council-lodge, and thus it is easy to perceive how the red man, with many of his old convictions and beliefs rudely shaken, should now be more disturbed and discontented than he has been at any former period.[8]

But nothing was done until 1874. In September of that year, Alexander Morris, Archibald's successor as Lieutenant Governor of Manitoba and the North-West Territories, travelled to Lake Qu'Appelle to induce the Cree and Saulteaux of that area to surrender 195,000 square kilometres of territory and sign Indian Treaty No. 4.

Lieutenant Governor Morris found the Indians belligerent and not willing to even talk about a treaty until one overriding matter was settled: the sale of the Hudson's Bay Company territory to Canada. The Indian spokesman at the Qu'Appelle talks, Gambler, pressed an impatient and condescending Morris for an explanation of the sale. How was it, the Indians wanted to know, that their land could be sold without even their knowledge, let alone their consent?

Morris replied that the treaty commissioners had nothing to do with either the company or the sale. God had given the land to the Queen, who allowed both the company and the Indians to use it. In any case, all the company had been paid for was the land that surrounded their posts, not the whole country.

For several days Gambler refused to talk about the treaty, demanding more explanations from Morris and, presumably, some indication the Indians would be compensated for the sale. Morris grew tired of Gambler's intransigence and professed not to know what he was trying to get at. Then Paskwāw, a leading Cree chief in the area, pointed at one of the Hudson's Bay Company officers with the treaty party and put the Indian demand in language Morris understood. "You told me you had sold your land for so much money, 300,000 pounds. We want that money."[9]

Once it was clear the Indians would receive nothing as a result of the sale, the Cree and Saulteaux Indians agreed to accept a treaty on the basis of Treaty No. 3, which Morris had signed the previous year with the Indians of the Lake of the Woods area of Ontario. There was some argument about the amount of money given to chiefs and headmen as a reward for signing the treaty and about the amount of annual annuities to band members. Morris refused to budge on any of his new treaty proposals, which included lower annuities than those in Treaty No. 3. There was little discussion of providing farm animals and equipment, a provision that had been included in the treaties because of Indian demands when Treaty No. 3 was signed. The Treaty No. 4 Indians demanded assurances from Morris that their cousins, the Métis, would be dealt with fairly.

Under the terms of Treaty No. 4, the Qu'Appelle Indians were granted reserves sufficient to allow one square mile for each family of five. The Indians were to receive annual payments of $25 for each chief, $15 for each of four headmen per band, and $5 for all others. To help them make the transition to farming, families were to receive equipment such as hoes and spades and seed. Each band would receive a yoke of oxen, one bull, four cows, and various saws and tools. The Treaty No. 4 Indians would receive $750 worth of ammunition and twine for making fishing nets each year. Each chief and headman who signed the treaty received tokens in the form of uniforms, medals, and flags. The treaty also contained provisions prohibiting liquor on reserves, establishing schools, and guaranteeing Indian hunting rights in the territory they surrendered.

The treaty-making process had not been as smooth as the government had hoped. The Lake of the Woods Indians had held out for more than two years until the support for the transition to farming, which would become standard in subsequent treaties, had been granted. For a while, it looked as if the sale of the Hudson's Bay Company lands, something the commissioners could not negotiate, would prevent or at least unreasonably delay the signing of Treaty No. 4. When it came to the signing of the major treaty with the Plains Cree of the North-West, the government had learned from these experiences and tried to lay a surer foundation.

In the fall of 1875, the government sent Methodist missionary George McDougall to sound out the Saskatchewan Cree for treaty negotiations to take place the following summer. Most of the Cree were amenable to discussing the proposed treaty with McDougall, with one major exception. Big Bear, a man the missionary regarded as a notorious malcontent, told McDougall: "When we set a fox-trap we scatter pieces of meat all round, but when the fox gets into the trap we knock him on the head; we want no bait, let your Chiefs come like men and talk to us." McDougall found most of the chiefs anxious to make a deal with the whites, but he reported an undercurrent of discontent. "Though they deplored the necessity of resorting to extreme measures, yet they were unanimous in their determination to oppose the running of lines, or the making of roads through their country, until a settlement between the Government and them had been effected. I was further informed that the danger of a collision with the whites was likely to arise from the officious conduct of minor Chiefs who were anxious to make themselves conspicuous, the principal men of the large camps being much more moderate in their demands."[10]

Two chiefs were particularly willing to come to terms, anxious to begin the transition to farming. Mistawāsis and Starblanket were leading chiefs among the House People branch of the Plains Cree, so called because they tended to cluster around the houses of the Hudson's Bay Company posts, particularly Fort Carlton. The company and the missionaries portrayed and promoted both these chiefs as powerful individuals among the Cree and as particularly amenable to and malleable by the whites. Mistawāsis and Starblanket were quickly singled out to smooth the negotiations for the major treaty with the Cree, Treaty No. 6.

Fort Carlton in 1877, looking southwest from a point on the Prince Albert Trail. [Glenbow-Alberta Institute]

When Lieutenant Governor Morris arrived back in the North-West in August 1876, some elements of the Cree, Saulteaux, and Métis population tried, briefly and not very seriously, to prevent his entry into the Saskatchewan country. As he neared Fort Carlton, designated for the treaty negotiations, the first chief Morris met was Beardy, a leading chief of the Parklands people, who were camped at Duck Lake just east of Fort Carlton. Beardy refused to negotiate the treaty unless the talks were held at Duck Lake, a request Morris refused because he was on his way to see Mistawāsis and Starblanket, whose support he could count on.

Despite the troublesome beginnings, the negotiations for Treaty No. 6 were relatively smooth. For both the whites and the Indians, conditions had changed dramatically even in the two years since the signing of Treaty No. 4. It was obvious that the great buffalo herds had disappeared forever and the Indians were becoming very hungry. White immigration had increased dramatically, alarming the Indians and making it more imperative for the government to make a deal that would preclude violence between the natives and settlers. At Fort Carlton in 1876, where two thousand Cree had gathered, Morris was much more patient, much less condescending, and much more compromising than he had been when he met the Cree and Saulteaux at Qu'Appelle. The Indians, too, had learned something about treaty-making. There would be no stonewalling from them, but more discussion of the specific articles of the treaty. In 1876, it was critical for both sides that an arrangement be reached.

According to Peter Erasmus, the half-breed selected by the two Fort Carlton chiefs to interpret the proceedings, Morris was surprised by the hard line some of the Cree leaders took during the negotiations for Treaty No. 6. Shortly after talks began, Poundmaker, a headman of one of the River People bands, objected to the provision of reserves that represented one square mile of country for each family of five. "This is our land! It isn't a piece of pemmican to be cut off and given in little pieces back to us. It is ours and we will take what we want," Erasmus quoted Poundmaker as saying. The interpreter, who did not have much respect for Morris and his entourage but who also did not side with the more radical elements among the Cree, recorded the Lieutenant Governor's reaction when many of the Indians seemed to approve of Poundmaker's belligerence. "The Commissioner was visibly shaken by this demonstration that erupted at the beginning. His assumption had been that the Indians had completely adopted his treaty terms, which by his own words he was not authorized to change in any form. I thought to myself, 'A boxer sent into the ring with his hands tied.'"[11]

After the initial posturing, the Cree settled in to do some remarkably successful negotiating on the factor that mattered most to them: the fear that the transition to farming would not be as easy as the whites claimed. Poundmaker and another headman, Badger, acted as spokesmen for the group that wanted the treaty to include a provision guarding against hunger in case the Indians' farms did not produce sufficient food quickly enough. In the Cree council before the Indians went back to negotiations with Morris, Mistawāsis said he sympathized with the concerns of the dissidents but he saw no solution other than to accept the treaty and trust the goodwill of the whites.

I have heard my brothers speak, complaining of the hardships endured by our people. Some have bewailed the poverty and suffering that has come to Indians because of the destruction of the buffalo as the chief source of our living, the loss of the ancient glory of our forefathers; and with all that I agree, in the silence of my teepee and on the broad prairies where once our fathers could not pass for the great number of those animals that blocked their way; and even in our day, we have had to choose carefully our campground for fear of being trampled in our teepees. With all these things, I think and feel intensely the sorrow my brothers express. I speak directly to Poundmaker and The Badger and those others who object to signing this treaty. Have you anything better to offer our people? I ask, again, can you suggest anything that will bring these things back for tomorrow and all the tomorrows that face our people?[12]

Starblanket backed his fellow chief's pleas that the treaty be accepted. "Can we stop the power of the white man from spreading over the land like the grasshoppers that cloud the sky and then fall to consume every blade of grass and every leaf on the trees in their path? I think not."[13]

Poundmaker and Badger could neither bring the buffalo back nor stop the white man. But they could threaten to hold out until the treaty was changed to include some protection against hunger. The next day, Poundmaker began negotiations by requesting such a clause. But Morris told him the government could not give the Indians daily rations. It would cost too much and encourage laziness. "I cannot promise, however, that the Government will feed and support all the Indians; you are a great many, and if we were to try to do it, it would take a great deal of money, and some of you would never do anything for yourselves."[14]

The Cree did not want to be spoonfed, Badger replied. They just wanted some protection against hunger during the transition to farming. They were uncertain of the effects of making the change and wanted some assurance they wouldn't starve in the process. "We think of our children. We do not want to be greedy but when we commence to settle on the reserves we select, it is then we want aid."[15]

James McKay, one of the treaty commissioners and Manitoba Minister of Agriculture, replied in a condescending tone in Cree, accusing the Indians of demanding too much and questioning their sincerity. The Cree were insulted. "I did not say I wanted to be fed every day," Badger told McKay. "You, I know, understand our language and yet you twist my words to suit your own meaning."[16]

McKay's ill-considered outburst changed the tenor of the negotiations. Mistawāsis, so anxious to sign the treaty, rose to defend the radical Badger. "It is well known that if we had plenty to live on from our gardens we would not still insist on getting more provision, but it is in case of any extremity, and from the ignorance of the Indian in commencing to settle that we thus speak; we are as yet in the dark; this is not a trivial matter for us."[17]

The Cree won their point. Treaty No. 6 contained the clause whose vague wording would soon make it the most controversial of all the treaty provisions: "That in the event hereafter of the Indians comprised within this treaty being overtaken by any pestilence, or by a general famine, the Queen, on being satisfied and certified thereof by her Indian Agent or Agents, will grant to the Indians assistance of such character and to such extent as her Chief Superintendent of Indian Affairs shall deem necessary and sufficient to relieve the Indians from the calamity that shall have befallen them."[18]

The Cree wangled other concessions from Lieutenant Governor Morris, in the form of increased assistance during the first three years farming on the reserves, more livestock, and more farming implements. In lieu of some of the demands he felt he could not grant, Morris gave the Indians something they had not asked for: a horse, harness, and wagon for each chief. Morris did not make any extraordinary compromises. Some of the increased farming provisions had already been granted to Manitoba Indians under Treaties No. 1 and No. 2 in the so-called "outside promises" which had not come into effect until 1875. But the Saskatchewan Cree had done much better than the Cree and Saulteaux under Treaty No. 4.

Despite his success, Poundmaker was still not happy. He would sign the treaty, he announced, because the majority of his band wanted it signed. But he was not convinced the treaty provided all the assistance he might need. "From what I can hear and see now, I cannot understand that I shall be able to clothe my children and feed them as long as the sun shines and water runs."[19]

On August 23, 1876, Treaty No. 6 was first signed near Fort Carlton. A few days later at Duck Lake, Chiefs Beardy and One Arrow of the Parklands People accepted its provisions. The treaty commissioners then travelled north to Fort Pitt, where Chief Sweetgrass and the Cree of that area were easily persuaded to sign, but not before Chief Pakan made a request that would become a leading principle for many Cree politicians. Pakan wanted one huge reserve extending along the north shore of the North Saskatchewan River for many of the Plains and Woods Cree bands, not the relatively small and separated reserves that would be alloted individual bands. Lieutenant Governor Morris said he had no power to discuss such a request and the matter was dropped for the moment. Pakan misunderstood Morris and thought his request had been granted.

Poundmaker in 1886. Many whites regarded him as the epitome of the "noble red man." [Glenbow-Alberta Institute]

As the commissioners prepared to leave Fort Pitt on September 12, Big Bear arrived. He had not been informed of the time and place of the treaty talks, he told Morris. Because his people were all still out on the plains, he had no mandate to negotiate. But he promised to consider the treaty and to confer with his band.

With the signing of Treaty No. 6, the Cree at Forts Carlton and Pitt surrendered their rights to an enormous area of land, 315,000 square kilometres extending almost from the border between modern Manitoba and Saskatchewan to Jasper House in the middle of the Rocky Mountains, excluding the Treaty No. 4 area and the Blackfoot country. When Treaty No. 7 was signed the next year with the Blackfoot-speaking peoples, the Canadian government had treaties covering the whole of the North-West into which the whites were immigrating.

There were still large numbers of Cree who had not surrendered their land. Big Bear had not signed and the other leading chief of the Prairie People, Little Pine, did not attend the negotiations. None of the most numerous of the Plains Cree people, the westernmost bands that tended to congregate south of Edmonton, were represented. But by 1879, even those chiefs who intended to hold out as long as possible had taken treaty, with the critical exception of Big Bear.

There was one other group not represented at the treaty negotiations: the Plains Métis. At talks for both Treaty No. 4 and Treaty No. 6, the Cree sought assurances that their cousins would be dealt with and in his official report, Morris recommended that the government come to terms with them:

> There are a few who are identified with the Indians, but there is a large class of Métis who live by the hunt of the buffalo, and have no settled homes. I think that a census of the numbers of these should be procured, and while I would not be disposed to recommend their being brought under the treaties, I would suggest that land should be assigned to them, and that on their settling down, if after an examination into their circumstances, it should be found necessary and expedient, some assistance should be given them to enable them to enter upon agricultural operations.[20]

Unlike the treaties the United States signed with its Indians, the Canadian government did not require that the Indians take their reserves immediately. They were allowed to continue to live as nomadic hunters.

Some of the Plains Cree bands moved to their reserves and began farming as soon as Treaty No. 6 was signed. Many others took reserves relatively quickly but only half-heartedly took up farming, going back to the plains to search for buffalo each spring. Some, including Big Bear's band, stayed on the plains, intending to take a reserve only as a last resort. The Cree were slow to settle not only because of their inclination to the plains but because the government was deliberately slow to provide the farming assistance the treaties stipulated. The treaties said a band's farming equipment was not to be provided until the reserves were actually surveyed. Consequently it was economical for the government to delay the surveys. In the late 1870s, white immigration into the North-West still had not reached the level at which it was impracticable to have some of the Cree bands roaming the plains.

By 1878 many if not most of the Plains Cree people had gathered near the NWMP post of Fort Walsh in the Cypress Hills, which run north of the international boundary on the border between modern Alberta and Saskatchewan. The few remaining buffalo had been gradually moving south. In 1878 they were avoiding the western Canadian prairie partly because a series of prairie fires had burnt large sections of their grazing land near the international border. Some said the Americans had deliberately set the fires to keep the animals in their territory. There were still a few small herds in Canada just northeast of the Cypress Hills. As a result the Cree gathered near the border, where they were anything but alone.

The Cypress Hills were at the edge of Blackfoot country and, with what buffalo remained in either the United States or Cree country, the Blackfoot-speaking peoples also gathered there in the late 1870s. Sitting Bull's Sioux, who had crossed into Canada after their defeat of Colonel George Custer at the battle of the Little Big Horn in 1876, settled temporarily at Cypress. Their presence in the Cypress Hills attracted elements of other American Indian peoples and presented a major problem for both American and Canadian authorities. Stoney and Saulteaux bands, traditional allies of the Cree, and Sarcee, allied with the Blackfoot, were also camped there, as were Plains Métis from both sides of the border.

The gathering of so many natives, many of whom harboured violent jealousies against one another, was an explosive situation in anyone's view, with the Blackfoot in particular vocally complaining that the Sioux had driven the buffalo away from them. In early 1878, NWMP Commissioner James F. Macleod reported:

> The result of this condition of things was a large band of Blackfeet were gradually getting closer to the Sioux, who were, by degrees, making their way up from the south-east in pursuit of buffalo, while other bands of Indians and half-breeds were pressing in both from the north and south. The most extravagant rumors reached me from all directions. A grand confederation of all the Indians was to be formed hostile to the Whites, every one of whom was to be massacred as the first act of confederation. "Big Bear," a non-treaty Cree Indian chief, was said to be fomenting trouble amongst our own Indians.[21]

Big Bear had decided the only way to come to better terms with the whites was to stand up to them with a united force of all Indian peoples, regardless of the old animosities. If the success of such ideas was improbable in 1878, it would have been unthinkable only a few years before. Despite sporadic efforts at peace-making and temporary truces, the Blackfoot-speaking peoples and the Cree remained mortal enemies. The Blackfoot and the Sioux had always mistrusted one another. But after the treaties, conditions worsened so rapidly and so visibly for all the Indians that Big Bear's proposals made sense, at least to some of the prominent chiefs. A combined army of Cree, Blackfoot, and Sioux could easily have kept the whites out of the Canadian North-West. But Big Bear probably had no plans for a military solution to the Indian problems. Even if they had re-captured the North-West, with the buffalo obviously on the verge of extinction, there was nothing the Indians could have done with the country. The Indians needed the whites but they also needed much more favourable terms from their new rulers. A powerful political confederation, Big Bear believed, might be just the lever to force concessions.

NWMP Commissioner Macleod had a more realistic view of the situation than most white officials in the North-West. He told Ottawa:

The several Treaties which have been made are no doubt of the utmost consequence, for by them we have secured the Indian title, but if each one of them was carried out in its entirety [sic], if each and all of their provisions were fulfilled, even to the satisfaction of the Indians affected by them, the danger I apprehend would not be averted. It is not that the Indians are disaffected towards the rule of the Government; they appreciate that rule, and never cease expressing their gratitude for the paternal care the Govern-ment is taking of them; but in some parts of the country they are already brought face to face with starvation, and in other parts where buffalo are more or less numerous the poor creatures are very often in want of food. Hungry men are dangerous whether they be Indians or Whites, and I think it is a wonderful thing how well the Indian has behaved under all the circumstances of the case.[22]

Big Bear pressed some of his demands on Edgar Dewdney, the new Indian Commissioner of the North-West Territories, at the Treaty No. 6 annuity payments in the summer of 1878. For several days, he tried to persuade Dewd-ney that the treaty payments should be much increased. The *Saskatchewan Herald* quoted the chief as saying: "Before the white man came, the Indians had everything they wanted; now that the Government had taken their land it should provide for them, which could be done by increasing the amount now allowed them."[23] At the Blackfoot treaty payments, their leading chief, Crowfoot, made a similar demand.

As Commissioner Macleod realized, the demands extended beyond keeping treaty provisions or renegotiating the treaties. For the hungry Indians, the coincidence of the disappearance of the buffalo and the arrival of the white settlers was awesome. The buffalo had provided them with the staple of their diet and with the skins for both clothing and housing. With the buffalo gone and the whites to blame, they believed, not unreasonably, that the government owed them a living, regardless of the formal arrangements. In early 1879 at Duck Lake, Chief Beardy militantly promoted that view. The *Saskatchewan Herald* reported that "the views held by the Beardy on the rights of labor and property are such as would not disgrace the most extreme communist leader, and not only does he refuse to work himself, but he will not permit any of his young men either to work or hunt; he is a chief, he argues, and he and his band must be fed by the government." If his demands were not met, Beardy said he would seize the trading post in the community of Duck Lake and help himself. As a result, the NWMP stationed a detachment at Duck Lake.[24]

In 1879, the buffalo had all but disappeared from Canada and many of the Cree and Blackfoot-speaking bands went to American territory. Hunting was not much better there, and the Canadian Indians faced constant hostility from American ranchers, soldiers, and Indians. They returned, starving, across the border in the fall. Conditions were no better north of Cypress, even for those Indians who were trying to make a living on reserves. Throughout the year, large numbers of Indians visited the new territorial capital of Battleford to press their demands for food and treaty revisions. Even Blackfoot, Blood, and Sarcee ventured far into Cree territory and met Indian Commissioner Dewdney at Battleford. The Indians were destitute except for their horses, which they were parting with quickly. In June 1879, the *Saskatchewan Herald* reported: "Horses can be bought at Battleford now for a mere song, owing to the hard times on the plains. The Indians have brought in large numbers of good beasts, which they sell readily for two or three sacks of flour or other provisions."[25]

As the Blackfoot visited Battleford, about a thousand Cree had wandered to Blackfoot Crossing, east of Calgary, in search of food. When Dewdney visited the Crossing in July 1879, he reported:

> On arriving there, I found about 1,300 Indians in a very destitute condition, and many on the verge of starvation. Young men who were known to be stout and hearty fellows some six months ago were quite emaciated and so weak they could hardly work; the old people and widows, who, with their children live on the charity of the younger and more prosperous, had nothing, and many a pitiable tale was told of the misery they had endured.[26]

The Indian Department officials responded to these desperate pleas by issuing, often grudgingly, small quantities of provisions. The rations supplied the Indians, editor P. G. Laurie told his *Saskatchewan Herald* readers, were often no better than nothing. "The condition of these Indians is deplorable in the extreme. Accustomed all their lives to a diet consisting largely of animal food, the rations of flour and tea they receive here leave them but one remove from starvation." The lack of a general government response to the Indians' plight and the delay in surveying the reserves and helping the Indians start to farm was beginning to worry the white settlers in the North-West. Laurie, a staunch Conservative, editorialized: "It is probable that most of the members of the Dominion Cabinet will visit Manitoba this season. They should come up here and explain to the Indians why provision was not made to carry the treaty obligations into effect."[27]

The white authorities were most concerned in mid-1879 with the Sioux both at Cypress Hills and congregating around the settlement of Prince Albert and the Cree who had not yet taken reserves, particularly Big Bear. There was also growing dissatisfaction among those who should have been complaining least. At a meeting in August 1879, Mistawāsis and Starblanket, the two chiefs responsible more than any others for the signing of the treaty and the two who had been most anxious to try the new way of life, complained to Indian Commissioner Dewdney that the treaty provisions had not been fulfilled. They said their reserves had not been surveyed as they had directed and the farming assistance had not been forthcoming in anything like the quantity and quality promised. Starblanket told the Indian Commissioner:

We have often been talking of the promises we got, and when we saw that they were not carried out in their spirit, we made representations to the Minister; but they were as if they were thrown into the water. We are very glad to meet you now, as you come with full authority to act. We will not touch on anything, but the promises which have not been fulfilled. We are very much pleased with the aid given us, as we hear of starvation on the plains, there being no buffalo. We are only beginning to be able to support ourselves, and it will take time to do so fully. We want what aid Government can give us. We have endeavored to fulfil our part of the treaty.[28]

Tom White, publisher and editor of the Montreal *Gazette* and a prominent Conservative Member of Parliament, was among the witnesses to the meeting between Dewdney and the two Fort Carlton chiefs. From his own observation, White reported that most of the Indians' complaints were justified, though he blamed the situation on the Liberal government that had been in power from 1874 to 1878. What equipment and animals the Indians received under the treaty provisions were of such obviously inferior quality that the Indians had understandably refused to take delivery of some of it, White reported. "It is an unfortunate impression to get among the Indians that the treaties are made simply as a means of getting peaceable possession of the country, and to be kept with the least regard to their welfare."[29]

By the end of 1879, Dewdney was admitting that the Indians faced a real crisis, but he was proposing few solutions. He pleaded that everyone, especially Indians, be patient. Things could not get much worse, and once the natives learned to live as white men their suffering would cease. "We have to view the disappearance of the buffalo as a solid, sober, serious fact. The Indian of the Plains has for generations solely depended upon this animal for subsistence. Habits formed under his mode of life have in a great measure unfitted him for civilized pursuits. The Government is doing much to assist him, and after a sharp trial, during which there will doubtless be not a little suffering, let us hope that the crisis will be overcome."[30]

Despite complaints from the Indians and some whites, the government had not been altogether displeased by the status quo. The longer the movement to reserves could be put off, the cheaper it would be, especially if Canadian Indians went chasing buffalo south of the border. Dewdney later privately recalled that he had actually encouraged the Blackfoot to follow the buffalo into the United States and that "their remaining away saved the Govt. $100,000 at least."[31]

Most whites in the North-West did not agree. They were alarmed by Ottawa's Indian policy, or the effects of the apparent lack of a policy. In early 1880, the town of Prince Albert felt itself besieged by bands of Minnesota and Teton Sioux who were ranging along the South Saskatchewan River north of St. Laurent and Duck Lake. In reporting that residents of his community had established a committee to look into Indian conditions, a Prince Albert correspondent of the *Saskatchewan Herald* said: "If the Dominion Government intends to carry out a starvation policy with the Indians, then we will be no better than our cousins across the line, whom we condemn so lustily for their "extermination" policy. We cannot allow the Indians to starve in our midst, and the Government cannot expect us to feed all of the Sioux nation who may take it into their heads to winter at Prince Albert. And there is no need that we should be burdened with them."[32]

It was not just ethics or economics that compelled the Prince Albert whites to take action. They feared for their lives and property, the *Herald*'s correspondent reported. "The Indians are very well behaved—much more so than our English, Scotch, or Irish, or Americans, under the same pressure. He starves better than they do; and if whites in the centre of civilization, in the most enlightened and Christian parts of the world, have their bread riots, what can we expect from the poor untutored, unenlightened Indian? He must be fed; if he does not get it he will take it; and he is in a position to do so. It is easier and cheaper to feed them than to fight them."[33]

Big Bear spent most of 1879 travelling throughout the Canadian North-West and Montana trying to drum up support for his Indian confederacy. On the one hand, many native leaders agreed his ideas made sense. But, although he successfully patched up some isolated quarrels between the nations and the Mounted Police successfully prevented others, the animosity among the different peoples proved too strong. Despite the best efforts of their leading chiefs, elements of various nations still raided others' camps, though there was nothing like the open warfare of previous years. And with a growing number of Indians chasing the same rapidly diminishing numbers of buffalo, nations accused each other of trying to drive the animals into their own territory. If prospects for an Indian confederacy seemed dim, it was still possible to draw together bands of the Cree people and their allies, who traditionally lacked cohesiveness. Big Bear and some other Cree chiefs came up with an alternative plan. In the fall of 1879, Chief Little Pine requested a reserve near the large Indian Department supply farm just north of Fort Walsh. Chief Piapot requested a reserve next to Little Pine's. Ten other Cree and Stoney bands requested reserves contiguous to those two. If Big Bear had taken treaty and done the same, most of the Cree nation would have been concentrated in the Cypress Hills, in effect creating an Indian territory. Initially, the requests were granted. But once government officials realized what the Indians were trying to do, the decision was abruptly reversed. There could be no Indian territory that would be a continuing source of international unpleasantness and that would give political muscle to some of the more militant chiefs.

At Fort Walsh during the spring of 1880, the situation was bleak not only for the Indians who congregated there but for the police who had to deal with them. NWMP Superintendent Leif "Paddy" Crozier reported:

About the middle of April the Indians commenced coming in large numbers from Milk River, on the American side, where they had wintered. In every instance they were starving. Many said they had but little to eat during the greater part of the winter, and would have come to the Fort sooner had they been able; men and teams were kept constantly on the road with provisions to meet and feed the starving camps as they arrived. The number of Indians increased daily, until at one time there were as many as five thousand about the Fort.[34]

By the spring of 1880, farming instructors had been appointed to help the Indians settle on reserves, one of the very few programs of assistance the government provided the Indians that had not been specifically granted in the treaties. Both the Indians and the white settlers in the North-West had been demanding instructors be hired for the obvious reason that the Indians knew very little about farming. Although the unsettled state of the Indians since the treaty signings had saved the government some money, it was becoming more critical to get them onto reserves. The uncontrolled and unpredictable disbursement of rations to starving Indians was at least a nuisance to the government, and as immigration increased so did public pressure from the North-West that the Indians be got out of the way. It was obvious when the treaties were signed that the buffalo were doomed, but the suddenness of their disappearance surprised government officials and even many old hands in the North-West. Both the government and the Indians had expected a longer breathing space between the treaties and the time it became imperative that the Indians move to farming on reserves.

Hiring farming instructors was only one of the plans the government had to induce the Indians to settle and it was the only one the Indians supported. The government believed that rationing the Indians just encouraged them to stay on the plains, compounding their own and the government's problems and making the eventual transition more difficult. In future, the Indians would have to work for their rations, a policy that would be progressively more strictly enforced and lead to often dangerous friction between the Indians and the Indian Department.

In early 1880, the *Saskatchewan Herald* set out what was to become the rationale for the new rations policy. "Not only must the Indian be shown how to work, but he ought to be impressed with the idea that if he does not work, and work well and faithfully, as the white farmer has to do, neither shall he eat. He must learn that farming is work—a labor that brings its own reward when honestly performed—and that while he has been fed this winter, he must hereafter look out for himself. There will no doubt be many cases in which further assistance will have to be rendered, but not on the extensive scale that has been practised this winter."[35]

Herald editor P. G. Laurie, like the officials of the government he supported, believed the Indian belonged to an inherently lazy race, that he would not willingly work but had to be forced to support himself. The whites could not, of course, regard hunting, the Indians' traditional occupation, as real work. North America had adopted the European view that hunting was merely an aristocratic pastime. "The experience of the past winter has shown that the liberality with which provisions have been issued has not been an unmixed good; in fact it has in many cases been productive of real harm, by giving the Indian the idea that to be fed, he has but to say he is hungry—that as the Government will provide for all his wants, he need make no effort to help himself."[36] To the Indians, that was all very easy for Laurie to say. His background fitted him for the white man's world in the North-West. He did not have to learn a radically different way of life in order to survive. His land and his very means of subsistence had not been suddenly removed.

The Indians, despite what they saw as their best efforts, were still starving. In June 1880, the *Saskatchewan Herald* reported that a group of Stoney Indians had been reduced to eating their horses on their way to Battleford to ask for help. A short time later, provisions were sent from Battleford to help Chief Mosquito's band of Stonies on their reserve near town. "When the first portion reached them they had been subsisting for a length of time on bulrushes, roots, and grass; and when the pork and flour were distributed, many who ate it were so weak that they became seriously ill in consequence of the sudden change."[37]

The Indians in the Battleford district were getting desperate and there was a real possibility of violence. Late in June, Mosquito's Stonies held a council with the Cree under Chiefs Strike-Him-on-the-Back and Poundmaker. The *Saskatchewan Herald* reported the result of this meeting as "a demand for an extravagant

66

amount of provisions, coupled with the suggestion that if it was not forthcoming 'they might be under the necessity of taking it.'" They held a meeting with their Indian agent, "which ended in their getting a large amount of provisions for immediate use without arriving at any understanding as to the future, other than that the Indians seem to think they have been invited here to be fed, and that there [sic] wants will all be supplied on demand." The large Cree bands at Bears Hills south of Edmonton were making identical demands and threats.[38]

At the treaty payments at the end of July, Poundmaker acted as spokesman for the Cree bands at Battleford and told Dewdney they needed substantially more oxen and cattle than the treaties provided. The Indian Commissioner agreed. "I have thought over that myself, and last year when travelling through the country I came to the conclusion that those who were working on the reservations in many cases had not enough teams to work with, while some had too many implements and others not enough." Poundmaker told Dewdney that if the government wanted to encourage the Indians to settle, it must do all it could to help those already on the reserves, regardless of what the treaty specifically provided. "The Crees that are not settled are watching those Indians that are now on the reserves to see if they can make their living out of the ground with what assistance the Government gives," Poundmaker said.[39]

Dewdney would not back all the Cree demands but he said he would recommend that Ottawa provide more cattle. The assembled Indians, including such unlikely supporters as the well-known warrior Wandering Spirit, all said they were pleased by the agreement Dewdney and Poundmaker reached. But the apparent compromise at Battleford was only a temporary lull in the struggle between the Indians and the government.

At Duck Lake in July, Chief Beardy tried to make good his threat to seize the local trading post. The Mounted Police prevented that but, apparently under their chief's orders, Beardy's Indians shot three government cattle, and the police were sent to make arrests. When NWMP Superintendent William Herchmer and his party arrived at Beardy's camp, "he was confronted by a large number of Indians armed with knives, which they brandished and threatened to use; and another portion of the band had guns, with which they tried to frighten the police by firing a volley over their heads."[40] But the police stayed calm and arrested Chiefs Beardy and One Arrow and several other Indians without a fight. The chiefs were subsequently acquitted and one band member was found guilty of killing the cattle, for which the Indians offered to pay.

For most of 1880, Chief Big Bear was in American territory working on his plans for a grand native alliance. In this he found a new and powerful ally. In the spring of 1880, Crowfoot, the leading chief of the Blackfoot-speaking peoples, and some of the Cree chiefs met exiled Métis leader Louis Riel, who was then living in Montana. Crowfoot recalled that Riel "wanted me to join with all the Sioux, and Crees, and half-breeds. The idea was to have a general uprising and capture the North-West, and hold it for the Indian race and the Métis."[41] Crowfoot said Riel took Chief Little Pine's copy of Treaty No. 6, trampled it under his foot, and said that the Indians deserved better.

Crowfoot's interpreter, Jean L'Heureux, remembered some of the details of Riel's invasion scheme. "The practical plan was to take opportunity of some horse difficulties of the Police with the half-breeds; attack and take possession of Wood Mountain Fort; they were then to make for Fort Walsh, and from the last place, make for Battleford. The Blackfeet were to take possession of Macleod. After that last exploit, Riel was to proclaim a provisional government."[42] Riel planned a council of the Indians and Métis for May 1880 in Montana, but the American authorities prevented it by announcing that those attending would be escorted back to Canada.

Big Bear and Crowfoot camped side-by-side that autumn and Riel again visited them. L'Heureux reported to Dewdney: "Riel and his frontier partisans are expected to renew their last year's tactics for fomenting trouble and half-breeding [sic] conspiracies with the Indians. He is only waiting at the Judith Basin [in Montana] the result of [General Nelson] Miles' campaign against the hostile Sioux, for a political campaign of his own whose program is 'That the N.W.T. is the natural property of the Indian and Half-breed, ought to be set apart for their exclusive use, ruled & governed by them alone.' That is his modest motto."[43]

The Canadian government got rid of one major problem in 1880. Most of Sitting Bull's Sioux were persuaded to return to the U.S., although the chief himself and a few followers returned for a while the next year. But the new alliance that seemed to be forming among the Blackfoot, Cree, and Métis was a source of considerable anxiety.

The authorities were understandably concerned about Big Bear's and Riel's activity. But as yet those efforts were just talk. In late 1880 and early 1881, the government had real trouble to worry about. The Indians were beginning to take out their anger on Indian Department employees, anger at what they saw as an oppressive and inconsistent government Indian policy.

At Frog Lake, north of Fort Pitt, Farm Instructor John Delaney was the first victim. When he refused rations to two Indians, he was horsewhipped. The Indians were sent to jail for two months. On Moosomin's reserve, near Battleford, an Indian who tried to stab the farm instructor received an identical sentence. At about the same time, Yellow Mud Blanket, Poundmaker's brother, was acquitted of a charge of threatening to stab a farm instructor in a dispute over provisions.

The additional cattle Indian Commissioner Dewdney had promised the Battleford Indians had not materialized. Poundmaker was angry and his band was hungry. In February 1881 he announced that if the Indians were not given extra provisions, he would kill one of the oxen the government had provided his band. He dared the police to arrest him. The previous year, Chief Beardy and

"WHAT IT MUST COME TO. (With the encroachment of civilization.) Officer—
'Here, you copper colored gentlemen, no loafing allowed, you must either work or
jump.'" This cartoon was published shortly after the rebellion but it is a particularly
apt, and blunt, portrayal of the feelings of Eastern Canada towards the Indians of the
North-West. Sir John A. Macdonald leading a horde of workingmen, backed by the
railway (smoke from a train engine spells "civilization" in the cartoon), pushing the
Indians into the ocean was a popular image. [The Toronto *News*, June 20, 1885]

some of his band had been arrested for a similar action. But Beardy's mistake had
been in killing cattle that had not yet been turned over to him, cattle that were
still unquestionably government property. When one of the Poundmaker oxen
was killed and no action was taken, other bands were encouraged to do the same.
In March, the *Saskatchewan Herald*'s P. G. Laurie editorialized: "These bands
have thrown down the gauntlet; they refuse to work, and declare that they will
not go hungry a day as long as there is an animal left on the reserves, and they
further give notice that they will not put in any crop this spring. These bands
fancy that they are the masters of the situation, as there seems to be no law to
punish any Indian for killing the cattle belonging to the band as a whole; and this
belief coupled with the idea that the police are too weak to make any arrests, is
making them quite saucy and independent."[44]

The government had instructed its employees to stop rations to those
involved in killing cattle but, as Laurie pointed out, that was no solution. It
simply confused the issue and delayed settling the real questions. "A vacillating
and temporizing policy has led the Indian to see that by persistent repetition
their most extravagant demands would be granted for a time, to be followed by a

withdrawal which to them seem without a cause. At one time fed liberally and promised almost everything they asked for, they were at another left on the verge of starvation; at one time encouraged to believe that the Government would do everything for them, they were at another bidden to go and hunt for themselves; so that they did not know what to do."[45]

Poundmaker was not a Plains Cree chief for all the usual reasons. He was not a great hunter like his uncle Mistawāsis, nor was he a great warrior like his friend Little Pine. His father had been a Stoney shaman, noted for his ability to make pounds and entice buffalo to their slaughter, hence the name which was passed on to the son. But Poundmaker, unlike many other Cree chiefs, was not particularly devout, although he did have a keen interest in history and delighted in collecting and telling the stories of his people. Poundmaker did possess to a remarkable degree one of the customary attributes of Cree chiefs: he loved to talk and he could do it very well. His friend, farm instructor and schoolteacher Robert Jefferson, recalled that "his bearing was so eminently dignified and his speech so well adapted to the occasion, as to impress every hearer with his earnestness and his views. Indeed, for the time being, I believe he impressed himself."[46]

As a young headman in the Red Pheasant band, Poundmaker made good use of his speechmaking ability at the Treaty No. 6 negotiations at Fort Carlton in 1876. In those talks that the white negotiators tried to carefully control and dispose of quickly, Poundmaker's was the leading voice among those who argued that the proposed treaty was not good enough and who pressed for more detailed explanations of its terms. At the treaty talks, Poundmaker argued strongly from an Indian rights position, promoting the view that Indians ought to be negotiating from a position of strength. Poundmaker's view did not prevail and he signed the treaty with the other chiefs and headmen. However, he had made quite an impression on the assembled Indians, especially on those who had doubts either about the treaty terms or the white man's inclination to carry out the treaty fairly.

Poundmaker emerged from the treaty talks as one who could argue with the whites on their terms and one who took a firm stand on Indian rights. For many Cree, Poundmaker seemed an ideal spokesman. The two main political leaders of the River Cree, Little Pine and Big Bear, didn't like talking to the white man and avoided white officialdom. But Poundmaker relished the opportunity for a battle of words with the whites. For the Cree at that point in their history, Poundmaker was important for another reason: he was closer than most to their traditional enemies, the Blackfoot. When Poundmaker was a young man, Chief Crowfoot had chosen him as an adopted son, to replace, in the Plains Indian custom, one of his own children who had been killed in battle. Since then, Poundmaker had spent some time with his adoptive father and had found an avocation in patching up quarrels between Cree and Blackfoot. It was becoming obvious to many of the Cree leaders, particularly Little Pine and Big Bear, that negotiating any truly favourable deal with the whites required a concerted effort by all plains peoples. To achieve this, old differences had to be smoothed.

For the whites, Poundmaker was a key figure for much the same reasons as he was for the Cree. They badly needed someone prominent among the dissidents with whom they could at least talk. If a powerful spokesman for Indian rights such as Poundmaker could be enticed to give the reserve system a try, it was likely that many Cree would desert the more radical leaders. For the whites, too, Poundmaker's appeal was in his appearance and his bearing. Portrayed as the epitome of the noble red man, Poundmaker was described as having qualities that would stand well in the white community: he was handsome, fashionable, and friendly, and he spoke well and freely. In a way, he looked and talked more like a white man than most Indians did. A newspaper reporter wrote of him:

> He is a noble looking Indian, and reminds one more of Fenimore Cooper's heroes than do the great majority of North-West Indians. His eyes are black and piercing. One moment they twinkle merrily at some humorous remark, and the next they flash with fire as something is said that is not agreeable to him. His nose is long and aquiline, while his lips are thin and his mouth devoid of that sensual character so peculiar to many Indians. His hair hung in one long plait for more than a yard down his back, and was tied round with a red bandanna handkerchief. The scalp lock was decorated with a mink skin, while from each temple there hung one long lock of hair twisted round and round with brass wire. He wore no coat, but his vest was richly decorated with brass-headed nails in true barbaric fashion.[47]

Poundmaker's personal following grew and he was named a chief and took a reserve in 1880 with 182 followers. At first he didn't stay on the reserve long. He was back on the plains looking for buffalo by the summer of 1881, but by then it was obvious there would be no more buffalo and that fall Poundmaker decided the Cree's only hope was a diligent effort to make farming on the reserves work. The turning point for the new chief came with the visit to the North-West of Governor General the Marquis of Lorne in the summer of 1881. Poundmaker accepted the job of guiding Lorne south from the Battleford area to the Blackfoot country and he was impressed by what he heard from the Governor General and his entourage. The new Lieutenant Governor, Edgar Dewdney, who also retained his position as Indian Commissioner, took that occasion to tell Poundmaker that rations for the Indians might be completely cut off in the coming year, or at least greatly reduced. Poundmaker decided that the whites were too numerous and too sophisticated for the Indians to resist. They had to make terms and the only basis on which to make terms was the flawed treaty.

When Poundmaker came back to his reserve west of Battleford after the

Lorne tour, his original fears of the inadequacy of the treaties were already too obviously true for comfort. There was just not enough assistance, in instruction or in equipment, to make farming work well on the reserves. Indian department employees were high-handed and arrogant in their dealings with reserve Indians, and those who had been powerful chiefs on the open prairie found themselves bossed around as ordinary workers. The government was trying to enforce a work-for-rations policy that the Indians believed was contrary to the treaty clause that promised assistance in case of famine.

The Indians believed the treaty guaranteed them a sufficient supply of food until they were well-established enough as farmers to provide for themselves. They had particular faith in the famine clause in the treaty, one of the few clauses that was a result of Indian demands. But the government took a radically different view of the famine clause. Government officials believed they were under no obligation to supply rations except in the case of a general famine. The Plains Indians had been consistently very hungry since the buffalo suddenly disappeared. Ottawa, however, refused to consider widespread hunger as the famine they interpreted the treaties to mean. Rations, in Ottawa's view, were a gift, not an obligation. It was also official Ottawa policy to use rations as payment for work.

On a day-to-day basis, individual Indian Department employees were free to dole out rations as they saw fit, and many used their prerogative to reward Indians for doing specific jobs or to punish Indians for disobeying Indian Department rules. As Robert Jefferson explained it, Hayter Reed, the Indian agent at Battleford in 1881, "had calculated to a nicety how much work a yoke of oxen and a plow were capable of performing in a given time and the Indian fell a good deal short of this. He had figured out how little food it was possible to get along with and the Indian was always hungry. The Indian was lazy, therefore he must have short rations; if he fell sick, there was the doctor who could give him pills but no food."[48] This was in marked contrast to the treatment the Indians received from the Hudson's Bay Company, with whom they had had a close relationship for two centuries before they found they had to deal with the government at Ottawa. Despite his obvious bias, Frog Lake trader Bill Cameron did not exaggerate when he explained the relationship between the Indians and the Hudson's Bay Company: "Their treatment by the Company had always been considerate and humane. If an Indian was sick he went to the nearest post and was supplied with food and medicine until he became well. When ready to go on a hunt he was outfitted with provisions, traps and ammunition, for which he paid in furs on his return. The Company made him advances in goods on account of his annuity and waited almost a year for payment, trusting entirely to his honesty for settlement of the debt. After a trade he always got a small present. When hungry he was never denied a meal."[49] The Hudson's Bay Company needed lots of healthy, happy Indians to gather the furs that provided the company its profits on the European market. On the other hand, the government's interest was keeping the Indians as far as possible away from the settlers. It would have suited the Indian Department best if the North-West had contained no Indians. Burdened with the natives, the government had to make sure they were properly subjugated so that they would not interfere with orderly settlement or the interests of the white businessmen who depended on the settlers.

The situation was so confusing and so disheartening that Poundmaker, the great orator, was almost at a loss for words. He did not know what advice to give his people. A united Indian effort was unlikely to stop the whites too long. The Big Bear-Little Pine scheme to establish a Plains Indian confederacy seemed as much a dream as ever. The Indians starved on the plains searching for non-existent buffalo. When they acquiesced to the treaty and went to the reserve they were little better off physically and had to endure a morally-debilitating second-class citizenship. Poundmaker gave a feast for his band on New Year's Day 1882, and in his speech the chief admitted he had no solutions except to plead that the Cree all stick together and support one another during the crisis.

Next summer, or at the latest next fall, the railway will be close to us, the whites will fill the country and they will dictate to us as they please. It is useless to dream that we can frighten them; that time is passed; our only resource is our work, our industry, our farms. The necessity of earning our bread by the sweat of our brows does not discourage me; there is only one thing that can discourage me,—What is it?— If we do not agree amongst ourselves; let us be like one man, and work will show quick, and there will be nothing too hard. Oh! allow me to ask you all to love each other; that is not difficult. We have faced the balls of our enemies more than once, and now we cannot bear a word from each other.[50]

The chief took his own advice. From the white point of view, all through 1882 Poundmaker was a model Indian. Unlike the previous year, he did not grumble or threaten Indian Department employees. He worked hard at farming and all but abdicated any role in Indian politics. He refused to cooperate in a demand from his neighbouring chief, Strike-Him-on-the-Back, that treaty payments take place at Battleford instead of on the reserves, long a matter of dispute between the Cree and the Indian Department. He quietly accepted a fine imposed on him for killing a calf. When *Saskatchewan Herald* editor P. G. Laurie visited Poundmaker's reserve in the fall, he reported:

The fields were generally free from weeds, potatoes and turnips were in very good order, while the grain crops appeared to have been properly cared for; but best of all, no idle Indians were seen lounging around—none were to be seen except in their fields at work—and their chief, dressed as becomes a Canadian farmer, with sleeves turned up, was busy, fork in hand, in securing his excellent crop of wheat. He seemed to take great pleasure in showing visitors around his extensive, well fenced and neatly kept field; and the chief need not feel ashamed to point out any corner of his grounds, as there are no weeds or noxious growth of any kind within his fences. It would be well if there were more such fields even in white settlements.[51]

This represented a very temporary lull. Despite the glowing reports, progress even on Poundmaker's reserve would not be enough to satisfy the Cree. There was still too little help from the government for the Indians to make the transition to farming quickly and smoothly. With rations all but cut off during the cold winter of 1882-83, many bands were pushed even closer to general starvation.

The Cree agitation that began soon after the treaty was signed occurred mainly at Cypress, Battleford, Qu'Appelle, and Duck Lake. Very little had been heard from the large bands in what is now Alberta. At Bears Hills, about eighty kilometres south of Edmonton, a concentration of Cree bands was led by two brothers, Chiefs Ermineskin and Bobtail, and by Chief Samson, who had inherited the mantle of the legendary Maskipitoon. Frustrated in their dealings with local Indian Department officials and disappointed by their lack of success farming on their reserves, those three powerful chiefs were the leading names in a strongly-worded letter sent in January 1883 to John A. Macdonald in his capacity as Minister of the Interior. Their eloquent, desperate plea contained a thinly-veiled threat.

Nothing but our dire poverty, our utter destitution during this severe winter, when ourselves, our wives and our children are smarting under the pangs of cold and hunger, with little or no help, and apparently less sympathy from those placed to watch over us, could have induced us to make this final attempt to have redress directly from headquarters. We say final, because, if no attention is paid to our case now we shall conclude that the treaty made with us six years ago was a meaningless matter of form and that the white man has indirectly doomed us to annihilation little by little. But the motto of the Indian is "If we must die by violence let us do it quickly."

The treaty had been broken, the chiefs told Macdonald. Promised farm implements and cattle had not materialized. Rations to the starving Indians had been cut off. The employees of the Indian Department were uncaring and arrogant. The Indians had fared no better in their dealings with Lieutenant Governor Dewdney, the man in charge of Indian Affairs in the North-West.

Why does not the head man of the Indians ever appear amongst us, he whom we call in our language the "white beard," and by the whites called Dewdney? He took a rapid run once through our country; some of us had the good or bad luck to catch a flying glimpse of him. He made us all kinds of fine promises, but in disappearing he seems to have tied the hands of the agents, so that none of them can fulfil these promises. This is the cause of our dire want now. We are reduced to the lowest stage of poverty. We were once a proud and independent people and now we are mendicants at the door of every white man in the country; and were it not for the charity of the white settlers who are not bound by treaty to help us, we should all die on government fare. Our widows and old people are getting the barest pittance, just enough to keep body and soul together, and there have been cases in which body and soul have refused to stay together on such allowance.[52]

If the plea of the Bears Hills chiefs made any impression on Macdonald, he never let on. Indian Department policy was to become more strict, the government believing that the main thing was to force the Indians, discontented as they were, to make a living on the reserves. If rations were given out as a matter of course, the Indians would simply rely on government largesse and not build the foundation they needed to make the transition to farming. Only when the Indians realized that there was a simple choice between farming and starvation would they progress. In effect, it was a policy of starving the Indians into submission, but many government officials honestly believed that in the long run it was for the Indians' own good. The Indians must be made as independent on their farms as they once had been on the plains. And the faster that was accomplished, the cheaper it would be. To increase economy, the government planned to decrease the aid provided to the reserves in the form of farming instructors and farming implements as quickly as possible, aid that many Indians protested was woefully inadequate in the treaties as they were written and which most bands said they had not received even to the extent the treaties stipulated. In his report for 1882, the Superintendent-General of Indian Affairs, John A. Macdonald, said his department's policy had been so successful that many Indians no longer needed help.

I am glad to be able to report that the advanced condition of the Indians, settled upon reserves in several localities in the Territories, admitted of the closing during the past season of the Instructor's [sic] farms in those localities. The object for which they were established, namely: the practical exemplification to the Indians of the manner in which farms should be managed, has been attained. It is hoped that next Autumn the Indians in several other localities will be sufficiently advanced to admit of a similar change being effected.[53]

As usual, with their chief administrator, Dewdney, safely ensconced in Regina, and the policymakers, Macdonald and Deputy Superintendent of Indian Affairs Lawrence Vankoughnet, far away in Ottawa, the local Indian Department officials bore the brunt of Indian anger, sometimes at the peril of their lives. A few Indian Department employees administered the policies the

Indians considered vindictive and outrageous so humanely and sympathetically that they actually earned the respect and friendship of those placed in their charge. But many more compounded their problems by making themselves as obnoxious as the government policies. At the Eagle Hills Stoney reserves south of Battleford, Farm Instructor James Payne's dislike of Indians was equalled only by their disgust for him. In January 1883 Stoney Chief Lean Man went to Payne's house to present the usual grievances and renew his pleas for more help for his band. Payne threw him out. Lean Man stormed back in and Payne threw him out again. When the farm instructor opened the door a third time, Lean Man had a cocked revolver pointed at Payne's head. Some other Indians grabbed the chief and saved Payne's life but neither the instructor nor the government learned anything from the incident. Payne stayed at the Eagle Hills, unwavering from the high-handed course that would eventually cause his death.

By June 1883 even Poundmaker was discouraged enough to reenter the Cree political scene. He put in his crop and headed south to consult with Big Bear before he went to Regina to make renewed demands to Lieutenant Governor Dewdney. This time Poundmaker had some tentative support from the white community. P. G. Laurie, who tended to gloss over Indian complaints and put the Conservative government's policy in a rosier light than reality warranted, realized how pivotal Poundmaker had become and worried about the effect of the chief's discouragement and his new agitation. Poundmaker "claims that while he has fulfilled his share of the compact entered into when he agreed to leave the plains and settle down, he has not received all that he understands he was to get. He is the only chief around here who has displayed any energy in his operations, or who conducts himself with dignity, and it would have a bad effect on the other bands of the district, if, from any fault not his own, he should be made to forfeit his high position as the most industrious, best behaved, and independent chief in the district."[54]

The Indian Department's biggest problem in the spring of 1883 was still the large congregation of Indians near the border at Cypress Hills, bands that had so far refused to take reserves and were being led by Chiefs Big Bear, Little Pine, Lucky Man, and Piapot. NWMP Commissioner A. G. Irvine had angered Ottawa by feeding the destitute Cree the previous fall. As long as the prominent dissidents remained in their favoured Cypress Hills, each spring they would attract large numbers of Cree who had already settled on the reserves. The Cree were relying on the NWMP post for sustenance and the only thing to do was close Fort Walsh.

Piapot and his band were among the first to be persuaded to move in the spring of 1883. The chief announced that he would settle at Indian Head, just east of Qu'Appelle, where, combined with Paskwāw's and several other reserves, there would be a concentration of two thousand Indians, just west of the group of Plains Saulteaux at Crooked Lakes. About eight hundred of Piapot's band were loaded into CPR boxcars at Maple Creek for the trip east. The train had not gone far when two boxcars, one of them full of Indians, slipped off the track and rolled down an embankment. The boxcar ended up on its side, its door blocked, and its ends had to be broken open to free the Indians. There were no serious injuries, but the Indians were understandably irate. Some of the Indians thought the accident was part of a plan to kill them all. They drew their knives and chased the brakeman, whom they held responsible, down the track. The brakeman escaped, tempers eventually cooled, and most of the Indians got back on the train to resume the journey. Those who had been in the overturned car decided to walk to Qu'Appelle. Piapot and his band didn't stay long at Indian Head. They were soon back at Cypress.

In June, shortly after Fort Walsh was closed, Dewdney went to Cypress Hills to meet the Cree chiefs. His interview with Piapot was discouraging. The chief loudly denounced Hayter Reed, who had just been promoted to Assistant Indian Commissioner and who was the strongest proponent of a harsh Indian policy. Piapot demanded food and announced he would hold a Thirst Dance for Treaty No. 4 Indians at which they would decide their strategy. Piapot also announced he was withdrawing from the treaty and he angrily left his treaty flag and medal with Lieutenant Governor Dewdney.

Closing Fort Walsh had an effect, although not exactly the effect the government had intended. The chiefs realized they could not subsist in the Cypress Hills and they would have to change their tactics. Piapot agreed to move back to his reserve. Little Pine and Lucky Man said they would go to Battleford to request reserves next to Poundmaker's for another concentration of two thousand Cree, just north of the Stoney reserves at the Eagle Hills. If the chiefs could not force the government to agree to contiguous reserves in the Cypress Hills, they still thought they could effect large concentrations around existing communities. Big Bear also agreed to move north. At the last moment, just as the Cree bands were leaving Cypress, Little Pine had second thoughts. He and his band crossed the border looking for buffalo. But by then, even on the American side of the border, there were only small, scattered herds of buffalo. By mid-July, Little Pine was back at the Cypress Hills.

Chiefs Big Bear and Lucky Man were at Battleford pressing their demands on John Rae, who had been promoted to Indian Agent when Hayter Reed moved to Regina to become Dewdney's assistant. On July 22, Big Bear made a long speech to the agent, a speech that P. G. Laurie thought was so much a litany of the usual, and in Laurie's mind outrageous, grievances that he didn't bother to report the substance of it. Big Bear ended his speech with a demand that his band be given beef. When Rae replied there was no beef, Big Bear demanded that an ox be killed. Rae refused that, and when the Indians threatened to kill one themselves, Rae threatened to throw them in jail. Laurie had grown tired of listening to the Indian appeals and in his words, the confrontation between the chief and the new agent was "a contest between the good nature of the agent and the gluttony and laziness of the Indians."[55]

As the Battleford Cree pressed their demands for provisions and contiguous reserves, the Bears Hills Cree made good the threat in their letter to the prime minister. They journeyed *en masse* to Edmonton and on July 23 demanded provisions from their agent, who replied that they would only be fed on their reserves. He finally compromised and gave the chiefs a small quantity of flour, saying that was all he had. The next day the Indians renewed their demands. When the agent said he had no more provisions, the Indians replied that there was plenty of food in the Hudson's Bay Company fort. They grabbed the agent and dragged him to the fort where he still stubbornly refused to give them food. The Hudson's Bay Company came to the agent's rescue by advancing provisions to the chiefs against their next treaty payment, the company's usual practice. That satisfied the Indians, who had been joined at Edmonton by other Cree and Stoney bands. Then they learned that the agent had sent for the police from Fort Saskatchewan, the main NWMP post in the area, just downstream from Edmonton. They waited for Inspector Sévère Gagnon and his detachment, then renewed their demands to the NWMP, with whom, like the Hudson's Bay Company, they had had traditionally better luck than with the Indian agents. Gagnon gave in and provided the Indians some supplies from his own stores. After a victory dance, the Indians went home.

By fall 1883, Chief Lucky Man managed to get a reserve next to Poundmaker's but the government balked when Big Bear, who had finally signed Treaty No. 6 the previous year, made a similar demand. It was one thing to have a concentration of large numbers of Indians; it was quite another to allow several powerful chiefs to be neighbours. Big Bear was eventually persuaded to move to Fort Pitt and find a place for a reserve there. Big Bear would be cut off from his fellow River Cree chiefs but there were already large concentrations of Woods Cree in the Fort Pitt area and Pakan's Whitefish Lake reserve was just to the west. When Lawrence Vankoughnet, Macdonald's Deputy Superintendent of Indian Affairs, toured the North-West in September, he gave Big Bear an ultimatum: either the chief must quickly select a reserve site near Fort Pitt or all assistance to his band would be cut off. When Chief Little Pine arrived back at Battleford later that fall, he fared a little better than Big Bear. He was not given a reserve, but he was allowed to winter next door to Poundmaker.

Vankoughnet's visit followed changes in the administration of the Department of Indian Affairs in the North-West that were bound to result in stricter adherence to Ottawa's policy. Hayter Reed, who had always taken a very hard line dealing with the Indians, had been promoted. He was second-in-command of Indian Affairs for the North-West, Dewdney's assistant. John Rae, a particularly unimaginative agent whom Reed had trained, was in charge at Battleford, potentially the most volatile point. Tom Quinn, whom the Indians regarded as the most stubborn and obnoxious of the Indian Department's employees and who was another Reed trainee, was sent to Fort Pitt to deal with Big Bear. There would be far less negotiating with the Indians. The work-for-rations policy would be far more universally applied. Bands would no longer be allowed to delay choosing reserves.

When Reed arrived at Battleford in November 1883 to make the annual treaty payments, he quickly put his no-nonsense approach into practice. Chiefs Lucky Man and Little Pine at first refused to take the payments until Reed listened to their complaints and negotiated some of their grievances. The Assistant Commissioner refused to talk with them. If they didn't take their money immediately and let him move on, there would be no payments at all that year, he told them. Reed's threat was undoubtedly illegal, a point he never let get in his way when he dealt with Indians, and he probably couldn't have carried it out. But faced with the prospect of getting nothing at all, the chiefs submitted to the bluff and took their money without having the opportunity of presenting their complaints.

For a short while in the fall of 1883, it looked as if the Indian Department's hard line, now far more consistent than in previous years, finally might have worked. Battleford was quiet. At Duck Lake, Beardy was bragging about his crops. At Qu'Appelle, Piapot had been prevented from holding a Treaty No. 4 Thirst Dance by threats to cut off rations and make arrests. And at Fort Pitt was the best news of all for the whites. Big Bear appeared to have become so domesticated that he had started a freighting business between Fort Pitt and Edmonton.

But just beneath the surface, the Indians were seething with resentment that began to show itself before the year ended. In December, the NWMP at Fort Macleod arrested a Cree on the Blood reserve. He was an emissary of Big Bear, sent to invite the Blackfoot and their allies to attend a joint council with the Cree. Nothing came of the proposed Cree-Blackfoot council but Big Bear was still working on plans for a major Treaty No. 6 council in the spring, as Piapot was making similar plans for Treaty No. 4. Big Bear was also still pushing for large concentrations of Cree reserves. On one of his freighting trips to Edmonton, Big Bear tried to persuade Pakan to renew his demand for a reserve that extended far further east than the one he had been granted. If he were successful, Big Bear would demand a reserve that stretched from the eastern boundary of Pakan's to Frog Lake, making a huge area stretching along the north shore of the North Saskatchewan River Indian territory. He also told Pakan, according to an Edmonton *Bulletin* report, "he would not go on a reserve until he saw all the implements, cattle and other matters that had been promised him, there first. The white men, he said, made many promises but they were very slow of fulfilment."[56]

Big Bear was also vocal in his attitude toward officials of the Indian

Department. It seemed that every time he complained, even to Lieutenant Governor Dewdney, he was told the local officials were just following orders. He was tired of dealing with a seemingly endless string of subordinates. Big Bear said he wanted to go to Ottawa where, if there was really some person in charge of Indian Affairs, the chief would find him and deal only with him.

CHAPTER FIVE

Confrontation 1884

The Métis were not prepared to go to war over their grievances, and the first real trouble of 1884 did not come from the discontented Cree either. The Plains Saulteaux had been relatively quiet during the Cree agitation. At the end of 1883, James Setter, farming instructor at the Crooked Lakes Saulteaux reserves about one hundred and twenty kilometres east of Regina, was fired for contravening government policy by giving rations to Indians who had not worked. In early 1884, the Cree and Saulteaux in that area were indeed very hungry. Edwin Brooks, a settler at Indian Head on the CPR line west of Crooked Lakes who had become friendly with Piapot and some of his band, wrote of their plight in a letter to his wife who was still back East. "There are lots of them dying on the reserve. They are really in a good many cases starving to death through the neglect of the Government to furnish them supplies. The Indians say they are going West next summer even if they have to fight for it, as they say it is better to die fighting than to be starved."[1] Indian Affairs officials had a much different perception of reality.

When Assistant Indian Commissioner Hayter Reed arrived at Crooked Lakes in January with Setter's replacement, Hilton Keith, he reported to Dewdney that the Indians on Saulteaux Chief Yellow Calf's reserve were actually pretty well off. They had ample opportunity to fish and hunt for small game and they had grain from their harvest. Reed left Keith with strict instructions to issue no rations except to the aged and to those who worked for them. The Indians, who had already protested Setter's removal, were indignant.

As Hudson's Bay Company trader N. M. W. J. McKenzie recalled:

> The Indians were making stiffer demands on Keith every ration day for more grub. Keith told me what his instructions were, and that he intended to carry them out. I said: "Keith, for God's sake, do not reduce their rations any lower, or there will certainly be trouble." He carried out the Assistant Commissioner's instructions. A few of the Indians died. The others came time and again asked for more grub which they were denied. Finally they broke into the government storehouse, threw out as much flour and bacon as they wanted, and threw Keith out on the top of it.[2]

It was February 18 when Yellow Calf led a group of about twenty-five warriors to see Keith. The instructor explained Reed's strict directives and said that all he could give them was ammunition for hunting. Then, as Keith reported to Dewdney, "they made a rush for the warehouse, I followed them and tried to defend our stores, whereupon I was knocked down kicked and bruised, and struck at, with a knife, by many of them, the knife ran across my leather coat thus saving me. They then all swarmed in like bees into a hive and stole right before my eyes, about sixty sacks Flour and 12 of Bacon."[3]

When the news of the incident reached Regina on February 20, Reed, acting in Lieutenant Governor Dewdney's absence, dispatched NWMP Inspector Burton Deane and ten policemen to the scene of the trouble. Whey they arrived at the reserves on February 22, they had difficulty finding any Indians. Finally Louis O'Soup, a leading agitator among the Saulteaux during the years they had spent at Cypress Hills, offered to direct the police to the house where many of the Indians were gathered. But O'Soup warned Deane, Hayter Reed reported, that negotiations would not be easy "as the Indians considered themselves justified in their action in that they, or many of them, were in want of food at the time they took it, and that they had not had an opportunity of laying their grievances before the Lieutenant-Governor."[4] Deane, wisely not wanting to provoke a confrontation, sent his men back to the farm instructor's house and, with an interpreter, went to talk to the sixty or seventy Indians gathered in a house near the river.

Deane, who made an effort to treat the Indians as children and use words of only one syllable, told them he had been sent by the Queen to find out why they had stolen the supplies. As he later recalled it, Deane told the Indians:

> The Great White Mother is very sorry to hear that her Indian children have done this wicked thing. She keeps a store of food on the Reserve so that her Indian children will not starve. She gives them of this food every two or three days, and expects that they will be content with what she gives them without money and without price. She feels quite sure that her Indian children would not have stolen her goods unless some bad men had put bad thoughts into their hearts, and she expects that those Indians who led the others in this bad act will give themselves up to be tried.[5]

If the Indians were insulted by Deane's condescending tone or his nonsense about the queen, or if it was even translated to them, they did not let on. The meeting lasted for more than two hours. In reply, the Indians said cutting the rations was a breach of faith, that they had only taken what hungry Indians rightfully deserved. But they promised to consider giving up their leaders for trial and would talk with Deane again the next day.

The next morning, NWMP Superintendent William "Billy" Herchmer arrived with ten police reinforcements and the entire police party started off to the house where the Indians had gathered. "When we came in sight of the house we could see that there were a number of armed Indians round about it. Some had shot guns, some had Winchester rifles, but every Indian present had a firearm of some sort," Deane recalled. Indian Agent Allan McDonald had arrived just before the police and Yellow Calf had told him the Indians would not allow themselves to be arrested. McDonald wanted to keep talking. But Herchmer, one of the many NWMP who were long on courage and short on common sense, formed the police into a line and, because they were not carrying rifles, ordered them to draw their pistols. The window of the house was knocked out and the space filled with guns. Indians appeared around the corners of the house. Agent McDonald was not about to take responsibility for the police action. "I'll have nothing to do with it," he said as he turned and left.[6]

Herchmer walked towards the house, watched by an incredulous Deane.

Herchmer had taken no more than a couple of paces towards the door when a big, fine looking and determined Indian who was guarding the door presented his double barreled shot gun full in his face at a distance of something like two feet. Herchmer stopped dead, as in my opinion he was well advised to do, for there was certainly murder in the dusky ruffian's eye. The other Indians followed his example and we were all covered. A movement on the part of any one of us would have precipitated a climax. As the seconds passed without an ulterior act it became evident that it remained with ourselves to force the situation or not.

I do not know what Herchmer proposed to do in the house even supposing the Indians had admitted us all. We had no warrant to arrest anyone—no information had been laid, and neither of us knew who the guilty parties were. Thus, from a criminal point of view, we had no locus standi [legal standing] whatever. We were, in effect, provoking the Indians to commit wilful murder by threatening to thrust ourselves into premises into which we had no right to force our way.[7]

Herchmer tried to force his way no further. He called for the chief. Yellow Calf appeared and held on to the door guard's shotgun as he talked to the policeman. A short time later, Indian Agent McDonald returned and defused the situation by suggesting everyone move to O'Soup's house for negotiations. At that meeting, Deane recalled, "the Indians, however, were no longer in the complaisant mood of the evening before—they had hardened their hearts, and resolutely refused to give up the offenders."[8] Superintendent Herchmer reported to Ottawa that Yellow Calf offered to give himself up to trial and replace the stolen flour but the chief said the young warriors who had actually carried out the raid would not allow themselves to be arrested, "that they would fight to the death—that they were well armed, and might just as well die then as be starved by the government."[9]

Hayter Reed arrived in the afternoon of February 24 to try to break the impasse, but it was not until the next day the Indians were persuaded to talk to him. O'Soup acted as spokesman at this meeting and told Reed the Indians had taken nothing except what they were due. O'Soup said, as Reed reported it, that many of the band "were in a state of great distress—having been a hunter all his life he knew that hunting had lately become impossible. Directly the surface of the snow became touched by a thaw no animal could be approached. So with fishing, it was not possible now to catch a single fish—well then—if hunting and fishing were out of the question and rations allowed were not sufficient to keep them alive what were they to do?"[10]

In a rare effort at negotiating with Indians, Assistant Indian Commissioner Reed reached a compromise. The government would not press charges of resisting the police if some band members gave themselves up on theft charges, for which they would be dealt with leniently. The Indians also apparently wangled a promise that rations would be increased, though Reed did not mention this in his official report. Yellow Calf and three others allowed themselves to be arrested.

At the trial on February 28, it was arranged to drop the charges against Yellow Calf. The other three pleaded guilty and received suspended sentences on a promise to pay for the stolen property. After the trial, Judge Hugh Richardson called Inspector Deane and Superintendent Herchmer into his chambers to ask them what they thought they were doing on the reserve without a warrant. Deane's answer was easy: "I simply obeyed orders which I received from my superior officer." Herchmer said nothing.[11]

The Indian Department's rations policy had backfired so completely that the usually intransigent Hayter Reed was forced to compromise, then make excuses to his superiors about why he had been uncharacteristically accommodating to the Indians. It was a matter of necessity, he argued. The Indians "knew their own power; they knew that the first gun shot would imperil the safety of every isolated settler throughout the whole North-West. They knew that the White mans [sic] iron horse is useless when the rails on which it travels have been torn up."[12]

Everyone knew the affair had been badly bungled, Deane recalled. "So far as the Government was concerned, the matter was promptly hushed up. Herchmer never made any allusion to it in any of his reports. I wrote the report which Hayter Reed sent to his department, and he struck out of it all reference to the complaints made by the Indians that they were starving."[13]

In his official report, Reed did make one mention of the Indians' condition. It was not the way Deane would have reported it, but Reed came close to reversing his former position that the Indians had nothing to complain about.

That the actual rioters were in a condition near starvation, I cannot admit for a moment, their appearance belies the supposition; and if their appearance did not, the well-filled Cartridge belts, and Winchesters would imply some means of provision; but it is certain that many of the Comparatively well to do, suffer from their Charity to the indigent and infirm. Sickness is more or less rife amongst them, there is not a ready market even for those who have grain to sell, and the present time of year is notoriously prolific of discontent.[14]

Late winter and early spring was the time of discontent among the North-West Indians for obvious reasons. It was then their food supply was at its lowest, especially after a hard winter. It was also the time when the bands had to consider what they would do when the snow melted. Would they stay on the reserves and plant or would they go to the plains and hunt? Would they make another attempt to hold meetings to consider concerted political action? The Crooked Lakes affair was only the first in a series of incidents in 1884 that brought the whites and Indians in the North-West perilously close to war.

News of the incident quickly spread among the Indians of the North-West. At Battleford, P. G. Laurie reported in the *Saskatchewan Herald* that "our Indians say they are as much entitled to increased rations as those of the Qu'Appelle District, and intend going to Regina to see about it."[15] Some of the Indians on Poundmaker's reserve decided a repetition of the Crooked Lakes incident would solve their problems, but the authorities at Battleford learned of the plans and sent a detachment of NWMP to protect the Indian Department storehouse on the reserve.

The Battleford Indians were waiting for Big Bear and his band to arrive for a council. Chiefs Lucky Man and Little Pine were camped at Poundmaker's and refused to budge no matter what rations Indian Agent Rae cut or what threats he issued. Rae anxiously pleaded that the government pass an order-in-council somehow making it illegal for Big Bear's planned gathering to take place and forcing the Cree back to their own reserves. He also prudently bought up all the rifles and ammunition available in the Battleford vicinity and the police force at Battleford was strengthened.

When Lieutenant Governor Dewdney visited the Qu'Appelle area reserves in late April, he found the Indians demoralized and discouraged with farming and he discovered there was some merit in their complaints, despite what his deputy had reported. He wrote Sir John A. Macdonald:

At Crooked Lakes I found that very little preparation had been made for the Spring work, and the Indians generally were depressed, a large number of new arrivals had wintered on the Reserves; and those who had raised any produce had been compelled to feed [them] grain and roots out of their stores, which they intended to keep for seed. When they were assured by me that seed would be supplied them, sufficient to crop all the ground, they would prepare; they took fresh heart; but complained they were short of ploughs, implements, and cattle, and on inspection I found such to be the case.[16]

Dewdney also found a great many sick Indians, especially on Cree Chief Pia-pot's reserve. He reported that "salt food aggravates these diseases, and all the Reserves are calling out for fresh meat, or if that is not to be got, ammunition, so that the Indians might get ducks. I have authorized a little tea, Tobacco, and ammunition for those that work; and have instructed the farmer [instructor], to issue a little tea to such every evening after the work is through, where it can be done."[17]

When he visited the Battleford area a couple of weeks later, just after Chief Big Bear arrived, Dewdney professed that he found Indian matters much more settled than he expected. In a speech to the citizens of the old territorial capital, Dewdney said his tour of inspection showed that "our old settled Indians and many of the late arrivals from the south were never so contented as they are at present; nor have they ever shown such willingness to work as they have this spring. On the two reserves I visited yesterday over one hundred acres have already been put in crop on each and this is entirely with Indian labor—men, women and boys all working with a good will. This certainly does not look like an Indian uprising."[18]

That was wishful thinking. All the danger signs were there but the Lieuten-ant Governor chose to ignore them. At a meeting at Battleford, Chief Pound-maker complained bitterly that he was not in charge on his own reserve, that the Indian Department stores and equipment rightly belonged to the bands and they should have control of them. He said the government's employees ought to be servants of the Indians, not the other way around. Poundmaker also complained that Indian Agent John Rae harboured ill will against him. His comments were noted briefly then ignored.

Dewdney and the other white listeners grew so tired of Big Bear's four-hour speech at Battleford that they stopped taking notes. He complained of all the treaty promises he said had not been fulfilled and repeated his vow not to take a reserve until more assistance was actually provided, not just promised. Big Bear complained that Sub-Indian Agent Tom Quinn at Frog Lake refused to give his band rations. Wandering Spirit, the war chief of Big Bear's band, complained about contradictory instructions from Quinn about taking a reserve. Big Bear's request that the Lieutenant Governor remain four days at Battleford to negotiate the Indian grievances was summarily denied.

When a number of Stonies from the Eagle Hills reserves arrived at Battleford to talk to Dewdney, he refused to see them and stopped their rations for eight days as a punishment for leaving their reserves without the government's permission.

Dewdney did make sure to report one part of Big Bear's speech to the prime minister. The chief had talked of his efforts to have a council of all the Cree particularly to press a demand for contiguous reserves. But, Dewdney told Macdonald, Big Bear had admitted he had failed, that the Indians would not

Thomas Trueman Quinn, Sub-Indian Agent for the Fort Pitt area, in 1884. To the Indians, he was the most obnoxious of the government's employees. To the government, he was the ideal personality to deal with Chief Big Bear's dangerous band. [Glenbow-Alberta Institute]

come together in one great council. The Lieutenant Governor should not have been so reassured by Big Bear's apparent lack of success.

While Dewdney was at Battleford, Cree Chief Piapot, Saulteaux Chief Yellow Calf, and Stoney Chief Long Lodge, with about seven hundred followers, left their reserves on their way to the nearby Paskwāw reserve for a Thirst Dance and council. The chiefs complained their reserves were too swampy, that the salty bacon they were usually provided was causing scurvy, and that treaty promises, especially regarding clothing and provisions, had not been kept. They said they wanted to have a council with as many Treaty No. 4 bands as possible to discuss the situation. The movements of the armed, angry, and hungry Indians greatly alarmed the white settlers in the Qu'Appelle area. A *Manitoba Free Press* correspondent reported from Indian Head on May 16: "A general feeling of alarm prevails. The Indians far outnumber the white inhabitants and the former, if exasperated, would have things all their own way." The whites recognized that Piapot's band was badly off and that their reserve site had been very poorly chosen, the newspaper's correspondent reported.

> The mortality among his band has been terrible. They had many deaths during the winter months. The bodies of the dead were strung up in trees as is the Indian custom. Spring found some fifty or more ghastly corpses dangling from limbs of trees surrounding the teepees of the remaining members of the band. Warm weather increased the number of deaths alarmingly. The deadly malaria arising from the sloughs in the vicinity carrying them off at the rate of seven or eight a day.[19]

Even Assistant Indian Commissioner Hayter Reed could no longer maintain the fiction that the chiefs' complaints were unjustified. If the words of the Indians and white settlers were not evidence enough, Dr. O. C. Edwards, sent by the Indian Department to investigate the situation on the Qu'Appelle reserves in early May, reported an alarming incidence of disease and death from a type of scurvy caused by a lack of fresh meat and proper rations. Chief Long Lodge refused to let Edwards treat his people, telling the doctor: "I want no government medicine, what I want is medicine that walks. Send 3 oxen to be killed and give fresh meat to my people and they will get better." Edwards backed the chief's prescription.

> I would recommend that, first, fresh meat be supplied them, as an absolute requirement in arresting the disease also that in addition potatoes be given them to eat and a quantity of rice be kept at each agency and that when one is sick and cannot take meat a proportion of rice be allowed. Many of those who have died this winter have died from absolute starvation. They were ill and could not eat the bacon and flour and having nothing else died. The only proper treatment of this disease [scurvy] whether on land or sea is fresh food

and vegetables and unless this policy is persued [sic] in the case of these Indians the disease will spread. It is useless to depend on supplying them with ammunition alone. It is good as far as it goes, but the ducks and [prairie] chickens are very scarce this year.[20]

Reed couldn't suppress the doctor's strongly-worded report. But when he sent it to John A. Macdonald, he blamed the situation on the Indians themselves. "No doubt the death rate is large but it must be borne in mind that the first seeds of their complaints were sown during the sojourning of the Indians in the Fort Walsh District, owing to immoral habits, and were it not for this fact the use of bacon would not have such a hurtful effect." Despite the dire condition of the Indians, Reed recommended only a very modest increase in the supply of fresh meat and potatoes and he suggested this could be accomplished economically by cutting back on flour and bacon. There was nothing essentially wrong with Indian Department policy, he told the prime minister. The amount of rations issued was sufficient to prevent starvation, but there was a question about the kind of rations. "Where the Doctor speaks of starvation the same does not mean that the quantities issued were not sufficient but that the Indians were unable to eat the bacon."[21]

On May 16 and 17, NWMP Commissioner A. G. Irvine and Hayter Reed visited the various bands moving towards Paskwāw's reserve. The chiefs told them them were not happy with their reserves, that the swampy land was exacerbating sickness among the Indians. But the negotiations with the Indians were not very successful, particularly with Piapot, who kept moving north. In Irvine's words: "Having explained to him that the Government would not permit armed bodies of men, whether Indians or whites, to roam about the country at large, and that he must well consider his future movements, we left him to reflect thereupon, and returned to Regina for an escort."[22]

On May 18, Commissioner Irvine and Superintendent Billy Herchmer left Regina for Qu'Appelle with fifty-four policemen and a cannon to head the Indians off before they reached Paskwāw's reserve. The expedition was designed more to reassure frightened settlers than it was to overawe the Indians. Irvine had pointed instructions from Dewdney to, at all costs, prevent Piapot from holding a council. Irvine was to arrest the chief on the slightest pretext, and to ensure that there was indeed a slight pretext, Hayter Reed had arranged for a member of Paskwāw's band to object to the council being held on that reserve so that Piapot might be charged with trespassing.

Piapot and Long Lodge learned of the police movements and tried to evade them, but Irvine caught up with them at dawn on May 21. The commissioner intended to be diplomatic and not bluster into a dangerous situation as his subordinate had at Crooked Lakes.

When within four miles of the camp, I rode on in advance with the interpreter. On nearing the camp I noticed that the Indians were still asleep in their lodges; an alarm however was quickly spread, when they all turned out, mounting their horses, and tearing down the lodges, evidently being under the impression that they were going to be attacked. I rode direct to "Pie-a-pot's" lodge, and told him, that I had not come with the intention of fighting them, but for the purpose of endeavouring to persuade him to return with his followers to their reserves. He then told me that he had been promised by Mr. Reed the Assistant Indian Commissioner, that fresh meat would be supplied this spring, for the sick Indians, but that they had not received it, and further that they had been promised Clothing by Mr. McKinnon the Farm Instructor on the reserve, which they had not received, and that these with other minor grievances were the cause of their leaving their reserves.[23]

Irvine wasn't about to try anything as foolish as carry out Reed's and Dewdney's wishes by arresting the leading No. 4 chief in the midst of so many angry Indians. In fact, with a little tact, things were much easier to work out. Irvine simply promised Piapot that if the Indians would move to Fort Qu'Appelle and camp there, Hayter Reed would come to meet them and discuss their grievances. When Piapot agreed, Irvine had prevented the Treaty No. 4 council without a dangerous confrontation. Even Irvine did not realize at the time how dangerous the situation really was. While he was talking with Piapot, Indians on neighboring reserves heard shots coming from the direction of Piapot's camp. It was a false alarm, but Indian Agent Allan McDonald later reported that the Indians were convinced the police had attacked Piapot and they had armed themselves for battle. Even the Indians on Muscowpetung's reserve, whom McDonald described as having no particular love for Piapot and who did not want any trouble, "if the worst had taken place they were going to help their own kind."[24]

Reed and Irvine met Piapot and Long Lodge at Fort Qu'Appelle on May 22. The chiefs agreed to go back to their reserves but from Irvine's accounts, the meeting appears to have been inconclusive regarding the Indian grievances, ending with Piapot pleading with Irvine to use his influence to get a new reserve for his Indians. In fact, whether or not he admitted it to Piapot, Reed had again been forced to compromise. At the beginning of the trouble, as the police left Regina, Reed told Irvine that Piapot might be permitted to look for a new reserve if he did not take his band roaming over the countryside with him. There was no guarantee he would in fact be allowed to select a new site; only that he might apply for one. However, Ottawa had begun to take a more moderate view of matters than its officials in the field. Lawrence Vankoughnet, Macdonald's Assistant Superintendent-General of Indian Affairs, had already telegraphed Reed that if Piapot were so dissatisfied with his reserve site, he should be allowed to select a new one.

Back at Battleford, it looked as if Big Bear's great council would take place after all. It would not be a council of all the Cree and there would be no Blackfoot delegates, but the Battleford bands were planning a Thirst Dance on Poundmaker's reserve for the middle of June, to be held under Big Bear's auspices.

Indian Agent John Rae had warned the previous December that Chiefs Big Bear and Little Pine were planning a council at the Battleford reserves. Although Big Bear's discussions with Dewdney in the spring had tended to reassure the government officials, Macdonald and Vankoughnet had instructed Dewdney to act quickly and sternly at the least sign of trouble at the planned Battleford council, in case any of the Indians acted in a "riotous disorderly, or threatening manner." In February, Vankoughnet wrote Dewdney:

> My own impression is that an example should be made of Chiefs or Indians who are guilty of such infractions of the law; and, as there is a considerable Police force now on the Saskatchewan, it appears to me that the arrest and transport of the guilty parties to prison, if convicted, should be a matter of comparatively easy accomplishment and that such a procedure on the part of the Authorities would have a beneficial effect upon the Indians generally in the North-West in deterring them from similar acts in the future.[25]

That policy was to come in handy very soon, but as many of those charged with carrying it out in the North-West knew, it was much easier said than done, especially for people sitting safely in Ottawa who did not have to wade into the midst of angry warriors led by such legendary and militant chiefs as Little Pine and Big Bear.

If Dewdney recognized the dangers his officials and the police faced in carrying out a policy of selective arrests, he did not tell Ottawa. In his reply to Vankoughnet, Dewdney said there would be no problem making the arrests. It was difficult, however, to persuade magistrates to hand down sentences that were not only in line with the law but that also coincided with the Indian Department's desire to make examples of agitators and get them out of circulation. "Magistrates are apparently disinclined to look any further than the evidence presented on the offence committed—and their punishment being only in relation thereto without regard being had to the desirability of keeping the prisoner away from his friends during an anxious time."[26]

By June 7, more than two thousand Cree had gathered at Poundmaker's reserve for the Thirst Dance and council and some of the Indians went to Battleford to stage a Hungry Dance. The local citizens responded generously with donations of food but the authorities were not impressed. Indian Agent Rae fined the Indians six days' rations for leaving their reserves without permission. *Saskatchewan Herald* editor P. G. Laurie was worried about concessions the government might make as a result of the renewed Indian agitation. There was little danger of serious violence, but compromise would only encourage the

Indians, he warned. It was time for the government to be resolute and to quickly single out and punish agitators. "The time for temporizing has passed away; give the Indians their rights, but nothing more."[27]

At Edmonton, *Bulletin* editor Frank Oliver was taking a much more pessimistic view of events. Oliver was all in favour of policies that kept the Indians from interfering with white settlement and business. He had good Liberal reasons for criticizing government policy, but his views happened to be a better reflection of reality than those of Conservative apologist Laurie. "The cause of the discontent is no secret to any person living in the North-West. Promises made when the Indians were strong and the whites weak are not carried out now that the whites have become strong and the Indians weak. While the Indians in a general way have been well treated there has throughout been a failure on the part of the Canadian government through its representatives to recognize the sacredness of a promise to say nothing of a treaty stipulation." If there were no change in government attitude, "all that is required is the occasion and a leader to land the North-West in the middle of a first-class Indian war."[28]

On the other hand, Oliver characteristically noted, a war with the Indians might not be altogether a bad thing. It would show them once and for all who was boss and bad publicity for the North-West might be better than none.

> If there was an outbreak tomorrow it would not last long, it would be easily quelled. It would bring money into and advertise the country, and it would result in the complete subjugation if not destruction of the Indians, so that from one point of view it would be a benefit rather than otherwise. But that is not the point. Treaty money is not paid, implements, cattle and rations issued and the salaries of agents, assistant commissioners, and commissioners paid in order to breed war. If that were the end to be attained it could be reached by much shorter means. The whole and sole end and aim of the existence of the Indian department is to preserve peace with the Indians, and if it fails in this as it seems likely to, it has been a fraud, and the money spent by it has been thrown away.[29]

As the Cree prepared for the start of their Thirst Dance on June 17, two Indians went to see John Craig, farm instructor on Little Pine's reserve. Then, Farm Instructor Robert Jefferson recalled, "a metaphorical bomb fell and burst in our midst." Jefferson, who held an even lower opinion of Craig than he did of most of the rest of his Indian Department colleagues, described the events.

> According to Craig's story, they had come while he was in the storehouse and demanded food; which demand he had refused with appropriate gestures. He could speak no Cree; they, no English. Craig seems to have lost his head, since the controversy culminated in his pushing the men out. One of the intruders then took an axe-handle that was near the door and struck Craig on

Frank Oliver. As a younger man in 1885 the fiery Oliver was one of the leading critics of government policy in the west. [Provincial Archives of Alberta]

the arm with it. This was an unpleasantness which at such a juncture, should have been avoided. Craig's arm was not injured, but his feelings were, so he took his case to the police.[30]

The five-man police detachment under Corporal Ralph Sleigh on Little Pine's reserve, which had arrived the previous evening to keep an eye on the Indians, went to the main Cree camp, on the boundary between the Little Pine and Poundmaker reserves. There, Chiefs Big Bear and Poundmaker said the Indians would rather fight than allow anyone to be arrested. They dared Sleigh to try to arrest the chiefs. The police prudently withdrew and sent word to Battleford.

This was just the excuse the hard-liners in the Indian Department had been looking for. A clearly illegal act had been committed and Big Bear and Poundmaker, the two leading agitators, openly defied the the white man's law. It was exactly the sort of trouble that must be nipped in the bud.

Indian Agent Rae recognized the precarious position in which his employers had placed him. He told Dewdney that if the politicians wanted to apply their Indian policy and uphold the law, they must

> make up their minds to fight the Indians, and send men, horses and cannon enough to give us a fair show. It is not feasible to expect that enraged Indians will quietly submit to the law which means among other things, arrests. To make them submit to arrests and obey the law generally under the present policy is to fight them, and orders to that effect should be sent if the present policy is to be carried out. Too much should not be expected of these new Indians who have never been on a Reserve. Although it is very easy to send orders from Ottawa I should like to see some of them run an agency under existing orders.[31]

Despite his worries, Rae left for the reserves the next morning, June 18, with NWMP Superintendent Leif Crozier and about thirty police. Crozier left his main force some distance from the Cree camp and went on with only a small party. When they reached the place where the Thirst Dance was taking place, Crozier, Rae, and Sleigh pushed their way into the tent. The Indians took little notice as Sleigh tried and failed to identify Craig's assailants. Crozier and his companions went back to the main force of police.

Crozier and Rae decided it would not be wise to attempt an arrest until the dance ended and Crozier made an alternative plan. He sent back to Battleford for the rest of his command, another thirty men. Then, to prevent pilfering, the police loaded the provisions from the Little Pine reserve storehouse on wagons, hitched up the agency's oxen, and began to move to the farm instructor's house on Poundmaker's reserve, which Superintendent Crozier intended to fortify and use as his base.

It was dusk when the little party set out to Poundmaker's reserve on a road that passed through the Thirst Dance camp. Robert Jefferson rode in the last wagon with Rae and Craig.

The road led straight through the camp and, as we wished our movements to be as unobtrusive as possible, we made a considerable detour round the circle of tents. Before we had got very far the Indians who had been commandeered to drive the oxen, deserted us. This journey made a lasting impression on me. At the beginning there was quite a suspicion that we would not be allowed to carry off the provisions without interruption. The desertion of our teamsters depressed interruption to molestation and we had serious doubts as to whether we should get through alive. These doubts showed themselves in agitation, in hurry, and in disorder. They received confirmation in the "warwhoops," the yelling and shooting that assailed us till we had passed out of hearing of the camp. I have since come to the conclusion that the Indians were merely trying to frighten us, as the bullets that whistled over our heads might just as easily have been sent into our midst. But we had other things to think of than motives or the dissection of circumstances, and everything sounded real enough at the time.[32]

Crozier and his party worked all night fortifying the instructor's little house. They pulled down an old log shack and built bastions at each end of the house. They piled sacks of flour and oats behind the logs to make their fortifications bullet-proof. They built earthworks behind the house as a corral for the horses. Jefferson worked as hard as anyone, but he was not impressed with the results of their efforts. "Neither of them was a bastion in much more than name. They were, in some sense, shelters in addition to the house from which men, too crowded to do anything but get in one another's way, could have fired at the enemy until the Indians rushed the place and massacred us all. The Indians had a very poor opinion of them."[33]

The reinforcements arrived late in the afternoon of June 19, but Superintendent Crozier delayed doing anything until late that night when the Thirst Dance ended. Then he, accompanied only by an interpreter, went to the Cree camp to try to persuade the chiefs to give up Craig's assailant. The negotiations lasted most of the night, beginning with a discussion of Farm Instructor Craig. Crozier reported that "they complained that Craig the Instructor had used them badly at different times and often, and that he had in the instance of this particular man refused to give him a little flour that he had asked for, when he was sick and had shoved him."[34]

The chiefs said they sympathized with Crozier's intent to solve the problems quietly and let tempers cool. But they warned the policeman that they could not speak for their young warriors who, in the large camp, were more in control than they were. Crozier was aware of the danger.

The Chiefs, including "Big Bear," were doing, or seemed to be doing all they could to have the man given up quietly; they said however from the first, they did not think their influence was sufficient to induce the young men to consent to this course, and if an attempt was made to take him forcibly, they felt sure bloodshed would follow,—Other people living about the reserve said the Indians meant war—and from what I saw myself, I knew that they were in a very bad temper. ... What made me most anxious to avoid a collision was the fear that the first shot fired would be the signal for an Indian outbreak with all its attendant horrors, and in the camp, Indians comparatively well disposed towards us would have been excited when the firing commenced and naturally would have joined their own people against the whites;—but more particularly was such a danger to be apprehended, if any of these ordinarily well disposed Indians, or their wives or children had been killed or wounded. From tribe to tribe would the disaffection have spread, until the whole Indian [race] was against the white population. To isolated settlers, such a condition of affairs would be terrible, without mentioning the extent to which such a condition of things would have delayed and prevented immigration.[35]

Crozier at first agreed to an Indian demand that Kāwēchetwēmot, the man who struck Craig, be tried in the Indian camp, but Poundmaker objected. If fighting broke out during the trial, some of their wives and children might be hurt, the chief argued. Crozier and the chiefs then agreed that Craig's assailant would be brought to the farm instructor's house that morning for trial there.

When the Indians didn't arrive on the morning of May 20, Crozier went back to their camp and talked with them until late afternoon. He finally persuaded the Indians to bring Kāwēchetwēmot to the instructor's house but when they came to the top of a hill about a kilometre from the makeshift fort, the warriors, numbering about two hundred, balked. They would go no further and they would not allow an arrest to be made. Crozier walked back to the house.

Crozier despaired of being able to negotiate Kāwēchetwēmot's arrest. He ordered his police, some on foot because they didn't have enough horses, to advance towards the Indians as he and a small group went ahead for one last attempt to make the arrest without using force. Crozier described the Indians as "intensely excited and making the most thrilling and indescribable gestures and noises—some of the older ones, including 'Big Bear,' shouting 'Peace, Peace.'"[36] Chief Lucky Man brought up Kāwēchetwēmot, who pleaded his case to Crozier. He had been sick and wanted provisions for himself and a sick child when Craig threw him out of the house. He wanted the matter dropped.

But Crozier could not leave without a prisoner and he made a grab for Kāwēchetwēmot, who dashed into the crowd of Indians, pursued by four policemen. The next few minutes were bedlam, later described in the *Saskatchewan Herald*.

Now ensued a scene of the most indescribable confusion and uproar, many of the Indians crying out "Now is the time to shoot," while others implored them to wait until the police fired the first shot. The mounted men, who had arrived in the meantime, extended in rear of the party on foot and were ordered to dismount and cock carbines—a manoeuvre which caused the Indians to scatter. In the melee two policemen, who belonged to the party on foot, were overpowered and disarmed. Indeed, for a few minutes things looked very darkly, and it was nothing short of a miracle that prevented bloodshed, for had a rifle or a revolver gone off accidentally in the scuffle, there is no telling what might have been the result, as firing would undoubtedly have become general and war to the knife have been declared.[37]

Even Poundmaker, who had been so pacific during the negotiations, was caught up in the excitement. He rushed at NWMP Inspector William Antrobus, a policeman he particularly disliked, and threatened him with a pukamakin, a war club with three butcher knives imbedded in its head. Someone pulled Antrobus back and the police covered Poundmaker with their rifles. The chief and some other Indians then rushed to a policeman who had become separated from his comrades, knocked him to the ground, and took his rifle.

Somehow, in the confusion, the police got not only Kāwēchetwēinot but also his brother, who had been with him on the visit to Craig. The Indians taunted and threatened the police as they dragged their prisoners to the instructor's house. But no shot was fired and no one was more astonished than Superintendent Crozier. "It is yet to me incomprehensible how some one did not fire, and it is more than fortunate they did not— Had a shot been fired by either the Police or Indians, I fear it would have been the signal for an engagement, and when that had taken place, it is hard to foretell what the consequences to the country would have been."[38]

With the warriors milling around the inadequate fort, Rae and Crozier decided to break Indian Department rules. To pacify the Indians, they would issue rations. The tactic worked. As the provisions were being doled out, Crozier took Farm Instructor Jefferson aside. He wanted the Indians to believe he regarded the events as only a minor incident, not as dangerous confrontation. Indian Agent Rae, the police, and their entourage would soon leave for Battleford, but would Jefferson be willing to stay at his post and pretend nothing serious had happened? Jefferson was not anxious to be put in that position but he agreed after Chief Little Pine took Jefferson under his personal protection. The farm instructor, his brother, and another man who had arrived with the volunteers were soon the only whites on the reserves. The Indians went home and they were all alone.

We did not sleep long that night; events were treading on each other's heels. In the early dawn of the summer morning, we were wakened by a thundering on the door. Indians, armed in all kinds of ways, were demanding their share of the "grub" that was being distributed. These, it appeared, had been overlooked the evening before, or they had gone home early to avoid trouble, or some other equally good reason was given for getting what they wanted. In any case, it behooved me as one in charge to repair such portentous omissions and heal up properly the wounded feelings of the Indians after such a providential escape. Of course, all this sounds tame and commonplace enough and it is only when connected with the wild character of the speakers and with every menace of voice and action, of appearance and demeanor reinforced by untiring pertinacity, that an estimate can be formed of the contract I found on my hands.[39]

Jefferson acted with a diplomacy unusual in Indian Department employees. He told the Indians that he had no authority to issue more rations and until he had permission he would give them none. On the other hand, he was only one man; they were numerous and could simply break into the storehouse and take the supplies if they really wanted them. But the Indians would not be the instigators. They wanted either Indian Department handouts or Indian Department intransigence, something they could respond to.

They had no intention of breaking into the store, however, as I soon found out; they wanted me to give it to them and were doing their best to frighten me into doing it. One lot would go away, and be replaced by another, who would repeat the general performance, with such variations as suggested themselves to the individuals. This continued from dawn till dark and I shall ever remember it as the greatest strain on my nerves that I had yet experienced. But they did not get anything and I went up several notches in the Indians' esteem.[40]

Kāwēchetwēmot appeared before Crozier, in his capacity as justice of the peace, for preliminary hearing on July 4, with Chiefs Little Pine and Big Bear in the audience. Crozier scored some points with the Indians by patiently listening to their stories and by criticizing the most convenient scapegoat in the affair, Farm Instructor John Craig. There was no doubt an assault had been committed, but, according to the *Saskatchewan Herald*'s report of Crozier's remarks, "Craig in this instance acted indiscreetly, and might easily have tided over the difficulty. Prisoner had a reasonable excuse, in being sick, for asking for rations, and a little discretion would have saved a very great deal of trouble at a most inopportune moment. Of course Craig had his orders, and orders must be obeyed, but the discretion allowed him might have been exercised."[41]

Lieutenant Governor Dewdney was also very hard on Craig. He could not admit that the government's policy was the cause of an incident that almost resulted in war. He wrote to Indian Agent Rae that "Craig was too overbearing in his manner towards the Indians. An official may be particularly strict with those placed under his supervision still this strictness can be tempered by moderation in one's demeanor and thereby obviate many retaliatory measures on the part of the Indian."[42]

That was certainly not Craig's view. He told the preliminary hearing: "My orders with respect to giving rations are that I am to give them to the old and to the sick and to no others unless they work. I am not allowed to deviate from these orders in the remotest degree."[43] Kāwēchetwēmot was not sick enough to deserve rations and his promise to work the next day had not been sufficient, Craig said.

Kāwēchetwēmot's trial a short time later was a routine affair. Judge Charles Rouleau sentenced him to a week in jail, a relatively light punishment.

The incident had thoroughly shaken those charged with carrying out the Indian policy in the North-West. Agent Rae wasn't quite sure where matters stood. On June 23, he wrote Assistant Indian Commissioner Hayter Reed: "There is a good deal of excitement here & every one feels that until the leaders are taken there will be no peace here. I think myself that to give in to them and their demands will only put off the trouble for a while."[44] At the same time, he telegraphed Dewdney that everything was quiet, the Indians contrite and that he should be given the power to liberalize the rationing policy in specific cases.

In the *Saskatchewan Herald*, P. G. Laurie saw the results of the incident as a clear victory. "It has often been said that this summer would see a contest between the Indians and whites for supremacy, and those who thought of it as probable looked forward to a collision in which precious lives would be lost, property destroyed, and the progress of the country arrested. The struggle has taken place, and has resulted in a complete mastery of the Indians—a decided victory, bloodless, but none the less complete."[45]

But NWMP Superintendent Crozier warned that perception might be too superficial. He wrote Dewdney: "Just at present the Indians seem quiet, though there is among them a great deal of discontent, and my opinion is, that in their present temper, an attempt to arrest one of them, or perform any duty not agreeable to them would lead to trouble again; for they seem to have made up their minds to resist any interference with them, even to the length of going to war."[46]

Agent Rae was firm in his conviction that the Indian policy could not be strictly applied under the circumstances. The government must either liberalize the Indian policy or spend its money on sufficient military strength to enforce it harshly. As well as soldiers, some cannons and a couple of Gatling guns would be useful, he told Dewdney.

After his experience in the front lines of enforcing the Indian policy and after long talks with Rae, Crozier shared the Indian agent's views. He told Dewdney that "considering all that is at stake it is poor, yes, false economy to cut down the expenditure so closely in connection with the feeding of the Indians, that it would seem as if there was a wish to see, upon how little a man can work, and exist." If the situation did not change dramatically, "if some such policy as I have outlined is not carried out, there is only one other—and that is to fight them, by doing so, the country no doubt would get rid of the Indians and all troublesome questions in connection with them in a comparatively short time, but, in changing to that policy, we must be prepared for the change. (Settlers in the country should know that such a change is to take place, for they would suffer most in case of an outbreak now)."[47]

Dewdney, as usual, vacillated. He sympathized with the difficulties and dangers his subordinates in the field faced. He recognized that ripples in the smooth running of his territory, particularly in the shape of a real or threatened Indian war, might severely retard his hoped-for advancement to the federal cabinet. But his first loyalty was to his superiors in Ottawa. He wrote John A. Macdonald that some slight relaxation in the rules for specific cases might not endanger the general policy, but he seemed uncertain of his own views, wanting to leave the really hard decisions to others. "As a general principle it may be well to carry out rigidly the rule that unless an Indian works he is to receive no assistance still the time often arises when this rule must be of an elastic nature and the Indian humored but under cover of a pretext which will lead him to the belief that (the rule) is not being broken."[48]

The hardliners in the Indian Department, particularly Assistant Indian Commissioner Reed in Regina and Deputy Superintendent of Indian Affairs Vankoughnet in Ottawa, believed even slight modifications would prove disastrous. Crozier's pleas were ignored and although Indian Agent Rae was regarded as a very loyal employee, he was dismissed as alarmist and too anxious to protect his own hide. Vankoughnet told Dewdney agents might be permitted some minor flexibility but only if there resulted "no loss of prestige by too much concession."[49]

Reed wanted the rationing policy applied more harshly, with proportionally more provisions going to those Indians whom the agent judged to be working harder and, presumably, who were less inclined to be political agitators than others. He was becoming particularly worried about Poundmaker and instructed Rae to watch the chief closely and have him arrested at the first opportunity. Then Poundmaker should be taken to Regina for trial because Charles Rouleau, Battleford's magistrate, was too lenient.

Whatever slight modifications were made to the general Indian policy or in dealing with particular bands, there would be absolutely no relaxing the rules for Big Bear's band. Shortly after the Kāwēchetwēmot incident, Chiefs Poundmaker, Big Bear, and Lucky Man decided they all ought to pull up stakes and move to new, contiguous reserves at Buffalo Lake, northeast of Calgary on the edge of Blackfoot country. That site had some of the same natural and political

NWMP at Edmonton. At the time of the rebellion most of the 500 Mounted Police were scattered throughout the Territories in small detachments like this one. [Provincial Archives of Edmonton, E. Brown Collection B 1946]

advantages for the Cree as Cypress Hills. It was a traditional camping place for both the Saskatchewan and Alberta Cree and for many of the Plains Métis.

Agent Rae was almost inclined to back that proposal. It would have removed the whole dangerous lot from his doorstep. But word came very quickly from Ottawa. There was absolutely no way Poundmaker and Big Bear would be allowed to settle too close to one another. For the Indian Department, the first priority was forcing Big Bear onto a reserve near Fort Pitt. There would be absolutely no variation in the rationing policy until the leading chief was actually settled. And the Department's sub-agent at Fort Pitt, Tom Quinn, was just the kind of inflexible personality who could do the job.

Despite the series of dangerous confrontations, by mid-1884, the Indians had succeeded only in whittling away at the edges of the Indian policy, Piapot by moving his reserve and the Battleford Cree by forcing some changes in the rationing policy. The general policy remained intact.

It is easy, in retrospect, to sympathize with Agent Rae's fears of being in the front line of enforcing an Indian policy he believed was dangerous, if not impossible, to apply. And there is no doubt that many Indians sickened and died, that tribes and bands had their culture and political life destroyed by what was in effect, at least for many of them, a policy of starvation. It was not unreasonable for those members of Piapot's band in the 1883 train wreck to believe that the government's policy towards them was one of genocide.

But it is not that most of the policymakers were being deliberately malicious. Some of them honestly believed there was only one course of action open. They thought that there could be no minor relaxation of the rules. If the policy had changed at all, Indian Department expenditures would have risen quickly and dramatically. Already burdened by the mushrooming costs of the CPR and in the midst of economic bad times, the voters of Ontario and Quebec would not likely have accepted a new drain on the federal coffers for the North-West, as humanitarian and far-sighted as those expenses may have been. The policy the North-West Indians so detested in the 1880s was not so much a policy of John A. Macdonald's government as it was the policy of the Canadian people. It is also no accident that the two people most responsible for putting the policy into practice fundamentally supported a hardline approach. Hayter Reed cared little about anything except furthering his own career. He was glad to tell Ottawa what it wanted to hear. Lawrence Vankoughnet tried to impose Eastern Canadian experience with Indians on the vastly different situation in the West. His attitude dovetailed with the prevailing desire for a simplistic, inexpensive solution to the Indian problem.

CHAPTER SIX

The Return of Riel

There was a growing desperation among the South Branch Métis who gathered at Abraham Montour's house on March 24, 1884. Their years of pleading for their rights had yielded nothing and, unless they did something dramatic, their prospects of achieving these rights seemed dim. The thirty Métis who attended that meeting were first sworn to secrecy; then their chairman, Gabriel Dumont, made a speech. Louis Goulet recalled Dumont saying that Governor General Lord Lorne, during his visit in 1881, had promised to take up the Métis grievances with Ottawa.

> He emphasized that the governor, during his visit, had promised the Métis he would put their case before the government and that he himself would see to the settlement of their just claims. Well, that was many years ago, Dumont went on, and we have nothing to show for it, in spite of all our demands and petitions to Ottawa, in spite of all the approaches we made and caused to be made to the government. In conclusion, Dumont told us: "And let me tell you, my friends, that's not the end of it. The government will never give us anything! They stole our land with promises and now when they've got control, they're laughing at us. They don't intend to grant us the slightest thing in return for the soil where generations of our ancestors sleep. No. We'll never get anything from them, until we take matters into our own hands and force the government to give us justice."[1]

Goulet recalled that Dumont doubted he could lead an agitation that had grown so large and so critical, despite his proven talent to lead his people. Sending petitions and pleading with the authorities was one thing; actually forcing the government to do something was beyond the old buffalo hunter's capabilities. But he had a solution. He told the meeting: "There's one man who could do what I wanted to do, and that's Louis Riel. Let's bring him back from Montana." Dumont's suggestion and his synopsis of the situation fell on eager ears, Goulet said. "We all agreed with everything Dumont had said. As far as I was concerned, those were questions I'd been thinking about for a long time, but, just like Dumont, I didn't have the qualities it takes to lead a movement."[2]

The one man in the group with considerable experience in dealing with the white man's politics and the government at Ottawa also felt inadequate to lead the increasingly militant movement. "The problem with us Métis right now,"

Charles Nolin said, "is that we're like a cart with only one wheel. If we want to get moving, we'll have to go find the other one we need, in Montana, beside the Missouri."[3]

All those at the meeting, the leading men of the South Branch communities, expressed similar sentiments but some had reservations about where heightened agitation was likely to lead, Goulet recalled.

> Abraham Belanger argued that forcing the government's hand in order to get our rights was no small matter. He was the only one who talked of the possibility of taking up arms as a kind of warning, but nothing more. "I don't think this is the way to go about it," he said, "and as far as I'm concerned, I've got nothing to complain about, all my children got what was coming to them in Manitoba." Baptiste Boucher argued that it would be no good to wait. The main thing was to get Riel here as soon as possible so we could hear what he'd advise us to do.[4]

The South Branch Métis briefly discussed sending a delegation to see Riel but when they invited Louis Goulet to be a member, he declined because of business commitments. Actually, he had another reason for refusing, one that he did not admit at the meeting.

> I'd never liked Riel. My father had opposed him during the Red River troubles in 1870. I myself had wrangled with him more than once over trading liquor. He was dead against it. Because of all that past history, I was afraid my presence in the delegation might do more harm than good to the Métis cause. In all justice to the memory of Riel, I'm happy to say that after I got to know him better I realized there was no such worry. Riel wasn't the kind of man to hold a grudge or drag up old disputes. But I didn't know as much that evening.[5]

The Métis realized that to increase the effect of their agitation they would have to broaden it. They recalled that the success of their Red River efforts was largely the result of a coalition between the French-speaking and English-speaking half-breeds. Towards the end of April, they invited some English half-breeds to a meeting at Isidore Dumont's house at St. Laurent. This time it was a public meeting where the Métis and their English-speaking cousins again set out their grievances. They established a committee of three French-speaking and three English-speaking members to consider the next step. After only a half-hour of deliberation, the committee reported and proposed "that a delegation be named and ready to leave in fifteen days to go to Louis Riel and that the public be asked to bear the cost of the expenses." Gabriel Dumont, representing the French, and James Isbister, a legendary name among the English half-breeds, were to be the delegates.[6]

The delegation did not leave at the proposed time. The English and French

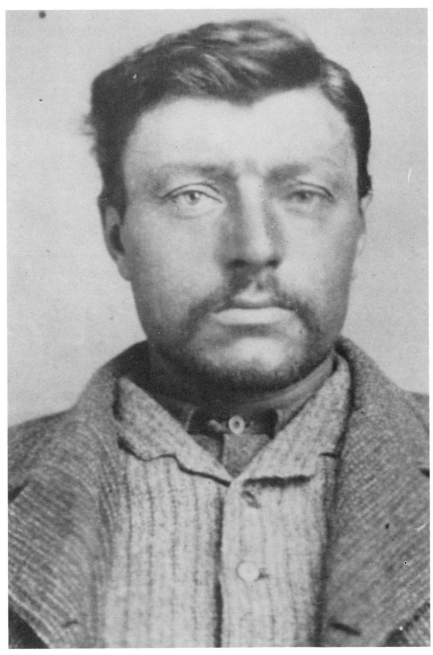

Michel Dumas, one of the delegates who invited Louis Riel to the North-West, photographed at Fort Benton, Montana, in 1885. [Montana Historical Society]

decided to take the time to cement their relationship and to put their grievances in a precise form that was acceptable to both parties. On May 6 they held a meeting attended by half-breeds from a wide area at the Lindsay school house, near the trail between Prince Albert and St. Louis, the community at the northern limit of what the Métis believed was their territory. That meeting passed several resolutions specifying the grievances, then unanimously decided "that a delegation be sent to Riel to get his advice on the resolutions that have been adopted in the various public assemblies so that these resolutions will have their effect." After seeing Riel, the delegates could change or expand the resolutions if they thought it appropriate and then travel from Montana to Ottawa to present the demands to the government.[7] The half-breeds were unable to raise enough money, so the Ottawa part of the trip was cancelled.

In the Métis' minds, although perhaps less so among their English counterparts, the delegation had only one task: persuade Louis Riel to come back to Canada and lead their movement. The Lindsay meeting's last instruction to the delegation was to invite Riel to the North-West and assure him of a sympathetic and enthusiastic reception. In addition to Dumont and Isbister, Moïse Ouellette and Michel Dumas were chosen as delegates.

Riel was soon aware of the feelings of the South Branch and of the delegation's mission. At least two letters were written to him in May, both signed only with initials. M. C. W. wrote "Dear Cousin" to tell him:

The movement began some four months ago, meeting on meeting. We wish to establish Union between the French and English which was no easy thing at first sight. You know the English—they wanted to revolt at once. We wanted to bring you to them as they have great confidence in you. They are numerous and they regret very much the events of 1870 in which they took part against you. At the present time they are the hottest in your favor. Therefore, dear cousin, it may be said that the part of the N. W. which we inhabit is Manitoba before the trouble, with this difference that there are more people, that they understand better and that they are more decided.[8]

Another writer, who signed himself T. L. but who has been identified as schoolteacher Octave Regnier, told Riel:

None of us feels capable of undertaking so great a protestation against a despotic authority. Altogether we turn our regards towards you in whom are our dearest hopes and our greatest confidence, excepting some sore heads of Prince Albert who wish to pass for great minds and who fear to be ruled by you. We therefore elect you as our chief. We all call on you loudly to come to our help, appreciating you as the only one able to defend us. Not only the Métis in general beg you to hear their prayers, but also those of other nations who do not know you beg us to convey to you the same wishes.[9]

In their enthusiasm, the Métis exaggerated the support they were receiving from the English half-breeds and the Indians. The Métis believed they were on the verge of a great advance in their movement. Not all their supporters agreed. Bishop Vidal Grandin wrote his clergy that the Métis, "pushed by a certain Charles Nolin, have made a terrible blunder. They have sent a deputation to Louis Riel to bring him back to act as their leader with a view to opposing the government. They would not listen to Father André, nor to the governor, nor to anybody. They are going to compromise everybody, give themselves a bad name, and will be unable in the future to obtain anything from the government."[10]

The delegation to Riel arrived on June 4, 1884, at St. Peter's mission on the Sun River in Montana, near Great Falls, where the Métis leader had been teaching school for a little more than a year. Riel was at daily mass when they arrived that evening and they waited for him at his home with his wife and two small children. Riel was anxious to get back to Canada and back to politics but he did not want to seem too eager. He asked the four delegates to wait a day for his answer.

On June 5, Riel presented the delegation with a carefully-composed written reply to their request for his assistance. "Your personal visit does me honor and causes great pleasure. But on account of its representative character your coming to me has the proportions of a remarkable fact. I record it as one of the gratifications of my life. It is a good event which my family will remember. And I pray to God that your delegation may become a blessing amongst the blessings of this my fortieth year."[11]

Riel doubted he could help the North-West half-breed cause by trying to give them advice from across the border, but he had another reason for agreeing to go back to Canada. The government, Riel said, owed him several lots of land under the Manitoba Act and "something else," which he did not specify but presumably included his claims for compensation for the time he governed Manitoba, for stepping aside to allow Sir George Cartier's election, and for helping the Canadian cause during the Fenian scare of 1871.

"My claims against them are such as to hold good, notwithstanding the fact that I have become [an] American citizen. Considering then your interest and mine I accept your very kind invitation. I will go and spend some time amongst you. By petitioning the government with you perhaps will we all have the good fortune of obtaining something. But my intention is to come back in the fall."[12] Riel asked the delegates to wait for a short time while he prepared his family for the journey and made arrangements to quit his job.

As Riel prepared to leave, the invitation to him was already having one of its desired effects. The prospect of Riel back in Canada frightened the authorities. On June 6, after visiting the South Branch that day, Lieutenant Governor Edgar Dewdney recorded in his diary: "Charles Nolin made a speech thanking me for coming to see them and mentioned several alterations which they wished to be made to the North West ordinances. I replied and that ended the meeting which was very orderly. No mention of grievances as I was told they had sent a mission to Louis Riel and they did not like to say anything until they heard from him."[13]

Dewdney did not admit it in either his diary or a subsequent report to John A. Macdonald, but he was chagrined that Nolin had not presented him with a list of grievances. And he was apprehensive. A short time later, he wrote Father André seeking reassurance. While the delegates were in Montana, a prominent person, who remained anonymous when the government published his correspondence, wrote Ottawa that Riel ought to be prevented from reaching the South Branch.

> In my opinion, and it is also the opinion of Rev. Father André, who is the superintendent of the Roman Catholic missions on the Saskatchewan, that these delegates should be shadowed and if Riel accepts the invitation and attempts to cross the boundary line he should be made a prisoner. The Rev. Father agrees with me that if Riel is not allowed to enter the country, the influence we can bring to bear on the body of the people will counteract the influence of that section of them who are leaders in this movement.[14]

But Riel and the delegates travelled north without incident. On July 5, they arrived at Tourond's Coulee, about twenty-five kilometres south of the village at Batoche's Crossing, the point that the Métis now considered the southern limit of their territory. They were met by a cavalcade of fifty wagons and the Riel family spent the night at the Tourond farm, where Riel introduced himself to the South Branch Métis, many of whom he had known in Manitoba. On his way to the North-West, Riel had found time to stop at a newspaper office. Montana's *Sun River Sun* reported that "Mr. Riel says that he is an American citizen, and that he considers the land over which the stars and stripes wave his home, and now only goes to assist his people as much as lays in his power, and after which—be it much or little—he will return to Montana."[15] That was a theme Riel would consistently echo in the last half of 1884.

The day after their arrival, the family moved on to Louis' cousin Charles Nolin's substantial home at St. Laurent, where they would stay for the next few weeks. There, on July 8, Riel held his first public meeting in Canada since 1870. He told the Métis how happy he was to be back with them.

> The kindness which you show me, and which I know you feel towards me, pleases me as much as it honors me. Your voice is more than friendly, it is the voice of loving compatriots. That voice is very sweet to me for it is not the loving compatriots that I listen to. I say to you: it is the voice of my country. You are happy to see me again, you say. You prove it. And I, what a joy have I in shaking your hand and saluting you. You have the kindness to mention what I did for Manitoba. True, I did my best to ensure its happiness. If I

succeeded so well, it was because I had in you solid, generous, brave, independent supporters.... Whatever place my name may occupy in history, after God I shall owe you my reputation. You never abandoned me in any difficulty.[16]

Riel said he was impressed with what he had seen on the South Branch. "Small in numbers, the French Canadian Métis people have made a grand struggle. I am glad to see them at peace; enjoying prosperity. Let me congratulate you on your increase; on the vigor you have acquired in the short space of ten years." But he reminded his audience that he was no longer a Canadian and that he expected to stay on the South Branch only briefly. "I thank you for the delicate and flattering invitation to remain with you. It would be assuredly most sweet to me to pass my life in the midst of such grateful compatriots. The love I have for my native country is strong enough to keep me here, but the adopted country to which I belong has taken hold of my heart. I have promised it my devotion. I belong to it as long as I live."[17]

The delegation that brought Riel to Canada described the success of its mission at the same meeting. In part, the delegates reported that Riel "inspires us with the greatest confidence, as his intentions are to help us, but if we understand him well he will help us without any wish on his part to embarrass the Government."[18] The pacific nature of Riel's speech at Nolin's, *Le Manitoba* reported, disappointed some of the more belligerent Métis.[19]

A few days after his speech to the Métis at Nolin's house, Riel journeyed the short distance north to Red Deer Hill where, in a speech at the Lindsay school house in the midst of English half-breed communities, he tried to cement the relationship between the two groups. "I salute you with all the cheers of my heart, because your different interests are finding the way to the grand union: the grand union of feelings, of views, of endeavours, without which a people can never have any influence, without which a people can never accomplish any thing of importance and without which you could not be happy."[20]

The English-speaking half-breeds received Riel enthusiastically, and most of the South Branch Métis were overjoyed to have their old champion back. Riel's former secretary, Louis Schmidt, who had recently been appointed to the government land office in Prince Albert, wrote *Le Manitoba* as soon as Riel returned. "It is said that Riel has arrived with his family. May it be his intention to remain permanently in our midst. This man can do nothing but good for his compatriots, and he is the only one who will obtain everybody's support in any kind of dispute. His is a great name among both the French and English half-breeds, and it is undeniable that his influence, well directed, will be of immense assistance to them."[21]

Even Father André, who had had initial misgivings, was delighted with Riel's presence and his behaviour. He tried to reassure Lieutenant Governor Dewdney.

Riel and delegates have arrived from across the line. The news may surprise and alarm you about the tranquility of the country, but you can set your mind quiet about that and have no fear of any disturbance in the country. You know I am [not] known to be a friend of Mr. Riel, and I looked to the event of his arrival among us as a danger for the peace of our community, but now I do not entertain the least suspicion about Riel causing any trouble. He acts quietly and speaks wisely . . .

You will receive alarming reports about the danger in which the country is in consequence of Riel's arrival. Do not believe a word. Those persons will be very glad that you should commit some rash act. They will send and advise you to have Riel arrested. For God's sake, never commit such an act before you have good motives to justify such an act. A good many persons will urge you to send here 200 or 300 policemen. They will be glad to see Government go to expenses, because that will be so much money put in their pockets. Nothing so far requires one man more to keep the peace of the country. The half-breeds, English as well [as] French, understand too well the foolishness and the consequences of rising in a rebellion against the Government, and Riel seems really to act by good motives and to have no bad design. A man will not bring his wife and children along with him if he intended to raise a rebellion, and Mr. Riel has brought his wife and two little children with him, and that is the best proof that he has no bad intentions.[22]

Although there might have been little to fear from Riel himself, just under the surface the North-West was ready to explode, Father André cautioned Dewdney. All might be well if the government left Riel alone. If anyone tried to interfere with the Métis leader's activities or tried to have him arrested, the half-breeds and Indians would join in open rebellion, Father André warned.

In case his opinions had not sunk in, Father André wrote Dewdney again two weeks later to say that nothing had happened to change the situation. Riel "has acted and spoken in a quiet and sensible way every time he has had opportunity of appearing before the public, and no one can point out any act or word of his which is liable to create any disturbance in the country."[23]

Riel appeared to be immensely popular both among the English and French, Father André wrote. But the Métis leader did have his detractors, particularly among the white community, some of whom had bitter impressions of the events of 1869 and 1870. Those critics realized they must tread a very careful line. They hoped to reap some of the benefits of the agitation in the North-West but they could not let it get out of hand. And they could not afford to offend Riel or the Métis too deeply. The Conservative Prince Albert *Times* editorialized:

We do not wish to reproach Mr. Riel for having come here, because we think the blame attaches much more to those who were sufficiently ill advised as to invite him. The invitation once extended we could hardly expect the idiosyncracy of that gentleman's character to allow of his refusing what naturally appeared so flattering to himself, but none the less do we most unhesitatingly express our opinion that his presence is a great mistake, and unreservedly condemn the action of those more immediately in our midst who from a spirit of curiosity, unseemly jocularity or any other cause have seen fit to endorse his presence by requesting him to hold a meeting in our town.

Riel's presence would split the protest movement, not mould it, the *Times* said. He was certainly the wrong man for the dissatisfied whites to pin any hopes on. Some settlers had "let the utterly false impression go forth to the world that Prince Albert is so destitute of able, educated, experienced and intelligent men as to require the guidance of an alien French half-breed. What can be said for the judgement of men who expect their petitions and demands to be favourably received at Ottawa when associated with the name of a man already outlawed?"[24]

Riel had been invited to Prince Albert, by far the biggest community in the North-West, by a group of businessmen. Some of them were probably merely curious, as the *Times* suggested, but many others were looking for new ways to put pressure on Ottawa and a few believed that a coalition between the half-breeds and the whites was possible. Most of them were staunch Liberals who were not only opposed to the Conservative government but who had had all sorts of arguments with it about North-West policy, particularly land policy. Some of their complaints echoed the complaints of the Métis. Fundamentally, as Riel realized, the grievances of the Prince Albert settlers, although strongly held, were much more superficial and administrative than the demands of the Métis.

Riel thought the proposed Prince Albert meeting was premature. He knew that in Prince Albert there were people who would rather see him hang than hear him speak. The movement he was leading had just begun; there had been little chance for the whites to observe its course and to understand that Riel was no threat to them. Before they had that chance, Riel did not want someone standing up in the middle of his speech to denounce him as a rebel and murderer and set back his organizing efforts. He wrote his Prince Albert friends thanking them for their invitation. "I wish to assist you all, and to render service even to those who regard me with dislike. Many do not know yet the line of conduct which I would like to follow. It is better that they should have some time to understand me. It may happen, if you postpone your hospitable meeting, in place of whisper of dissent, we may have the pleasure ere long, of being assured of the complete unison of the people of Prince Albert. There is reason to hope that the feeling may become universal."

But a meeting held too soon could split the Prince Albert movement, he warned. "I know that as your guest I would be perfectly safe with such a respectable body of men as those who have signed the invitation, I would feel far above any insult that could be offered to me. But for the sake of avoiding even the slightest trouble, in order to allow no germ of division to weaken our basis of action, I beg leave to be excused. Please, consent to put off the meeting."[25]

The Prince Albert agitators were not easily dissuaded. They rewrote their invitation in the form of a petition signed by eighty-four Prince Albert residents. And Father André, still caught up in the South Branch euphoria over Riel, couldn't sit on the sidelines. He wrote Riel pleading with him to change his mind. "Opinion is so pronounced in your favor, and you are so ardently desired, that it will be a great disappointment to the people of Prince Albert if you do not come. So you must absolutely come; you are the most popular man in the country and, with the exception of four or five persons everyone awaits you with impatience. I have only to say to you: come, come quickly."[26] Riel could not very well refuse such a plea from the leading priest in the country. The meeting went ahead as scheduled on July 19.

Riel's apprehensions were not realized. Father André reported to Lieutenant Governor Dewdney: "Riel came down last Saturday, and he received a really hearty and enthusiastic welcome from the people of Prince Albert. The meeting went out quietly, only one man tried to raise a row, and he was put out quickly. There was a mass meeting, such as Prince Albert has never seen; people came from the country to meet Mr. Riel, from everywhere, and they went back struck with the quiet and gentle way he spoke to them."[27] Riel estimated the crowd at five hundred.

The one dissenter was Captain Richard Deacon, a member of the Red River Expeditionary Force, who tried to tell the Prince Albert settlers "to be careful who they selected as their leader, for Mr. Riel had been a failure before, and they had no guarantee that he would not be so again." Riel's supporters cut Deacon off and "the majority of the meeting got uproarious, attempts being made to lay hands on Mr. Deacon. Quietness was restored after a time by the prompt interference of Sergt. Stewart and constables of the Mounted Police who were present. Mr. Riel then returned to the hall, which he had left during the disturbance." Deacon later apologized for causing the row but said that if he had been allowed to continue, he would have said: "That as Judge Lynch was deservedly unpopular on this side of the line, he [Riel] was safe to come and go as he pleased. He also said he had grievances in common with others, but would bear with them rather than work in connection with him or with those connected with him."

In his speech, Riel urged all dissatisfied people in the North-West to form a coalition to press their case on Ottawa.

I know that you are laboring under serious governmental difficulties. Were you to tolerate your situation without seeking true remedies, the state of your affairs would become worse and worse. And in a comparatively short time, it would become evident to the calculating observations of the Capitalists that your future is not taken care of. Allow me a suggestion. Instead of petitioning for your rights severally; instead of making a particular struggle for each of your rights, thereby wasting energy and losing time, would it not be better to apply for them all in block.

But he emphasized, the *Times* reported, that his were peaceful intentions. "He wished them to understand no trouble would have his sanction, as he was for peace, believing that their object would be gained faster if they acted orderly and peaceably." The white settlers, Indians, and half-breeds in the North-West needed, as a first step, their own government. Riel urged his audience to petition Ottawa to establish provinces in the North-West. "The Indian had been robbed of his living by the advance of civilization, and they ought to receive ample compensation. Emigrants came out here and paid far too much for the land, buying from the Government and the Hudson's Bay Company, which was not theirs to sell. The first, not the only, thing they needed, but as it would lead to the other things, was free and responsible government. The present government was too far away to properly act."[28]

In his report to Dewdney, Father André described Riel's suggestions at the Prince Albert meeting: "He wants the half-breed to have a free grant to the land they occupy; he wants to agitate to have the three districts of Saskatchewan, Alberta, Assiniboia, erected into provinces, or at least to have each district represented in Parliament; he wants the land laws amended to suit more the rapid settlement of the country."[29] A few days later, Riel delivered much the same speech at the English half-breed community of Red Deer Hill, just south of Prince Albert, where he again urged a cautious process of negotiations with Ottawa.

His reception at Prince Albert delighted and surprised Riel. He wrote his brother and his brother-in-law in Manitoba: "Not long ago I was a humble schoolmaster on the far away banks of the Missouri. And here I am today in the ranks of the most popular public men of the Saskatchewan. Last year no one wanted me in influential political circles in Manitoba. This year the people circulate my words in the heart of the North-West. Bankers invite me to their table. And their goodwill makes them applaud in appreciation. They applaud me with the crowd."[30] Government officials in the North-West were not among that crowd. They were at least apprehensive, if not thoroughly alarmed.

Just before Riel arrived back in Canada, the Sub-Indian Agent in the Carlton area, Ansdell Macrae, sent urgent messages to Lieutenant Governor Dewdney warning that considerable stores of arms and ammunition belonging to the Militia Department in the vicinity were unprotected.

It would not appear that any sinister motives actuate the half-breeds, though they are undoubtedly in a disturbed, and excited condition; but they are so unstable, and susceptible to the influences of their leaders, that they might be led into the commission of indiscretions, which would terminate in acts of a serious nature; and therefore if the government is not thoroughly advised of their intentions, it might be well to put out of the possibility of reach, such dangerous tools as those referred to.[31]

A few days later, the militia units at Duck Lake, Fort Carlton, Battleford, and Prince Albert were disarmed and a Prince Albert correspondent of a Winnipeg newspaper reported: "This is probably owing to Riel's presence there. This action is regarded here as injudicious, as no trouble is expected unless the half-breeds are excited by measures such as these."[32] Exaggerated rumours had reached Ottawa and the government had decided a month previously to disarm the militias. Prime Minister Macdonald wrote Dewdney in July: "We have information from the Manitoba Govt and other sources of a plot to seize the militia arms all over the country. There is a Combination of Farmers, Indians, Blackguards, Half Breeds and Fenians across the line that cannot be disregarded."[33]

Macrae and Dewdney had another worry in July 1884. Chief Beardy had called a council of all the Carlton-area Cree for the end of the month. Chief Big Bear was on his way back to Fort Pitt when a messenger from Beardy caught up with him and invited him to attend. Worse, Beardy had also invited Riel. Despite his pleas to Ottawa, Dewdney had no way of preventing the Indians from attending the councils. Ottawa had explicitly denied him the means. The Lieutenant Governor advocated "the initiation by the Government of a policy which has not hitherto been applied towards any of our Indians—that of preventing them from moving about at will throughout the Territories and the undersigned questions the advisability of adopting such a policy," Assistant Superintendent of Indian Affairs Lawrence Vankoughnet explained to John A. Macdonald. Under the treaty provisions, nothing could be done unless the Indians broke the law but they should be watched closely, he said.

> Should these Indians move off their Reserve and if they cannot be induced by moral suasion to return, if a sufficiently large number of Police follow them and watch their movements and upon the first unlawful act being committed by them make an arrest of the parties concerned therein and bring them to justice immediately before the commanding Officer of the Force, who would have the power of sentencing the offenders to imprisonment, that it would probably have the effect of causing these Indians to be glad to return again to their Reserve.[34]

As the police who had been involved in the Battleford incident already knew, that was very easy to say in Ottawa but dangerous to put into practice once large groups of Indians gathered.

A few days before the Duck Lake council, Riel met the chiefs. According to reports that reached NWMP Superintendent Crozier at Battleford, "He is said, though I have no official information to that effect, to have told the Indians that they had 'rights' as well as the Half Breeds, and that he wished to be the means of having them redressed."[35]

After talking with Riel, the Carlton-area Cree began their council on July 31 at Beardy's Duck Lake reserve. All the Indians from the area were present but the only outsiders to attend were Chief Lucky Man from Battleford and Big Bear, who gave a speech listing the broken promises of the whites and pleading with the Cree to form a united front.

> I have been trying to seize the promises which they made to me, I have been grasping but I cannot find them. What they have promised me straightway I have not yet seen the half of it. We have all been deceived in the same way. It is the cause of our meeting at Duck Lake. They offered me a spot as a reserve. As I see that they are not going to be honest I am afraid to take a reserve. They have given me to choose between several small reserves but I feel sad to abandon the liberty of my own land when they come to me and offer me small plots to stay there and in return not to get half of what they have promised me. When will you have a big meeting. It has come to me as through the bushes that you are not yet all united, take time and become united, and I will speak.[36]

Big Bear went on to make an unusual proposal. Every four years, one Indian should be chosen to speak for all the Indians of the North-West to the white man.

After the nearly-disastrous incident during the Battleford council, the Duck Lake council was anticlimactic. It was important for bringing the Carlton chiefs together with Big Bear and, just prior to the meeting, with Riel. But, except for the suggestion that an Indian spokesman be chosen every four years, it broke no new ground. At Duck Lake, as at Battleford, the most significant series of events involved a confrontation with the whites and with the strict rules of the Indian Department.

On August 6, some of Beardy's men went to Fort Carlton to ask Agent Macrae for provisions for the council, a request that could not be granted for that would mean both wavering from the work-for-rations policy and condoning exactly the kind of meeting the government wanted so much to prevent. But the Indian Department policy was vulnerable and the Indians were increasingly dissatisfied. The next day, the council sent Chiefs Mistawāsis and Starblanket to renew the demand. Refusing those two chiefs, who were supposedly the leading supporters of the Indian Department among the Indians, would have been to insult the whole Cree nation, not just the radicals that chiefs like Big Bear and Beardy controlled.

Agent Macrae kept his wits about him and promised rations only if the Cree would move their council to Fort Carlton and invite him to attend. The Cree at first hesitated, but hunger necessitated agreement. Macrae told Dewdney that the Indians aired all their usual grievances: the treaty promises had not been kept, cattle and farm implements they received had been too few and of inferior quality, the government had not yet established schools for them, and the government refused to invoke the famine clause of the treaty. After saying they were "glad that the young men have not resorted to violent measure," the chiefs told Macrae they were reaching the end of their rope. "It is almost too hard for them to bear the treatment at the hands of the government after its sweet promises." They made a vague threat. They would "wait until next summer to see if this council has the desired effect, failing which they will take measures to get what they desire."[37]

At Beardy's council the Cree had again aired their complaints, but they were not much closer to the fundamental changes they wanted. Big Bear left the council with only moderate progress towards his goal of uniting the North-West Indians in their defiance of the whites. Now he had to consider a new factor: the possible merger of the Indian and Métis agitation. A united front of Cree and Métis, of Big Bear and Riel, would have been a significant force in the North-West in 1884. But from Big Bear's perspective, an alliance with Riel and his people was even more difficult than an alliance with the Blackfoot. Blood had flowed between the two great Indian nations of the North-West in skirmishes over territory and horses. The Cree were friendly with the Métis, but Big Bear and Riel had philosophical and political differences over which it might have been more difficult to compromise than it would have been for the Cree to come to terms with their traditional enemies.

On his way back to Fort Pitt, Big Bear stopped at Eastwood Jackson's home in Prince Albert for another meeting with Riel. Jackson, the North-West's first druggist and one of the leaders of the white agitation, later recalled that "Big Bear during the conversation complained that the conditions of the treaty had been violated by the Dominion government. He expressed his confidence that when the half breeds had secured their rights, they would assist the Indians to obtain theirs."[38] Neither Big Bear nor Riel commented on their talks but as the chief passed Battleford on his way to Fort Pitt after the meeting, the *Saskatchewan Herald* reported that "the old man does not seem to have been favorably impressed with the prospects held out to him there."[39]

In all the petitions and drafts of petitions Riel wrote in the fall of 1884, he mentioned the aboriginal rights of the Indians, but for Big Bear it was too much lip-service and not enough support. The Indians were wary of joining the Métis agitation from fear that their cousins were untrustworthy, that the Métis would use the Indians as pawns in the battle for their own rights.

If the Indians distrusted the Métis, Riel had very serious political problems in joining his agitation with theirs. He had refused to attend the Duck Lake council, meeting only the chiefs before it actually began. Even then he did not want to be committed to specific action. Judge Charles Rouleau made inquiries

116

Some prominent participants in the North-West Rebellion trading at Fort Pitt in the fall of 1884. Left to right: Four Sky Thunder, King Bird, Bad Arrow (also known as The Worm), Iron Body, Chief Big Bear, Angus McKay, _____ Dufresne, Louis Goulet, Stanley Simpson (with book), NWMP Const. G.W. Rowley (seated), Alex McDonald, NWMP Corp. Ralph Sleigh (on cart), _____ Edmund, and Henry Dufresne. Noticeably absent is Sub-Indian Agent Tom Quinn. [Glenbow-Alberta Institute]

and discovered that the Duck Lake chiefs planned to draw up a petition to be sent to Ottawa and had asked Riel's help. He agreed only to help them put it in the proper form; he would not advise them about what to put in the petition.[40] Riel realized that in the frontier society, the greatest crime he could commit in the eyes of the white settlers was inciting the Indians. And he feared that if things got out of hand, he could no more control the Indians than the government could.

In September Big Bear returned to Fort Pitt, where his band was supposed to receive its annual treaty payments. He found himself right back into the old argument with Agent Tom Quinn. Big Bear would not take the government's money until Quinn slaughtered some beef for a feast for his band. Quinn refused. Big Bear insisted. The two of them argued for three days before Hudson's Bay Company Factor Angus McKay, who thought Quinn was being unnecessarily intransigent, said he would kill one of the company's cattle. The agent reluctantly accepted that offer and the payments were made, but it was a very sullen-looking group of whites and Indians who posed for what has become a famous photograph.

The Duck Lake council had little impact in itself, but the coincidence of the growing farmers' movement in Manitoba, dissatisfaction among white settlers in the North-West, the Indian councils, and Riel's return was enough to thoroughly alarm Ottawa and its representative, Lieutenant Governor Edgar Dewdney, particularly after the Kāwēchetwēmot incident at Battleford. In August 1884 the government had a golden opportunity to defuse the agitation or at least control it to some extent.

A federal cabinet minister was on his way to the South Branch—not just any cabinet minister but one of the two most powerful French Canadian politicians in the country. Sir Hector Langevin, the Minister of Public Works, was touring the West and was scheduled to visit the country north of Regina. The Métis were anxious to meet him. Riel scribbled notes for his speech to the minister. "And finish by acknowledging his visit as a marked proof of good will towards the North West and principally of this section of the North west; and by expressing their hope that he, as a minister of the Crown will help the administration to which he belongs to ameliorate in a good measure the present condition of affairs amongst all classes of the people."[41]

Riel would not give his speech. At Regina, Langevin decided not to bother travelling the three hundred and fifty kilometres over muddy trails to Batoche. Upon leaving Regina, Langevin travelled by rail to Calgary. He had been wined and dined by Conservative Associations throughout the West, and he would return home to tell the Eastern Canadian public that in his entire trip he had met only two dissatisfied settlers, an unfortunate bit of rhetoric that came back to haunt the government. No one thought to tell the Métis why the minister would not meet them. No one even bothered to tell them Langevin had changed his plans. To the Métis, Riel's presence seemed to have done no good. Even in the company of their militant, high-profile leader, the Métis had still not jolted the government to recognize their existence.

The Métis didn't know it, but the government had wakened to the danger signs in the North-West. Early in September, Macdonald wrote Dewdney to say that he would propose increasing the size of the North-West Mounted Police and that the government would try to resolve the half-breed grievances that winter.

In September, Dewdney decided that the unrest should be thoroughly investigated and commissioned Judge Charles Rouleau, North-West Council clerk Amédée Forget, and Assistant Indian Commissioner Hayter Reed to do the job. He also received reports from NWMP Superintendent Leif Crozier.

Forget, who was well-liked in the Métis community, reported that the agitation was not as noisy as it had been when Riel first arrived. But appearances were deceiving, he said. The Métis had widened their demands and as the agitation progressed it would be harder to satisfy them. What Forget found most alarming was that the Métis had had a serious falling out with the priests. Riel and Father André were engaged in bitter debates. Forget suggested some immediate aid be given in the form of schools and help with farming and that work be begun quickly on settling the larger matter of Métis rights to land.[42]

Rouleau reported that the rumours of a Métis-Indian alliance were exaggerated and that such an alliance would be more difficult to form than it seemed. He agreed with Forget that some obvious progress must be made immediately in settling the half-breed complaints. "At all events, I would in your place impress the Govt. with the advisibility [sic] of settling that question of the half-breeds under the shortest delay possible."[43]

The reports all agreed on the situation at the South Branch. Everyone, including Riel, was peaceably inclined but their demands were increasing and their resolve was growing. The Indian situation was fundamentally different and more dangerous, Dewdney was told. It would be a bad winter for the Indians and for the Métis. Crops were not looking good, Rouleau reported. He pleaded with Dewdney to liberalize the rations policy, something that clearly contravened Indian Department rules.

> Unless the Govt comes to the help and assistance of the indians with *food and clothing*, there will be great misery and starvation among them during this winter. On almost all the reserves, the crops are a failure, and in order to avoid perhaps some depredation on their part during the winter, I would humbly suggest that more supplies than usual should be bought; that the indian agents should be given more latitude in the exercise of their judgment, when provisions and clothing are necessarily required or needed by the indians.[44]

Rouleau was known as a man who did not much like Indians. However, his pleas on their behalf were in marked contrast to the opinions of Hayter Reed, who travelled with him during their investigations. Reed was willing to advance his career by responding to the anti-Indian mood in Ottawa. In fact, he went so far in his anxiety to please that many of his recommendations were dismissed in Ottawa as outrageously immoral and sometimes illegal. His attitude strengthened the hand of the hardliners who demanded a harsh policy toward the Indians. Here was a man who knew the conditions in the North-West, who knew the Indians, and who was advising Ottawa to take extraordinarily repressive measures. The Macdonald government's Indian policy looked tame by comparison.

Reed told Dewdney that if the government could keep Big Bear at Fort Pitt, there was nothing to fear from the Indians at least until spring. Everyone was waiting to see how the government would answer the Métis petitions. Chief Poundmaker was becoming more troublesome and an excuse ought to be found to arrest him and send him for trial at Regina. At Battleford, Judge Rouleau had proved himself too lenient in the Kāwēchetwēmot case, Reed said, and he should not be trusted with something as important as putting Poundmaker in jail. Reed told Dewdney that there ought to be enough police on hand to put a stop to any large gathering of Indians and he urged that the work-for-rations policy be strictly enforced and expanded to more conspicuously reward those Indians who toed the government line. Reed also wanted orders issued to the NWMP prohibiting them from providing rations to Indians under any circumstances.[45]

Edgar Dewdney's favourite advisor on Indian matters in 1884, however, was not Reed. Peter Ballendine was a former Hudson's Bay Company employee whom Dewdney liked to call his "secret agent" among the Cree, although it is doubtful how secret his mission actually was. Ballendine was supposed to travel among the bands and report on their activities and inclinations. The Indians trusted Ballendine and he did his job well.

Ballendine told Dewdney that most of the chiefs wanted to keep a discreet distance from the Métis agitation. Although Big Bear was his old recalcitrant self, most of the other chiefs told Ballendine they would have little to do with Riel, at least for the present. Like Rouleau and unlike Reed, Ballendine correctly gauged the difficulties of forming a Cree-Métis alliance. That was a comforting thought for Dewdney, but other parts of Ballendine's reports were not reassuring.

The Indians recited a litany of complaints to Ballendine, most of them involving the rations policy and the quality of Indian agents and farm instructors. Even Chiefs Mistawāsis and Starblanket echoed the grievances. "Both the chiefs are much dissatisfied with their agent and Instructor. Since the [annual treaty] payments they say that not more than 40 lbs. of flour has been issued to them. They say they they think that they are imposed upon, being good-natured Indians. The two Chiefs stated to me today that there is a many a time they are very angry but always hold themselves not to say anything, fearing they may excite their young men and other friends." The two Fort Carlton-area chiefs complained to Ballendine that their crops were failing and they demanded the government invoke the famine clause of the treaty. Ballendine backed some of the Indians' demands, particularly those of Mistawāsis and Starblanket. "I would recommend that the two chiefs should be assisted better than they have been. I am sorry to say that the whole Band are really starving as far as I can see. I think they are justified to complain." But he also went along with Reed's suggestion that a pretext be found for arresting some of the leaders if trouble seemed likely.

Chiefs Big Bear and Beardy were planning a Thirst Dance and council to be held at Duck Lake the following summer, Ballendine reported. And this time, the Qu'Appelle Cree and those from the Edmonton area were expected to attend. On the other hand, Poundmaker had become disillusioned with the Indian and Métis movement. He had refused Little Pine's request that he visit the Blackfoot and he told Ballendine he would have nothing further to do with the agitation. The whites were too quick to blame him for anything that went wrong, Poundmaker complained. But Poundmaker told Ballendine that Chief Little Pine was working hard to bring the Blackfoot into the Cree agitation. "Poundmaker stated to me the other day that Little Pine said so much as if he had made arrangements with the Blackfoot Indians to come here this summer and give us trouble."[46]

Ballendine harshly criticized many of the Indian Department employees. With a little tact, it would not be difficult to get the Indians, even Big Bear, settled down, he said. But some agents and instructors were making trouble for the government by unnecessarily annoying the chiefs. Ballendine's activities sparked an angry complaint from Agent Tom Quinn at Frog Lake, one of the people the criticism was particularly aimed at.

Most of the reports in the fall of 1884 gave the government the impression that murder and mayhem were not imminent. But most of them also said that the government must act immediately—not next week or next month—to at least appear to be satisfying some of the Indian and Métis demands.

NWMP Superintendent Leif Crozier, fresh from near disaster at Battleford, put it most bluntly. He had received a pessimistic report from Sergeant Harry Keenan at Batoche. Keenan had learned that at a meeting of the South Branch Métis council Charles Nolin had

> proposed that the Halfbreeds make certain demands on the Govt and if not complied with, they take up arms at once and commence killing every white man they can find and incite the Indians to do the same. . . . The crops here are almost a total failure and every thing indicates that the Halfbreeds are going to be in a very straitened condition before the end of the coming winter, which of course will make them more discontented and will probably drive them to an outbreak and I believe that trouble is almost certain before the winter ends unless the government extends some aid to the Halfbreeds during the coming winter.[47]

Crozier warned Lieutenant Governor Dewdney that "prompt measures should be taken to allay if possible the existing dissatisfaction and at the same time precautionary measures should be taken to ensure against either Indians or Halfbreeds becoming unmanageable. If matters go on as they are or if some such course as suggested is not acted upon in my opinion everything points to an overt act or more probably acts being committed during the winter, I think in different parts of the district at the same time."[48]

But the government should be careful what precautionary steps it took, Keenan told Crozier, for they might have the opposite of their intended effect. Increasing the police force at Fort Carlton in October "created considerable uneasiness amongst the people, the more so as some person circulated the report that their object here was the arrest of Riel and his principal followers. The Halfbreeds were greatly excited and asserted that any attempt to take Riel would be resisted by an armed force."[49]

All this did not fall on deaf ears, but the government preferred to arm itself in case of an outbreak rather than take quick steps to prevent one. Prime Minister Macdonald ordered NWMP comptroller Fred White to prepare to enlist more men, to arrange for the NWMP to take its orders from Lieutenant Governor Dewdney in an emergency, and to consider going to the North-West himself. "I don't apprehend myself any rising, but with these warnings it would be criminal negligence not to take any precautions," Macdonald told White.[50] Minister of the Interior David Macpherson seemed more concerned with Ottawa politics than with conditions in the North-West. He promised Dewdney that the cabinet would soon consider the half-breed complaints but he did not appear to think there was any real urgency.

At the end of October, Inspector Francis Dickens wrote Superintendent Crozier from Fort Pitt to say that Big Bear's band was calm. "Unless the rations are stopped I do not anticipate trouble. Should however the Sub Indian Agent receive orders to discontinue the issue of rations the Indians might and would probably try to help themselves from the Store in which case there might be a collision between them and ourselves."[51] Despite all the warnings, about a month later Assistant Superintendent of Indian Affairs Vankoughnet told Dewdney to reduce the rations to Big Bear's band. Too often the Indians received rations without having to work for them, he complained. If this treatment continued to be accorded Big Bear's band, Indians who were working for rations might become more discontented and join Big Bear. Vankoughnet also complained about the practice of giving gifts of food to Indians before talking with them.[52]

By this time, Dewdney realized there might be serious Indian trouble on the horizon, exacerbated by just the sort of measures Vankoughnet advocated. He wrote an uncharacteristically sharp reply to Macdonald's assistant, demanding that the rations policy be tailored to meet the reality of the North-West, not the idealistic images about civilizing Indians that were prevalent in Ottawa.

Dewdney particularly defended giving gifts of food when he or his officials visited the Indians. It was a traditional practice in Indian society, carried on successfully for many years by the Hudson's Bay Company, he argued. Far from demoralizing the Indians as Vankoughnet suggested, the practice was simply a fact of North-West life. The Indians would refuse to talk to the Indian Department officials if it were discontinued, he said.

Dewdney blamed the Indian troubles of 1884 directly on the decision to stop the rations to Big Bear's band. If the chief had been contented he would not have tried to stir up trouble and the Indians in the North-West would be much quieter, Dewdney wrote.[53]

Throughout the fall of 1884, Riel worked on drafts of petitions. The first effort he presented at a meeting on September 5 at St. Laurent to Bishop Grandin, who had been complaining the Métis had not specified their demands. The list presented to Grandin contained all the usual Métis requests: responsible government in the North-West, guarantees of the rights of pre-survey squatters and old settlers, a land grant of 240 acres for each Métis in the North-West, and proper rations for the Indians. The point about Indian rations, which was coupled with a demand that the government "make the Indians work as Pharaoh had made the Jews work," was dropped in the formal presentation sent to Grandin a couple of days later.[54]

The petitions to Grandin also contained an extraordinary scheme to extinguish aboriginal title, particularly Métis title, in the North-West. "That two million acres be set apart by the government for the benefit of the half-breeds, both Protestant and Catholic. That the government sell these lands; that it deposit the money in the bank, and that the interest on that money serve for the support of schools, for the construction of orphanages and hospitals, for the support of institutions of this type already constructed, and to obtain carts for poor half breeds as well as seed for the annual spring planting."

As a further guarantee that the benefits from extinguishing the aboriginal title extend past his generation, Riel also asked "that a hundred townships, selected from swampy lands which do not appear habitable at the moment, be set aside by the government and that every eighteen years there take place a distribution of these lands to the half-breed children of the new generation. This is to last 120 years."

That wasn't all. Riel added a postscript to the letter to Grandin. "This is what we ask while we wait for Canada to become able to pay us the annual interest on the sum that our land is worth and while we wait for public opinion to agree to recognize our rights to the land in their fullest extent." After he sent the petition to Grandin, Riel expanded the demands in a version addressed to the federal cabinet. That version was never sent, but North-West Council clerk Amédée Forget described it briefly in his report to Dewdney.[55] The government would have been astonished if it had ever received the full extent of Riel's demands.

There were, in Riel's estimation, 1.1 billion acres of land in the North-West Territories. If there were one hundred thousand Indians and one hundred thousand Métis, then "is not each Métis and each Indian found to own at least 11,000 acres of land." Presuming that undeveloped Indian land was worth 12.5 cents an acre, each Indian was owed $1375 for extinguishing his title. If more developed Métis land was worth 25 cents an acre, then each Métis was owed $2750. Riel did not want these sums paid. He would be content if the government paid the Indians and Métis an annuity equivalent to the interest on those sums if they were invested at an annual rate of five per cent. That worked out to a payment each year of $68.75 for each Indian and $137.50 for each Métis.

His calculations were only approximate, Riel intended to tell the cabinet. But they gave some idea of Métis rights and provided some understanding of "the profound distress in which the Dominion of Canada plunges us by taking possession of our lands and not giving us the adequate compensation we expect of it."[56]

Riel's proposals for extinguishing aboriginal rights were dropped from all subsequent versions of the Métis petition. There were some obvious problems with the scheme. It would have required a huge government undertaking and a vast amount of money. It would have been out of the question for Ottawa to consider it.

There were also political problems for Riel with the early versions of the petition. It was very much a purely Métis document. The uncertainty about including a demand for better rations for the Indians did not bode well for a Métis-Cree alliance. In the aboriginal title sections, the Indians were reduced to second-class status by placing a lower value on their lands. And the Indian chiefs, if they had known about it, would not have taken kindly to Riel's reference to the Pharaoh. There was little in the petition to appeal the white settlers either, a deficiency that would be corrected in subsequent drafts, and some of Riel's white supporters were beginning to react strongly to his emphasis on aboriginal rights.

After meetings between the French- and English-speaking half-breeds during the fall, they finally sent their petition to Ottawa on December 16, 1884. The first point dealt with rations for the Indians. "The Indians are so reduced that the settlers in many localities are compelled to furnish them with food, partly to prevent them from dying at their door, partly to preserve the peace of the Territory." The second point was a demand that the half-breeds of the North-West receive 240 acres of land, as they had in Manitoba.[57]

Other points dealt with the rights of old settlers and squatters, a complaint that too high a price was charged to secure additional land after a settler had taken a homestead, a complaint about customs duties, a plea that North-West residents get preference in bidding on contracts for public works and government supplies, a proposal for a trade route via Hudson Bay, and a suggestion that elections be held by ballot. They also included complaints about the treatment of the provisional government of 1869-70 and demands that the North-West be divided into provinces which would control their natural resources and be represented in the federal cabinet. The petition suggested the residents of the North-West be allowed to send delegates to Ottawa with a bill of rights to negotiate their entry into Confederation. "In conclusion, your petitioners would respectfully state that they are treated neither according to their privileges as British subjects nor according to the rights of people and that consequently as long as they are retained in those circumstances, they can be neither prosperous nor happy."

Riel's young secretary and collaborator Will Jackson wrote a covering letter to the federal Secretary of State.

From your knowledge of the matter referred to, you will perceive that the petition is an extremely moderate one. I may say in fact that to the Canadian and English wing of the movement a more searching exposition of the situation would have been much more satisfactory. The opinion has been freely expressed that our appeal should be directed to the Privy Council of England and to the general public, rather than to the federal authorities, on the ground not only that our previous petitions would appear to have gone astray, but that even the benefit of federal representation might be largely neutralized by the placing of obstacles in the way of our choice of leaders, or the disregard of those leaders even when elected, as was done in the case of Manitoba.[58]

Jackson presumably referred to Riel's inability to take his seat in the House of Commons in the early 1870s.

By December 1884 Father André had become thoroughly disgusted with and fearful of Riel, particularly because the Métis leader was beginning to talk about reforming the Roman Catholic Church, in part so it would be more supportive of the Métis efforts to establish nationhood for themselves. Father André was a hardworking and respected priest who had a genuine fondness for the Métis but he was too much swayed by the passions of the moment. He had been as pleased as the Métis when Riel first began his political work at the South Branch. Only a few months later, the priest had radically changed his mind. Riel and Father André were both emotionally volatile, especially on the topics of religion and politics. Father André later described the depth of the feeling involved in his arguments with the Métis leader.

Our people considered him a hero and identified in him the qualities that distinguish a genius and all the virtues which characterize a saint. But under his mask hid a diabolical pride and an immeasurable ambition. At the bottom of his heart was a secret hatred for all authority except, to be sure, his own.... I had terrible struggles with him, and I aroused his anger so much that he lost all control of himself; he became in those moments truly a maniac, twisting himself into contortions in a rage that rendered him unrecognizable. I contradicted him openly in front of the people and pointed out the dangers that would face all equally. I did not hide my belief that this agitation could only end in war, that it would bring down upon them all sorts of evils and cover the country with ruin and blood.[59]

Father André had almost despaired of dealing with Riel when he accidentally stumbled on the one way to get rid of the agitator. At a meeting with the priest on December 12 at St. Laurent, Riel mentioned, as he had many times before, that he had personal claims against the federal government. He was owed land under the Manitoba Act, payment from the government for the time he governed Manitoba, and some payment or at least recognition for stepping aside so that Sir George Cartier could be elected and for helping during the Fenian scare in 1871. Father André recognized the opportunity. What if the government paid Riel's claims? Then, the Métis leader said, he would head back to the United States, his adopted country.

Father André said he would do what he could. Riel told the council of South Branch Métis about the conversation. Napolean Nault recalled: "We talked at length about the figure to ask. Charles Nolin thought $100,000, but finally we agreed to settle for $35,000, the sum which was thought necessary to purchase a printing press and all the equipment to start a newspaper."[60]

Father André was back on December 23 with David Macdowall, the member of the North-West Council for the District of Lorne, which included the South Branch. The two were ready to talk dollars and cents with Riel. Macdowall reported to Dewdney:

> His claims amount to the modest sum of $100,000, but he will take $35,000 as originally offered, and I believe myself that $3,000 to $5,000 would cart the whole Riel family across the boundary. . . . if the Government would consider his personal claims against them and pay him a certain amount in settlement of these claims, he would arrange to make his illiterate and unreasoning followers well satisfied with almost any settlement of their claims for land grants that the government might be willing to make, and also that he would leave the N. W. never to return.[61]

Father André and Macdowall preferred to interpret Riel's motives during the negotiations as pure avarice, but Riel did not care for money. He was always poor, always worried about his family's financial welfare, and constantly borrowing from friends. He kept himself that way. No matter how much money actually came his way, it inevitably slipped through his fingers. It was difficult for even Riel's most strident critics, whose numbers were growing, to believe the Métis leader would sell out his people for pieces of silver, an allusion that must have occurred to Riel.

Macdowall may have misinterpreted what Riel said about the Métis' willingness to accept a settlement. When he was asked if settling his personal claims would change the Métis grievances, Father André later reported that Riel answered evasively: "If I am satisfied the half-breeds will be."[62] It is not clear whether he meant that all the Métis grievances would be ameliorated or, as is more likely, that the Métis would be satisfied with Riel's personal settlement. Macdowall and Father André gave Riel's statement the interpretation most favourable to their hopes.

Father André was not known for his searching analysis of situations; he was more swayed by momentary emotions. Macdowall had been only peripherally involved in the politics of the South Branch, to the extent that a promise to bring some of the Métis land grievances to the attention of the authorities helped him win election in 1883. Neither man understood Riel, his politics, or his motives. From the time he returned to Canada, in many of his letters and speeches Riel mentioned he was an American citizen and intended to remain one. That statement was often coupled with a declaration that he had personal claims against the Canadian government. Riel did not dwell on either point; he just was careful to mention each. No one, in particular Father André and Macdowall, seems to have understood what he was getting at.

Riel, to whom ethics were fundamental even in political life, believed that no American citizen had a right to engage in political agitation in Canada. The fact that he had personal claims that he believed had been widely acknowledged gave him the right to cross the border into the North-West. His personal claims were the foundation of his political legitimacy. He best expressed his position in October in a letter to James Wickes Taylor, the American Consul at Winnipeg.

As [an] American citizen, I could not have accepted an invitation to come and act in any political movement, on this side of the line. But I am personally interested in the treaty [the Manitoba Act] which took place, in /70, between the East and the West of British North America and as one who has thus a personal right to ask for the fulfillment of that treaty, I have come to try and get from the Canadian government what they owe me. And as a witness of the people, I am willing to give them, as they ask for it, the help of my testimony concerning the conditions upon which this country has been entered in the canadian Confederation.[63]

Father André could not admit that a priest would be involved in such an odious enterprise as to try to bribe someone he found troublesome, but that is what the negotiations with Riel amounted to. Father André rationalized the situation. Riel's claims became legitimate in Father André's mind, and that confirmation encouraged Riel.

Father André made anguished pleas to Dewdney that the government come to a settlement with Riel. "I strongly advise not to look to some paltry thousand dollars when the peace of the country is at stake," he wrote the Lieutenant Governor.[64] The government did not take Father André's advice. In February 1885 John A. Macdonald, who was not known to spare expense to buy loyalty, put a stop to the negotiations. He wrote Dewdney: "We have no money to give Riel and would be obliged to ask for a Parliamentary vote. How would it look to be obliged to confess we could not govern the country and were obliged to bribe a man to go away? This would never do. He has a right to remain in Canada and if he conspires, we must punish him. That's all."[65]

It would have suited Riel best if his personal claims had never been noticed, even though he had to consistently mention them. As long as they remained outstanding, in his own mind he retained his political legitimacy. But the moment the authorities began to talk seriously about settling his personal grievances, his political base was eroded. Macdonald's demur was a green light, if not a red flag.

CHAPTER SEVEN

The Eleventh Hour

When he was writing and re-writing the petitions of the fall of 1884, and trying to get the Métis, the English half-breeds, and the white settlers to sign them, Riel's closest collaborator was not a fellow Métis but young Will Jackson of Prince Albert, who had become Riel's personal secretary and his link with the white community.

Orthodoxy and William Henry Jackson did not go together. As a boy in the small Ontario town of Wingham, he was known as an exasperating practical joker. Boyhood acquaintances later told stories of an arrogant young Will carrying knives and pistols and threatening adults. He was tolerated because he showed signs of brilliance. In the home above Gething Jackson's store, Will, his brother, Eastwood, and his sister, Cicely, were brought up in a strict religious environment. Both his grandfathers had been Methodist ministers in England, and for a time before they built a church in Wingham, the Methodists held their services in the Jackson home. Will's mother Elizabeth, and his father, Thomas Gething, were very well-read and believed strongly in the value of education. Gething Jackson was also a dedicated Reformer, an admirer of progressive social movements and the men, like William Lyon Mackenzie, who made them. Gething Jackson, who took Will to his first political meeting when he was eleven years old, ensured that his children had a keen appreciation of the right to oppose oppression and that they understood it was God's wish that they support the underdog. Will was only sixteen when he enrolled in classics at the University of Toronto in 1877. He did well in his studies, but in 1879 his family, whose business in Wingham was bankrupt, decided to move west to Prince Albert, where Will's pharmacist brother, Eastwood, planned to open a drug store. There was no more money for Will to attend school. He withdrew in his fourth year and joined them shortly after they arrived in Prince Albert. He first tried to homestead near the forks of the North and South Saskatchewan Rivers, but Will wasn't much of a farmer and he soon moved to help his father in a farm implement business on Gething's homestead a few kilometres east of the forks.

Will Jackson used his family's political philosophy only as a starting point. By the time he left university, he had gone far beyond his father's Liberalism. He leaned towards political theorists who prescribed quick and comprehensive cures for the social ills that he had learned about on Gething's knee. When the agitation was dangerously accelerating in the early months of 1885, a friend later quoted him as saying: "If it came to the knife, the merchants and lawyers would be the first to suffer."[1] For all his moral support of social reform, that statement, characteristic of anarchist sentiment at the time, would have appalled the elder Jackson.

With his interest in politics and protest movements, it is not surprising that Will took up the cause of the white settlers against the Ottawa government almost as soon as he arrived in the North-West. For their part, the farmers were glad to have the well-educated, well-spoken young man on their side. Will was a good writer and an enthusiastic and energetic speaker, exactly the kind of person the reform movement in the North-West needed. In the spring of 1884, Will became one of the first to join the North-West Settlers' Union.

Will Jackson was easily impressed by new people and new ideas. When he found a cause that appealed to him, Will embraced it thoroughly, passionately, and suddenly. When Louis Riel arrived at the South Branch in July 1884, Jackson, then secretary of the Settlers' Union, was one of the first to visit him. Here was a golden opportunity for the impressionable young activist, the chance to be associated with a legendary and militant champion of the underdog, the sort of person Will loved so much to read about. He knew how vehemently the majority society in Ontario hated Riel. That only added to the Métis leader's prestige in Will's eyes. "In my boyhood days," his neighbours portrayed Riel "as a Cut-throat, an outlaw, bold braggart, and indeed the embodiment of nearly all that is evil."[2] When they first met, Riel and Jackson talked all night and quickly became fast friends. Riel recorded a prayer in his diary: "We thank You, through Jesus, Mary and Joseph for having watched over the following people until now, and we beg You through Jesus, Mary and Joseph to take care of them always, if You please: my friend William Henry Jackson, whom I have chosen as a special friend, and all his well-meaning followers."[3]

Through his friendship with Riel, Jackson found himself drawn closer to the Métis and it became an even more urgent political task for him to forge an alliance among the white settlers, English half-breeds, and Métis. His activities brought Will to the attention of the authorities. In the fall of 1884, he wrote Riel: "It seems the police have an eye on me. They told the man who drove their horses that they had sure evidence against me. They say Riel is not a bad fellow only he is liable to be seduced and led astray by 'that young Jackson.' Ain't I a big man?"[4] Riel replied in a letter to Eastwood Jackson a few days later: "If your brother finds himself unsafe, tell him that the french Halfbreeds invite him to come and remain this way amongst us. And if we are to be arrested, we will be together."[5] Will took up the invitation in November when he moved into Moïse Ouellette's home at the South Branch. Riel and his family were also staying there. Jackson's ties to the Métis became closer when he fell in love with sixteen-year-old Rose Ouellette, Moïse's daughter and Gabriel Dumont's niece, as passionately as he had embraced any political activity.

The Métis were impressed with Jackson for much the same reasons as the white settlers liked him. "As Jackson had acquired the reputation of being the best-educated man in the country, everyone greatly respected his opinion," Philippe Garnot recalled.[6]

Jackson wrote the covering letter with the petition sent in December 1884 complaining that previous pleas had been ignored and warning against interfering with Riel's leadership. Early in January 1885 Jackson was delighted to receive a letter from Ottawa. It was a simple acknowledgement that the petition had been received, but Jackson wrote Riel: "The mere fact of an answer is a very good sign considering the bold tone of my letter and our audacious assumption that we are not yet in Confederation, an assumption, which, it seems to me, they have conceded in their letter."[7]

In his enthusiasm and optimism, Jackson was reading far too much into the government's reply, just as he had over-estimated the depth of the feeling of the white community in his letter to Ottawa. But at least the federal government had finally communicated with the North-West agitators. Previous appeals, as Jackson said, had gone unacknowledged, a common problem for any group in the North-West that tried to deal with Ottawa. Even Conservative Associations and the government's own advisors in the North-West frequently complained about the lack of official notice.

By the beginning of 1885, the Métis had made only moderate progress towards getting their grievances settled, but they had put their views in a comprehensive and specific form and Ottawa had taken note. And they were pleased to have their legendary leader back among them. On New Year's Day, the Métis of the South Branch held a banquet for Riel at which they presented him with a house, some money, and an illuminated address thanking him for his efforts on their behalf and calling him the "veritable father of the French population of the vast North-West Territories...like the tribunes of Ancient Rome, the courageous spokesman for the people...the founder of Manitoba."[8] Riel graciously thanked his comrades, then proposed toasts to Queen Victoria and the Métis women.

The South Branch Métis were pleased with the progress of their movement but their impatience grew quickly as they waited for government response to the specific points in their petition. At the beginning of February, NWMP Superintendent Crozier, at Father André's request, telegraphed Dewdney. "Great discontent at no reply to representation.... Urge government declare intention immediately."[9] Father André added his own plea in a letter to Lieutenant Governor Dewdney. "The government certainly takes upon itself great responsibility in thus delaying so long to redress the grievances of the halfbreeds and rendering them the justice to which they are entitled." It would be the last letter he would write on the matter, Father André said, because "I have already written twice, ere this, but I presume my letters were not received because neither was acknowledged."[10]

Unknown to Father André and the Métis, the government had already declared its intention. On January 28, the cabinet passed an order-in-council authorizing the Minister of the Interior to appoint a three-man commission to make a list of North-West half breeds "with a view of settling equitably the claims of half-breeds in Manitoba and the North West Territories who would have been entitled to land had they resided in Manitoba at the time of transfer and file their claims in due course under the Manitoba Act, and also of those who, though residing in Manitoba and equitably entitled to participate in the grant, did not do so."[11]

Minister of the Interior David Macpherson soon telegraphed Dewdney, repeating the wording of the order-in-council. The Lieutenant Governor immediately recognized the dangerous shortcomings in what the government had done. There was no specific action mentioned except making a list of half-breeds. There was no concession to, or even mention of, any of their grievances. Even the contentious matter of river lots had not been dealt with. Dewdney knew that the government action would not only disappoint the Métis, it might incite them. The Métis might view the message as a government attempt to buy time at a point when their agitation seemed to be reaching a climax, hoping that the vague promise to investigate the claims would permit enough of a delay that the proposed commission, in the absence of sustained pressure, would be allowed to accomplish little. He resolved not to send Macpherson's message on to the South Branch. In a draft of a letter to Macdonald, Dewdney said: "To send the telegram as worded by Sir David would spur the bulk of the French Half Breeds who are making demands that they have nothing to expect. They would at once work on the English Half Breeds to help them start a fresh agitation which would make it more difficult to carry out the views of the Govt."[12] If the government appeared to be stalling or if it was not willing to give in to some of the Métis demands, it would be better to do nothing at all until the spring, when the Métis would be too busy planting to have time for politics, Dewdney thought. He was trying, belatedly, to infuse official Ottawa with a dose of North-West political realism. It had little effect. Dewdney's previous overly-optimistic reports that all was well under his guiding hand were part of the problem, part of the reason that whatever the Macdonald government could do for the North-West in the spring of 1885 would be far too little, far too late.

Dewdney sent his own version of the government's telegram to David Macdowell at Prince Albert to pass on to the Métis, a deliberately vague version that he thought sounded a little more optimistic. "Government has decided to investigate claims of half-breeds and with that view has already taken preliminary steps."[13]

The Lieutenant Governor's apprehensions were well-founded. When Charles Nolin showed Riel the reworded telegram on February 8 at St. Laurent the Métis leader hit the table and angrily exclaimed: "In 40 days, Ottawa will have my answer."[14] Forty days later would be March 19, 1885.

Despite their mutual affection and agreement on so many points, it gradually became apparent that Louis Riel and Will Jackson had one difference of political opinion so fundamental it threatened to destroy all their efforts. Jackson eagerly accepted Riel, who was to call himself "Prophet of the New World," but he had another political hero, the radical American economist Henry George, whose work was immensely popular in the 1880s. George, who was known as the "Prophet of San Francisco" and who believed that he was divinely inspired, wrote that the great mistake mankind made was to adopt private ownership of land. God had given the earth to mankind in common and, although individuals were free to use the land to create wealth by their labour, it was evil for individuals to claim ownership of any piece of land. This evil was expressed as rent or profit that resulted solely from land ownership. Rent, in George's philosophy, was responsible for all human misery and inequality. In Jackson's mind and in the minds of many others, particularly those in the labour movement at the time, Henry George provided a clear explanation of one of man's fundamental problems and better yet, what looked like a simple solution. George's work also contained a sophisticated criticism of racism, for native people often lived close to his ideal. George thought North American natives believed the earth belonged to God, that no man could claim ownership of any part of it and so, in native society, they were free to enjoy their fruits of their own labour unfettered by the evil rent.

But George's writings were diametrically opposed to any notion of aboriginal rights to land while the theories of Louis Riel rested on land ownership for his people. As Riel later explained his philosophy:

In England, in France, the French and the English have lands, the first was in England, they were the owners of the soil and they transmitted to generations. Now, by the soil they have had their start as a nation. Who starts the nations? The very one who creates them, God. God is the master of the universe, our planet is his land, and the nation and the tribes are members of His family, and as a good father, he gives a portion of his lands to that nation, to that tribe, to everyone, that is his heritage, that is his share of the inheritance, of the people, or nation or tribe.[15]

Using George's propositions of the evil of rent, Jackson criticized what he saw as the absurdity of Riel's authority for a foundation of a Métis nation, that God had allotted nations land that they owned and could pass on to the individual ownership of their citizens.

If the Indian has the right to demand rent, and the white man to pay rent for the use of the soil, then the white half of the Halfbreed has the right to pay rent to the Indian half; that is, the Halfbreed has simply the right to use the soil, without paying rent, and without receiving rent, even if the ownership is admitted, and if the ownership of the human race is admitted, he is in just the same position, for then neither the Halfbreed nor anyone else has the right to pay or receive rent. The position of the Halfbreed, therefore, is the same in either case.[16]

Young Will may have been easily led into versions of political philosophy, but once there, he hung on tight. Fundamental contradictions between his heroes, Riel and George, were not easy to take. The dispute climaxed early in 1885. Jackson was busy gathering signatures for a North-West Bill of Rights and a new petition to Ottawa, one that would expand the agitation and particularly appeal to white farmers. Jackson's plan was "to organize every settlement & the N.W.T. convene a central congress in about two months and take our case direct to the throne. In the meantime we will send down a softly worded petition which will leave them under the impression that if they remove some of our present grievances, we will cease to agitate."[17]

Jackson's new petition listed all the usual grievances but it neglected any mention of aboriginal land rights. Jackson arrived at the South Branch on February 14 to collect Métis signatures and, in Eastwood Jackson's words, "Riel (by whose advice they were guided) opposed the petition, attacking it on the basis of Halfbreed ownership, and my brother being equally determined on the other side, the argument lasted all night, and became so fierce that Riel lost his self-control."[18]

Will Jackson's politics were far too radical to be accepted by the constituency he claimed to represent, the dissatisfied businessmen and white farmers of Prince Albert, but his split with Riel on the issue of aboriginal rights illustrated a fundamental difference of opinion between the natives and the newcomers in the North-West. A claim to aboriginal rights to land was the basis of all Riel's political activity. The whites, while most of them agreed the government was considerably indebted to the Métis and Indians, did not want the notion of aboriginal rights carried so far that it might jeopardize their own land holdings. On the other hand, many of the South Branch Métis were only lukewarm to the notion of Métis aboriginal rights. Unlike most Métis in other parts of the North-West, they had always refused to base their claims for a land settlement on their kinship with the Indians. In a way, Will Jackson was closer to the views not only of the dissatisfied whites but also of the South Branch Métis than Louis Riel was on the issue of aboriginal rights. But Jackson's philosophy was too academic and too radical for either community to accept wholeheartedly.

In late February 1885 Riel began to move away from cooperation with the white community. However, to keep the agitation growing as it seemed to be nearing a climax, Riel had to solidify his base of operations among the French- and English-speaking half-breeds. At a meeting at Batoche on February 24, Riel announced that he wanted to go back to the United States. Ottawa had not responded to the Métis pressure any more than it had when he was not leading them. His usefulness in Canada had ended, Riel said. Most of the Métis believed

Riel really did intend to go back to the United States. All the time he had been in the North-West Riel had laid the foundations for that belief with his references to his American citizenship. It is more likely that Riel was grandstanding, trying to ensure that the Métis would follow wherever he led. Philippe Garnot, a French Canadian who owned a tavern and boarding house at Batoche, recorded that when Riel made his announcement, "a cry arose from the whole assembly: 'No! No! No! No!' An old man got to his feet and said, 'If you leave, nephew, we will all leave with you.' Charles Nolin would have cried 'No!' all day if someone had not stopped him." When the clamour subsided, Riel asked: "But the consequences?" Several Métis answered: "We will suffer the consequences."

The three priests in attendance were just as enthusiastic as the Métis, Garnot said. "The Reverend Father Fourmond spoke and approved everything that had happened and told the people that they had acted wisely in not letting Riel leave. Father Moulin explained his ideas in almost the same terms as Father Fourmond. But Father Végréville was more explicit, claiming to have himself been the promoter of the movement."[19]

Riel's priestly support quickly evaporated. In the evening of March 2, he went to see Father André and demanded: "You must give me permission to proclaim a provisional government before twelve o'clock tonight."[20] The priest, of course, refused and after a heated exchange, Father André told Riel to leave. The next day, accompanied by a group of armed Métis, Riel told a meeting at the English half-breed community of Halcro, south of Prince Albert, that the NWMP intended to arrest him. He pointed to his armed comrades and said: "These are the real police."[21] Riel made no direct mention of taking up arms but he recorded in his diary at about that time:

O my Métis people! You complain that your lands have been stolen. Why, how can it be that you have not yet recovered them? You hold all the cards, you are strong enough. All you have to do is take your lands. The foreigner cannot resist you. Pray God to grant you His Spirit; and the moral force of His wisdom, together with the divine courage of the Sacred Heart of Jesus, will make you surmount all difficulties. O Sacred Heart of Jesus, help the Métis people to take up arms; help them to use them well, and to gain Your successes, victories and triumphs.[22]

While he and Riel were plotting and arguing about political strategy, Will Jackson had been considering Riel's pleas that he convert to Catholicism. It was not an easy decision for a man so steeped in Catholic-hating Methodism to make. On the other hand, conversion would tie him closer to his adopted people, the Métis, and make it possible for him to marry Rose Ouellette. At the Halcro meeting on March 3, after being convinced that Protestantism was a sin and the Pope the true leader of all Christians, Jackson announced he was resigning his position in the Settlers' Union to devote himself to religious studies. Two days later, his appalled father visited Will at Riel's home but he got nowhere arguing with Riel and his new religious disciple and left convinced "a religious mania had taken possession" of his son.[23]

Riel had decided to try to repeat the Red River insurrection. On March 5, he held a secret meeting with a group of prominent Métis and presented them with an oath:

We, the undersigned, pledge ourselves deliberately and voluntarily to do everything we can to

1. save our souls by trying day and night to live a holy life everywhere and in all respects.

2. save our country from a wicked government by taking up arms if necessary.[24]

Joseph Ouellette, Gabriel Dumont, Pierre Gariépy, Isidore Dumont, John Ross, Philippe Gariépy, Auguste Laframboise, Moïse Ouellette, Calixte Lafontaine, and Napolean Nault all signed. Charles Nolin refused. Riel told Nolin "he had decided to take up arms and to induce the people to take up arms and the first thing was to fight for the glory of God, for the honor of religion, and for the salvation of our souls." Nolin protested against a rash decision. He proposed that a novena, nine days of public prayers, be held so the Métis could consult their consciences.[25] The novena would also be in honour of the cure of Nolin's wife, who had been sick all winter but had recovered after praying to Our Lady of Lourdes. The Métis and their priests deemed the cure a miracle.

Riel opposed Nolin's suggestion but he promised to take it to a meeting of the leading Métis. The next day, a small group met at Riel's house and adopted Nolin's plan. The novena would begin on March 10 and end on March 19, forty days after Riel had received the government's reply to the Métis petition.

Riel announced his intention to form a provisional government at a large public meeting at St. Laurent on March 8. England and Russia were about to go to war, he said. It was a good time to press the North-West complaints when Imperial troops would not be able to come to the aid of the Canadian government. An anonymous correspondent to a Toronto newspaper reported: "Nolin and Riel then moved that, as the Government had for fifteen years neglected to settle the half-breed claims, though it had repeatedly (and more especially by providing for their adjustment in the Dominion Land Act of 1883) confessed their justice, the meeting should assume that the Government had abdicated its functions through such neglect; and should proceed to establish a provisional Government."[26]

The meeting passed a ten-point "Revolutionary Bill of Rights," probably the one that Will Jackson had been working on, which duplicated some of the items in the petition sent to Ottawa in December. It did not mention aboriginal rights but the section dealing with settlers' land patents presumably covered the river-lot question.

1. That the half-breeds of the North-West Territories be given grants similar to those accorded to the half-breeds of Manitoba by the Act of 1870.

2. That patents be issued to all half-breed and white settlers who have fairly earned the right of possession on their farms.

3. That the provinces of Alberta and Saskatchewan be forthwith organized with legislatures of their own, so that the people may be no longer subject to the despotism of Mr. Dewdney.

4. That in these new provincial legislatures, while representation according to population shall be the supreme principle, the Métis shall have a fair and reasonable share of representation.

5. That the offices of trust throughout these provinces be given to residents of the country, as far as practicable, and that we denounce the appointment of disreputable outsiders and repudiate their authority.

6. That this region be administered for the benefit of the actual settler, and not for the advantage of the alien speculator.

7. That better provision be made for the Indians, the parliamentary grant to be increased and lands set apart as an endowment for the establishment of hospitals and schools for the use of whites, half-breeds, and Indians, at such places as the provincial legislatures may determine.

8. That all the lawful customs and usages which obtain among the Métis be respected.

9. That the Land Department of the Dominion Government be administered as far as practicable from Winnipeg, so that settlers may not be compelled as heretofore to go to Ottawa for the settlement of questions in dispute between them and the land commissioner.

10. That the timber regulations be made more liberal, and that the settler be treated as having rights in this country.

Riel told the meeting, in the words of the newspaper correspondent, "that no hostile movement would be made unless word was received from Ottawa refusing to grant the demands in the bill of rights. If, however, the Government should appoint a commission to deal with the half-breed claims and pledge itself to deal with the questions affecting white settlers, then the Provisional Government, on obtaining reasonable guarantees that this would be done, would disband. Bloodshed was to be avoided unless the provocations amounted to life or death for the revolted settlers. In the meantime, the authority of the Dominion would be repudiated, and supplies collected to provide against the emergency of war."[27] Even by this time, Riel may not have known that the government intended to appoint what it called a Half-breed Claims Commission. It was not until March 4 that Dewdney finally told Father André that the commission was to be appointed.[28] In any case, Riel wanted a commission empowered to do much more than just make a list of half-breeds.

The Métis appointed a committee to gather supplies from the neighbourhood. Riel and Dumont sent runners to the Indian bands to tell them what had happened and ask for support.

At Battleford, NWMP Superintendent Crozier didn't wait for instructions. On March 12 he dispatched twenty-six of his Battleford garrison and one field gun to reinforce Fort Carlton. Under the headline, "Incipient Rebellion," the *Saskatchewan Herald* told its readers NWMP were tight-lipped but there was no doubt the police movements were in response to the growing agitation on the South Branch.

> From the information in our possession it appears that Riel has resumed the role of agitator, delivering inflammatory speeches in which he urges his followers to demand from the Government a recognition of what he says are their 'rights.' In his latest oratorical efforts at Duck Lake he is said to have pointed out that England was now engaged in a gigantic foreign war, and that this was their opportunity, as she could not spare any troops to fight them.
>
> According to their own talk, the deluded men intend to re-enact the old-time scenes at the barricade at St. Norbert [Man.], by deciding that on the 15th March they will put a stop to all traffic across the South Branch. A more suicidal programme for their own interests it would be hard to decide on.[29]

Crozier, who had been diligent in his efforts to keep tabs on the South Branch agitation, had already warned his superiors what was likely to happen. The desperate tone that grew with each letter he wrote caused Dewdney to dismiss most of what he said as exaggerated. On February 27, Crozier had written a straightforward letter to Dewdney, disregarding the niceties that might be expected of a policeman addressing the Lieutenant Governor. "Could not a surveyor be sent out *now*, if it is intended to allow the Halfbreeds their land as they wish to have it laid out in place of the regular blocks as surveyed throughout the country. Then there is the question of the Halfbreeds being allowed scrip as granted in Manitoba. I must strongly urge that these and other matters already reported upon be attended to at once. Delay causes uneasiness and discontent, which spreads not only among the Halfbreeds but the Indians." If his advice were not followed, Crozier warned, "it would not be surprising if the whole country were kept in a continual commotion, if not worse, during the coming spring and summer."[30]

When he arrived at Fort Carlton on March 13, Crozier telegraphed Dewdney: "Halfbreed rebellion likely to break out any moment. Must be prepared for consequence. Troop must be largely reinforced. French Halfbreeds alone in this section number seven hundred men. If Halfbreeds rise Indians will join them."[31] Dewdney replied that he was ready to support Crozier's efforts. He told the policeman that the government had prohibited the sale of arms and ammunition to Treaty No. 6 Indians.[32]

At Regina, Dewdney had already been considering what to do. He wondered if it would be wise to reinforce Crozier's command with police from the territorial capital. On March 12, as he was receiving alarming messages from Crozier and considering sending more police north, Dewdney met with Hudson's Bay Company Factor Lawrence Clarke, on his way to Prince Albert from Winnipeg, to brief him on the South Branch situation and seek his advice. Dewdney did not record the discussion that would soon have unfortunate and unforeseen consequences.

Eastern Canadian newspapers, most of which had paid little attention to the North-West even after Riel's return, quickly realized they had a hot news story on their hands. The Toronto *World*'s headline on March 13 was typical: "Ripe for a Rebellion." The *World* was among the first to jump on what would soon become a popular bandwagon. "Whether the agitation will develop into anything serious it is yet too early to predict, but it is sincerely to be hoped that the government will take prompt measures for its suppression, and give Mr. Riel if he is ever again proven guilty of an overt act the short end of a rope."[33]

On March 14, Dewdney received reassuring telegrams from Lawrence Clarke, then at Fort Qu'Appelle. He had talked with people who knew the situation and found that the rumours were exaggerated, Clarke said. "More talk than fight. Quiet enough now. . . . No danger anticipated. . . . Riel will not get Indian support."[34] At Fort Carlton, the police reinforcements were finding the situation uneasy but there was no real sign of open rebellion. On March 17, the day Crozier ordered twenty more men and much more ammunition and arms from Battleford, William Laurie, P. G. Laurie's son, reported from Fort Carlton: "The Half-breeds, I am informed, can muster eleven hundred men able to carry arms, and are talking very boldly, although they say the commission of any overt act is postponed until after the Lenten season; while others say they have given the Government until after the arrival of this mail for an answer to their memorial."[35]

Louis Riel and most of the South Branch Métis attended mass at St. Laurent on Sunday, March 15. Father Vital Fourmond used the occasion to sermonize on rebellion. "I concluded with the declaration that absolution would be refused to all those who took up arms."[36] After mass, Riel criticized the priest for meddling in politics, but the Métis leader had gone beyond worrying about what the priests were doing and saying. If the Church of Rome would not support the Métis in their struggle for justice, the Métis would abandon the church, Riel had decided.

Riel's religious opinions had been decidedly unorthodox for many years. After he came to the North-West, while it still seemed the priests might support the Métis movement, he had kept his thoughts on religion mostly to himself, proposing only a few changes in ritual and religious practice and staying away from questions of doctrine. When the priests formally opposed the right of the

Métis to assert themselves in arms, there was no longer any need to keep his opinions quiet and throughout March Riel gradually told the Métis that the church needed more than just reforming, it needed radical change.

Riel began presenting himself as a prophet. In Riel's mind, his prophetic mission had been sanctioned by Ignace Bourget in a letter the Ultramontanist Bishop of Montreal had written to him in 1875. "God, who has always led you and assisted you until the present hour, will not abandon you in the dark hours of your life, for He has given you a mission which you must fulfil in all respects."[37] Riel carried that letter with him for the rest of his life and chose to interpret it as meaning that he was a genuine prophet, although Bourget would later say he was reading too much into it. When the time was right, on receiving a message from God, Riel was the messenger to tell the world that Rome had fallen and the Holy Spirit now resided in Bishop Bourget, the new Pope.

Lawrence Clarke arrived at the South Branch on March 17. The Métis wanted to know if he had any news about a government response to their petition or bill of rights. According to some white settlers who knew of the affair, Clarke replied "in a domineering and authoritative manner" that the only response would be that "the government were sending up five hundred men to take Riel."[38] Clarke later denied saying any such thing but the story was quickly and widely circulated. Father Fourmond heard that the police were coming "to exterminate the Métis, their wives and their children."[39] For the Métis, Clarke's statement was a declaration of war.

Clarke wasn't far wrong. Early in the morning of March 18, NWMP Commissioner A. G. Irvine left Regina for Fort Carlton with almost a hundred men. Before Irvine began his march, Crozier wired Dewdney that things were quieter and there was "no cause for alarm now."[40] Dewdney wrote Hudson's Bay Company Commissioner Joseph Wrigley in Winnipeg to reassure him. It looked as if Irvine's force would not be needed to put down a rebellion but their presence would be beneficial, he told Wrigley. "I think it is better to have a good force in the north this summer & so show the agitators that the Govt. won't stand any nonsense & it will assist us very materially in handling our Indians."[41] But late on March 17, Crozier changed his mind and requested reinforcements. "Rumor tonight Indians being tampered with. Large force should be sent without delay that arrests may be made if necessary to prevent further and continuous trouble from Riel and followers."[42] George Ness, a farmer and magistrate at Batoche, had arrived at Fort Carlton to say that Gabriel Dumont was trying to persuade the Cree at One Arrow's reserve just east of Batoche to join the Métis.

When Ness neared home on March 18, he found his Métis neighbours all carrying arms and talking of a mass meeting that was to be held that night. That prompted an urgent telegram from Crozier to Dewdney. "Send as many men as possible immediately. Mass meeting half breeds tonight. Report of immediate trouble. Must stamp this out."[43] Ness crossed the river and reached the Kerr Brothers' store, where he found a large number of Métis and met Gabriel Dumont. To Dumont's question of where he had been, Ness lied and said he had only been as far as Duck Lake. Dumont, who probably suspected that Ness had gone to give information to Crozier, said "I will take you prisoner. I says you can do what you please. I says, if you want to kill me, I am ready." Ness wasn't harmed but he was kept prisoner in the Kerrs' store.[44]

Saskatoon physician John Willoughby and half-breed trader Norbert Welsh stayed at Batoche overnight on March 17 and learned "that certain parties were to be arrested, the telegraph wires cut, etc."[45] The two left Batoche for Saskatoon in the morning of March 18 but Welsh wanted to see Riel. On the way south they met Gabriel Dumont, who told them Riel was at Joseph Vandal's house just north of Tourond's Coulee. Riel had left by the time they arrived. They went back north and caught up with him at Baptiste Rocheleau's house, where they stopped for an early dinner.

Willoughby and Riel, who had met before, exchanged pleasantries. "After a few casual remarks, silence ensued. Riel soon arose and paced the floor in front of me. At that moment about seventy armed men drove up to the door. Can you imagine my feelings? I had no revolver and decided to let them take me quietly. Welsh sat with his navy pistol in his hand under his coat. Riel faced me, and exclaimed, 'The time has come, doctor, when it were better for a man to have been good.'"

Willoughby didn't understand but Riel was eager to explain. He had decided to begin the rebellion before the novena ended. "He and his people were going to strike a blow to get possession of the country, which had been stolen from them and misruled by the Canadian Government." There would be a new government for the North-West, Riel said, "a God-fearing Government. His Parliament would not be after the style of the one at Ottawa, where men present to smoke cigars and lounge about reading-rooms. He and his people had many times petitioned the Government for redress, but the only answer they received was an increase in police. He said, 'I also have my police whom you see at the door, and one week from to-day that little Government force will be wiped out of existence. Saskatoon will also be wiped out.'" He would attack Saskatoon in retaliation for the citizens of that town offering volunteers to the police during the Battleford Indian troubles of the previous year, Riel said.[46] "'Go home to Saskatoon, tell the people to pray to God—it is their only hope. You know Louis Riel and his past history.' He spoke as if he was leader at the head of the rebels. He said: 'You remember the rebellion 15 years ago. That was nothing to the rebellion that this will be. The time has come when I am to be ruler of the Country or perish in the attempt. You are an educated man, and you know that when I, Louis Riel, stand before you and say this, I mean business.'"[47]

Willoughby and Riel talked for two hours. The Métis leader expected the half-breeds and Indians of the United States to join the rebellion. When they had control of the country, they would divide it into seven parts, giving one part to various peoples from whom Riel expected help, the Bavarians, the Poles, the Italians, the Germans, the Irish, and the Irish and German people living in the United States.

The conversation ended with Riel advising the doctor "to prepare for eternity and as I was going back to Saskatoon to advise many people to do the same."[48] After Riel and the Métis left Rocheleau's, Willoughby and Welsh hurried south towards the telegraph station at Clarke's Crossing, where they found the Métis had already cut the wires, preventing communication with Prince Albert and to the east. But the lines to Battleford were still open so Willoughby related what he had seen and heard to NWMP Inspector William Morris, who was in command there.

When Riel and the Métis left Rocheleau's, they went back to Batoche. As they neared the village, they discovered that Gabriel Dumont had taken more prisoners, John Lash, the Indian Agent for the Carlton district, and his interpreter, William Tompkins. Riel went up to Lash. "He says 'I will have to detain you.' I asked on what grounds he was going to detain me and he said the rebellion had commenced and that they intended fighting until the whole of the Saskatchewan valley was in their hands."[49] The prisoners were taken to the church of St. Antoine de Padoue at Batoche.

Riel and the Métis moved just south of the village to the Kerr Brothers' store, where they took arms and ammunition. They promised not to arrest George and John Kerr if they stayed in their store. When Riel arrived at the church, he was met by a large crowd of Métis and he made a speech, declaring himself a prophet and announcing he was taking over the church.

Riel and some of the Métis then crossed the river to the Walters and Baker store. The Métis leader went up to Henry Walters and said: "Well, Mr. Walters, it has commenced." He asked Walters for all the arms and ammunition in the store. "He asked me to give them up quietly and peaceably, and said that if they succeeded in the movement they would pay me, and if they did not the Dominion Government would pay for them. It would be all right either way."[50] Walters and his helper Joseph Hanifin were held in the second floor of his store where the other prisoners were also housed later that night. The little Métis army, numbering probably about fifty or sixty, was busy all night securing the Batoche area. At about 10 P.M., they arrested Métis Louis Marion, who had refused to join the movement. When Marion arrived under guard at Walters' store, Riel said to him: "Unhappy man, think of your soul & not of earthly things."[51] But Marion refused to change his mind and was kept with the white prisoners. At about 4 A.M. some of the Métis came across and arrested Peter Tompkins and John McKean, who had been sent out near Duck Lake to repair the telegraph line the Métis had cut.

March 19, 1885, was one of the biggest days in the lives of both Will Jackson and the Métis nation. At the end of the nine-day novena, on the feast day of St. Joseph, the patron saint the South Branch Métis had chosen the year before, Jackson was baptised in the church of St. Antoine de Padoue at Batoche. Most of the population of the South Branch communities attended the baptism. Riel had directed the men to come armed, to fire a salute in honor of the convert, he said. The guns greeted another momentous event: the formation of the ministry and army of the Provisional Government of the Saskatchewan.

Will Jackson took Joseph as his baptismal name, the only one of his names he would keep until his death. Jackson faced yet another crisis of confidence the day before his baptism. Riel told his young follower of his plans to break with Rome and establish his own church, with Bishop Bourget as the new Pope and Riel proposing himself as "Prophet of the New World," endowed with priestly authority. After having made the agonizing decision to accept the Church of Rome, Jackson didn't know what to do when his religious mentor told him he was about to convert to a false religion. "There was no middle course. If he spoke the truth then I must accept him in place of the priest—lose my soul even as the Jesus of old, on the other hand if he were an imposter or deluded fanatic then to accept was damnation, for he would be an anti-Christ. I at first temporized. I accepted his statement in silence with a straight countenance but a dubious heart."[52]

Choosing between Riel and the priests was not just a religious matter for Jackson and the Métis of the South Branch. The major difference between the two, Jackson said, was the passage in St. Matthew where Christ says: "Think not that I am come to send peace on earth: I came not to send peace, but a sword." Riel translated that for his followers and in his communication with the government authorities as: "Justice commands us to take up arms." Jackson, already alienated from his family, was also worried about the verse in St. Matthew that followed: "For I am come to set a man at variance against his father, and the daughter against against her mother, and the daughter-in-law against her mother-in-law."

Jackson resolved to join the Roman Church, deciding for the moment that Riel was not the prophet he claimed to be. "After a night of terrible agony enhanced by the supposed proximity of the opposing troops and my consequent liability to a speedy call to answer God according to my choice, I concluded that Mr. Riel was presumptuous & wrong and confessed my non-rejection of his proposition as a sin to Father Moulin." Then he went to tell Riel what he had decided. "To my surprise he rec'd my decision with calmness and said that he left me as free in regard to leaving Rome for him as he had left me in regard to leaving Protestantism for Rome, but told me that I would suffer for my lack of faith."[53]

With most of the Métis fighting force and some Indians gathered for the baptism, Riel made a speech in the church after the service. England, he said, was about to go to war with Russia and could not rush to the Canadian government's aid. It was the best time for the Métis to challenge the government's authority and defend their territory. The Métis formed themselves into companies of ten men and one captain, modelled on the organization of the buffalo hunt. The twenty Indians at Batoche formed their own company. Charles Nolin, suspected of informing the police about the Métis plans and whom Riel wanted to use as a lever to force the priests to his side, was arrested that day and in the evening he was brought to trial before the Métis council at the church. Philippe Garnot attended the trial.

Riel then made a long speech accusing Charles Nolin of treason and said that it was necessary to make an example and it was necessary that Nolin be condemned to death: but he asked council not to fix a date of execution, since it was necessary to leave a way to save himself and that way would be in the hands of the clergy. If the clergy would consent to join him and to approve the resort to arms, Nolin would be freed. The council, for their part, refused to condemn Nolin for different reasons, and when it was put to a vote, Nolin was freed by a large majority and Riel was the first to congratulate him and to take him back into favor. He went even farther. He made a speech in which he said that he had done his duty in arguing the case against Nolin. But that he was proud to see that the council had acquitted him and that he proposed that Nolin be elected as a member of the council of the Provisional Government of the Saskatchewan and he was elected unanimously.[54]

In addition to Nolin, fifteen others were named to the council: Pierre Parenteau, as chairman, Gabriel Dumont, Baptiste Boyer, Moïse Ouellette, Donald Ross, Albert Monkman, Ambrose Jobin, Baptiste Parenteau, Pierre Henry, Norbert Delorme, Damase Carrière, Maxime Lépine, Baptiste Boucher, David Tourond, and, as secretary, Philippe Garnot. Riel was not a member of the council, or at least not a member like the others. As the Métis' prophet, he was a kind of *ex officio* leader in matters spiritual and political. He called himself *exovede* which he coined from Latin to mean "out of the flock." Riel called the council the Exovedate.

After the Nolin trial, Riel had a long discussion with Duck Lake storekeeper Hillyard Mitchell, who had arrived at Batoche in time to attend the baptism.

I told him I came to find out the cause of this trouble, what it meant, and said that he need not look upon me as a spy as I simply came as a friend of the half-breeds to give them some good advice, and try to get them to go home. He went on explaining the cause of the rising. He said that the half-breeds had petitioned the government several times to have their grievances redressed but never got a proper reply, and the reply they were getting now was, 500 policemen to shoot them. I told him the whole thing was a false rumor, that no police were coming. There always had been false reports and I looked upon this one as not true. He said it did not matter whether it was true or not, that the half-breeds intended to show the government that they were not afraid to fight 500.[55]

The next day Mitchell talked with Riel again, and this time the Métis leader asked him to go to Fort Carlton and demand that NWMP Superintendent Crozier surrender the fort. Mitchell refused to carry that message but said he would try to arrange a meeting between Riel and Crozier. Mitchell went to Fort Carlton that same day to make arrangements for the meeting. By this time, about fifty volunteers had arrived from Prince Albert to reinforce the Fort Carlton garrison. Among them was English half-breed Tom McKay, who had already decided to go on his own to Batoche to find out what was happening and try to persuade some of his Métis friends to abandon the rebellion. When Crozier asked Mitchell to take a message back to Riel, McKay eagerly went along. The two emissaries from Fort Carlton travelled most of the night and reached Batoche early in the morning of March 21.

Some of the people at Batoche had not really believed Lawrence Clarke's story about the five hundred police on their way to arrest Riel. When messengers reported that Commissioner Irvine was indeed on the road heading towards Batoche with a large party, the Métis council sent a party of twenty men off towards Humboldt to intercept the police. At the Hoodoo mail station, about eighty kilometres east of Batoche, the Métis party took the goods from the small store that Irvine had counted on to replenish his supplies. They returned to Batoche later that day with two new prisoners, the operator of the Hoodoo station and farmer Tom Sanderson, who had just escorted as far as Hoodoo a courier from Crozier to Irvine.

When McKay and Mitchell arrived at Batoche from Fort Carlton, Riel was in very bad humour. McKay said:

> There appears to be great excitement here Mr. Riel. He said, no; there is no excitement at all, it was simply that the people were trying to redress their grievances, as they had asked repeatedly for their rights, that they had decided to make a demonstration. I told him that it was a very dangerous thing to resort to arms. He said he had been waiting fifteen long years, and that they had been imposed upon, and it was time now, after they had waited patiently, that their rights should be given, as the poor half-breeds had been imposed upon. I disputed his wisdom, and advised him to adopt different measures.

Riel was in no mood for debate about grievances or the consequences of taking up arms. He tongue-lashed McKay, called him a traitor, and said that his was likely to be the first blood shed. "He became very excited, and got up and said, you don't know what we are after— it is blood, blood, we want blood; it is a war of extermination, everybody that is against us is to be driven out of the country."[56]

Riel then put McKay on trial for treason in front of the Métis who were assembled in the little house that they used as a council chamber. The trial had barely begun when Riel changed his mind and went upstairs to talk to Mitchell. Riel was still eager to berate Mitchell about the needs of the Métis and the justice of their cause, but after a while he relaxed and he and Mitchell got down to business. Riel would not agree to meet Superintendent Crozier himself but said he would send two emissaries to negotiate. When they came back downstairs, Riel apologized to McKay, at first in the Cree language. The Métis leader told the English half-breed "he did not mean it to me personally, that he had the greatest respect for me personally but that it was my cause he was speaking against, and he wished to show he entertained great respect for me. He also apologized in French to the people there and he said as I was going out that he was very sorry I was against him, that he would be glad to have me with them and that it was not too late for me to join them yet."[57] And back McKay and Mitchell went to Fort Carlton.

In Riel's mind there could be no negotiation. The South Branch and surrounding territory was Métis country and Crozier ought to leave it gracefully. With the now-confirmed stories of the police marching on Batoche from the southeast and the Métis army not numerous or well-organized enough to fight on two fronts, Riel needed either Fort Carlton abandoned or its garrison his prisoners. Later on March 21, the council sent Charles Nolin and Maxime Lépine to Carlton with a letter addressed to Crozier and signed by Riel.

> Major [Crozier]: The Councillors of the Provisional Government of the Saskatchewan have the honor to communicate to you the following conditions of surrender: You will be required to give up completely the situation which the Canadian Government placed you in at Carlton and Battleford, together with all Government properties.
>
> In case of acceptance you and your men will be set free on your parole of honor to keep the peace. And those who choose to leave the country will be furnished with teams and provisions to reach Qu'Appelle.
>
> In case of non-acceptance we intend to attack you, when to-morrow, the Lord's day is over, and to commence without delay, a war of extermination upon those who have shown themselves hostile to our rights.[58]

A short distance east of Fort Carlton, Nolin and Lepine met Tom McKay and another man sent by Crozier to negotiate. But there was little talking. Crozier's two messengers bore a message similar to that from the Métis council: If the rebels allowed their leaders to be arrested, they could go free. With nothing accomplished, the negotiators returned.

At this point, the English half-breeds of the area around Prince Albert were in an enormous quandary. To side with the police was out of the question. They sympathized strongly with the Métis. But they did not want to go to war over the grievances. They feared the Indians. They did not want the struggle to widen to include the white settlers supporting the police, a turn of events which would put them in a very dangerous position.

On March 20, the English half-breeds met at the Lindsay school house, about twenty-five kilometres south of Prince Albert, to consider their position. Meeting chairman Tom Scott, no relation to the Thomas Scott executed by the Red River provisional government in 1870, was one of the most prosperous farmers in the area. He was not a half-breed himself but he was considered the leader of the English half-breeds during the agitation. A few days before the Lindsay school house meeting, Scott had tried to dissuade Prince Albert residents from joining the volunteers being enrolled to reinforce the garrison at Fort Carlton. His greatest concern was that white settlers joining an armed conflict might signal a race war between whites and half-breeds into which the Indians would be drawn.

At the Lindsay school house on March 20, the English half-breeds decided to send a delegation to the South Branch. They wanted to know what the Métis planned. They also wanted to know, if worse came to worst, how they could defend themselves against the Indians. Those who attended the meeting were discreet in what they said and resolved that night. The meeting ended with three cheers for the delegation and three cheers for Louis Riel.[59]

Scott and the delegation returned to their communities a few days later with a letter from Riel and the Métis council.

> The Ottawa Government has been maliciously ignoring the rights of the Original Half-Breeds during fifteen years. The petitions which have been sent to that Government on that matter and conserning [sic] the grievances which all classes have against its policy are not listened to, moreover the Dominion has taken the high-handed way of answering peaceful complaints by reinforcing their Mounted Police. The avowed purpose being to confirm in the Saskatchewan their Government spoliation & usurpation of the rights and liberties of all classes of men except these assistant oppressers the Hudson's Bay Company and Land Speculators.[60]

It was a relatively mild letter asking for English half-breed help in the fight. It ended with the admonition: "Justice commands us to take up arms."

For Crozier at Fort Carlton, the English half-breeds posed a significant military problem. Their communities straddled the trail between Fort Carlton and Prince Albert, both Crozier's line of supply and reinforcement and, if necessary, his line of retreat. Early on the morning of Sunday, March 22, Crozier and Tom McKay asked Edward Matheson, the Anglican minister for the area south of Prince Albert who was to hold services at Fort Carlton, to visit the English half-breeds and try to ensure they would not interfere with the police.

Matheson realized it would be impossible to persuade them to actually side with the police against the Métis. The best he could hope for was to persuade them to remain neutral in the conflict.

Later that day, he arrived at the Lindsay school house just as people were leaving a church service. He began a meeting that continued later that night at the neighbouring St. Catharine's Church where, after a discussion during which several people said they were ready to get their guns and join Riel, Tom Scott proposed a motion calling on the Prince Albert volunteers to lay down their arms and let the matter be decided solely between the police and the Métis.[61] Before that motion could be debated, the meeting secretary, William Craig, proposed a more moderate course of action, one that still would not put the English half-breeds in opposition to their Métis cousins. That motion, which was passed unanimously, read in part:

> First—That the members of this meeting continue to sympathize as they have always done with the French Halfbreeds in their desire to obtain their legal rights by all constitutional means
>
> Second—That they do not approve of the resort to arms or the raising of the Indians and wish to remain neutral.[62]

As that motion was being discussed, Scott apparently lost his temper and left the meeting in a huff. The next day, Scott had calmed down and Edward Matheson had called another meeting of the English half-breeds, again at the Lindsay school house. Although there was still no hope of bringing the English half-breeds to the fight alongside the Métis, they passed stronger resolutions. The meeting declared, unanimously:

> That while heartily sympathizing with the French half-breeds in their endeavours constitutionally to get redress of their many grievances, we cannot endorse their present attitude in taking up arms for that purpose, and we hereby beg them not to shed blood;
>
> That the opinion of this meeting is that, had the Government been just with the settlers, this disturbance would never have been;
>
> And further, had the influential citizens of Prince Albert joined the movement, instead of ignoring it, had they advised the Government instead of exciting it against the people, it is the opinion of this meeting that the Government would have settled all grievances ere this;
>
> That we, the English half-breeds and Canadian settlers, while advocating peace and remaining completely neutral, as regards resorting to arms, do not for one moment lose sight of our grievances and will henceforth use all lawful means for the redress of same.[63]

A draft of the resolution was even more to the point: "The government has refused to treat with settlers, till one party could bear it no longer, and will have their rights or die."[64]

Scott was pleased with the results of that meeting. He wrote to the Métis that "the voice of every man was with you, and we have taken steps which I think will have a tendency to stop bloodshed and hasten a treaty."[65] But the Métis did not want just English voices with them; they needed their guns. After receiving the resolution of March 22 passed at the St. Catherine's Church, the Métis council, disappointed though they were, replied diplomatically. "Situated as you are it is difficult for you to approve (immediately) of our bold but just uprising, and you have been wise in your course." The council went on to list briefly the North-West grievances against the government and alluded to the Métis' influence over the Indians, which the English half-breeds feared. "We are sure that if the English and French half-breeds unite well in this time of crisis, not only can we control the Indians, but we will also have their weight on our side in the balance. Gentlemen, please do not remain neutral. For the love of God help us to save the Saskatchewan." A postscript added: "If we are well united the police will surrender and come out of Carlton as the hen's heat causes the chicken to come out of the shell. A strong union between the French and English half-breeds is the only guarantee that there will be no bloodshed."[66]

The reply was delivered to the English half-breed communities on March 24 by Albert Monkman with a party of about twenty Métis, including Charles Nolin. They held another meeting at the Lindsay school house that night, with Monkman arguing for armed support and Nolin arguing for peace. The English half-breed intention was still to avoid bloodshed, although some of them told Monkman they were willing to fight. The meeting resolved to do nothing until it was clearer what course events would take.

While the negotiations with Crozier were going on, Will Jackson was still grappling with his religious dilemma. For Jackson, it was a choice of staying neutral or going to war. If he chose Riel's religion, Jackson would declare war on his family and friends, some of whom were then prisoners of the Métis.

I remained in horrible suspense increased by the necessity of choosing between the two parties in the approaching encounter. To one side I was allied by blood, to the other by the ties of religion, friendship and concurrence in certain political views. To this was added my natural horror lest in the excitement of the crisis the white prisoners, with several of whom I had been on the most intimate terms, should be sacrificed as hostages prior to the expected conflict of extermination with the body of police whom Lawrence Clarke had reported as being in full march upon Batoche from the south.

But Jackson became convinced that Riel was both a prophet and able to read his mind. Just after he came to this conclusion, it was confirmed in Jackson's mind for "on coming downstairs (in Mr. Champagnes house) I was met by a Sioux Indian who saying 'This is the house of my children' suddenly appeared & shook hands enthusiastically as if he had been sent to congratulate me on my clearer perceptions."[67]

Their religious differences settled, Riel and Jackson went right back to work arguing about aboriginal land rights and trying to write new drafts of the rebel political platform. Riel believed that since Will had accepted him as a prophet, he would also accept his political theory, including the Métis right to a land base. But Jackson, who still had lingering doubts on the aboriginal land rights question, was also confronted with a similar notion he had trouble accepting, that God had asked Riel to divide the North-West into sections to accommodate several different nationalities. The effect of Riel's powerful personality and his new role as religious leader were too much for Jackson. He could not just repudiate the political philosophy he believed in so firmly but neither could he admit that Riel might be wrong. During one of their arguments,

> I felt however that the fault of our disagreement lay with me rather than with him and asked him to pray that I receive more light & clearer views, we accordingly stopped short and while he was praying a peculiar convulsion or something of the kind seemed to take possession of me under the influence of which I became rigid & helpless sinking back upon the bed on which I was sitting. Mr. Riel asked me to continue my writing and I attempted to do so but found that very old ideas maintained the uppermost place in my mind and I again sank back willing to die on the spot. Mr. Riel and some of the attendant councillors then rubbed my limbs until I recovered but I believe from a remark which I fancied I caught from Mr. Riel's lips that he considered me hopelessly prejudiced against his views.[68]

Though he remained loyal to the rebel leader, that was the end of Jackson's collaboration, and it also marked a considerable cooling of relations between him and the Métis who had so warmly embraced the educated young man with the big political ideas.

The Métis rebels reaped an unexpected windfall on March 22. Four freighters carrying Hudson's Bay Company flour to Fort Carlton camped that night only a few kilometres from Batoche. They were apparently unaware that rebellion had broken out and were surprised when three Métis appeared to tell them that Riel ordered them to go to the town the next morning. The freighters were allowed to leave with their teams but the Métis kept the 140 bags of flour.

On March 23, Commissioner Irvine and his party of police reached the Hoodoo mail station, where they found that the rebels had already appropriated the supplies and police sentries reported rebel scouts nearby. It was rumoured that the rebels were sending five hundred men to attack the police and Irvine decided not to go directly to Fort Carlton but to take the fork in the road just east of the South Branch and head directly for Prince Albert. To confuse the rebels, he also sent rumours toward Batoche that the police were on their way to attack Riel's stronghold, unwittingly bolstering Clarke's injudicious bragging that already he had many of the Métis convinced that they had to defend their homes.

PART TWO

Conflagration

CHAPTER EIGHT

The Fighting Begins: Duck Lake

The wary negotiations with Superintendent Crozier had failed. For all practical purposes they had not even really begun. Crozier was not about to abandon the fort in the face of a simple declaration that the Métis wanted it. The police, augmented by zealous citizen volunteers, were sitting tight. On the South Branch, everyone was waiting for the five hundred police Lawrence Clarke said were coming to arrest Riel and Dumont. The provisional government had firmly established its authority throughout the small territory the Métis recognized as their own, along the east side of the South Branch of the Saskatchewan River from Tourond's Coulee in the south to St. Louis in the north, a distance of about forty kilometres. Just holding that territory and their few prisoners would not be leverage enough to prevent an attack by a large force of police or soldiers, but capturing Fort Carlton and holding its garrison hostage might the key, Riel and other leading Métis reasoned, to force Ottawa to make terms with the provisional government instead of resisting the Métis efforts with an armed force.

One-third of the way between Batoche and Fort Carlton was the small village of Duck Lake, almost ten kilometres west of Batoche, just east of Beardy's reserve. Duck Lake was a community of very mixed loyalties. While its merchants and white population looked to Crozier at Fort Carlton to protect them from the army at Batoche, its Métis residents wanted the provisional government to protect them from the police. The Métis were concerned that Crozier appeared to be using Duck Lake as a base to keep watch on their activities. Duck Lake also had strategic importance. In a fight, both Crozier and the Métis would need the provisions and arms in Hillyard Mitchell's store there. The Métis believed that an attack might come south from Prince Albert along the trail on the west side of the river and pass Duck Lake on the way to Batoche. Whoever held Duck Lake controlled the trails both from Prince Albert and Fort Carlton.

On the evening of March 24, the Métis council considered and rejected a proposal to move its army to Duck Lake. Gabriel Dumont argued strongly in favour of the move. He told Riel: "You are giving them too many advantages. They come from Duck Lake up to the crossing to spy on us. And so, why don't we take Mitchell's store? We have taken up arms and we have done nothing else. If we want to push things further, we will at least need provisions."[1] The Métis fighters had already decided that if they had to fight, theirs would be a purely

NWMP Superintendent Leif Crozier in 1880. Friends called the Irishman "Paddy."
[Glenbow-Alberta Institute]

defensive action and they were unwilling to move out of the territory they could traditionally claim as their own. "But this same evening," Philippe Garnot wrote, some women from Duck Lake "came before the council and said that after dark they had heard everybody complaining along the road and that they feared that the police were going to come and take away several people by force to Carlton."[2] Faced with this new information, the council took another vote. Six members were in favour of moving and six voted against the proposal. Riel broke the tie[2] and the Métis moved toward Duck Lake. The next afternoon Dumont left Batoche at the head of a group of the Métis' best fighters.

Before they arrived, Mitchell, warned of their approach, locked his store and went to Fort Carlton to join Crozier's force. Magnus Burston, an English half-breed who lived at Duck Lake, told Dumont Mitchell had fled and when Dumont threatened to break down the store's door, Burston produced the keys. Inside, they found some provisions but no arms or ammunition. Burston, who had told Mitchell a few days earlier that the Métis intended to shoot him as a spy, had taken much of Mitchell's stock to his own house. The Métis council had previously ordered Burston to seize the goods from the store but they apparently were unaware he had done anything and it is likely he was not acting in their interests.

Shortly after Dumont's party left for Duck Lake, Riel had decided to move the rest of the Métis fighting force and the prisoners they held to the village. When they arrived, Dumont and a few scouts moved west to the Fort Carlton road to ensure the police did not surprise the Métis at their new headquarters at Duck Lake. The scouts crossed the end of the lake on the ice and reached Beardy's reserve, where they stopped to feed their horses and drink tea with their Cree friends. Dumont sent Baptiste Arcand and Baptiste Ouellette to watch the road.

At about ten o'clock that night Crozier, worried that the Métis might try to intercept Commissioner Irvine, sent Prince Albert Deputy Sheriff Harold Ross and surveyor John Astley down the Fort Carlton road to watch the activity at Batoche. Before they left Fort Carlton, Ross and Astley were told that Duck Lake had been quiet all day and the rebels had apparently made no move towards the village. They were also warned that Chief Beardy said he was annoyed by the comings and goings of police scouts. They moved slowly and warily through the reserve without seeing any lights or hearing any sounds until they were in sight of the village of Duck Lake.

Shortly after midnight, Arcand and Ouellette came galloping back to Dumont and the other Métis. Two men had passed them, riding along the road towards the village without seeing the Métis scouts. Dumont and four others set out at a trot, intent on taking two more prisoners. When they reached a long hillside at the edge of a wood almost at the eastern edge of Beardy's reserve, they could see clearly in the bright moonlight two riders ahead of them. The Métis galloped down the hill. Ross yelled at Astley, "They are upon us." The Métis had come up so suddenly and frightened them so thoroughly that Ross would later report that Dumont's five-man scouting party was an army numbering between sixty and a hundred; Astley thought there were between sixteen and twenty men. Ross and Astley tried to escape, but the Métis were too close and going too fast. Dumont caught up to Ross, whom he didn't recognize at first. "Don't try to escape or I'll kill you," Dumont told the deputy sheriff in Cree. "I'm a surveyor," Ross replied. "You're a liar," Dumont said as he pulled Ross off his horse. Astley was galloping away and for a moment the Métis, blocked by Dumont and Ross on the road and the crusted snow on both sides, couldn't pursue him. He almost got away but his horse stumbled and its rider fell.[3]

When the scouts returned to Duck Lake with their prisoners, they found that Riel and other members of the Métis council had decided the fears the women had expressed to the council were exaggerated. They were preparing to move the Métis army back to Batoche. But, as Garnot later recalled, the two prisoners said the police planned to come to Duck Lake that day to seize the provisions in Mitchell's store. So the Métis remained at their new headquarters and Dumont went back to Beardy's reserve to rejoin his scouts and watch the road.

At four o'clock in the morning on March 26, a party of police and volunteers were getting ready to leave Fort Carlton to secure the provisions at Mitchell's store. Crozier had planned the expedition, which was to be led by NWMP Sergeant Alfred Stewart, the day before. He was still unaware that the Métis had taken Duck Lake. Stewart dispatched four policemen to make sure the road was open and followed about an hour later with eight sleighs and eighteen men. English half-breed interpreter Tom McKay rode about half-way between the main force and the four scouts.

Dumont and the scouts saw no one else on the road for the rest of the night. At daybreak they decided the police would not risk sending out scouts again and they returned to Duck Lake. They had put their horses in the barn and had just started breakfast when someone shouted: "Here comes the police." Patrice Fleury ran to the barn and grabbed a horse. As Fleury galloped toward the Fort Carlton road, Jim Short and Edouard Dumont were close behind. Gabriel Dumont's horse was stuck in a snowbank. Farther up the road, two of the police scouts threatened to shoot Fleury unless he stopped, but the Métis yelled that he wanted to see Tom McKay and he kept going. The police turned and galloped back towards their main party with Fleury close behind and the two Dumonts and Jim Short hurrying along the road but well behind the others. When McKay saw what was happening, he galloped back to warn the police escorting the sleighs, then went back along the road to stop the scouts and Fleury.

McKay shook hands with his friend Fleury and told him the police intended to take Mitchell's goods. Fleury warned McKay that the Métis had already taken possession of Duck Lake and would not give it up without a fight. McKay agreed to take the police back to Fort Carlton and turned around to go back to the sleighs. By this time, the rest of the Métis had caught up with Fleury, and Gabriel Dumont was not about to let McKay and the police off so easily.

Dumont dismounted and walked towards the police. One of the policemen aimed his rifle and shouted: "If you don't stop, I will kill you." "I'll kill you first," Dumont replied as he shouldered his own rifle. The policeman, who was sitting in one of the sleighs, put the rifle across his knees and Dumont kept advancing. Dumont leapt at the sleigh and knocked the policeman from his seat with the barrel of his gun. As Dumont lifted his rifle, one of the fingers of his glove accidentally pulled the trigger and the gun went off into the air.

> Then Thomas McKay rushed at me saying "Be careful, Gabriel." I answered him, "You'd better be careful yourself, or I'll blow your brains out." And I flung myself upon him. He turned his horse which had its back feet sunk in snow, and it reared up. I gave McKay a push in the back with my rifle. He spurred his horse and it gave a leap forward and got away. Meanwhile, McKay kept telling me, "Watch out Gabriel" and I kept repeating too, "You'd better be careful yourself, or I'll slaughter you" and I followed him with my gun.[4]

As the police retreated, Edouard Dumont jumped into the last sleigh. He tumbled out and the sleigh ran over him but didn't injure him. Fleury had better luck. He managed to get into the same sleigh and rode in the back for a short distance. He later said he did that to prevent his comrades from shooting the policemen as they retreated. The Métis wanted to chase the police but Dumont thought they were too few to do any damage and he led them back to Duck Lake.

As the sleighs moved back to Fort Carlton, Sergeant Alfred Stewart sent a courier to tell Crozier what had happened. Crozier still intended to wait for Irvine before he took the offensive but the volunteers, who had little military experience but who were anxious to put a stop to the Métis movement, prodded him. "Are we to be turned back by a parcel of half-breeds? Now is the time, Crozier, to show if you have any sand in you," taunted Lawrence Clarke, the man who had goaded the Métis by bragging that five hundred police were coming to arrest Riel. Crozier still was not convinced. He believed the Métis army at Duck Lake numbered three hundred, far larger than any force he could muster before Irvine arrived with reinforcements. But when Clarke, backed by other over-eager citizens, called him a coward, Crozier relented and moved out of Fort Carlton at about 10 A.M. with a force numbering fifty-six policemen and forty-three volunteers and teamsters, and a seven-pounder cannon.[5]

Shortly after leaving Fort Carlton, the police and volunteers met the party returning from the confrontation with Dumont. The whole force went on to the reserve, where they waited at Chief Beardy's house while Crozier talked to the chief. Beardy said he would have nothing to do with the uprising, and he didn't admit that many of his young men had joined the Métis.

The Métis scouts had just resumed their breakfast at Duck Lake when the shout was heard again: "Here come the police." The Métis were not expecting the police to return so soon and initially there were only twenty-six of them who rode out to stop Crozier's force before it got too close to the village.

When the Métis got to the Fort Carlton road, they saw police scouts near where the confrontation took place earlier in the day. Volunteer Alex Stewart, who was with the scouts, shouted, "Enemy here!" and galloped back towards the main force.

> The enemy then gave the war-whoop, which made the air ring, and put after me at full race. There was one Frenchman who came up alongside of me as I was retreating, and tried to catch my bridle reins. I drew my revolver on him (a N.W.M.P. 6-shooter, self-cocker, 44 calibre) and told him to go back or I would blow his brains out, and he skipped back like a streak of lightning. None of the rest could come anywhere near me. I would look back every little way to see if any of them were going to shoot or still coming. I could see them coming over the hill like bees, and all shouting. The Indians were all painted up like demons, as were also some of the French half-breeds.[6]

Like most other participants, in the excitement Stewart vastly over-estimated the rebel force. He thought he was followed by two hundred Indians and Métis.

As his scouts were chased back to his lines, Crozier stopped half-way down a long incline and divided his force. A group of police took the horses to some bush on the north side of the road, and the volunteers and some more police moved into a larger clump of trees on the south. The sleighs formed a line across the road broadside to the oncoming rebels.

Dumont had sent some of his men to chase the police scouts, but they were not to shoot because the Métis had decided they would not fire first. The main party of Métis and Indians went into a large shallow depression just to the north of the road where they and their horses would be shielded from the police guns and cannon.

Gabriel's brother Isidore and Asiyiwin, one of Beardy's headmen, walked from the hollow across an open field towards the troops carrying a white flag. Seeing this, Crozier walked towards them to parley and, when he called for an interpreter, Gentleman Joe McKay joined him. The two parties met in the middle of the field, half-way between the opposing forces.

In Métis eyes, the police had reached the boundary of a foreign country. They might do the prudent thing and slink back to Fort Carlton, or they might be goaded into firing first. The Métis and Indian soldiers were under strict orders from Riel, the provisional government council, and even the aggressive General Dumont himself, to hold their fire. Crozier was in a similar position. He had to assert the police authority and secure the Duck Lake stores, and the citizen-volunteers in his force were too trigger-happy for his comfort. He did not want to be held responsible for starting a war. Elements on both sides of the field near Duck Lake were anxious to shoot each other but neither side wanted to fire first.

"Who are you?" Crozier asked the two emissaries. "Crees and half-breeds. What do you want?" Asiyiwin replied. "Nothing," Crozier said, "we only came to see what was wrong."[7]

Asiyiwin, who was notoriously nearsighted, carried no weapons. McKay was loaded down with rifle, cartridge belt, and huge revolver. Why, Asiyiwin wanted to know, if the police did not intend to start a fight, was the English half-breed carrying a small arsenal? With that, he grabbed McKay's rifle. If he had managed to seize it, he would have scored a bloodless coup and McKay would have been shamed. But McKay would not let go, and he struggled with the Indian as Isidore Dumont kneeled and raised his rifle to his shoulder.

As they watched the short struggle, the police and volunteers noticed that more men had come up from Duck Lake and moved into a small house south of the road in front of the woods that sheltered them. Some thought they heard a shot, or at least saw a puff of smoke from the rebel lines. Someone shouted to Crozier, "We are being surrounded." Crozier, realizing the attempt to parley was futile, had already turned and started back towards his force when McKay, jerking his rifle from the Indian's grasp, suddenly drew his revolver and shot Isidore Dumont dead. He turned the gun on Asiyiwin and left him lying in the snow mortally wounded as he and Crozier ran back to their comrades. When he heard McKay's shot, Crozier raised his arms and gave the order: "Fire away, boys." The North-West Rebellion had begun.[8]

As Métis and Indian reinforcements trickled in from Duck Lake, the rebel force grew to two hundred, but many of them were badly armed. Some of the Indians had only sticks as weapons.

The police took cover behind the sleighs and in the trees, but the inexperienced volunteers tried to rush from their cover towards the house the Métis had occupied. They became bogged down in a metre of snow and very quickly suffered most of the casualties of the battle. Louis Riel had arrived in the hollow on the north side of the road which was not deep enough to shield a mounted man. He refused to get off his horse and, as the bullets whizzed by, he waved a huge crucifix and invoked God on the side of the rebel fighters. Exposed to the enemy fire, Riel was not hit. His followers thought he must truly lead a charmed life.

Gabriel Dumont was not as lucky. "Since I was eager to knock off some of the redcoats, I never thought to keep under cover, and a shot came and gashed the top of my head," he later recalled. "I fell down on the ground, and my horse, which was also wounded, went right over me as it tried to get away. We were then 60 yards from the enemy. I wanted to get up, but the blow had been so violent, I couldn't. When Joseph Delorme saw me fall again, he cried out that I was killed. I said to him: 'Courage. As long as you haven't lost your head you're not dead.'"[9]

Alex Stewart was wounded shortly after the battle began.

I got back to the troops' position and jumped off my horse alongside of the ammunition sleigh, and there was a young Canadian fellow named Gibson (20 or 21 years of age) who drove the ammunition sleigh. He was in the act of rising from his seat to get out when he received a ball through the heart. He threw up his hands, gave a sigh, and fell on his shoulder, striking my feet. His legs caught on the side of the box. I lifted him clear of the sleigh and laid him down alongside. Unbuttoning his coat I saw he was shot through the heart. I picked up his rifle (I having only a revolver with me) and took his cartridges from him and commenced firing over the seat of the sleigh. Joe McKay came to me and asked me to hold his horse while he would have a shot. I got up and took the lines, and just then I received a ball sideways, striking me a little below the neck, on the top of the chest. It knocked me down, keel upwards.[10]

The police tried to bring the old cannon they brought from Fort Carlton to bear on the house from which the rebels were decimating the volunteers, but it had only been fired twice and done no damage when, in the excitement, the gunners loaded a shell without powder, rendering the gun useless.

As Dumont lay in the snow, his cousin Auguste Laframboise fell beside him. "I crawled and dragged myself over to him, saying to myself: 'I am always going to say a little prayer for him,' but wishing to make the sign of the cross with my left hand, since my right side was paralysed, I fell over on my side and, laughing I said, 'Cousin, I shall have to owe it to you.'"[11] Laframboise was already dead.

By this time, the police and volunteers, alarmed by the number of casualties in so short a time, began to load their sleighs to retreat. Edouard Dumont had taken command after his brother was wounded and he "shouted to our men to follow and destroy them. Riel then asked, in the name of God, not to kill any more, saying that there had already been too much bloodshed," Gabriel recalled. "However, there was a captain whom the police called Morton, a good shot, who was behind a tree and had killed two of our men; he was hit in the back while trying to get away. As he was screaming and suffering horribly, Guillaume Mackay thought he did him a service by shooting him in the head."[12]

Volunteer Charlie Newitt had bayoneted one of the rebels and, as he was trying to pull the bayonet out of his victim, was shot in the leg. As his comrades left the field, Newitt kept shooting. Then, according to Dumont, "Philippe Gariépy threw himself on him, wrenched his gun and bayonet from him and tried to hit him with his weapon. One of our men restrained Gariépy, and urged him to have pity on the miserable creature who was taken to Duck Lake."[13]

Crozier was in full retreat. He could not risk picking up the bodies of the volunteers who died in the battle and he had to leave some sleighs, arms, and ammunition behind.

When the sounds of the Duck Lake battle were first heard at Batoche, Madame Patrice Caron had just begun to wash her floor. When the firing stopped, she was only half-finished. The battle lasted only about thirty minutes but in that time, Will Jackson's prediction that lawyers and merchants would die first had come true. Prince Albert lawyer Skef Elliot, son of an Ontario judge and nephew of Liberal leader Edward Blake, lay dead on the field with his law clerk Bill Napier, nephew of British General Sir Charles Napier. Saloon and billiard hall proprieter Bob Middleton and hardware merchant Dan McPhail were also among the dead. Among the wounded was the volunteers' leader, Captain H. S. Moore, nephew of Sir Francis Hincks, veteran of the British army and a wealthy mill owner. Nine volunteers and three police were killed. Five rebels died in the battle. Asiyiwin was taken to Mitchell's store at Duck Lake, where he died later that evening. The rebels captured fifteen rifles, about five hundred rounds of ammunition, some sleighs, and the wounded volunteer Charlie Newitt.

When the rebel army arrived back at Duck Lake shortly before noon, Charles Nolin had disappeared. Isidore Dumas arrived at Duck Lake shortly after the battle began, escorting the prisoners to the Métis' new headquarters. As he arrived, Nolin galloped past yelling, "The Holy Sacrament! The Ciborium! The Holy Sacrament!" Dumas assumed Nolin wanted the ritualistic articles so that a last communion could be given those dying on the battlefield, but Nolin ran off down the Prince Albert road and it was the last the Métis would see of their one-time leader until the rebellion ended.[14]

Four of the five rebel dead had been close relatives of Gabriel Dumont. When he arrived back at Duck Lake, Dumont ordered all the prisoners taken out into the yard. He and some of his Indian allies wanted to kill them in revenge, but Riel intervened, as he had done when his troops wanted to pursue and pick off Crozier's force as it retreated in disarray to Fort Carlton. He ordered that there would be no more bloodshed until he decreed it.

The Métis council met all the rest of the day and into the early morning of March 27 to decide what to do next. They argued about sending new emissaries to Crozier to see if his surrender could be arranged, then they rejected that plan. They did send prisoner Tom Sanderson to Fort Carlton to tell Crozier he could pick up his dead on the Duck Lake battlefield without being molested. Then they escorted Bill Tompkins, the captured interpreter for Indian Agent John Lash, and Deputy Sheriff Harold Ross to the battlefield and allowed them to put the bodies in the little house from which the rebels had killed most of them.

The Hudson's Bay Company had built Fort Carlton in the last decade of the eighteenth century to be a major North Saskatchewan River outpost on the way to Fort Edmonton, which was built at about the same time. Although the Gros

Ventres Indians had destroyed neighbouring South Branch House, just north of what would become Batoche, the company was obviously not concerned about defense when it chose the location of Fort Carlton. On the south and east, Fort Carlton was closely bordered by steep treed hills ninety metres high, a contrast to the expanse of low sand hills just to the east. The route north from the fort was a steep climb for about one and a half kilometres on a single-lane cart trail through thick woods. The site was pretty, but it was also absolutely indefensible. It was said that twenty marksmen could hold a force of two hundred inside Fort Carlton indefinitely. Attackers would be able to shoot down into the fort itself from the tops of the hills.

NWMP Commissioner Irvine and his force arrived at Fort Carlton at 3 P.M. on March 26, about half an hour after Crozier led his tattered command into the fort. Irvine was furious Crozier had acted so impetuously.

The force spent the rest of the day at Fort Carlton looking after their wounded, two of whom died shortly after they returned, and wondering what to do next. The next day, Irvine expected the rebels to press their advantage, and when he received Riel's promise that the police could retrieve their dead, he thought it was a ruse and would not risk sending another party to Duck Lake. Tom Sanderson then offered to do it by himself. Crozier and Irvine were so wary of the rebels they not only would not loan him a team and sleigh to do the job, but they imprisoned Sanderson as a Métis spy. In the morning of March 27, Irvine called a council of officers to consider abandoning the indefensible post. That plan pleased the citizen-volunteers. Although eager before the shooting actually began, they had now had enough of battle and wanted to retire to the relative safety of Prince Albert where, in any case, they would be needed to defend their families if the rebels took the offensive. The officers decided to evacuate at three o'clock the next morning. They also considered burning the buildings and those supplies they had to leave behind so they would not fall into rebel hands, but this idea was rejected when someone pointed out that the sight of the flames could bring rebels from Duck Lake to attack the force as it retreated to Prince Albert. Even without a fire to tip them off, Irvine feared the rebels might discover his plans and try to prevent his retreat. He kept his intention to evacuate as secret as possible even within the fort, and for the rest of the day no one was allowed outside without a special pass.

Hudson's Bay Company Factor Lawrence Clarke immediately began taking an inventory of Fort Carlton's goods as the police and volunteers loaded them into sleighs. There were far more provisions in the fort than the sleighs could hold and a large number of sacks of flour were ripped open and their contents spread on the ground and covered with coal oil in the fort's square.

At about 1 A.M., as men were still working loading sleighs and destroying flour, some volunteers were busy on the second floor of the non-commissioned officers' quarters near the main gate of the fort making hay mattresses to put in the sleighs for the wounded. The night was cold and the volunteers had a fire going in the old wood stove in the middle of the room to warm themselves and the wounded. Suddenly some of the hay near the stove blazed, and in seconds the building itself was on fire. The fire spread so quickly in the old frame bunkhouse that it was difficult to get the wounded to safety. There was little hope of putting the fire out or preventing it from spreading to other buildings. The main warehouse and another large building soon caught fire and the flames spread along the eastern palisade, blocking the fort's gate. With half-loaded sleighs, Irvine and his force escaped by breaking through the northern palisade. Lawrence Clarke was almost left behind. He had fallen asleep in one of the buildings and at the last moment Irvine remembered to wake him up. By the time he got outside, the buildings were a mass of flame and he was the only person in the fort. In the snow, it took them four hours to stumble the one and a half kilometres to the top of the hill and on to the Prince Albert road.

As Irvine had been warned it would, the fire drew the rebels to the fort, but they gave no thought to following the small force. By the time they arrived, the fire had almost died out, leaving some buildings, including the Hudson's Bay Company store, and a substantial stock of goods untouched. When local farmer William Diehl arrived at about 7 A.M., "there were about a dozen or fifteen French Half Breeds in the Fort and they were hard at work pillaging and carrying out goods and whatever else there was that was moveable and each one seemed to be making a pile of stuff for himself. They had even taken a number of the doors and windows out of the buildings."[15]

Sioux Chief White Cap and his family on their reserve near Saskatoon in the summer of 1885. The news of the rebel victory at Duck Lake persuaded White Cap's band to join the Métis at Batoche. At the left is White Cap's son, Blackbird, who was captured during the rebellion (p. 228). [Glenbow-Alberta Institute]

As he began the seventy-kilometre march to Prince Albert, Irvine was thoroughly frightened. He was pessimistic and angry about the turn events had taken since Crozier's ill-advised foray. Before leaving Fort Carlton, he wired Lieutenant Governor Dewdney: "Officer commanding militia enroute to this point should be warned that on no account to come by Batoche's Crossing. Force should be five times as strong [as proposed]. Fifteen hundred should be sent in at once."[16] When he passed that message along to the prime minister, Dewdney added another admonition: "Rebels are good shots."[17] Dewdney also suggested a reward be offered for Riel's capture.

The authorities also knew how the news of the important victory at Duck Lake would affect the rebels' efforts, a fact Irvine had considered when he decided to abandon the fort. Dewdney's assistant, Hayter Reed, wired on March 27: "Emissaries going all over country after engagement evidently to influence Indians. Fear he [sic] will succeed in great measure. All Duck Lake Indians joined rebels."[18] Farther south, the Sioux at the reserve north of Saskatoon were preparing to move north to Batoche under Chief White Cap.

At Prince Albert, the frightened townspeople had been busy fortifying the Presbyterian church. Father André was almost out of his mind with worry, not only for the community of Prince Albert, but also for the Métis. The day of the Duck Lake battle, he recorded in his journal:

> My God! What will become of our poor unfortunate Métis? They must have seriously offended God to bring down upon themselves a punishment as terrible as that which threatens them! And, in spite of all the news, they persist in their blindness and obstinately resolve to fight. But I can hardly believe they will do so when they are surrounded on all sides by forces double their numbers and better armed. We can scarcely breathe, so great is our anxiety to know the outcome of this struggle which can only be disastrous whichever side is victorious.[19]

News of the Duck Lake fight arrived at Prince Albert in the afternoon of March 27. Its citizens, already thoroughly alarmed, now expected the rebels, especially the Indians, to swoop down on their community and massacre them all. The news from Duck Lake, Father André recorded, "has spread terror in Prince Albert; the inhabitants are maddened by fear. They expect any minute to see Riel with his band of Métis followed by the Indians pounce upon us and put all to fire and blood." That night most of the townspeople and many from the surrounding countryside and outlying communities took refuge at the entrenched Presbyterian Church. Father André was even more pessimistic than other panic-striken Prince Albert residents, and he kept himself busier than most. But he found time to record his feelings in his journal and to assign blame in an outburst of indictment from one who had worked hard on Ottawa's behalf to get rid of Riel and soothe the Métis.

Now that blood has been shed the war will take on a more savage and cruel character. Our poor Métis will be exterminated. The government will stop at nothing to put down this rebellion and God only knows what ordeals we will be put through. Our sad predictions have not been mistaken: our poor people are irretrievably lost. The government of Canada must be severely blamed and condemned for having brought this war on the country. It is their delay in redressing the grievances of the Métis and their refusal to listen to the advice given to them that has brought on this trouble that will end God-knows-how![20]

As he helped the nuns he supervised at the Prince Albert convent on the south edge of the town prepare to move to the fortified church, Father André believed, "Riel's faith has not been extinguished to the point where he would dare to capture those holy women who have shown no animosity against him."[21] But Indians were another matter. The Prince Albert residents' fears were not limited to the Batoche-area Cree bands that were known to have either joined the Métis or were sympathetic to them; there were persistent rumours that the Sioux near the town would rise. Even the most seasoned North-West whites did not understand the Indians very well. They believed these people, especially the Sioux, were savages whose minds could not be expected to make a distinction between soldiers and women and children. Father André prepared the nuns for death. Before they set out for the Presbyterian church, he gave them Viaticum, a little-used form of last rites usually reserved for the elderly or gravely ill who face imminent death. "Father André came to confess us. He then told me that he had quite decided and that he would give us Holy Communion as Viaticum, and thus consumate all the Sacred Particles. The Father with a voice trembling from emotion told us to make this Holy Communion with extraordinary fervour as the last in our life and in reparation for all those tepid ones of ours; it was to be now for us our Holy Viaticum and in giving us the Sacred Host, he used the words for the dying," one of the nuns recorded.[22]

Commissioner Irvine arrived back in Prince Albert on March 28 to a mixed reception. The townspeople were overjoyed that the armed force had returned, but they were appalled by the visible reminder of violent death. The nuns watched the little force march into town. "Was it sadness or joy that reigned in every heart?... Almost like a funeral train did that procession again pass our windows, now numbering 9 less of our brave citizens & bearing in it several wounded."[23] Irvine's reputation dropped among Prince Albert residents, who were indignant he had not taken Riel's invitation to retrieve the bodies from the battlefield. Their sons, brothers, and neighbours, they thought, would by now all be scalped and unspeakably mutilated. Prince Albert residents persuaded Irvine to release Tom Sanderson so that he, teamster Bill Drain, and Eastwood Jackson could go to Duck Lake to pick up the bodies. Jackson was not altogether trusted but he was their best bet to make the foray into the rebel camp and come out again unmolested. Riel respected Jackson and owed him favors for his help earlier in the agitation, and his brother, Will, had been one of the rebels' key people. Eastwood had an ulterior motive for making the trip. Sanderson had told him that Will had become insane and that Riel was keeping him under guard. Eastwood and the rest of the Jackson family found that easy to believe. Converting not only to Catholicism but to a version of that hated religion propounded by rebellious half-savages was surely sign enough of insanity in one who had been brought up in a strict Methodist environment. Despite their liberalism and their support for progressive social movements, those were lines that members of the Jackson family could not cross if they were in control of their senses. Eastwood decided to rescue Will. He would ask Riel to release his obviously deranged brother to the custody of his family.

Once the troops had returned, the citizens abandoned their makeshift fort. That evening of March 28, Father André was back home at the southern outskirts of the town talking with some friends

> when, looking out of the window, I saw a rider and a band of horses coming at full gallop toward Prince Albert. They hurled themselves forward as though pursued by the enemy. I went out to ask the cause of this movement; the men arrived pale and with wild eyes, and passing in front of me they cried: "Come on! They are coming. The French and the Indians!" Immediately, from the outside, I called to the Sisters to come out and save themselves since the enemy was arriving. The poor sisters were in bed and while they were getting dressed I ran toward the fort to look for a wagon. I arrived out of breath at the fort where Mr. Clarke had already obtained a wagon for them. The greatest disorder and confusion reigned in the town. Families in tears and panic-striken with terror came out of their houses; everywhere there were cries of terror and despair. I waited for the Sisters. They arrived half-dressed and trembling with fear. It is difficult to paint a picture of the spectacle that met our eyes; men and women were in mortal terror and waited to see the Indians and the Métis fall upon us to slaughter us and put all to fire and blood.[24]

The alarm was first sounded between nine and ten o'clock that evening. Little Ida Clarke was in bed when

> the church bell rang out and suddenly my father burst into the room. He said something to my mother and snatching me up, put on my cloak and stockings and stuffed my boots into his pocket. Wrapping a shawl around the baby and with one of us on each arm he and my mother ran for the fort. They took the short cut through a low spot covered with a foot of melted snow, my mother running a few feet ahead, a coat over her nightdress and overshoes on her otherwise bare feet. At the deepest part of the pool I leaned over my father's

shoulder to feel in his pocket for my beloved red kid boots. Inside the stockade was a scene of confusion. The bell in the steeple rang faster and faster. Women huddled their children in their arms and men, with blanched faces, loaded guns and gathered ammunition.[25]

Many of those in the church believed the nuns would be a particular protection against the Catholic Métis and they clung to the sisters' clothes and recited prayers in the crowded, dimly-lit room. Ida Clarke remembered that "when things were at their worst a gun under a bench in the manse kitchen went off by accident. Women fainted and children screamed. My mother was laid on the dining room table. I cried because I thought my mother was dead." Ida's mother gave birth that night to a son who died before daybreak.[26]

A few hours later, the frightened townspeople learned that it had all been a false alarm. One of the scouts placed just south of town thought he saw some Indians hiding in the bushes and, made extraordinarily impressionable by fear, he believed he had discovered the advance force of the entire rebel army. It had been one too many false alarms for Father André. The priest had not slept in days. His mind was bursting with confusing thoughts of the fanatic Riel, with worry for the Métis and the nuns, with anger at those responsible for the misfortune, and with confusing notions that somehow he could have done more to prevent the violence. On the way back to the convent, as he walked beside the nuns' sleigh, Father André broke down in hysterical laughter and had to be relieved of the half-dressed child he was carrying as he trudged through the deep snow.

Eastwood Jackson and his two companions reached Duck Lake on the afternoon of March 29. They retrieved the bodies with surprisingly little difficulty although the Métis, angered by Crozier's refusal to pick them up in the first place, refused to help. At Duck Lake, Eastwood met both his brother and Riel. Will, in Eastwood's opinion, was clearly but inexplicably demented, although Tom Sanderson said he appeared much more in control of himself than he had when they last met. By this time Will wanted to leave the Métis, but Riel refused to allow him to accompany Eastwood back to Prince Albert.

Will had had a falling-out with his Métis friends and by the time Eastwood arrived he was in an uncomfortable position. On the evening before the Duck Lake battle, Will Jackson had followed Riel's party across the river. But his underclothes were dirty and "it seemed to me that I was not worthy to participate in the new order of things & I accordingly went back to get a fresh change." Back at Batoche, he borrowed some underwear from George Fisher but then went to Albert Monkman, who had been left in charge, and demanded another suit of clothes, quickly because Will wanted to get back across the river and catch up with the Métis. But Monkman, probably fearing that Will's actions were not altogether rational, took him prisoner.[27] From then on, the Métis weren't quite sure what to do with their young white collaborator. Riel refused to release Will to his brother and Eastwood didn't press the matter, believing, he said later, that travelling with the bodies of his acquaintances killed at Duck Lake might be too much for Will's disturbed mind.

At Duck Lake, Riel and Eastwood talked of the battle. The Métis leader sympathized with the Prince Albert residents who had lost family members, but he took Eastwood into the room where the five rebel dead lay and said they had died defending their homes, that they had not sought the war but had been fired on by the police and volunteers. Riel was angry that the whites of the North-West would fight against him. "I explained to him that we could not take up arms against Canadians," Eastwood Jackson recalled. Riel replied that if the whites could not shoot their own kind, at least they should remain neutral and not shoot at their Métis friends either.[28] He gave Jackson a letter to the Prince Albert whites explaining his position that the rebel fight was solely against the Hudson's Bay Company and the NWMP. "If the Police could be isolated from the people of Prince Albert we would make them surrender easily enough I think, we would keep them as hostages, until we have a fair treaty with the Dominion," Riel told the whites. "Join us without endorsing our taking up arms, if you feel too much repugnance to do it, but send us delegates to meet ours, we will discuss the conditions of entering into confederation as a province." Riel still saw the struggle in the light of the events of 1869-70, but he warned that if the whites didn't help, things might get out of hand, "Indians will come in from all quarters and many people will cross the line early this spring, and perhaps that our difficulties will end in an American 4th July."[29]

Eastwood Jackson and his companions arrived back at Prince Albert without Will on March 30, but with the bodies of the nine volunteers and Charlie Newitt, the wounded man the Métis had taken prisoner. Riel had asked Jackson to take Newitt because the Métis could not provide the medical attention his leg wound needed.

The Jackson family was still anxious to get Will away from the rebel camp. Two days after his return to Prince Albert, Eastwood learned that his brother was at Fort Carlton with a party of Métis and their white prisoners in charge of Albert Monkman. Riel would not part with his young collaborator, Eastwood believed, but his friend Monkman might be induced to let Will go. Commissioner Irvine refused to give Eastwood a pass to go to Fort Carlton to try to rescue his brother. In Irvine's mind, the rescue mission was just a cover story for a plot to give the rebels information about the situation in Prince Albert. But after Eastwood's mother and the Anglican bishop at Prince Albert interceded, Eastwood got his pass and left for Fort Carlton on April 4. When he arrived the next day, Eastwood found that the rebels had burnt what was left of the fort and gone back to Batoche. Eastwood reached the rebel headquarters with little difficulty but negotiations with Riel for Will's release were inconclusive.

On April 8, Eastwood made a formal plea to the rebel council for Will's release. By this time, Will Jackson had decided "that God wished me to go and live among the Indians partly by way of penance and acquiring a natural method of life partly to become a bond between them and the whites." When he was at Fort Carlton, he had tried to escape to an Indian camp. "My attempts to get away to the Indians were regarded as the effect of insanity by the half-breeds who trusted me, and as attempts to desert to the Police by those who did not. Hence I was kept under strict watch & ward."[30] Riel undoubtedly understood that if he were allowed to go, Will likely wouldn't stay with Eastwood long but would take off for the Indians at the first opportunity. Riel would be apprehensive of the trouble Will Jackson would cause himself if, as was likely, he attempted to lecture the Indians on either politics or religion. Riel wanted to keep Will in a kind of protective custody but there were new considerations. Some of the rebel Métis and Indians had become convinced that Eastwood was a spy for the police and they told Riel that if he allowed the Jacksons to leave, they would follow and kill them. Michel Dumas told Eastwood the council had agreed to let the brothers leave, but Riel vetoed the decision and Eastwood, not trusted by either side, found himself a rebel prisoner.

CHAPTER NINE

Mobilization

Three days before the fighting erupted at Duck Lake, the government in Ottawa became sufficiently alarmed to send the Major General commanding the militia, Frederick Dobson Middleton, to Winnipeg. The only militia units between the Great Lakes and the Rockies, the 90th Winnipeg Rifles and the Winnipeg Field Battery, were ordered to a state of readiness, while preliminary arrangements were made with the Hudson's Bay Company for supplies for a larger force. Ottawa doubted the seriousness of the situation. Any hint that the government was taking the situation seriously might alarm potential settlers and investors, so Middleton claimed in a newspaper interview in Toronto on the eve of his departure that the trip was a routine inspection planned months before. The press generally ignored this effort to downplay the outbreak. RIEL'S REBELLION was already a headline and newspapers from Winnipeg to New York on March 24 filled their columns with reports of an alleged battle between the NWMP and the rebels near Fort Carlton.[1] The details were uncannily close to those of the actual battle of Duck Lake, but the reports were two days early.[2]

The man responsible for organizing Canada's military response to the rebellion was a lawyer from Quebec City who was almost exactly the same age as Riel. In every other respect they could hardly have been more different. Joseph Philippe René Adolphe Caron came from a family that was at or near the centre of power in French Canada from the Conquest to the mid-twentieth century. Caron's grandfather was a member of the Lower Canadian Assembly as was his father, René-Edouard Caron, who was also at various times Mayor of Quebec City, Speaker of the Legislative Council, Judge of the Court of Queen's Bench, and Lieutenant Governor of Quebec. Caron's nephew, Louis-Alexandre Taschereau, was to be Premier of Quebec from 1920 to 1936. Adolphe Caron was neither the most nor the least successful of this clan, but he had a firm grasp of the basic elements of survival and power in the Canadian politics of his day: partisan loyalty and control of patronage. Had the rebellion not raised him to prominence, he would undoubtedly have remained one of those obscure cabinet ministers whose work behind the scenes keeps the political machinery functioning.

A dark-haired, handsome man with an imposing mustache, Caron was completely bilingual and, according to no less an authority than John A. Macdonald's gossipy and snobbish secretary, Joseph Pope, the Carons fitted easily into the society of the capital. Macdonald was a close personal friend in spite of the difference in their ages, and loyalty to the Chief was Caron's firmest political principle. Macdonald, for his part, was more inclined to take an objective view of his junior colleague. "Caron is too much influenced by his hates—a fatal mistake in a public man who should have no resentments," he told Sir John Willison.[3] In spite of Caron's loyalty and his display of competent and even resourceful management in 1885, he was never offered a more senior portfolio.

Caron's appointment as Minister of Militia and Defence in 1880 was not because of any special interest on his part in military affairs. He was chosen rather for his skills as a manager of patronage because Militia and Defence in the 1880s was regarded, more than most of the others, as a patronage department. Defence was not a high priority for the government and parliament each year grudgingly voted a bare minimum budget for the military. The British garrisons had been withdrawn in 1870 and if Canada was attacked by the United States, the only possible aggressor, a successful defence by Canada alone was out of the question. With luck Canadians might hold out long enough for the British to send help, as they were pledged to do. The British would maintain their commitment to Canadian defence only as long as Canada showed some signs of willingness to defend herself. The annual militia budget therefore represented the Canadian parliament's considered judgement of the least amount necessary to show the British that an attempt at self-defence was being made. If the money had to be spent, most members of parliament were determined to extract the maximum political advantage from it.

The Militia Act of 1868 theoretically made every Canadian male of sound mind and body between the ages of sixteen and sixty subject to military service. This group, which was counted once in 1869 and then forgotten, was supposed to constitute a Reserve Militia. The really functional portion of the Act was the provision that up to 40,000 volunteers could be organized into battalions as the Active Militia and trained for up to sixteen days every year. The pay for militiamen was insignificant and employers often refused to let their employees participate if it meant losing time from work. Enthusiasm was the chief characteristic of the volunteer. Public feeling against "standing armies" was intense in Canada but the Militia Department soon found it necessary to create a tiny permanent force in disguised form to maintain training standards. The so-called "artillery schools" which were established at Quebec City and Kingston to train gunners were, in fact, permanent artillery batteries. They were so successful that in 1883 the concept was expanded to include infantry and cavalry schools as well, although the cavalry schools were not operational by 1885. The permanent force was limited to a total of 750 men in all branches.

The Militia was commanded by a Major General who had by law to be a British regular officer at the time of his appointment. The chief source of tension

Arthur T.H. Williams, the most popular officer among the troops in the North-West.

within the Militia Department lay in the conflict between the commanding officer and his staff, who wanted a smaller but better-trained Active Militia, and the MPs for rural constituencies, who wanted more battalions, trained or untrained. A militia battalion and drill shed in every rural constituency meant that the money spent on defence was spread as widely as possible, and money spent locally translated into votes on election day. A very large number of the honourable members also had direct connections with the militia in that they were themselves officers or former officers. This group, known as the "Colonels' Lobby," strongly resented what they considered to be the pretensions of the better-organized and trained city regiments. In 1883 open conflict erupted between the militia commander, Major General Richard Luard, and some of the rural colonels, notably Arthur Williams, Tory MP from Port Hope. Caron reacted to this squabble by coming down decisively on the side of the colonels. Luard was persuaded to resign and make way for an officer more tolerant of the demands of patronage.[4]

Both the militia and the permanent force were armed with Snider-Enfield rifles of British manufacture. These were single shot converted muzzle-loaders that fired an enormous .57 calibre bullet. They had a barrel fully a metre long and were correspondingly heavy and clumsy. Their rate of fire was slow and they were inaccurate. Their virtues were that they were cheap and almost indestructible even in the hands of untrained recruits. The Sniders were unquestionably obsolescent; the British had already replaced theirs with the Martini-Henry, which had a much higher rate of fire, and Winchester repeaters were readily available. Inevitably some armchair generals in and out of Parliament clamoured for the militia to be reequipped with one or the other before facing the rebels. Only enough Martini-Henrys could be obtained to equip one company of the 90th Winnipeg Rifles immediately and the government wisely ignored demands for complete reequipment, which would have meant unacceptable delays and new elements of confusion among green troops. Officers were armed with revolvers that they supplied themselves.

The artillery units were equipped with nine-pounder muzzle-loading field guns (guns that fired a shell weighing nine pounds). These were sturdy, easily-handled weapons but had a very slow rate of fire, since each shell had to be filled with gunpowder by hand during the action and fuses cut to the correct size. Perhaps because of the modest firepower of his artillery, Middleton suggested at the beginning of the rebellion that the government purchase two Gatling guns in the United States. This was hastily arranged and these primitive machine guns played a highly visible part in the campaign. What was almost entirely lacking in 1885 was any means of moving the militia to the field of battle, feeding and supplying them while they were there, and taking care of the wounded. Caron

Artillery captain R.W. Rutherford titled this sketch "Cow Boy Cavalry." It is an accurate representation of the corps of scouts raised in the North-West to fight the rebels. [Glenbow-Alberta Institute]

did a very commendable job of improvising these services on the spur of the moment, ensuring that the money spent went to friends of the government whenever possible.

General Middleton arrived in Winnipeg on the morning of March 27 and left almost immediately for Troy station on the CPR line, the point at which the Carlton Trail branched northward in the direction of the trouble. One contingent of the 90th Rifles was already there, and Middleton took with him the second half of the battalion and the Winnipeg Field Battery. He was in constant touch with Caron in Ottawa by telegraph and was able to confirm the rumours that had been circulating in Winnipeg that the Mounted Police had suffered a defeat at Duck Lake. Middleton immediately requested that all the regulars and the better urban militia battalions be called out and sent west immediately. Orders went out from Caron's office that same day for the mobilization of the Queen's Own Rifles and the 10th Royal Grenadiers in Toronto and the 65th Mount Royal Rifles in Montreal.[5] The following day the 9th Voltigeurs in Quebec City were mobilized along with a composite unit known as the Midland Battalion, made up of men from several rural Ontario units.

Several offers to raise companies of scouts in the North-West were hastily accepted. Towns which had requested rifles to arm home guard units were now informed brusquely that all armaments would probably be needed for the militia and that only General Middleton could authorize the distribution of equipment. The Hudson's Bay Company officials in Winnipeg were warned to arrange supplies for large numbers of men, and Ottawa leaped at the CPR's offer to get the soldiers west. There were large uncompleted gaps in the main line through Northern Ontario, but these could be bridged by sleighs or by even having the men march between completed sections of track. The crisis in the West was a heaven-sent opportunity for the railway, which was on the verge of bankruptcy and could not have survived without an immediate loan from the government. Such a loan had been unthinkable up to this point because the CPR had already absorbed vast sums of public money. In its new role as saviour of the integrity of the nation, however, the railway was once again acceptable. The loan went through in the nick of time. The decision to use the CPR imposed serious hardships on the troops and was almost certainly unnecessary. There would have been no difficulty shipping the men through the United States; most of the ammunition and supplies went that way anyway.

On Monday, March 30, some six hundred men in two trains left Toronto at noon. This first contingent of troops from the East had been assembled as a result of a weekend of frantic activity. Lieutenant R. S. Cassels of the Queen's Own Rifles was roused from his bed at 1 A.M. on Saturday, heard the news of Duck Lake, and went off to track down the men of his company.[6] The newspapers reported that newfangled gadget, the telephone, was being used to help assemble the men but few people had them yet. Once the battalion was

Riel! Poundmaker! Big Bear! Clear the Track!

HURRAH FOR THE NORTHWEST !!!

IMPLEMENTS OF PEACE TO SUPPLANT THOSE OF WAR

The above illustrates the handsomely decorated train of TWENTY cars loaded with HARVESTING BINDERS shipped on Saturday, the 11th instant, for the North-West by The Massey Manufacturing Company. This Train contained 240 of the Famous Toronto Light Binders, which have been so completely successful and have given such perfect satisfaction as to win the highest admiration of the Farmer from coast to coast. It also contains 1 large quantities of Binder Twine. This is the THIRD ANNUAL TRAIN shipped this instant, via the G T R and Albert Lea routes, and arriving at Winnipeg on Wednesday afternoon. Aside from this Train, THE MASSEY MANUFACTURING COMPANY have already sent 16 Car Loads to Manitoba this Season, and there are several others yet to leave. Flattering reports of the Toronto Light Binder in the Harvest of 1885 are already coming in.

This train was a standing feature many advertisers used in the 1880s. But when the Massey Company adapted it for use with a North-West Rebellion theme, they forgot to change the initials on the coal tender. G.T.R. stands for Grand Trunk Railway, Ontario's great railway and the CPR's great rival. [Toronto *Globe*, July 22, 1885]

VOLUNTEERS!

ATTENTION!

THE OLD ADAGE SAYS

"An Ounce of Prevention is better than a Pound of Cure"

NOW!

If you would save yourselves a world of suffering and pain, incident to the hardships you will have to endure, such as being soaked to the skin while on march, or chilled through by sleeping on damp ground in camp, or from the many minor accidents that can befall you, such as sprains, cuts, &c., while serving your country in the present crisis.

DON'T FAIL

to provide yourself with a few bottles of the "Old Reliable"

PERRY DAVIS' PAIN-KILLER

TAKEN INTERNALLY,

It cures Dysentery, Cholera, Diarrhœa, Cramp and Pain in the Stomach, Bowel Complaint, Painter's Colic, Sudden Colds, Sore Throat, Coughs, &c.

USED EXTERNALLY,

It cures Bruises, Cuts, Burns, Scalds and Sprains, Swellings of the Joints, Toothache, Pain in the Face, Neuralgia and Rheumatism, Chapped Hands, Frost bitten Feet, &c.

THE PAIN-KILLER is put up in 1 oz., 2 oz. and 5 oz. bottles, retailing at 20c, 25c and 50c respectively; large bottles are therefore cheapest. Sold by medicine dealers everywhere.

DAVIS & LAWRENCE CO. (LIMITED) MONTREAL.
General Agents for Canada.

Perry Davis' Pain-Killer was one of the most popular all-purpose remedies in the 1880s and volunteers would have been wise to take this ad's advice and stock up. If Perry Davis' really didn't cure all, it at least made symptoms, including facing enemy bullets, easier to bear. It was a soothing mixture of alcohol and opium. [*Manitoba Free Press*, May 7, 1885]

BUFFALO BILL,

"He is king of them all." Gen. E. A. Carr.

AT

WOODBINE PARK.

3 Days, Aug. 22, 24, and 25,

Afternoons only. Performance given, rain or shine.

BUFFALO BILL'S WILD WEST

FIRST AND LAST TIME IN CANADA.

Giving an exact exhibition of Western border life.

THE GREATEST NOVELTY OF THE CENTURY.

Gates open at 1 p.m. Performance at 2.30 p.m. The following are a few of the numerous FEATURES: The Renowned Sioux Chief,

SITTING BULL,

and staff, WHITE EAGLE and 52 Braves. The One-legged Scout Spy, FRISKING ELK. The great Markswoman from the Western Border, Miss ANNIE OAKLEY. Largest HERD OF BUFFALO ever exhibited. Great Indian buffalo hunt, known as "The surround." The Phenomenal Boy Shot, JOHNNY BAKER. Cowboy Kid, "PETE LOVELL," the unequalled Cowboy Shot, shooting at impossible dollars, and nickels. MUSTANG JACK, the Champion Jumper, jumping over a horse 16 hands high. BUFFALO BILL will shoot at clay pigeons from traps; also with revolver, gun, on foot and on horseback, at full speed, at glass balls. BUCK TAYLOR, king of the Cowboys, in several requisites on and issuing wild cattle, and riding bucking horses wilder than ever. YELLOW HAND'S DEATH by Buffalo Bill. Grand BATTLE SCENES similar to

Fish Creek, Cut Knife, and Batoche.

Music furnished by the famous Cowboy Band. We fulfil every promise.

CODY & SALSBURY.

Admission 50c., Children, 25c. Grand street parade Saturday, August 22nd, at 10 a.m.

When Buffalo Bill Cody brought his famous Wild West Show to Canada in the summer of 1885, he made certain to include "grand battle scenes similar to Fish Creek, Cutknife and Batoche." That year, Sioux Chief Sitting Bull and sharpshooter Annie Oakley were the star attractions. Gabriel Dumont would later join the entourage. [Toronto *Mail*, August 19, 1885]

173

mustered, the quota of 250 men had to be selected and equipment issued. This took most of Saturday and Sunday, and Cassels found that he barely had time to say good-bye to family and friends. In Toronto the competition for places in the militia contingent was intense. "We are the stuff," the Toronto *World* reported the adjutant of the 10th Royals as saying. "The Queen's Own are nice at amateur theatricals in the Grand, but if there's fighting to be done we are the men to regulate the breeds."[7] After the train carrying the Queen's Own left Toronto, a head count revealed that twenty-three extra men had smuggled themselves aboard.

The departure of the troops from every major city was the occasion for outpourings of public enthusiasm and sentimentality. One company of the Queen's Own made up entirely of undergraduates from the University of Toronto celebrated their departure by meeting with veterans of the company who had served against the Fenians in 1866 and singing songs in Latin. In Quebec City the 9th Voltigeurs attended mass at the Basilica before marching through the streets to the station cheered on by an estimated twenty thousand spectators. In Toronto the crowds in King Street for the departure of the first train were so heavy that sizeable sums of money were being offered just for a place to stand in a doorway to watch the sendoff. Clergymen of every persuasion rose to the occasion and delivered orations in support of the military effort, including Rabbi Phillips, whose encouraging words for the two Jewish militiamen of the Queen's Own were reported prominently in all the Toronto papers.[8] The troops were somewhat relieved to get on the trains and escape the crowds.

A week or so later the Midland Battalion, made up as it was of contingents from the relatively untrained rural units, found that mobilization did not proceed quite as smoothly. Private Joseph Crowe recalled:

We were soon ordered to fall in for inspection by some officials, and then were taken to the stores for a hand out of clothing etc. The clothing that we had on was as poor a fit as you can imagine. Some of men had never drilled or soldiered before, and knew nothing of order or discipline. Most of us had been "smelling the cork," and as a result there were quite a few that had to be put in the guard room for the night. The next day we were furnished with brand new uniforms from head to foot. The shoes were of red leather. We were issued the following clothing: a scarf or muffler, leggings made of strips of cloth about four inches wide which we circled around our pants up from the boot tops to the knees giving us a natty appearance. Each man was given a knapsack with a canteen on top of it, and a new rifle. We next received an oil cloth sheet, and a very large overcoat which were folded together and then folded neatly on the back of the knapsack. The whole equipment weighed about twenty-five pounds. One mistake was to issue Glengarry caps for a trip of this kind as they were of little use as far as being protection from the weather. The barracks at Kingston reminded us of a large prison. We were placed in large rooms to sleep on a hard dirt floor. This was most uncomfortable for most of us who were used to a soft bed. The men were hard to control since a great number of them had never been under military rule, and an order was never obeyed without question. I remember an officer going on his rounds at "lights out," and he received a severe blow from a boot which someone threw in the dark at him.[9]

When the battalion was finally on the move by train through Northern Ontario, one private evidently had second thoughts about the adventure. While the train was moving about forty kilometres per hour he suddenly jumped from his seat and dove through a closed, double-paned window and out into the snow.[10] By the time the astonished authorities got the train stopped, he had disappeared. Eventually he made his way back to his home town of Bowmanville, unhurt except for a few minor cuts.

Although newspapers were reporting temperatures as high as twenty-one degrees Celsius in parts of the country in the first week of April, Northern Ontario was bitterly cold. Nighttime temperatures dropped as low as thirty degrees below zero Celsius as the first trainloads of troops were going through, and had moderated only slightly by the time the Midlanders made their journey. The first two days of the trip were easy enough although the troops were somewhat crowded in their colonist cars. The major delays came at meal times, when the train would often have to stop for several hours while the men ate in shifts.

As the end of track at Dog Lake approached there were some hints of the ordeal that lay ahead in the first sixty-four kilometre gap. The last two hundred

The first troops dispatched to the North-West in 1885, the two artillery schools and the Queen's Own Rifles, embark on sleighs for the trip across one of the gaps in the Northern Ontario rail line in this sketch by artillery captain R.W. Rutherford. [Glenbow-Alberta Institute]

kilometres of track had been constructed so hastily that the spaces between the ties were not yet filled with ballast and the train could not go faster than ten or fifteen kilometres per hour. The snow alongside the tracks in some places was higher than the roofs of the cars. Fifty-five large sleighs holding ten men each were waiting at the end of track. The journey through the gap was fairly easy in places where the railway roadbed had already been graded, but often the sleighs had to leave the right of way and make their way on rough trails through the bush. Heavy snow and potholes a metre deep waylaid unwary teamsters and dumped men and equipment into the drifts. About half way across the gap there was a construction camp where the troops could be fed. As soon as this was completed they pushed on to the beginning of the track. The crossing of the first gap took about sixteen hours.

The first contingents through, "A" and "B" Batteries and the Queen's Own Rifles, paused at the aptly named Camp Desolation, where the track began again. They stayed only long enough to eat before climbing onto the trains to resume their journey. The units that came later stayed overnight at the camp. An enormous seventeen-metre by thirty-five-metre tent had been erected at the camp but the temperatures were so low that many preferred to sleep in the open where they could build fires to help supplement their meagre blankets. Private Crowe found that this too had its drawbacks.

> We spread our rubber blankets on the crystallized snow. Earlier in the day the snow had changed to hail the size of large peas, and it had been very hard to walk on it and almost impossible to make a beaten path. On the rubber blanket we placed a woolen blanket laid on it and placed our other blanket over us. Most lay with their feet toward the fire. I slept very little. Some slept soundly only to be awakened when their rubber blankets slid down the incline, or their feet inside of their boots became so hot the soles of their boots started to smoke. They would jump up more asleep than awake, tear open their laces and get the boots off.[11]

After Camp Desolation there was a stretch of 190 kilometres of track that most of the troops found to be the worst part of the trip. The only rolling stock available was flatcars with sides and seats hastily constructed of rough boards. Ten or eleven hours in open cars at sub-zero temperatures was an agonizing experience. Some of the men had to be lifted bodily from the cars at the end of the run, and there were some cases of frostbite severe enough to require amputation.

The second gap of twenty-nine kilometres required about six hours marching. Then the troops got back on the train once again and were taken as far as Jack Fish Bay, where most spent the night in a large empty warehouse. "It is a night of luxury," Dick Cassels wrote, indicating how drastically standards had changed only two days out from Toronto.[12] Others slept in the hold of a half-sunken schooner frozen into the ice of the bay and were equally pleased. From Jack Fish Bay there was a march of forty-two kilometres over the ice of the lake, followed by more open cars to McKay's Harbour. There the CPR maintained a hospital where the worst cases of frostbite and illness could be left behind for treatment. Eighty kilometres farther on, at Nipigon, the last gap in the track began. The fourteen kilometres took about three hours to cover on foot, not much in comparison to the other gaps but quite enough for men who had for four days been alternately frozen and then baked by the sun, slept very little, and eaten irregularly. Sun and wind in the open cars left faces swollen and blistered. Some men were snow blind. At last Port Arthur was reached and the men could relax in the luxury of Pullman cars for the twenty-four hour run to Winnipeg. Amazingly, in just over two weeks since the first shots at Duck Lake, more than three thousand men with all their equipment had been shipped to the West and were ready to be deployed.

In the meantime General Middleton had sized up the situation and reached some basic strategic decisions. He met with Lieutenant Governor Dewdney at Qu'Appelle on March 31 and seems to have relied heavily on his advice. The Lieutenant Governor was convinced that the rebellion was, so far at least, a very localized affair which was heavily dependent upon Riel's leadership. If this were true, the logical course was to march as quickly as possible to the rebel headquarters and snuff out the uprising before it could spread. Middleton's plans reflected this analysis. He would leave Qu'Appelle for Batoche immediately with the 90th Rifles, the Winnipeg Field Battery, and a party of scouts raised locally by former NWMP officer Jack French.[13] Together with the NWMP and volunteers at Prince Albert, Middleton believed that he would have no difficulty coping with a contemptible band of half-breeds. The forces on their way from the East could follow as soon as they arrived.

Middleton was far more concerned about the possibility of his troops suffering from starvation than from Métis bullets. With the weather warming, the trails would dissolve into a morass under any traffic. There was no natural feed for the horses along the way at this time of year. For a wagon to reach Clarke's Crossing from the railway, fully half the load was taken up by food for the horses that drew it. Teams and teamsters by the hundreds were needed to keep the troops in the field. The Hudson's Bay Company handled this along with its other supply responsibilities, paying sub-contractors $10 per day per team, of which the teamsters, mostly local farmers, got $5 to $6. The farmers were delighted at this unexpected windfall. It was too early to get on the land and in any case cash from the government was a much surer thing than a crop that might be destroyed by drought, frost, or insects.

Even so, the supply of teamsters was not endless and the trails could only support limited traffic, so when Middleton heard that a fleet of river steamers was available at Medicine Hat, his most severe logistical problem seemed solved.

Half the troops could continue past Qu'Appelle by rail to Swift Current. Here a supply base would be established under the command of Major-General John Wimburn Laurie, and both troops and supplies could be loaded on the boats and sent downriver to meet Middleton and his men. Crews for the boats were rushed by special train to Medicine Hat. As the trainloads of men began to arrive from the east, "A" Battery, forty men of "C" Company Infantry School, and the 10th Royal Grenadiers left the railway at Qu'Appelle and marched off in pursuit of Middleton. "B" Battery, the rest of the Infantry School men, and the Queen's Own Rifles under the command of Lieutenant-Colonel William Otter continued to Swift Current to join a party of fifty Mounted Police under Superintendent William Herchmer. The French Canadian battalions were close behind the Toronto contingent and Middleton, who distrusted them on both military and political grounds, sent them on to Calgary, where the citizenry were clamouring for protection. Major General Thomas Bland Strange, a retired British officer who had a large ranch near Calgary, had been put in charge of Alberta's defences. Strange had served for some years in Quebec and, unlike his superior, believed that French Canadians made excellent soldiers. He was delighted to have the Quebec regiments under his command. More militia battalions had been mobilized in Ontario and the Maritimes and were on the way but were ordered to stop at Winnipeg.

Calgary was not alone in its vociferous demands for troops but General Middleton was quite prepared to ignore all the others until April 10, when word arrived of the massacre at Frog Lake. This threw a different light altogether on the plight of the settlers cooped up in nearby Battleford. Middleton remained convinced of the correctness of his basic strategy but realized that a substantial gesture would have to be made in the direction of the besieged town. Otter and his troops, waiting at Swift Current for the water to rise enough to get the loaded steamboats down river, were ordered to march to Battleford at once.[14] Some of the troops that had been ordered to halt at Winnipeg were ordered west to take the place of Otter's men. The Midland Battalion, marching through the streets of Winnipeg under orders to go into camp there, were halted almost in mid-stride, turned around, and marched back to the train. By April 10, the basic outline of the campaign had taken shape. Three columns of troops were converging on the valley of the Saskatchewan unchallenged by the rebels.

CHAPTER TEN

Battleford and Frog Lake:
A Spring of Blood

The citizens of the town of Battleford knew they were in grave danger the moment rebellion began to spread in the North-West Territories. The one-time territorial capital that boasted a substantial and thriving business community was just east of the reserves of two of the most powerful and militant Cree chiefs, Poundmaker and Little Pine. Several other Cree bands were nearby, and the unpredictable Stonies were at the Eagle Hills about thirty kilometres to the south. The town was one hundred and eighty kilometres southeast of Frog Lake, a safe distance in normal times from where the acknowledged leader of all the Cree and the tribe's foremost political activist, Big Bear, held together an often-warlike band of malcontents. The large NWMP fort boasted palisades that had been carelessly built with large gaps between the poles. The fort sat on a large hill overlooking the "old town" across the Battle River to the south. The fort itself was just a short distance south of the North Saskatchewan River which the Battle River joined not far downstream. A "new town" was expanding around the fort, away from frequently flooded Battle River flats where much of the old town was located.

The fort commanded an impressive view of the old town and the surrounding countryside, but it was a long way from the river and had no internal water supply. In the spring it was cut off from the main settlement. The Battle River bridge was taken down each year as the ice began to break up and was not replaced until the river was clear. At the end of March 1885, there was strong ice in the centre of the river with running water at both shores. To cross from the town to the fort involved taking one boat to the ice in the middle of the river and another to the opposite shore or struggling across the rapidly flowing river at a low point. The citizens thought so little of the fort's defensive possibilities that when they first met to consider their dangerous situation near the end of March, they decided to ignore the fort and instead to fortify and defend Judge Charles Rouleau's substantial home near the old Government House just across the river in the old town. To add to their worries, Superintendent Crozier had taken the bulk of the NWMP Battleford garrison with him to Fort Carlton, leaving only a skeleton staff in defence of the fort and town.

The citizens of Battleford were as ill-prepared as their fort. Few of them had any military training and they were not at all equipped to negotiate with the natives, who could easily raise a substantial army. Indian Agent John Rae didn't

SASKATCHEWAN RIVER
COUNTRY

Frog
Lake

ALTA
SASK

Frog
Lake
*Massacre Site

Onion Lake

N. Sask. R.

Old Fort
Pitt *

Frenchman
Butte

Area of
main map

ALTA
SASK

N. Sask. R.

Big Gully Creek,

0   100   200   300
MILES

like dealing with Indians. In fact he was petrified of them. He was easily persuaded of the worst possible scenarios when it came to those in his charge, and his alarmist and inaccurate reports during the past year had done little to enlighten his superiors. It is difficult to see why he was put in such a key location in the first place except that he was, despite his complaining, a loyal employee and he was John A. Macdonald's cousin. Inspector William Morris, the NWMP officer in charge in Crozier's absence, was an unimaginative disciplinarian, disliked and distrusted by many of the townspeople. He shared Agent Rae's attitude toward Indians. Judge Charles Rouleau considered himself a well-read, refined man in a backward country. He knew where savages placed in the social order and he was fond of saying so. P. G. Laurie, the editor and founder of the *Saskatchewan Herald,* who had worked in Winnipeg and had known Louis Riel in 1869 and 1870, had once been on good terms with the Indians. He had professed a great admiration for their race and had had a special fondness for Chief Poundmaker, whose considerable talents were a common theme in Laurie's newspaper. But a couple of years before, Laurie had radically changed his mind. He was, in 1885, coming more to the racial views of Rouleau and other Battleford citizens, and Poundmaker was no longer his friend. There were two men in town who had considerable experience with the Indians and who enjoyed a mutual respect with them: Hudson's Bay Factor William McKay and Peter Ballendine, Lieutenant Governor Dewdney's "secret agent."

Battleford learned of the Duck Lake fight late on March 27, but the Indians knew about it first and they quickly considered their position. That afternoon, Mistaynew, a Cree friend of Factor McKay, reported that he had met some Indian messengers. "The Indians from all over the country, they told me, were gathering at Poundmaker's and would soon march in a body on Battleford."[1] Rouleau scoffed, but P. G. Laurie at once prepared to move his family into the NWMP barracks, where Inspector Morris was not being very helpful. Merchant James Clinkskill complained "no definite information could be got from those in authority as to what was transpiring, nor would they give us any advice as to what we should do in the event of the little town being attacked."[2] Morris lowered his stock even farther in the eyes of the citizens when he decided that his duty was to help Crozier. He dispatched twenty-five of his forty-three remaining policemen and twenty-five of those who had enrolled in the Battleford home guard to Fort Carlton. The angry and frightened citizens reacted by removing their volunteers from Morris' command and firing telegrams at Lieutenant Governor Dewdney, appealing for immediate help. "At least one hundred men should be thrown into here with every dispatch," one telegram told Dewdney.[3] In Agent Rae's active imagination, it was not only hundreds of local Cree warriors who were advancing on the town. Big Bear's Cree and the dreaded Blackfoot were also on the way, he told his boss. But there was little the Lieutenant Governor could do. There were no reinforcements anywhere near

Battleford and Dewdney would not interfere with police or military arrangements. He fell back on threatening the Battleford Cree. "Let it be known that hundreds of men and heavy artillery are on the road," he wired Rouleau.[4] The next day, Factor McKay sent a messenger west towards the reserves as the townspeople held their breath.

Agent Rae wasn't enthusiastic about visiting the Indians on their own turf, especially if trouble was brewing. But on March 28 he swallowed his nervousness to do his duty and set off south for the Eagle Hills to the Stoney reserves of Chiefs Mosquito and Bear's Head. There, they met Farm Instructor James Payne, a man the Stonies heartily disliked even though he had married a daughter of Chief Bear's Head. After they talked with the Indians, Payne recorded: "Visited reserve and had a talk with all. Indians spoke of their loyalty to the whites and their desire for continued peace."[5] Rae was just as impressed. In a report, he said, "I visited the Stonies, and gave them also tea and tobacco. They seemed glad to get it, and had no complaints to make. Their instructor [Payne] said: 'I believe the Crees are up to mischief and in case you need assistance the Stonies will fight for the whites. They told me so.'"[6] It was one of the few times Agent Rae allowed himself to be reassured by the statements of people he believed were treacherous savages. As usual, he was wrong. For Payne it was a fatal misjudgement.

When he got back to Battleford, Rae was overjoyed with the apparent success of his mission to the Stonies. He was still terribly frightened of the Indians he had not talked to, the powerful Cree bands then gathering under Poundmaker, but he thought that rumours, some of which he himself had started, might have got a long way ahead of the facts and he had some hope that the trouble would blow over.

But the next day, March 29, it was readily apparent that trouble was indeed on its way. Factor McKay's messenger returned with bad news and it was later reported that Indians in war-paint under Poundmaker and Little Pine were camped thirteen kilometres from town. Settlers from the surrounding countryside flocked to town, "settlers with their families from the surrounding country who reported that the Indians had left their reserves and were on the war path. In many instances these settlers had had their houses ransacked and their contents either destroyed or carried away, and the stock driven off by the marauding redskins. The women and children were in a state of terror, and eager to get behind the palisades of the fort," said one Battleford resident.[7]

Judge Rouleau didn't wait for McKay's messenger to return. In the morning of March 29, he gathered his family, threw a few belongings into a wagon, and prepared to head south towards Swift Current. He was going to ensure troops were sent quickly to Battleford, Rouleau said, an excuse that caused snickers among the townspeople. When he learned of the considerable Indian army on the road, Agent Rae quickly discarded his optimism and prepared to join the judge. But Rae, as the Indian Department's representative in the area, could not be allowed to leave. In the afternoon, Rouleau's small party set out without the Indian agent as most of the rest of the town moved into the fort, causing considerable consternation for Inspector Morris, who tried to accommodate the refugees. Merchant James Clinkskill was one of those who moved his family from the south side of the river.

Gathering some clothing, etc. together we hastily took a meal and prepared to take refuge in the Police barracks. All our horses were off on a trip to Swift Current for goods for the Spring. I only had a little pony my wife used to drive and a buckboard. Every one else owning teams were using them themselves to take their belongings to a place of safety, so I was unable to take any of our trunks which had been packed. My wife carried her jewel case and an old family bible, an heirloom, in her hands, the clothing on our backs was all we could take.[8]

The frightened settlers shivered in their makeshift quarters in the fort as rain and sleet fell that night on Battleford. Judge Rouleau and his party spent the night of March 29 at Payne's home, where the farm instructor told them the Stonies were painting themselves and planned a dance the next day. Things were looking a little more ominous. Rouleau was nervous and he left Payne's place hurriedly shortly after daybreak, none too soon, as it turned out. Shortly after 10 A.M., a group of Stonies arrived. Itka "asked Payne for some shot and flour; he would not give me any; my son wanted to go shooting; then my heart got bad and Payne got vexed and I told him not to get vexed; he said he would not give me flour for ten days; I went away and got my gun and came back; then the instructor took hold of my arms, and I said he had better loose me or I would kill him; I got my arms free and shot Payne."[9] Payne was a stern and uncompromising taskmaster and the Indians' dislike of him bordered on hatred. When Itka killed him, it marked the end of a long-standing feud.

From Payne's home the group of Stonies set off for Battleford to join the Cree. About halfway there, they came across Barney Tremont as he was greasing his wagon to go to town. Tremont was a rancher who kept so much to himself that his closest neighbours and the Battleford merchants with whom he did business could hardly remember his last name, let alone spell it. He was born in Belgium and had come to the North-West from the United States, where his brother had been killed by Indians. One thing his friends did know for certain about Barney the Belgian: he hated Indians and would threaten them whenever they came near his ranch. When the Indians arrived on the evening of March 30, Man Without Blood

met the white man on the road near his house; the Man with the Black Blanket told me to kill him; I said I would; I saw him leaning on a waggon; two Indians were coming towards him...going to the white man's house;

The death of James Payne. R.W. Rutherford sketched Payne's homestead on the spot and reconstructed the events. [Glenbow-Alberta Institute]

there were four Indians standing there; I walked up beside them and the Indians asked who that white man was; I said I did not know; did not listen to what they said; one of my brothers had a bow and arrows and the other had a gun; My brother asked, "Why don't you go and kill him?" I got his gun and loaded it and walked over and killed the white man.[10]

The Indians made sure he was dead. They put another bullet in the head of the lifeless body and an arrow in the heart.

The morning of March 30, the Battleford settlers awoke to see an Indian army across the river on the hill above the old Government House. "The hills are black with redskins," one settler wired the *Manitoba Free Press*.[11] Poundmaker and the other chiefs had realized that the time was opportune to push the government for concessions. Embroiled in the Métis uprising to the east, Ottawa and its agents might be induced to bow to a show of force by the Battleford Cree. They thought they could at least pry increased supplies and rations from the government coffers, if not force a change in the arrogant, demeaning manner in which the government and the local whites treated them.

Robert Jefferson and two other farm instructors had caught up with the Indians on the evening of March 28 while they were holding a council on the Young Sweetgrass reserve. After the council, Chief Young Sweetgrass met the instructors and told them, in Jefferson's words, that "he was not altogether in sympathy with the meeting, but could not separate himself from what the whole people seemed to have set their hearts on doing, and that on the morrow they intended going down to Battleford to interview the agent, since they deemed that this was a crisis that would give their requests as great force as demands. He did not anticipate any trouble. They did not seek it." The Indians were hungry and frustrated. Chief Poundmaker, who once had promised to give the white man's way of life a try, had concluded that the whites promised everything but delivered only disease and hunger. Poundmaker told his brother-in-law Jefferson: "Of old, the Indian trusted in his God and his faith was not in vain. He was fed, clothed and free from sickness. Along came the white man and persuaded the Indian that his God was not able to keep up the care. The Indian took the white man's word and deserted to the new God. Hunger followed and disease and death." Poundmaker said the Cree "have returned to the God we know. The buffalo will come back, and the Indian will live the life that God intended him to live."[12]

When he saw what was happening on the morning of March 30, Agent Rae wired Dewdney: "Poundmaker and Little Pine with two hundred Indians all armed broke into the house of the Finlayson Brothers farmers last night and took everything they could carry away. Two houses in the old town also broken into. Indians from other reserves expected in today. Women & children also. Most of the farmers inside barracks which is fairly well fortified. Expect to have a Council with them today."[13]

Poundmaker sent a messenger to the fort across the river. The Indians had come to town to see their agent, he said. They wanted some additional provisions. That was certainly not all Poundmaker hoped to accomplish but it was an opening to negotiations. Agent Rae offered to meet Poundmaker and the other chiefs on the north side of the Battle River, midway between the fort and the river. But that would be under the guns of the fort, cut off from their comrades. The chiefs refused.

Rae had no option but to go to see the Indians on their side of the river. He, with Factor McKay and Peter Ballendine, walked down the long hill from the fort to find a boat. When they got to the river, a Métis woman called in Cree to McKay from the opposite bank. "Don't come across! The Indians are going to kill you people on sight." When that was translated, Rae had had enough. He turned around and went back up the hill and would refuse to emerge from the safety of the fort. But McKay and Ballendine were not about to be deterred by vague, second-hand threats and, in any case, they were on much better terms with the Cree than Rae was. They found some chiefs and councillors near the Indian Department office. "What's the matter here?" asked Poundmaker. "The houses seem all deserted." McKay knew that Poundmaker knew why the houses were deserted. Understanding the whites better than the whites understood the Indians, it was the Cree way of putting the whites on the defensive at the opening of negotiations: profess ignorance, innocence, and weakness, and force the white man to explain, make the proposals, and expose the limits of his understanding, while all the time being in a position of strength and knowledge.

Poundmaker extended the tactic. The Cree came to town to learn about the fight at Duck Lake, he told McKay. The Indians already knew far more about the battle than the whites did and they had found out sooner, but McKay was forced to patiently explain how it was that the white man, who portrayed himself as all-powerful in the North-West, had been defeated by a motley group of badly-armed natives. And McKay repeated the standard threat. "You may succeed in killing some whites," he said, "but your success will be shortlived and they will be avenged. Don't think you can beat them. For every white man killed, when you Indians are hiding in the woods, fearing for your lives, a hundred if necessary will come. They will be here, more of them, when all the fighting is over, than when it began and your sons and daughters will pay." The Cree knew very well that would be true in the long run, but as they talked to McKay, they were intent on enjoying a victory, short-lived as it might be. They had cowed the whites, forced them to retreat without firing a shot. Some of the Cree in the group at the Indian office took up that refrain, crowding around McKay and taunting him.[14]

When they finished the initial posturing, the first thing the chiefs wanted to know was why their agent had not come to meet them, why, when they most needed them, were the Indian agents nowhere to be found? McKay couldn't tell them that Rae was too frightened to cross the river, so he sent an Indian messenger to the fort to invite the agent to attend the meeting. Rae, of course, never showed up. When the negotiations moved on to the question of food, McKay was in a position to make a gesture himself. The factor doled out enough provisions from the Hudson's Bay Company store to give the Indians a meal. If he had not agreed to open the store, the Indians would have simply helped themselves but it was important for McKay, and for the company he represented, to show that he sympathized with hungry Indians. All that McKay was willing to do was alleviate simple hunger. When it came to demands for blankets, clothing, arms, and ammunition, he balked and the negotiations ended.

After Factor McKay arrived back at the fort, Agent Rae wired Lieutenant Governor Dewdney. "Indians willing to go back to reserves tomorrow if their demands for clothing and sugar, tobacco, powder and shot are complied with. Strongly [urge] you to give me full authority to deal with them as we are not in a position at present to begin an Indian war."[15] Having no way of fighting the war Rae warned about, Dewdney replied the only way he could. "You have full authority to deal with Indians. Use discretion and ask Poundmaker to meet me at Swift Current with copy of any arrangement you make. He can bring a couple of his best Indians with him. His expenses will be paid & I guarantee his safety."[16]

Rae had given Dewdney the mistaken impression that he was involved in face-to-face negotiations with the Indians. The Lieutenant Governor wired Prime Minister Macdonald, General Middleton, and other officials: "Am treating with the Indians at Battleford by wire. I think I shall come to a satisfactory understanding."[17] Dewdney was actually negotiating with Agent Rae, who had not spoken to an Indian. Talks would not resume with McKay and, not surprisingly, Poundmaker was not about to accept the Lieutenant Governor's invitation to a meeting.

The Indians began to enjoy the astonishing situation in which they found themselves. The white interlopers, who had always been so concerned with pushing the Indians back into confining reserves, now appeared to have given back to the Indians an entire town. "The Indians are behaving as if they owned the country," said the *Manitoba Free Press* correspondent.[18] They wandered about the town with a mixture of curiosity and delight, examining and having complete control of the abandoned community. As P. G. Laurie reported it:

> The Indians had a big council all afternoon, and the evening and night were spent in carting away goods of all kinds from the shops of the Hudson's Bay Company and Mahaffy & Clinkskill and raiding and destroying the private houses. The desolation wrought is only equalled by a fire of whose work we say there was "nothing saved." The devilish ingenuity displayed in the destruction of things that were of no use to them would put to the blush a city mob—a thing usually put down as the extreme of everything that is mad and unreasoning. They had a high time generally.[19]

At about 3 A.M. on the morning of March 31, George Applegarth, the farm instructor on the Red Pheasant reserve south of Battleford, was awakened by a knock at his door. It was a party of Cree who said the Stonies were on their way and would kill the farm instructor if he didn't leave quickly. Applegarth bundled up his family and headed off towards Swift Current. Almost as soon as they left, the Stonies arrived and ransacked the house. The Stonies continued on their way to Battleford, plundering farms and verbally abusing but not physically harming settlers they met.

When Battleford residents peered from the fort to the town across the river on March 31, there was not a Cree to be seen. They had loaded as many provisions as they could into their carts and moved to a camp about three kilometres from town, where the Eagle Hills Stonies joined them. James Clinkskill, with Rae, McKay, and Ballendine, went down to the riverbank to have a look.

> We saw two men standing in front of a building a little way up from the river that the H. B. [Hudson's Bay Company] had been using as a temporary sale shop. We shouted to them and just as they started to come down toward us, some rifle shots were fired in our direction from out of the underbrush on the other side, this was a signal for our hasty retreat to cover. We were standing in the open on the river bank. Hampered as we were with heavy overcoats, carrying a heavy snider rifle, a belt around our waists filled with cartridges that had ounce bullets in them; it was a wild scamper, we slashed through a pool of water and half-melted snow that lay between us and the barracks. I shall never forget the sight of my companions floundering through the water breathlessly hastening to get out of range. I must confess I did exert myself too in the run, but the sight of us all scattering in different directions, each scared he was a target for a bloodthirsty Indian was comical in the extreme.[20]

Their fear turned to anger when they discovered that a couple of mischievous Irishmen who happened to be on the other side of the river had fired the shots to see what confusion they could cause.

The Indians no longer held the town, but its residents stayed safe in their fort. On April 1, they scored a small victory. A cannon shell lobbed from the fort dispersed three men who had been seen loading plunder from one of the stores into a buckboard. A party from the fort went across the river and captured the horse and buckboard.

One of the few things that worked well in the confines of the Battleford fort, overflowing with more than four hundred people, was the telegraph. Battleford residents crowded the wires with anxious messages to everyone they could think of. Most of those pleas for help eventually reached General Middleton. In the general's view, the Indians and the overwrought and exaggerating settlers were interfering with his plans for a grand show of strength that would cow the arch-rebel Riel. Middleton had no interest in dividing his forces, but he had to make some pretence of bowing to the pressure. While Middleton was at Qu'Appelle,

> I received here a message from [Minister of Militia] Mr. Caron informing me that he had heard Battleford was to be attacked immediately by six hundred Indians, and asking me to make arrangements to meet this danger, which, though not believing in their necessity, I had already done by ordering Lieutenant-Colonel Herchmer, with fifty men and one mountain gun, to proceed at once from Regina to Battleford. I continued to receive such urgent appeals from Superintendent Morris at Battleford that I telegraphed to him that I would march on Battleford from Clarke's Crossing, after disposing of Riel.[21]

Middleton's overly-optimistic messages were misinterpreted at Battleford to mean that he was sending immediately an entire column of troops to the town's relief, which was certainly not part of Middleton's plan. Herchmer didn't get to Battleford. After a couple of days on the trail, he turned back at the swiftly-flowing, icy Saskatchewan River.

As the plight of the Battleford settlers became known to their friends in other parts of the North-West, political and military authorities found themselves deluged with demands the siege be lifted. Although Riel was threatening neighbouring communities, as yet the Métis had not strayed outside their own part of the country. At Battleford, however, the poorly-protected white settlers were actually surrounded and in imminent danger from the Indians who, in the minds of white North-West residents, were far more treacherous and blood-thirsty than the Métis. At Winnipeg, as the *Manitoba Free Press* described the situation, "the general feeling in the city is that Battleford should be the first place to receive assistance, as they are not in a position to hold out as long as the force at Prince Albert, the latter being much stronger. The suffering of the poor women and children, hemmed within the walls of a dilapidated barracks, and momentarily expecting to be hacked to pieces by a blood-thirsty horde of yelping savages, can be better imagined than described."[22]

At the end of March, the residents of Battleford received one piece of extraordinarily optimistic news. From Fort Pitt NWMP Inspector Francis Dickens wrote to Indian Agent Rae on March 30. "Big Bear is away hunting(?) [sic] Indians all quiet at present. Some say they heard during the winter that something important was to happen after Easter. There is no chance of them getting up to Battleford anyhow."[23] Had Dickens known why Big Bear was out hunting, he might have been very worried. Big Bear's band at Frog Lake would not wait until Easter.

The community of Frog Lake was not what anyone would call thriving. It sat all by itself, an outpost on a road to nowhere else, about ten kilometres north of the North Saskatchewan River, just west of the Third Meridian, 110 degrees longitude, the line that would divide the provinces of Alberta and Saskatchewan. It was a subsidiary to Fort Pitt, about fifty kilometres southeast on the river, but closer to timber and to the Indian reserves. Trader William Bleasdell Cameron thought the community was in a pretty spot; others would say it looked pretty desolate. The site of the Frog Lake community marked the boundary of the territory of the Woods Cree, who had taken two large reservations around the lake, just at the end of the timber towards the Saskatchewan River, the main trading route. In 1885 the Frog Lake community boasted a Hudson's Bay Company store, a Roman Catholic church, George Dill's store, a small North-West Mounted Police barracks, a blacksmith shop, and various stables and houses. At the end of 1883 Chief Big Bear had been cajoled into moving to a spot just north of the Frog Lake settlement and just east of the grain mill John Gowanlock and William Laurie, son of Battleford's P. G. Laurie, would begin building on Frog Creek in 1884.

With his boss, Jim Simpson, at Fort Pitt and little business to do, Bill Cameron closed the Hudson's Bay Company store at Frog Lake early on March 28. He walked over to Frog Creek, intending to skate down to visit his friends John and Teresa Gowanlock at their home near the half-built mill. Cameron was only twenty-two years old, but he had been in the North-West since 1881. In the winter of 1884-85, he and George Dill had formed a partnership to trade with the Frog Lake Indians. Cameron built a small store at the Frog Lake settlement, but early in 1885 he left Dill and went to work at the Hudson's Bay store there. Cameron was a friendly, observant young man who was fluent in Cree and, unlike most other whites in the area, counted several Indians among his friends. After the bright sunshine and warmth of the previous few days, Cameron found himself skating through a veneer of water and slush on top of the ice of Frog Creek. He had not gone far before his clothes were soaked and he decided to abandon his visit to the Gowanlocks and walk back home. As he passed Big

Frog Lake trader Bill Cameron with Horse Child, Chief Big Bear's youngest son, in the summer of 1885. [Glenbow-Alberta Institute]

Bear's camp, Cameron saw the band was in council and he went to see what was happening.

> I noticed the tense, serious looks on the faces of the warriors smoking the long stone pipe round the fire in the centre as I entered the lodge. I saw at once that this was no ordinary social affair. I pulled once or twice at the pipe when it came to me in its course round the circle and I heard and understood enough, though the talk—in the Cree tongue—was guarded, to make it clear that subdued excitement burned in the breasts of the Indians—that they were contemplating some eventful step.[24]

The Indians had received some news and Big Bear's band were apparently making some proposals to their Woods Cree neighbors. Cameron watched as the Plains Cree war chief, Wandering Spirit, gave his shirt to Longfellow, a brother of a Woods Cree chief. The young trader felt uncomfortable at the Indian council. He was evidently not very welcome and he soon left.

Cameron did not know that what the Cree were discussing was the remarkable news of the defeat of the police at Duck Lake. The whites in the community would not know about the battle for several days. Nor did Cameron know that a soldiers' tent had been erected and, by Cree custom, the war chief was in control of the camp. Chief Big Bear did not know this either. In a deliberate attempt to prevent the trouble he felt was brewing, trouble Big Bear felt was largely the fault of local Indian Agent Tom Quinn, the chief and two of his sons had gone north hunting.

Thomas Trueman Quinn was one of several Indian agents distinguished by a dislike for Indians. The Indian Department did have some sensible, sympathetic employees in the North-West in the 1880s but Quinn, whose responsibilities included the most troublesome of the Cree bands, wasn't one of them. Although his mother was a Cree half-breed and he himself married a Cree woman, his feelings about the Indians had been formed many years before. His father, a trader and U.S. Army interpreter, had been killed in the terrible rampage known as the Minnesota Massacre of 1862, and teenager Tom Quinn had barely escaped with his own life.

When Quinn began work as an Indian agent in the Canadian North-West, the Cree named him Sioux-Speaker. As they got to know him, they gave him two less complimentary names, Dog Agent and The Bully. Informally, the Indians knew Quinn as "the man who always says no." Quinn was arrogant, boastful, and harsh in his dealings with the Indians. No one doubted his personal courage, but he seemed to have an astonishingly short supply of ordinary good sense.

In March 1885, Big Bear finally selected a reserve site west of Frog Lake. That site was acceptable to the government, but the band had not yet made any move towards their new home and the government was trying to limit the band's rations until they did. Agent Quinn used rations as payment to Big Bear's band for work they did helping to build Gowanlock's mill. When the Cree complained the rations had run out, Quinn refused to provide more until they did more work. According to Métis Louis Goulet, who spent some time at Frog Lake, Quinn and Farm Instructor John Delaney were conspiring to use rations for another purpose. They knew that Big Bear's band would soon be forced to move to their reserve site a few kilometres west. When that happened, the land north of the Frog Lake village on which the band was camped would be open for homesteading. Quinn and Delaney used rations to pay Big Bear's Indians for clearing the land around their camp, hoping they could acquire and sell the cleared land to settlers, Goulet said.[25]

Big Bear went hunting on March 28 because Agent Quinn had said no again. The hungry band had asked him for more rations, particularly fresh meat. Big Bear, worried about the growing anger among his people and about Quinn's intransigence, set off north hoping to provide enough fresh meat for a feast that would cool tempers at Frog Lake.

Shortly before midnight on March 31, NWMP Constable Billy Anderson galloped to Frog Lake from Fort Pitt with the terrible news of the defeat at Duck Lake. He brought a message from Inspector Dickens suggesting the whites at Frog Lake immediately move to the safety of Fort Pitt, or "if you think it a better plan, I will take my men at once to Frog Lake and extend what protection I can to the settlement."[26] Quinn and Cameron walked the short way from the NWMP barracks to the Roman Catholic mission to tell Father Léon-Adélard Fafard the news. On the way, Quinn suggested that Cameron leave for Fort Pitt that night but the young trader replied that with Jim Simpson already at the fort, he couldn't leave the Hudson's Bay store unattended. In any case, he told Quinn, "These Indians aren't going to kill me, whatever happens. I'm not trying to influence anybody, though. Anyone who doesn't feel safe, should leave, I'm thinking."[27]

At the mission, Father Fafard rejected the plan to abandon the community. The whites, by staying, would show they had confidence in the Indians, he argued. Agent Quinn replied: "If that's how you feel, I'll stay, too, though I did think that to go to Pitt would be wisest for us all." The men went back to Farm Instructor John Delaney's house, where most of the rest of the community, including Corporal Ralph Sleigh, who was in charge of the Frog Lake police post, were gathered. Father Fafard's point of view prevailed, but the assembled whites also decided that Sleigh and his detachment of six police should leave for Fort Pitt immediately. That small group would not be much protection against the Cree warriors and their presence might just complicate matters. The Cree would be less likely to start shooting at civilians, they reasoned. Just before daybreak, the police left with their sleigh full of ammunition from the Hudson's Bay store. Cameron thought it wise to get the ammunition out of the community, but he also had the presence of mind to leave a little bit in the store so the Indians wouldn't realize what he had done.[28]

Early the next morning, Agent Quinn sent a message to the Big Bear camp. He wanted to meet the Indian leaders. War Chief Wandering Spirit; Big Bear's son, Ayimāsis; Four Sky Thunder; and Miserable Man soon joined Quinn, Cameron, and other whites. It was April 1, the white man's "big lie day," Wandering Spirit joked as he entered Delaney's house. Ayimāsis addressed the Indian Agent:

We have had bad advice from the half-breeds this winter. They said they would spill much blood in the spring. They wished us to join them. They have already risen; we knew about it before you. They have beaten the soldiers in the first fight, killing many. We do not wish to join the half-breeds, but we are afraid. We wish to stay here and prove ourselves the friends of the white men. Tell us all the news that comes to you and we will tell you all we hear. The soldiers will come, perhaps, and want to fight us. We want you to protect us, to speak for us to their chief when they come.[29]

Ayimāsis, Big Bear's son, in exile in Montana about 1900. There, he was known as Chief Little Bear. [Glenbow-Alberta Institute]

Quinn thanked Ayimāsis for his sentiments, then said: "The fighting is far from here. Stay on the reservation and no one will bother you. I will see that you do not want for food." But Quinn said he could do nothing until he talked to Big Bear and he refused a specific request for more rations. The Indians said they would send for their chief and they shook hands with the whites as they left. "I'm glad Wandering Spirit seems friendly," Quinn said to Cameron. "So long as he stays quiet we have nothing to worry about."

Cameron was not so sure. He was wary of Wandering Spirit. "Tall, lithe, active, perhaps forty years of age, of a quick nervous temperament which transformed him at a stroke in moments of excitement into a mortal fiend. He was a copper Jekyll and Hyde—a savage no more to be trusted than a snake."[30]

After supper, Cameron left his home in the Hudson's Bay Company store to walk to Quinn's house, a short distance east of the main settlement. On the way, he stopped at the Delaneys', where several whites had gathered. Cameron was irritated by their easy, joking conversation. "Plainly these people did not sense the gravity of our position. It seemed to me no time for flippant talk."[31]

When he arrived at Quinn's, Cameron found that Big Bear, who had returned in the afternoon from his hunting trip, had led another Indian delegation to see the agent. Big Bear was having no better luck prying increased rations from the agent than the Indians had had earlier in the day, and he let his anger show, referring to Quinn as the "Dog Agent" and wondering whether his colleagues had lied when they told him the agent wanted a meeting. If Quinn was unwilling to grant their demands for food, why had he been called back from his hunting trip? Big Bear then said he had heard rumours from the south and he wondered if Quinn knew what was happening. "You heard the story already," the agent snapped. But he had to patiently read the message Inspector Dickens had sent and admit the half-breeds had defeated the police in battle.[32]

Wandering Spirit suggested that all the whites leave the community and leave the Indian Department storehouse intact with its contents in Indian hands. That, of course, was out of the question but Ayimāsis offered Quinn a compromise. If it were too much to ask that the agent bend his rules to give food to the Indians, he could present the supplies to Big Bear as a gift. That way, he would be simply honouring the venerable chief, not giving in to pressure. In the Cree tradition, Big Bear would use the supplies to make a feast for his people. Quinn would not lose face and the Indians would be satisfied. But the agent was beyond reasoning. He would give rations neither to the warriors nor to the chief.[33]

Big Bear talked of his meetings with Riel in Montana about five years before and he recalled: "When I was in the Long Knives' [Americans'] country I had a dream, an ugly dream. I saw a spring shooting up out of the ground. I covered it with my hand, trying to smother it, but it spurted up between my fingers and ran over the back of my hand. It was a spring of blood."[34]

Quinn still thought nothing was seriously amiss. He had had similar discussions with the Indians and had refused to bow to demands for increased rations many times before. He did not think the situation had changed, even though there was now open rebellion in the North-West. Cameron was far from reassured. He told Quinn, "Something's troubling Big Bear; he behaves queerly. I'm sure no harm's to be anticipated from him personally. I'd like to feel as sure about the others." Quinn replied, "Well, Cameron, they might kill me, but they can't scare me."[35]

Cameron and the other whites did not know that Big Bear had lost control of his band and the warriors were on the move. As the chief went home to bed, Little Bear, a prominent member of the warriors' society, led a small party to the house of Isidore Mondion, a half-breed minor chief of the Woods Cree who was very friendly with the whites in the community. Big Bear's warriors didn't want Mondion passing any information to the whites that night, he was told as Little Bear pointed his rifle at him. Mondion tried to grab the gun but the other Indians pulled knives and overpowered him. They tied him up and left him under guard.

A short time later, Ayimāsis led another group of warriors to Quinn's house. They broke in through a window and went upstairs to the agent's bedroom.

Quinn's wife jumped up between her husband and the Indians and called for help. Her brother, Sitting Horse, and her uncle, Lone Man, a son-in-law of Big Bear, were staying with the Quinns to protect them. They rushed into the bedroom and pointed their guns at the intruders. It was a stalemate and, as Ayimāsis was forced to leave, he warned: "Wandering Spirit will deal with you." About two hours later, at daybreak on April 2, the war chief himself arrived at Quinn's house. He broke the lock on the front door and called for Quinn to come downstairs. Lone Man offered to defend his relative but Quinn realized resistance was useless. He would meet the war chief "and never will they be able to say Sioux Speaker was afraid to face them!" Wandering Spirit took Quinn prisoner and appropriated his guns and ammunition.[36]

Ayimāsis had gone west to Gowanlock's mill. There, half-breeds Louis Goulet and Adolphus Nolin, Charles Nolin's son, were having breakfast with William Gilchrist, Gowanlock's clerk, and a number of others. The Gowanlocks were still at Delaney's house in the village. Ayimāsis rushed in, grabbed Goulet, and dragged him outside. He ordered Gilchrist to open Gowanlock's store, which he did, and the Indians plundered the contents. Then Ayimāsis took all his new prisoners towards the Frog Lake community.

As they rode towards the Frog Lake by way of Big Bear's camp, the sun sat on the horizon facing them. Goulet enjoyed the spectacle. "The sun was rising, one of the most beautiful springtime suns I'd ever seen in my life. I don't know why, but I started to think, 'This may well be the last sunrise I ever see. That's why it looks so beautiful.' I didn't mean to think that thought and it got me angry. Just when I was about to start cursing myself out, the sight of the camp took my mind off my sad notions and the Indians escorting us began whooping and singing out war chants. When the sun comes up bright and beautiful like that, it's a sign they'll win their battle."[37] The rising sun really was impressive that morning and Goulet was not the only one who noticed. Bill Cameron would entitle his famous book *Blood Red the Sun*, based on the scene that morning. When they reached the village, Goulet and his companions were allowed to stable their horses and visit their friends.

Ayimāsis went on to Delaney's house, where he took the farm instructor, his wife, the Gowanlocks, and also interpreter John Pritchard prisoner. Indians, who crowded into the house, told the frightened whites they would protect them from the Métis. When Walking Horse, a Woods Cree employed at the Hudson's Bay store, sleepily answered a knock on his door that morning, he found his brother-in-law, Four Sky Thunder, there. "I'm surprised that my brother-in-law is still sleeping," the Plains Cree said. "Didn't you know they have already taken the agent?" After a short discussion with Four Sky Thunder, Walking Horse rushed to the store and into Cameron's bedroom. He jolted the trader awake. "I think it will be bad today," he said. "They've taken the horses from the government stables already." As Cameron went downstairs, Ayimāsis and twenty warriors appeared, demanding ammunition. Cameron was thankful he was able to say there was some in the store. The Indians gathered what powder, bullets, and knives they could find and left for the nearby NWMP barracks, where some of their companions had started a dance and were busy appropriating whatever they could find that the police had left behind. Soon after, Wandering Spirit sent a messenger to demand that Cameron go to Quinn's house. There he found all the whites of the community surrounded by Indians.[38]

Wandering Spirit renewed his demand for fresh meat. This time Quinn was in no position to refuse but he was still, astonishingly, so stubborn that he could not just give in. He asked Farm Instructor Delaney if there was an old ox that could no longer be used as a draught animal. Delaney sensibly replied that he just happened to have just such a thing. As Delaney told them where they could find the ox to butcher, the Indians wondered where this useless animal had been hiding during their earlier impassioned and threatening requests for meat. Wandering Spirit ordered Cameron back to the store to dispense tobacco to the Indians, who had already sacked George Dill's little store southeast of the settlement. Quinn had to remain in his own house and the rest of the whites were sent to Delaney's.

Cameron had breakfast about 9:30 that morning at Jim Simpson's house with Father Fafard; Father Félix Marchand, who was visiting from Onion Lake; and Henry Quinn, Tom's nephew, who was the village blacksmith. Shortly after the priests left to prepare their Holy Thursday service, Cameron went back to his store and a short time later Wandering Spirit appeared, decorated in his war paint. "Why don't you go to the church?" he said to Cameron. "Your friends are already there." Cameron had had no intention of attending the Roman Catholic service but he could not ignore an order from the war chief. He was kneeling with the congregation when

> there came the rattle of musketry from the door and looking out from beneath my arm I saw Wandering Spirit enter. He moved cat-like on his moccasined feet to the centre of the church and dropped on his right knee there, his Winchester clutched in his right hand, the butt resting on the floor. His lynx-skin war bonnet, from which depended five large eagle plumes, crowned his head; his eyes burned and his hideously-painted face was set in lines of deadly menace. Never shall I forget the feelings his whole appearance and action excited in me as I watched in stupefied amazement while he half-knelt, glaring up at the altar and the white-robed priests in sacrilegious [sic] mockery. He was a demon, a wild animal, savage, ruthless, thirsting for blood. I doubted then that we should any of us ever again see the outside of the chapel.[39]

Louis Goulet remembered Wandering Spirit walking up and down the aisle of the church, firing his rifle at the windows and door.

Outside it was like a pack of wolves. While looting the stores, the Indians had helped themselves liberally to liquor and spirit waters, and obviously the alcohol was having an effect. The Indians came in and out of the church, singing, shouting, howling and beating drums, storming around and strutting in underclothes and suits they'd taken from the stores and the prisoners. Father Marchand closed the door at one time, but Wandering Spirit opened it five minutes later. At that, Father Fafard turned around to face us and said it was too much, he couldn't continue in all that uproar.[40]

As the congregation left the church, Goulet hung back to talk to Father Fafard. Little Bear came up and demanded that the priest hurry to catch up to the other prisoners. When Father Fafard said he wanted to lock the church first, Little Bear hit him in the face with the butt of his rifle, cutting him badly under the eye. Goulet jumped on the Indian but the priest broke up the fight.

King Bird, a son of Big Bear, had joined Cameron on his walk back to the store and asked him if he sided with Riel or the police. Cameron replied diplomatically. "The half-breed war is far from us. Let them fight it out between themselves. Here we are all friends." Quinn dropped in on the way back to his house. It had finally dawned on the Indian agent that he was in the middle of no ordinary confrontation. "If we live through this we'll have something to remember for the rest of our days," he told Cameron.[41] At the village, Wandering Spirit asked Gowanlock's clerk, William Gilchrist, the same question King Bird had asked Cameron. Gilchrist didn't think to lie or to be as diplomatic as Cameron. He said he sided with the government, of course. "That's all I wanted to know," replied the war chief.[42]

Wandering Spirit ordered all the whites to Delaney's house, which stood next to the police barracks where the Indians were dancing. As Cameron arrived, his friend Yellow Bear asked him for a hat he had seen in the store. "King Bird danced up to me, the Hudson's Bay flag over his shoulders. We had always been good friends. 'I'm cold,' he said. He shook, but not from cold; the day was warm and pleasant. It was from suppressed excitement. He came closer and added meaningly, in a whisper: 'Don't stop around here!' "[43]

Cameron did not want to stay but he couldn't disobey the war chief. Yellow Bear's request gave him the excuse he needed and he persuaded the Indian to accompany him back to the store. Halfway there, Wandering Spirit stopped them and ordered Cameron to go with the other whites. But Yellow Bear intervened and the war chief left Cameron with an admonition to do his business quickly and get to Quinn's house. As they passed Simpson's house, they saw Big Bear visiting the trader's wife. Yellow Bear got his hat and Cameron was locking his store again when Miserable Man appeared with an order from Quinn for a blanket. The Indians had already taken all the blankets so Miserable Man demanded something comparable. As Cameron went back into the store, he didn't know how extraordinarily lucky he was.

Louis Goulet, Charles Gouin, and Henry Quinn, who had not been ordered into Delaney's house, sat on a packing case watching the proceedings. "It was getting hard to be optimistic. The Indians were getting drunker and drunker, more and more provoking. The crazy games they were playing with firearms, an accident was sure to happen. Catastrophe wasn't far down the road," Goulet recalled.[44]

At Delaney's house, Wandering Spirit ordered all the whites to go to the new camp the Plains Creek had established on Frog Creek about one and a half kilometres from the settlement. Big Bear had agreed to the move on the condition that the whites would not be harmed and the whites were resigned to their position as prisoners of the warriors. But Tom Quinn refused to budge. He had had enough of doing what the Indians demanded. And Wandering Spirit had had enough of Quinn. "You have a hard head. When you say no, you mean no, and stick to it. Now if you love your life you will do as I say. Go to our camp." When Quinn again refused, the war chief said: "I don't know what kind of a head you have that you do not seem to understand. I may as well kill you." With that, Wandering Spirit raised his rifle and put a bullet in Quinn's head.[45]

Charles Gouin, the Indian Agency carpenter, was walking towards Quinn. Wandering Spirit told Bad Arrow to shoot him. Bad Arrow protested but the war chief insisted so "I raised my gun and fired where I would not kill him; I shot him in the shoulder and he fell and lay on the ground; I asked him if I had killed him and he shook his head; I made him a sign to close his eyes and sham dead."[46] Miserable Man had run out of the store, followed closely by Cameron and Yellow Bear. Cameron looked from the small hill where the store stood across the trail to Delaney's house. "Dust and smoke filled the air; whoops and shrieks and the clatter of galloping hoofs blended in a weird and ghastly symphony. High over all swelled the deadly war-chant of the Plains Crees, bursting from a hundred sinewy throats. I heard the peculiarly-ringing voice of Wandering Spirit calling on his followers to shoot the other whites and burst after burst sounded the death knell of my friends."[47]

Big Bear rushed out of Simpson's house near where Cameron was standing and yelled: "Stop. Stop."[48] But it was no use. Miserable Man ran to where the wounded Gouin was trying to raise himself. As Calling Bull described it, "Miserable Man came forward and shot him in the chest; he fell and shook a little while and then ceased to move and died."[49] By this time, most of the whites were about fifty metres north of Delaney's house on their way to Big Bear's camp. Teresa Gowanlock was walking beside her husband and behind the Delaneys when "I saw an Indian aiming at my husband by my side. In a moment he fell, reaching out his arms towards me as he fell. I caught him, and we fell together. I laid upon him, resting my face on his, and his breath was scarcely gone when I was forced away by an Indian."[50] No one knew who killed Gowanlock. Then a shot from Bare Neck's rifle struck Delaney, whose wife called for a priest. As Father Fafard knelt over the doomed farm instructor, Bare Neck shot him too. Bad Arrow grabbed Mrs. Delaney to save her from the same fate. Wandering Spirit shot Father Marchand as that priest turned to help.

Three of the whites in the little group had tried to flee, running up the trail towards the Indian camp. John Williscraft, Father Fafard's lay assistant, did not get far. Kāwēchetwēmot, the man who nearly started a war the year before by assaulting Farm Instructor Craig, rode after Williscraft and shot him only a short distance from the main group. Henry Quinn saw Williscraft fall and managed to slip away unnoticed into the woods and run towards Fort Pitt. Kāwēchetwēmot and a group of Indians then pursued trader George Dill and Gowanlock's clerk William Gilchrist, who were running beside the road about forty metres away. Thunder followed the other Indians. "As I went along I heard Wandering Spirit call out to the other Indians to shoot all the whites, what was the delay for; after that I saw Dill and Gilchrist running, and a white dog with them." A bullet from Kāwēchetwēmot's gun felled Gilchrist, and Thunder saw Dill stop and turn around. "He seemed to have given up hope and to have stopped running; he was looking in the direction of the Indians."[51] Iron Body was in the group closest to Dill and later recalled: "Little Bear fired at Dill and I fired too and missed and Red Skin knocked Dill down. It was Wandering Spirit who urged us to do this because he was the cause of it all. Wandering Spirit did this because he was jealous of other Indians who wanted to go on a reserve, while he did not want to. He was afraid after he had killed Quinn and he wished to drag others into it."[52]

Some of those who had been chasing Gilchrist and Dill came back to where a large group of Indians were gathered around the dying Father Fafard. Most of the Indians kept their distance but Sawayon walked up to him. "I went quite near him, and I saw blood running on the ground and I stepped back. He was breathing because his back was moving up and down as a person breathing. He was lying on his face with his hands folded under his head. I saw the wound near the back of the neck and I saw the blood running. I thought the bullet had passed through the side of the neck. When the Indians came where Father Fafard was lying, Manachoos [Bad Arrow] said: 'He is still breathing. Shoot him.'"[53] Walking the Sky, who had been brought up by the priest, stepped forward and shot Father Fafard in the top of the head.

Nine whites lay dead or dying in the snow. The whole thing had taken, one Indian recalled, "only about as long as it would take a person to smoke a pipe."[54]

Throughout the killings, Bill Cameron's extraordinary luck stayed with him. His friend Yellow Bear took him to Mrs. Simpson. The trader's wife and another woman wrapped Cameron in a big red shawl and took him with them to Big Bear's camp. The warriors didn't notice the young clerk disguised by the shawl and walking with the women. Louis Goulet watched Mrs. Simpson "going by with Cameron under one arm. She was Gabriel Dumont's sister, a big, fat woman, strong as any man. Cameron could hardly keep on his feet, every step was a stagger. I thought he was wounded, but no, it was fear made him that way. Mrs. Simpson had to drag him, or carry him more like it."[55]

Some of the Indians moved off towards their camp with the two white women and some half-breed prisoners. Others had moved to the church a short distance west. They did not know that Father Marchand was the only one of their nine victims who was still barely alive. Masanēkwepān, the seventeen-year-old son of Woods Cree chief Onēpohayo, was listening to a conversation between his father and Chakwapokes, a Big Bear warrior, in a field near Frog Lake. Chakwapokes, riding Delaney's horse, had come to tell the Woods Cree chief the news. "We took all the whites early this morning but we are not going to hurt them," Chakwapokes said. While they were talking, "all of a sudden and like thunder we heard several shots, one after the other down towards the Agency."[56]

Chakwapokes turned and galloped back towards the community. Masanēk-wepān ran after him, through Frog Creek. "I heard several more shots while running from the creek. As I reached the bluff just north of the Agent's house, I met a young woman from Big Bear's band crying at the top of her voice. 'All the Priests are killed and all the white people are killed.'" Masanēkwepān ran on and found Father Marchand

Inaccurate in detail, this *Canadian Pictorial and Illustrated War News* re-creation of part of the Frog Lake massacre was based on accounts of eyewitnesses. *The War News*, published by Grip, was criticized at the time, and since, for embellishing rebellion scenes.

lying helpless on the ground with blood streaming from his throat. He was still alive, breathing slowly. I said to him: "I am very sorry but it must be God's will." I took some grass to try and wipe away the blood which was coming from a gash in his throat. This was not very satisfactory, so I took my black silk handkerchief and tied it around his neck. He had his eyes closed but was still breathing as the blood trickled away from his throat at intervals. As I was bandaging him up, I noticed that he struggled hard to get his breath. He had his robe on with a watch chain on one side and a cross on the other. I stayed with him till the last.

After the priest died, Masanēkwepān, joined by his uncle, walked past the other bodies to Delaney's house, then over to the church. "When we got there everything was damaged. I saw two kegs of wine that the Church had had. I saw the Indians open these kegs and drink of the wine. The rest they poured out on the ground. A few of Big Bear's Indians clothed themselves in the Priests' robes. I joined in with them as they were having a good time." Onēpohayo arrived and took his teenage son in tow, scolding him for engaging in the plundering. They walked to Simpson's house.

It was awful to be there. Big Bear's men were dancing upstairs and breaking things to pieces. My father who by this time began to show annoyance pushed his way through and went to the stair. He got half way up but could not get any further as there were too many Indians. I tried to follow him. My father called to Big Bear and said "I am surprised that you would allow your men to carry on like this. Are you people crazy or what is the matter. Your mind cannot be right. If I had known of this I would have given you twenty-five head of cattle to kill instead of massacring the white people the way you have done besides all the damage. All of you men get down and take nothing away from this house.... If you do not like my talk take a gun and shoot me." I was getting afraid and excited as I expected my father any moment to come tumbling down the stairs a dead man. No shooting, however, took place. The men dropped everything and left the house. My father shut the door behind.[57]

Big Bear's Indians moved to the Hudson's Bay store. Onēpohayo despaired of being able to prevent any more looting and he and Masanēkwepān began walking home. They had not gone far when they saw the Indians move back into Simpson's house.

The Woods Cree chief arrived home with his son to find that his wife had been taken to the Plains Cree camp a virtual prisoner. When they walked into their teepee in the middle of Big Bear's camp, "as soon as mother saw us she broke into tears, 'All of us will be killed now this day,' she said. Tears came into my eyes in pity of my mother. After we had comforted her by saying that we thought everything would come out all right, she prepared something to eat; but

I could not eat after all the excitement. I said I would go out and look for the horses. This was merely an excuse on my part as I did not want to show my nervousness."

Masanēkwepān went to a hill overlooking the approach to the camp from the south. "I had not been sitting there long when I saw Indians bringing over two white women they had captured and made prisoners. The women were walking ahead, the Indians following behind. A short distance back of these Indians came two squaws with a large shawl outstretched between them and under which was Mr. Cameron."

The two white women had been dragged, terrified and crying, through the woods and creek to the camp. The Indians who had unceremoniously pulled them away from their dead husbands thought they were saving the women's lives. But Teresa Delaney and Teresa Gowanlock were in mortal dread of the Indians, fearing not only for their lives but petrified with notions of indignities they might suffer in Indian captivity. Masanēkwepān ran back to tell his father what he had seen. He had hardly arrived when Mrs. Delaney and Mrs. Gowanlock were brought to the Woods Cree chief's teepee. "As they came up, one of them fainted and fell to the ground. Mother brought out some water and gave it to her. Father said: 'I am glad that you have been brought here. I will see that you are not harmed.'"[58]

Cameron was initially taken to another teepee, where he found himself in the company of Walking the Sky. The Indian held out Father Fafard's watch and asked Cameron to read it. It was eleven o'clock. The distraught Cameron was soon taken to Onēpohayo's teepee where he mumbled to the Woods Cree chief: "It is hard. It is hard. It is hard. Maybe I'll be killed today."[59] Onēpohayo promised to speak for Cameron and the two white women captives and try to keep them out of danger.

Louis Goulet got Big Bear's permission to go back to the village and put the bodies of the victims in the church basement. He and some helpers "gathered up the remains of Father Marchand, Father Fafard, Gowanlock and Delaney. It was no small chore. We were covered with blood in no time. To lift Father Marchand, André Nault had to take him by the feet and I reached under his arms. The bullets had ripped his skull open. When we lifted him his head fell back and his brains ran into one of my boots. That little picture stuck in my mind for a long time." The warriors prevented them from moving any of the other bodies.

Late that same morning I heard some Indians having noisy fun in front of Pritchard's house. One of them was saying, "You've been a thorn in our side for a long time, haven't you? You never wanted to give us anything to eat. Well here you go; now we're gonna pay you like you deserve." Curious, I went to have a look. He'd opened Quinn's clothing and rammed a sharpened willow stick into him. Tom Quinn was a hard man, always abusing his help and the Indians. Those Indians hated him and that's why they took revenge on his body with such indecency.[60]

The safety of Mrs. Delaney and Mrs. Gowanlock was further guaranteed later in the day when Louis Goulet, John Pritchard, and Adolphus Nolin formally purchased them from the Indians. After his boss, Jim Simpson, arrived at Big Bear's camp from Fort Pitt, Cameron was housed in the teepee of one of the trader's stepsons. They were kept captive, but the whites and half-breeds were allowed the freedom of the Indian camp as long as they didn't try to escape. The warriors had promised to do them no harm and, although they still faced constant danger from some individuals, with the help of their Indian and half-breed friends, the whites were relatively secure. With the addition of the Woods Cree, the camp contained about two hundred lodges and the Indians spent the few days after April 2 dancing and feasting. Big Bear's band had gained control of the substantial herd of cattle belonging to the Woods Cree and these provided more fresh meat than they needed.

In the afternoon of April 2, Charles Quinney, the Anglican minister at Onion Lake, which was situated about half-way between Frog Lake and Fort Pitt, visited his friend Half Blackfoot Chief on the neighbouring Cree reserve. By this time Half Blackfoot Chief undoubtedly knew of the killings, but he didn't tell the minister. He did say that the Frog Lake Cree planned to kill Quinn and the other whites. Then the Indians would move on Fort Pitt. There were only twenty-five police there and the Indians no longer needed to fear the white man, Half Blackfoot Chief said.

At the same time, the Onion Lake Indians were gathering at the home of Farming Instructor George Mann. They told Mann they were upset that Indian Agent Tom Quinn had not come to visit them that morning as he had promised. Then they moved their camp to straddle the main road to Fort Pitt. About nine o'clock that night, some Indian friends came to Mann's home to tell the instructor about the killings at Frog Lake and warn him that he, too, was to be killed. Mann couldn't escape by the main road, so the Indians offered to show him a back trail to Fort Pitt. The instructor put his family in the back of a buckboard and started off. One of Mann's children remembered the journey: "After driving for some time and through a large swamp of snow and water, Father found he was driving in a circle, decided to stop until the moon rose, to get the direction of Fort Pitt. While waiting we could hear the shrill war whoops of the Indians, and firing of guns. They were plundering our home and the warehouses. We were afraid that at any moment our horse might winnow [whinny] or the dog, which had followed us, would bark and reveal our whereabouts."[61]

When the moon rose, Mann got his bearings and reached Fort Pitt without incident at about 1 A.M. bearing the first report of the Frog Lake killings to the little garrison. The Hudson's Bay Company Factor at Fort Pitt, William

McLean, was one of the first to get the bad news. He later told a reporter that "a terrible scene of confusion ensued. The residents at once commenced barricading Fort Pitt with sacks of oats, and everything they could lay their hands on. They tore down the outbuildings so that they would not afford cover to the enemy, and tried to dig rifle pits but found the ground too hard."[62]

At about five o'clock on the morning of April 3, Anglican Minister Charles Quinney and his wife were roused from bed by an Indian at their window. He told them to get away quickly or they would be killed. They dressed hastily and Quinney opened his front door "and about 20 Indians rushed in and began removing the clothes from the bed and taking everything they could lay their hands on. We were escorted to the reserve by armed Indians who were instructed not to allow any person near us." A short time later, they were taken to the Manns' home. "We arrived at the farm wet and weary, and found the Indians in possession of the house, which they had pillaged. They had already killed cattle and gave us beef for dinner. We were subjected to the hugging and kissing of old hags who said that our kindness to them and their children now saved our lives, and that the farm instructor had only escaped in time to save his scalp." The Indians held a council to consider what to do with their captives. They decided that the Quinney family could borrow a horse to go to Fort Pitt on condition an escort accompany them to bring the animal back.[63] When the minister and his wife arrived at the fort, Factor McLean and NWMP Inspector Dickens went out to talk to a chief who had accompanied them. They offered a reward to anyone who would bring the Frog Lake captives to Fort Pitt.

Henry Quinn had also arrived and the population of Fort Pitt then numbered forty-four civilians and twenty-three police who, for the next couple of weeks, would live in daily dread of an attack. Not much really happened. Chief Little Poplar and his band arrived on the south bank of the river on April 7 and seemed friendly enough. Dickens refused to let them cross but sent rations to their camp.

On Easter Sunday, April 5, some of the Indians had returned to the community at Frog Lake, where they burned the church and some of the other buildings. As the priests' bodies burned in the church basement, the smoke rose in the shape of a man. As it ascended, it briefly took the form of a horse. It was a bad omen.[64]

The Fall of Fort Pitt

On April 2, the day of the Frog Lake killings, the Battleford Indians had moved west to Poundmaker's reserve and the townspeople breathed a little easier. But they still had no intention of moving back to their homes and they settled in at the fort. They felt reasonably safe though, as Battleford merchant James Clinkskill recalled, still uneasy and not very comfortable.

> The situation inside the barracks was getting acute. There were about one hundred able-bodied men with about three hundred women and children. The difficulty was to get shelter for them and food for so many. A number of the women and children were housed in the Quartermaster's warehouse, which was outside the stockade. In the night time frequent alarms sounded, when every man took his appointed station at a loop-hole made in the stockade. When these alarms were given the women and children had to clamber over a stile [ladder] to get inside, some of the women in their excitement throwing the children over. This could not continue.[1]

Those women and children were eventually housed in a large tent erected in the middle of the fort while some of the others crowded into NWMP Inspector William Morris' house. The newly-formed home guards were given the Indian Department's warehouse as a barracks, where sleep, Clinkskill said, did not come easily. "The old gag of selecting the softest plank to lie on for the night was slightly altered in this case. The [warehouse] floor consisted of whip-sawed logs, all thicknesses, with wide spaces between and it was a case of selecting the least uneven planks to lie on and which had the smallest spaces between, these spaces had the faculty of allowing a draft of cold air to shoot up that seemed to cut your flesh like a knife."

A temporary bridge had been constructed across the Battle River and what was left of the provisions in the town, mostly bacon and flour, had been brought to the fort. "These supplies were piled up in the centre of the square, covered with tarpaulin, and a strong guard over it. We began to feel better at the sight of enough food to do us for a time. The flour was all right but the bacon displayed all the colors of the rainbow, and tasted rank, however it was eatable if you had a strong appetite and a vigorous digestion."[2]

On April 3, things had quieted down to such an extent that Inspector Morris ordered a foray to a nearby camp of half-breeds. A group of police went out that afternoon and arrested the entire camp, about ten men with their wives, children, horses, and wagons. The captives, along with two other half-breeds who had been captured in the town earlier in the day, were locked up and their families kept at a corner of the fort outside the stockade. There was so little evidence that any of them had broken any law that some were quickly released. At midnight that day, half-breed Alex Bremner galloped up to the fort to report that the neighbouring half-breed community of Bresaylor was in imminent danger of attack by the Indians and needed help. But, as P. G. Laurie recorded, "the reputation of the people he represented not being very savory and his stories contradictory, Col. Morris concluded he would be safer here and he was accordingly locked up."[3] On April 4, Battleford learned of the Frog Lake killings and a short time later, a large party of Indians returned to town to continue plundering and burning some of the buildings.

For the two weeks at the beginning of April, the besieged inhabitants of Battleford watched as groups of Indians came to town from time to time to continue the pillaging. From the stockade of the fort they could also see the flames and smoke of immense prairie fires and of some outlying settlers' houses set afire by the Indians. But the whites and Indians rarely came close to one another, except on April 8, when a few Indians on the flats near the Hudson's Bay Company store fired on water wagons sent down to the river from the fort. The wagons' escort returned the fire and a couple of shells were sent from the fort's cannon in a brief, brisk skirmish. Though they supposed they killed three or four Indians, none of the whites was hit. The townspeople settled in to the fort as best they could and everything worked remarkably well despite the overcrowding and the difficulties of getting and distributing food and water. They were always extremely edgy, and the faintest unusual noise at night was enough to call out the guard. Patrolling outside the stockade at night was the hardest task for Clinkskill. "Every little object in the semi-darkness seemed magnified in size, a little bit of weed seemed to be as large as a man, with your eyes strained, every nerve on edge, mistakes would occur. You had to watch the ground for fear of some Indian crawling up on you, naturally imagination gets busy. We were very much bothered by a lot of dogs sneaking around and pigs too. One night I called halt and challenged, it turned out to be a hog in search of food, the answer I got was a grunt. I am not allowed to forget this incident."[4]

The Battleford whites were besieged not by Indians but by their own fears of Indians, magnified by the killings of Farm Instructor Payne and farmer "Barney the Belgian" Tremont and of the nine whites at Frog Lake. Farm Instructor Robert Jefferson spent the month of April as captive guest at Poundmaker's camp and described the situation from that perspective.

During the whole of the outbreak, there was no organised attempt at besieging the barracks; indeed there were not enough Indians to do it. Such

206

men as thought fit prowled round the town at night, but at a safe distance. In the daytime when they would appear on the hills on the south side of the river they were saluted with bullets from watchers on the other side and at night they were too few to do any harm. Great consternation prevailed in the white camp but it arose altogether from the preconceived idea of Indian warfare and the barbarities that accompanied it. The Indians were not sufficiently worked up to attempt offensive measures.[5]

The combined Battleford bands had established their large camp on the plains just to the east of Cutknife Creek. They gathered all the cattle and supplies they could find on nearby reserves and farms. They also gathered up the community of Bresaylor, reasoning that the French half-breeds there, many of whom had participated in the Red River resistance, naturally belonged with the natives. Most of the whites and English half-breeds at Bresaylor had fled to Battleford and the French half-breeds who remained wanted nothing to do with either side in the conflict. They would not go to the fort and appear to side with the whites; neither would they willingly support the rebels. But they were in no position to resist the Cree warriors who took them and all their provisions to the camp at Cutknife Creek.

Poundmaker was appointed the political leader and chief spokesman for the combined bands. The Indians believed they had done their part. They had succeeded in establishing their supremacy in their own territory and all that was left was to wait for other native groups to do the same. Poundmaker believed that the Cree of Bears Hills to the west and Qu'Appelle to the east would make their own shows of force and that his adoptive father, Chief Crowfoot, would lead the Blackfoot in recapturing the south. The Métis would control their own territory on the South Branch of the Saskatchewan. The Indians had no thought of actually taking the offensive in force. Their military tradition was in horse-stealing raids or small forays to drive intruders out of what they considered their territory. They had no notion of the movement of armies or capturing territory in the European tradition. Poundmaker believed that for Riel and the Métis everything was going according to plan.

A soldiers' lodge was erected at the Cutknife camp but for the first two weeks of April the Indians were content to be relatively patient, dancing and feasting on captured cattle and waiting for news of the successes of the Métis army.

When fighting broke out in 1885, the people of the bustling community of Edmonton had better reason to panic than most North-West residents. Edmonton was a major trading centre, the most important Hudson's Bay post between Battleford and the Rocky Mountains, but it was a long way from any other large settlement and from reinforcements in case of trouble. Several of the half-dozen Cree bands in the area were a considerable distance from the town, but there was no substantial white settlement between the Indians and their trading and supply point, Edmonton. The town itself was poorly equipped to defend itself. The police garrison was stationed at Fort Saskatchewan, thirty kilometres northeast, and the old Hudson's Bay Company post was run-down, its stockade in no condition to withstand an attack. To add to the feelings of defencelessness, the telegraph line suddenly went dead at the end of March, just after tapping out the news of the police defeat at Duck Lake. The people of Edmonton at first didn't know what to think or do. They had had little warning of the agitation at the South Branch and they didn't know to what extent the local Indians and half-breeds were dissatisfied and likely to take up arms. They did know that if the trouble quickly spread, they would be in real danger.

At the Métis colonies near Edmonton, particularly St. Albert just to the north and Duhamel to the south, the inhabitants had been engaged with the federal government in spirited arguments about land rights, and some of the people of those communities were known to be very sympathetic to Riel's efforts. But Edmonton was relatively safe from the half-breeds, Hudson's Bay Company Factor Richard Hardisty telegraphed the company's Commissioner Joseph Wrigley in Winnipeg, because Edmonton's citizens were just as dissatisfied with Ottawa. "Decisions of Land Board regarding white claims at Edmonton has given general dissatisfaction. This being so they sympathize with breeds." The half-breeds were unlikely to start a fight with their own supporters, Hardisty said.[6]

The rebellion reached the area on April 3 when Cree of the Little Hunter and Blue Quill bands raided a government storehouse at Saddle Lake, about one hundred and thirty kilometres northeast of Edmonton, after receiving a message from Riel telling of the Duck Lake battle and from Big Bear's band about the killings at Frog Lake. The Big Bear Indians wanted the Saddle Lake bands to join them at Fort Pitt, about one hundred and fifty kilometres to the southeast. The Indians ordered their farm instructor to kill an ox for them and turn over his storehouse. When he refused, they grabbed him and broke open the storehouse.

With their telegraph line still down, the people of Edmonton found out about the Saddle Lake raid and the Frog Lake killings on April 7. They still had little idea of the plans of Indians in their neighbourhood, but they expected the worst. "When the Indians around Edmonton will rise appears now to be only a question of days. What they will do in that case, or what numbers they will be joined by, is something which can be better decided after the event," Frank Oliver editorialized in his Edmonton *Bulletin*. Oliver, a fierce Grit, knew exactly where to put the blame for the troubles.

A match will not fire a pile of green wood, but it will a pile of dry. Had the Saskatchewan country been in a satisfied condition a hundred such men as Riel might have come into it and the only harm resulting would have been to themselves. But when years of careful mismanagement of the control exercised by the Interior department, and department of Indian affairs had stirred up discontent among all classes, from the breech-clouted Indian to the hardworking farmer and well-to-do merchant or professional man, the pile was made ready for the fire brand, and the fire brand ready lighted came in the person of Riel.[7]

When they received the bad news, most of the male population of Edmonton gathered in Kelly's Saloon to consider their position. Things did not look good. The Saddle Lake outbreak itself was bad enough, but it had occurred too close for comfort to the reserve of the influential Pakan at Whitefish Lake, the Cree chief the Edmonton residents knew best and feared most. Because they had no telegraph communication, they talked about sending a courier to Calgary to ask for help. No one was willing to put up the money for the trip so they decided to wait for the arrival of NWMP Inspector Arthur Griesbach, who was on his way into town from Fort Saskatchewan, and ask his advice. Meanwhile, individuals busied themselves writing short pleas for help to Lieutenant Governor Dewdney, Prime Minister Macdonald, and any other influential friends they could think of back East. "Great excitement. Indians rising. Send reinforcements and arms at once," read the one Minister of Public Works Hector Langevin eventually received.[8] The mail courier from Calgary arrived while the meeting was in progress and reported most Indians friendly but the bands at Bears Hills, about a hundred kilometres south of Edmonton, were talking of going to war. If a large-scale outbreak occurred in the Edmonton region, it was likely to centre at Bears Hills. One of the chiefs there, Bobtail, had made his reputation in the buffalo hunts and had avoided the whites as much as he could. His brother and fellow chief Ermineskin was a brother-in-law of Poundmaker. The other main chief in the area was Samson, who was considered relatively friendly to the whites, although no one was confident he could control his large following of three hundred people if war broke out.

When Inspector Griesbach finally arrived, he chastized the assembled citizens for not sending the courier to Calgary when they first heard the news. But they still hesitated. A committee of defence was elected and they bickered and haggled about the price of a courier until midnight, when James Mowat offered to do the job for free if someone would give him a horse. Mowat set out south at a gallop with a message from the defence committee to General T. B. Strange, who had been put in command of the forces in Alberta: "Have wired Sir John. Indians on the war path. Send us men and arms immediately. Can't you help us at once?"[9] As Mowat rode for help, the people of Edmonton spent the next two days strengthening the stockade at the Hudson's Bay Company fort, moving most of the town's families into the fort, and enrolling and drilling a home guard.

Meanwhile, in response to a message from Big Bear's band, Bobtail had sent messages of his own to other chiefs in the Edmonton area asking if they would be willing to join the revolt. He had apparently received promises of support from the Stonies at Lac Ste. Anne and Rivière qui Barre, just northwest of Edmonton. Samson had gone off south to gauge the feelings of his fellow Methodists, the Mountain Stonies at Morleyville, and the Blackfoot-speaking nations.

Mowat, encouraged by the confusion and excitement at Edmonton, took his mission too seriously. He almost started the war he was supposed to help prevent. Father Constantin Scollen, the Oblate priest at Bears Hills, looked in amazement at the wake Mowat left as he dashed through the reserves early on April 8. "The climax of all was to see the Whites running for their lives. The courier from Edmonton to Calgary past through the reserve at steeple-chase speed. He warned all the Whitemen as he went along. Edmonton was preparing for a siege," Father Scollen wrote.[10] That day and the next, most of the few whites at Bears Hills and at Red Deer Crossing, about fifty kilometres south, packed up and hurriedly left for Edmonton and Calgary.

Father Scollen stayed at his post as excitement grew among the Bears Hills bands.

Just imagine the consternation of the Indians when witnessing all this commotion. Myself & Companion were the only Whites left. The Indians were amazed & frightened. They thought the Whites had received letters bearing terrible news, and were hiding the real state of affairs from them. In fact they thought that Louis Riel must be about to pass through with an army sweeping everything before him, and that the days of the Whiteman were at last numbered in the Northwest. I am not using hyperbolical language, but stating real facts. The Indians were actually beginning to have visions of the return of the good old times when they would once more be able to replenish their larders with the succulent viands of favorite bison. Such were the feelings of the majority.[11]

The priest met the Indians on April 9 and tried to calm the excitement by telling them that the whites would prevail no matter how many bands joined the revolt and by "dwelling strongly on the fearful consequences that any trouble on their part would entail." The chiefs and headmen agreed with Father Scollen but "the young men held an ominous silence which made me feel very uneasy. However, the meeting broke up with the understanding that all hands should continue their work as usual."[12]

But unknown to Father Scollen, and apparently also unknown to the chiefs, the hands of the young warriors had already been busy. They had organized a war dance, to be attended by members of bands to the north, in preparation for joining Big Bear at Fort Pitt. At the dance, in Scollen's words, "these young braves worked themselves into the belief that they must do something for the

Fine Day first gained fame as the talented young war chief of the combined Battleford bands. He went on to become an outstanding chief and shaman and one of the most important individuals in preserving Cree history and culture. [Glenbow-Alberta Institute]

national cause and the best thing they could do was to rob & pillage."[13] On April 11, led by war chief Ringing Sky, warriors raided the nearby Hudson's Bay Company store and a farmhouse at Battle River Crossing. The warriors' action committed the Bears Hills bands. The next day all the bands formed a combined camp on a war footing.

James Mowat reached Calgary on April 9 and there he met Lieutenant Governor Dewdney. When the Edmonton courier explained the situation, Dewdney wrote a letter to Father Scollen to try to help him calm the situation. The Cree captured the messenger bearing Dewdney's letter as he crossed the Battle River but Father Scollen happened to meet the party and persuaded them to give up their hostage. Armed with Dewdney's letter and one from Edmonton trader John A. McDougall, whom the Indians respected, Father Scollen attended the war dance on April 12 and found himself not very welcome. The priest was not the only observer. Two half-breed emissaries of the Edmonton townspeople had arrived to see what was going on.

Father Scollen interrupted the dance in an attempt to persuade the Indians that it would be folly to go to war. The young warriors weren't about to listen to the priest. "The young rascals who had caused all this annoyance saw my object & kept up the war dance as a protest they would not listen. The whole of the people, men, women & children, were gathered around the dancing lodge. I tried several times to get a hearing, but all to no purpose. The drums rolled; the young scoundrels fired shots over my head, and shouts went forth of 'No surrender! Riel! Riel!'"[14] The two other Edmonton representatives described the scene for the Edmonton *Bulletin*. "The dance was going on when they arrived, and was a rather exciting affair. Between the drumming, yelling, and firing of guns the chances of a general massacre seemed excellent. The Indians were decked in the clothes and finery taken from the H. B. [Hudson's Bay] store and were having a huge time generally."[15]

But Father Scollen found a friend in Chief Bobtail. The priest persuaded the chief there was little support for the rebellion and the Indians' foolish actions would have disastrous repercussions. Bobtail "jumped & made a raid on the drums, & in two minutes scattered the crowd who were making such a noise." This gave Father Scollen the opportunity he needed. He read Dewdney's letter and delivered a two-hour harangue in which the passionate Irishman "poured at them all the spleen with which they had been filling my heart during the few previous days."[16] His speech had effect and the camp broke up. Later, Chief Ermineskin persuaded the looters to give back what remained of the Hudson's Bay Company booty.

But it was an uneasy peace at Bears Hills. Indian Agent S. B. Lucas, who had fled at the first whiff of trouble, reported to Dewdney: "As it now stands the Bears Hills Indians are afraid of the consequences of their actions and will not move until they are joined by Indians from Battleford, the Blackfeet or Stonies from Lake St. Ann's. Should they receive help from these sources they will be joined by most of the Indians in this District, except perhaps Peccan [Pakan] of White Fish Lake, who may remain quiet. I have no confidence in the promises made by Bears Hills band. Ermine Skin admits that he cannot even control his men."[17] With their own war camp broken up, some of the Bears Hills warriors went east to join Poundmaker or Big Bear.

Big Bear's Cree were still in the vicinity of Frog Lake for almost two weeks after the April 2 killings. They were too busy dancing and feasting on their unaccustomed abundance to consider going too far. On April 13, the atmosphere in the camp was shattered when a sick and semi-delirious old woman named She Wins announced she would turn into a wehtikow, a cannibal, if someone did not kill her. For the Cree, this was a very serious matter for, as Louis Goulet explained it:

The Indians believe that when a person is about to turn wendigo, he or she lets out a scream and anybody within earshot is paralyzed. You don't even have to hear it, because it's not the wendigo's fault if people don't hear! You just have to be close enough, that's all it takes. The wendigo's scream paralyzes people, and that's how he can eat a whole camp, even if it takes a month or two to swallow everybody! That's not the most serious part of the whole business, though. When a person shows wendigo symptoms, he must be killed before the change actually takes place because it's difficult to kill a full-fledged wendigo! They have hearts of ice and the power to rejoin parts of their body and come back to life, even after their head's been cut off and they've been hacked to pieces. The best way to get rid of them is to have a Catholic kill them or else load the gun with some kind of holy object.

When She Wins announced she was about to turn wehtikow, Big Bear's camp was terrified. It was obvious she had to be killed immediately but no-one relished the dangerous and distasteful job. Finally, the Indians chose three men to do the deed. Some of the prisoners in the camp, including Goulet, helped carry the old woman well away from the camp. She sat on the ground crosslegged and threatened to turn wehtikow as the three Indians stood around, Charlebois armed with a club, Bright Eyes with a rifle and Dressy Man with a sword. Then, according to Goulet's story, Charlebois took his club,

> went up to her very cautiously, placed a shawl over her face, stood so he could make a quick getaway, and wham! Struck flush on the temple, the old woman fell on her side, still and trembling in every limb. Bright Eyes put three bullets into her body. Dressy Man lifted away her shawl and cut off her head with one powerful stroke of the sabre. Then, clutching it by the braids, he tried to throw the head over the clump of willows, but the braids caught in the branches and the head stayed hanging there with its hideous face swinging three or four feet above the ground, striking blind terror into the Indians, who ran away as fast as they legs would take them, without risking so much as a backward glance.[18]

But the Indians couldn't risk the head re-uniting with the rest of the body so they later burned the remains.

At about the same time as they had to deal with the wehtikow, the Frog Lake Cree held a council to plan an attack on Fort Pitt. Big Bear made a speech in which he urged the warriors to let the small garrison and the civilians get away from the fort unmolested, a plan Bill Cameron and Jim Simpson took credit for suggesting. After Big Bear spoke, as Cameron recorded it,

> several Indians followed and supported our plan. One man thanked us for the suggestion. It would be much simpler to lure the police out of the fort by fair promises and then surround and kill them in the open than to attack them

under cover of the buildings. Wandering Spirit said they had not spared our lives thus far to have us dictate to them what they should do in time of war. Imasees [Ayimāsis] said Riel's orders were to kill the police. As for the Plains Cree, they meant to fight. They had men enough to capture and burn the fort and kill everyone in it. If the police went they would take with them their guns and ammunition, things the Indians most needed.[19]

The next morning, April 14, Cameron watched as Big Bear's warriors prepared to go to Fort Pitt. He and Simpson had refused an invitation to go along. The warriors had not pressed that point but had warned the two Hudson's Bay Company employees that if any Indians were killed in the attack on Fort Pitt, their lives might be taken in revenge.

The warriors, mounted, assembled at the lower end of the camp. They, as well as their ponies, were decked in all their finery. With their paint and feathers, their polished weapons, gaudy blankets, beaded leggings and moccasins, they made a picturesque panorama against the setting of green grass and delicate aspens, the distant hills, the glint of blue waters in the lakes below, and immediately behind, the white canvas lodges with their smoke-browned tops and crossed poles. They came riding slowly around the camp, their war-chant rising weirdly on the fresh spring air, their ponies prancing under their flashy trappings. They reached the far end again, broke into a gallop and with wild cries and a crash from their guns, clattered away in the direction of Fort Pitt.[20]

Inspector Francis Jeffrey Dickens, the commander at Fort Pitt, was unquestionably the least inspiring officer in the NWMP in 1885. Only the famous surname of the third son of author Charles Dickens had kept Francis in the police for this long. Dickens was short, deaf, alcoholic, and completely tactless in his dealings with Indians. His superiors found him appalling and his fitness reports are filled with phrases such as "totally unfit to be an officer in the Mounted Police."

After Francis, whom his father had nicknamed Chickenstalker, had tried medicine, business, and journalism as a young man and failed at all three, his father found him a commission in the Bengal Mounted Police. Francis returned to England when his father died and after he had drunk up his share of the estate, his sister got him a commission in the newly-formed NWMP in 1874 through the Governor General of Canada, Lord Dufferin, who was a family friend. The Mounted Police kept Francis at headquarters, where he could be watched, until 1881. But then there was such a desperate shortage of officers in the field that Dickens was put in charge of a small detachment at Blackfoot Crossing. In the space of six months, Dickens managed to antagonize the Blackfoot so thoroughly that he and his men were almost attacked on three separate occasions. After the last incident, Dickens was put under the watchful eye of Superintendent Crozier. When Crozier was given command of the Battleford district in 1883, Dickens went with him and was assigned to Fort Pitt.

As Wandering Spirit led his warriors away to do battle, Chickenstalker Dickens was busy making one of the biggest mistakes of his bumbling career. He decided to send Frog Lake blacksmith Henry Quinn, Constable Larry Loasby, and Corporal David Cowan out to find out where Big Bear's Indians were, despite Factor McLean's advice that that was a foolish thing to do. "I told the captain [Dickens] plainly that to send them out was simply to lessen the strength of the fort by having three men killed, and to increase the force of the Indians by three stand of arms. If they had been experienced men it would have been different. They were the rawest of our stables."[21]

About three o'clock that afternoon, the two hundred and fifty Cree warriors appeared on the low hill just north of Fort Pitt. Big Bear was managing to hold the warriors in check, but only barely. He had persuaded them to let the police evacuate the fort. Bearing Big Bear's proposals, a small group of Indians approached the fort. Factor McLean went outside to meet them and they talked for about an hour. Big Bear wanted blankets for himself and supplies, arms and ammunition for his warriors. He would let the police retreat unmolested but if they tried to hold the fort, he couldn't guarantee the safety of the civilians. The chiefs also demanded that Factor William McLean meet them in council at their camp.

The Indians told McLean they wouldn't even need to attack the fort. They had brought forty gallons of coal oil from Frog Lake, more than enough to set the small stockade and the buildings it contained ablaze. McLean promised to discuss their demands with Inspector Dickens and, if they did not attack the fort that night, he would meet the chiefs at eleven o'clock the next morning. Dickens was in a very difficult position, one that was well beyond his capabilities. He did not want to just give up the fort and all it contained to the rebels. On the other hand, he didn't have even resources enough to put out the fire the Indians threatened to start, let alone resist a frontal attack. If a retreat across or down the river were attempted, the fort boasted only one leaky scow that would hold neither the civilians nor all the police supplies. And Dickens could not rely on guarantees from those responsible for the Frog Lake killings that the fort's civilians would be safe if the police left. In the end, the police commander abdicated his responsibilities, leaving McLean to do what he thought best and the rest of the inhabitants to defend themselves as best they could.

As the anxious defenders manned loopholes cut in the stockade, the Indians drove the fort's cattle to their camp and spent the evening singing, dancing, and feasting. The next morning, Big Bear, pessimistic about his attempts to avoid bloodshed, didn't wait for the parley with McLean. With the help of Henry

Halpin, the Hudson's Bay Company clerk whom the Cree had taken along as a captive, the chief sent an anxious letter to his friend NWMP Sergeant John Martin.

> Since I first met you, long ago, we have always been good friends. That is the reason why I want to speak kindly to you: please get off from Fort Pitt as soon as you can. Tell your Captain [Dickens] that I remember him well, for since the Canadian government has had me to starve in this country he sometimes gave me food. I do not forget the last time I visited Pitt he gave me a good blanket. That is the reason that I want you all out without any bloodshed. We had a talk, I and my men, before we left camp at Frog Lake and thought the way we are doing now the best, that is to let you off if you would go. Try and get away before the afternoon, as the young men are all wild and hard to keep in hand.[22]

After breakfast on April 15, McLean and his interpreter walked out to a point about halfway between the fort and the hill behind which the Indians were camped. There they met Indian emissaries who told them to go to their camp. McLean was reluctant to get out of range of the fort's guns, but he had little choice and accompanied the Indians. In council, the chiefs presented McLean with "a long confused list of grievances in the usual Indian style" and then told him "that the time had now arrived when they were going to kill all the redcoats and clear all the white people out of the country. I argued with them as to the folly of the idea." The Hudson's Bay Company factor tried to persuade the Indians to return to their reserves, that the government would take care of them. But the time was past when the Indians would listen to that sort of talk. It was now they, not the government, who controlled the country. During McLean's discourse on how severely the government would punish them if they persisted in the rebellion, "Wandering Spirit arose and walked towards me, putting cartridges in his rifle and put his hand on my shoulder and said 'That will do. You have said enough. We do not want to hear anything about the Government and if you want to live do as I tell you. Don't be stubborn, that is the reason why I shot the agent.' "[23]

McLean was in trouble enough, but just then Dickens' three scouts returned. They had done such a poor job that in the twenty-four hours they had been out of the fort they had failed to discover any trace of the large, loud party of warriors. They had been as far as Frog Lake and had wondered why Big Bear's camp appeared so quiet, but had not attached any significance to that fact. As they returned to the vicinity of Fort Pitt, they discovered the tracks of the war party. A nervous Henry Quinn, as he later told Bill Cameron, got off his horse to examine the hoof-prints, proof, he told Corporal Cowan, of his contention that there were Indians up ahead. "I said the Indians were ahead of us. Well, they are. They came down the trail as as we went out along the river," Quinn said he told

Cowan. And the blacksmith Quinn thought he had proof. "Here's the track of a shod horse—my uncle's mare that Wandering Spirit took the day of the massacre. I put those shoes on myself. I know them." But Cowan thought the tracks were of men from Fort Pitt who had been out rounding up cattle. After all, at Big Bear's camp the lodges had still been standing.[24]

As the three scouts came over a hill just out of sight of the fort, they stumbled right into the camp where the warriors were negotiating with Factor McLean. They were too close to turn around and make a run for it. The Indian camp was just to their left and a heavily wooded area to their right. They had no choice but to try to gallop right past the Indians to the safety of the fort. "Soldiers! Soldiers!" the Indians shouted as they rushed for the trail to cut them off. The scouts ran safely through the hail of bullets before the Indians could get to the trail, but Cowan's horse suddenly stopped and bucked. Cowan jumped off and as he began to run, a bullet in his heart stopped him. With the Indians running behind him, Quinn abandoned his dash for the fort and instead pushed his horse into the woods and poplar thickets that bordered the river. Constable Loasby kept going, with Lone Man close behind. A bullet struck the policeman's leg but he kept riding. Another bullet felled his horse. As Loasby tumbled to the ground, Lone Man jumped on top of him but Loasby was up quickly and, as his comrades in the fort covered his escape, tried to run for the fort on his wounded leg. Lone Man raised himself on one knee, aimed his rifle, and shot Loasby in the back. Under the fusillade from the fort, Lone Man crawled up to his victim and turned him over. "I thought he was dead . . . or I would have finished him." Lone Man cut Loasby's revolver belt off and as he was crawling back to the Indian lines, the policeman got to his feet and staggered towards the fort. When he got close to the stockade, two men rushed out and carried him in.[25]

Back on the hill, Louison Mongrain, one of the leaders of the Frog Lake Cree, walked up to Cowan, who was lying on his back, still alive. Mongrain pointed his rifle at the policeman. Cowan raised his hands and said: "Don't brother, don't." Mongrain put two bullets in his head.[26] The Indians cut out Cowan's heart and nailed it to a tree, a mark of respect for a brave enemy. Slippery Henry Quinn had again come through a brush with the Indians without a scratch. He was wandering along the river bank, unable to expose himself to get to the fort and hemmed in by the Indian camp.

The skirmish with the scouts left Factor McLean and Chief Big Bear despairing of being able to lift the siege peaceably. The chief was particularly anxious that McLean get his large family out of danger. If he could persuade his wife and children to come to the Indian camp with at least some of the other civilians, Big Bear might be able to restrain his warriors long enough to let the police escape, the chief told McLean. The factor then wrote a long, despondent letter which was delivered to his wife inside the fort. "Now, in the excitement, they have made me prisoner and have made me swear by Almighty God that I

The drawing of Fort Pitt is the only highly accurate feature of this *Canadian Pictorial and Illustrated War News* sketch. It was titled "Heroic Defence of Fort Pitt by Inspector Dickens" but there was no real defence of the fort and long before he was forced to abandon his post, Dickens had abdicated all responsibility.

will stay with them. Alas, that I came into the camp at all, for God only knows how things will turn out now. They want you and the children to come into camp and it may be for the best that you should. If the police cannot get off the Indians are sure to attack tonight, they say, and will burn the fort. I am really at a loss what to suggest for the best."[27]

This time, Inspector Dickens and the police agreed to leave. Big Bear gave them two hours. The police gathered what little they could take and, carrying the wounded Loasby, went down to the river to launch their scow. Water poured in between the boards that had shrunk during the winter. High winds and a blinding snowstorm had come up and the swiftly-flowing river was choked with blocks of ice. Just as it seemed they would not get away from the shore before Big Bear's deadline, Anglican minister Charles Quinney galloped up to the Indian camp to plead for an extension. Big Bear gave them another hour. As soon as she knew the police were safely in the river on their way to the southern shore, Mrs. McLean led the youngest of her nine children out of the fort. Her two oldest daughters were already in the Indian camp, having earlier left the fort unescorted to find their father. The other white civilians followed them unmolested. The moment the hour was up, Big Bear relaxed the reins and the warriors ran to the fort.

James Simpson's stepson, Louis Patenaude, described to Bill Cameron the scene when the Indians reached the deserted Fort Pitt.

218

Forcing the doors of the H. B. [Hudson's Bay] stores, the Indians rushed in. Each seized the first thing he could put his hands on. It might be a cask of sugar, a chest of tea, a princely fur, a bolt of calico, a caddy of tobacco, a keg of nails—it was all one. Off he rushed, set it down outside and hurried back for more. When he returned his first prize was certain to be gone; another—a weaker brother—had appropriated it. A woman might get hold of a fine wool shawl, some buck fancy it for his wife and she would be forcibly dispossessed. It was bedlam and war for the spoils, Indian expletives mingling with blows and outcries. Tins of Crosse and Blackwell's Yarmouth Bloaters, jars of pickled walnuts and pate de foie gras, imported at great expense all the way from London, were slashed open with knives, sniffed at and flung on the ground. The police hospital stores were got at. The red men evidently believed all medicines in use by the police were 'comforts'; they drank them, until one old man nearly succumbed. Then they decided the enemy had tried to poison them. They hesitated to use the sacks of flour piled in tiers for the defence of the fort; the police, they thought, might have mixed strychnine with it.[28]

In the spring blizzard, Henry Quinn dug a hole in the riverbank about one and a half kilometres upstream for shelter for a few hours. In the darkness, he thought it would be safe to move to the fort and he walked up to the palisade and shouted for Sergeant Martin. "But the police had left. The Indians were in possession, however, and fired on me. I ran down towards the river chased by about 20 of them. They wanted to kill me." He hid in the riverbank and for a few moments eluded his pursuers. Then Cree Isidore Mondion, standing on the edge of the bank, looked down and saw a pair of legs sticking out. "Henry," he said, "come out." Quinn emerged just as Wandering Spirit ran up and levelled his rifle at him. But Mondion put himself between Quinn and the war chief and declared that Quinn was his prisoner and he intended to spare his life.[29]

On April 16, some of the whites were allowed to go back to Fort Pitt to retrieve some of their personal possessions. The looting was still going strong. William McLean and his teenage daughters salvaged the family Bible and a copy of *Robinson Crusoe*. Amelia McLean played the last tune on the family's organ, scaring the assembled Indians, who thought the machine was full of vengeful spirits. They chopped up the organ and burned the pieces. The Indians found Hudson's Bay Company clerk Stanley Simpson's spare glass eye and gave it to a one-eyed comrade. When the Indian announced he couldn't see out of his new eye, Simpson explained that a blue eye wouldn't work for a brown-eyed man.[30]

The next day, the Indians burned the fort and set off back to Frog Lake with their large entourage of white captives.

CHAPTER TWELVE

Standoff at Fish Creek

The two weeks between April 10 and April 24 were the high point of the campaign for General Middleton. Out of a military organization designed mainly for coping with labour unrest, he had managed to conjure into existence an army in the field thousands of kilometres from the population centres of central Canada. Perhaps it was not the most formidable fighting force but it far outnumbered and outgunned the rebels. Middleton thought that success would be a simple matter of marching. It is quite evident from his telegrams to Adolphe Caron, Minister of Militia and Defence, that in mid-April he thought it likely that Métis resistance would melt away at the mere sight of his soldiers. At worst there might be a minor skirmish before the rebels dispersed or surrendered. The Métis made no effort to attack or harass his forces as they organized at Qu'Appelle and began to march toward Batoche. Middleton understandably interpreted their inactivity as a sign of fear-induced paralysis.

Physical courage General Middleton possessed in abundance, even if he was rather too ready to assume its absence in others. Born into an Anglo-Irish military family, Middleton was educated at the Royal Military College, Sandhurst, and went into the British Army in 1842. Promotion was excruciatingly slow in that era of unchallenged British military superiority, and even an officer of proven skills and outstanding bravery could find himself from time to time on half pay. Middleton experienced involuntary retirement in the 1860s in spite of the fact that he had distinguished himself during the Indian Mutiny, being mentioned in dispatches four times and recommended twice for the Victoria Cross, which was normally awarded for acts of near-suicidal recklessness. Service in Canada had rescued him from temporary unemployment and while posted in Montreal he married Eugenie Marie Doucet. In 1874 he returned to England as Commandant of Sandhurst and remained in that comfortable job for a decade. When that appointment came to an end, however, Middleton was in an awkward predicament. As a Colonel, aged sixty, he could look forward only to immediate retirement on half pay.

Canada offered Middleton an alternative to spending his remaining years in genteel poverty. The Canadian government needed a replacement for the prickly Major General Luard. The appointment was not one that would appeal to ambitious and energetic younger officers and there were not many outstanding candidates for the position, but it had considerable attractions for Middle-

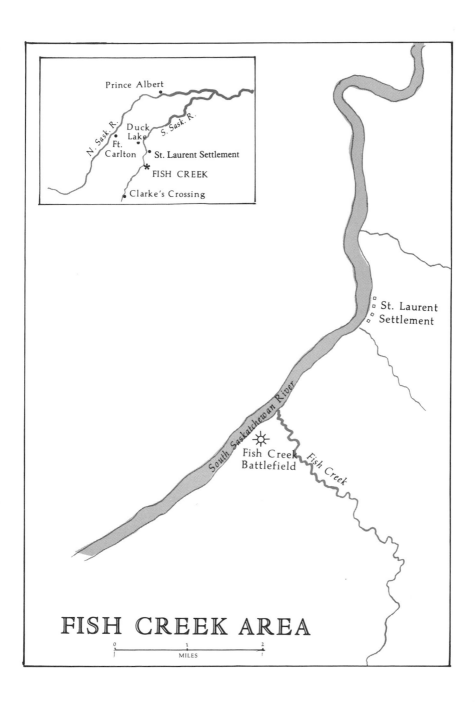

Prince Albert

N. Sask. R.

S. Sask. R.

Duck
Lake

Ft.
Carlton

St. Laurent Settlement

FISH CREEK

Clarke's Crossing

St. Laurent
Settlement

South Saskatchewan River

Fish Creek
Battlefield

Fish Creek

FISH CREEK AREA

0   1   2
MILES

General Fred Middleton, sketched by Capt. R.W. Rutherford inside Fort Battleford. Most artists portrayed the general as rather more portly, a reflection of the feelings of many Canadian militia officers who saw him as fat and pompous. [Glenbow-Alberta Institute]

ton. He would have the local rank of Major General, status in a colonial society that cherished all things British, and a job that was not particularly demanding. Middleton was well aware of the ramshackle structure of the Canadian military machine but, unlike Luard, his ambitions did not extend beyond applying a patch or two to stave off total collapse. His contempt for the fighting qualities of the Métis before the battle of Fish Creek was merely an extension of his real doubts about his own soldiers. He knew that the militia had little training and less experience and he worried that his green troops would panic and run under fire.

But if his assessment of the situation was correct, then real fighting would not be necessary. The mere appearance of strength would be sufficient to do the job. Lewis Redman Ord, the surveyor who published his account of the rebellion anonymously in 1886 as *Reminiscences of a Bungle*, loathed Middleton and usually overstated his condemnation of the general, but he caught his mood in the period before Fish Creek rather well. "He expected them [the Métis] to flee at the first sight of his Falstaffian figure; but alas for human expectations and vanity, the mighty and glorious name of Middleton familiar in our mouths as household words, known wherever the flag of Britain spreads its folds to the breeze, and used alike by Esquimaux and Maori to hush the restless infant, had not even been heard by these rude and ignorant sons of the plains."[1]

Even without resistance from the rebels, marching to the centre of resistance was not exactly a pleasant stroll through the countryside for the troops, mostly because of the weather and their own inexperience. They departed from Qu'Appelle early in the morning of April 6 with a good deal of dash and enthusiasm. French's Scouts were in front. Harold Rusden, a trooper in the unit, recorded the moment.

> Presently the General's aide came galloping up with orders to advance; then our Captain gave the order, "Troop will advance at a walk, march," and our little troop moved off—the first to leave Qu'Appelle, the last to come back. No sooner over the bridge than Captain Jack yelled, "Double," and away he went, the troops following helter skelter through mud and half-melted snow, splashing and throwing the mud everywhere. Up the bank of the Qu'Appelle; out of the valley, "Halt," then extending 100 yards apart covering the advance and flanks of the advancing troops.[2]

As the day wore on the weather grew steadily colder and it began to snow heavily. Boots and clothing, soaked from contact with the wet ground, froze, and the morning's enthusiasm dissolved. Camp was made early that day after a march of only twelve miles, and the troops spent a frigid night shivering in their tents, except of course for those on sentry duty, who shivered in their frozen boots, and not entirely from the cold. Throughout the night every bush in sight of the camp was mistaken for an enemy and challenged at least once, although no shots were fired. This was an experience that almost every soldier who did sentry duty during the rebellion was to encounter. Some were so embarrassed by the

The 10th Royal Grenadiers on their way to Clarke's Crossing. Most of the troops travelled by oxcart and on foot from the railway to the scene of the fighting. [Glenbow-Alberta Institute]

experience that they went out and chopped down the offending bushes in the morning.

The next day the march through the Touchwood Hills continued but on April 8 there was a halt while the column waited for "A" Battery to join and for the supply wagons to bring up additional food for men and horses. At the end of the following day's march, the Infantry School contingent arrived in camp. On April 10 the trail descended onto a flat and marshy glacial lake bed known as the Salt Plains. Mud and water were often up to the men's knees and most found this the dreariest part of the trip. The weather alternated between thawing and freezing and the troops often bedded down cold and wet. Wood for fires was in short supply, leaving the men only cold corned beef and biscuit to eat.

On April 13 the troops reached the telegraph station at Humboldt, and although both trail and weather had improved significantly, the men were tired and ready for a rest. Private Robert Allan of the 90th Winnipeg Rifles wrote, "My legs were never so stiff and sore in my life before. When I lay down for a few minutes I could hardly move when I got up."[3] The supply column was lagging behind once again and word had arrived that the 10th Royal Grenadiers were only a day or so back on the trail. For all these reasons General Middleton decided on another pause. During a two-day halt at Humboldt, Boulton's Scouts joined the little army. Boulton's Scouts were raised in Manitoba and commanded by Major C. A. Boulton, whom Riel had condemned to death and then reprieved in 1870. The day after movement resumed again the Grenadiers caught up with the troops.

Despite these additions, which brought his total strength to about nine hundred men, Middleton made a small but significant shift in his plans at this point. Instead of making directly for Batoche as he had originally intended, the column marched for Clarke's Crossing, fifty kilometres to the south. After the column left Humboldt, the troops noticed rebel scouts for the first time. Reports from NWMP Commissioner Irvine at Prince Albert were gloomy, and deserters from Riel's camp were telling wildly exaggerated tales of Métis strength. A halt to establish a firm base on the river before confronting the rebels seemed prudent. Although the supply column was functioning reasonably well, fodder was in short supply, a problem that might be solved if the steamboats could get down the river. The river remained too low and after nearly a week of waiting at Clarke's Crossing, Middleton's patience came to an end and he marched on Batoche.

In the weeks after Duck Lake, Middleton was not the only observer who failed to understand Métis inactivity. Father André, bitter opponent of the rebellion that he was, could not restrain himself from wondering frequently in his diary why the Métis were throwing away opportunities to attack.

After the defeat at Duck Lake, nothing would have been easier than for Riel to have descended upon Prince Albert which was defenceless—we could only

The first of Middleton's column reaches Clarke's Crossing. The general used this point where the telegraph line crossed the South Saskatchewan River as his base for the advance on Batoche. [Winnipeg *Sun*, Rebellion Number, 1885]

have opposed him with thirty well armed men—and the terror that this defeat spread was so great that he would only have had to appear for us to surrender without resistance. I truly believe that it would have required nothing more than to come to Prince Albert while the troops were shut up in Carlton, terrorized by the defeat they had sustained. Possession of Prince Albert would have won for them immense quantities of provisions and furnished them with arms and ammunition of which they have such a pressing need, and further, they would have had an immense assortment of merchandise that would have been a powerful bait for the Indians. The fame carried by this brilliant success would have brought all the Indians into the uprising and the Métis dispersed throughout the North-West would have been eager to join and the government of Canada, disorganized as it is in this region, would have had on its hands an insurrection difficult to suppress.[4]

Philippe Garnot, the French Canadian secretary of the Métis council, later wrote, "If they had followed up the advantages gained in the little battle of Duck Lake, the Rebellion, as they have named the affair, would not be over yet and could have lasted for ten or twelve years, and the ending, I believe, would have been very different."[5]

Since 1885 the most publicized critic of the failure to act has been Gabriel Dumont. In an account dictated in December 1888, Dumont claimed that Riel prevented him from taking the offensive against the advancing Canadian army.[6] He spoke rather vaguely of plans to attack Middleton soon after he left Qu'Appelle and even of blowing up the railway. Every historian who has written about the rebellion since has accepted Dumont's account at face value. The defensive stance of the Métis has been explained as the result of the hard-nosed military leader, Dumont, who knew what needed to be done and was eager to do it, being restrained by the pious and other-worldly Riel.

Examined more closely, it becomes apparent that this explanation is at best a gross oversimplification of the situation. Consider the situation of the Métis after Duck Lake and the fall of Fort Carlton. If they were to consolidate their position and have some chance of resisting the inevitable military response of the Canadian government, they must have weapons and food supplies. The obvious and only place to obtain those essentials was at Prince Albert. The town was defended only by the demoralized survivors of Duck Lake, huddled behind an improvised stockade of cordwood in the river valley. The position was if anything weaker than that of either Fort Carlton or Fort Pitt, which were notoriously indefensible. The terrified inhabitants of Prince Albert had no illusions about the weakness of their position and hesitated at first even to send out scouting parties because they expected immediate attack. But, to their astonishment, no attack came. The only rebels who came within gunshot of Prince Albert were a few deserters from Riel's camp seeking refuge. Instead of attacking Prince Albert, the Métis council had decided, on a motion by none other than Gabriel Dumont, to move back from Duck Lake to Batoche and to prepare to defend themselves there.[7]

In addition to supervising the construction of a defensive system of trenches and rifle pits around Batoche, Dumont seems to have been preoccupied with attempts to obtain support from the Indians. Letters and messengers went out in all directions from the Métis headquarters. The appeals for aid were largely fruitless. The Indians considered that each group should confine its efforts to its own territory. Riel was immersed in the details of his new religion, much to the irritation of council secretary Garnot. "The council remained occupied with religious matters and stayed inactive, although the enemy was gaining strength on all sides of us. It was truly disgusting to see a man of Riel's capacity and influence use that influence to deceive superstitious and ignorant people. He succeeded in making them believe he was a prophet and even had council pass a resolution recognizing him as a prophet."[8]

Garnot's complaint gives us some insight into the peculiar nature of the provisional government. It operated through consensus which was often achieved only after lengthy and occasionally bitter debate. Votes were usually unanimous when they were finally taken and it is rare to find more than one dissenting vote recorded in the minutes. Group decision-making covered everything from basic strategic matters to instructions for the cooks. On the day that General Middleton's force arrived at Clarke's Crossing, a mere two day's march away, the council passed numerous resolutions concerning the ownership of individual cows, issued ferry passes, and solemnly admonished some of its own members for absenteeism.[9] The council was clearly revelling in the intoxicating feeling common to the early stages of most revolutionary regimes that the popular will can be controlled and molded in the most minute detail to achieve the ends of the revolution. What is entirely absent from the deliberations of the council is any suggestion by Dumont or anyone else that attacks should be launched on the government forces which were gathering ominously in the south.

But there was a deeper reason than the concerns of the moment for concentrating on preparing to defend Batoche at the expense of carrying the war to the enemy. That reason lay in the Métis military experience going back almost to the beginning of the century. The identity of the Métis as a separate people had been forged to an important degree by successful battles which were celebrated in their songs and folk memory. Those battles shared a common feature: they were all defensive. At Seven Oaks in 1816 the Métis believed they were asserting their ancestral rights against interlopers. At Grand Coteau in 1857 they administered a crushing defeat to the Sioux when the Sioux mounted an all-out attack against the Métis buffalo hunt. During these annual hunts the Métis spent months on the open prairie in territory the Sioux considered to be theirs. To preserve themselves against their more numerous enemy, the Métis had to be tactical innovators. Their innovation was to fight from rifle pits dug in a circle around the camp where the women, children, and horses were located. Shooting from these entrenchments against mounted attackers made maximum use of the range and hitting power of the gun. Fighting from rifle pits gave the Métis an enormous advantage over the Indians, whose tactics were better adapted to the bow and arrow. In the crisis of 1885 the natural reaction of the Métis was to do what had worked in the past: dig in and wait.

The moves that seemed so obvious to all observers from Father André to Sir Sandford Fleming—attacking Prince Albert and harassing Middleton's lines of communication—were obvious only when filtered through European concepts of the nature and purpose of war. For Canadians in the late nineteenth century these concepts were so thoroughly assimilated that they were almost unconscious. They were nevertheless present and highly sophisticated as the result of centuries of writing and thinking on the subject. It was taken for granted that the aim in warfare was to attack and destroy the enemy's army as quickly as possible and as far away from your own territory as could be arranged. This idea was quite foreign to the experience of the Métis, who had always done best when they waited for the enemy to come to them.

The Métis also lacked the Indian attitude to war, which might have made them more aggressive. Carrying the fight to the enemy's camp was an important part of Indian warfare, although for different reasons than in the European case. Indians made war for reasons of individual status rather than for reasons of state. A warrior's standing could only be enhanced by demonstrations of courage and skill performed in the course of raids on traditional foe. But the Métis were careful to distinguish between their own brand of fighting and that of the

Indians. Their defensive tactics had proven devastatingly successful in encounters with the Indians in the past and the Métis were very conscious of that fact. When Dumont suggested ambushing the Mounted Police on their retreat from Fort Carlton to Prince Albert, Riel rejected it on the grounds that this was the way Indians fought. There were no further arguments.

In the month after Duck Lake there was a dispute between Riel and Dumont over strategy but it was very much more limited than historians have painted it. Dumont wanted to make a stand at the outer edge of the Métis settlement while Riel favoured concentrating the meagre rebel resources on Batoche. This difference of opinion, unlike the larger one, is not well documented but makes perfect sense in the light of Métis experience. The place where Dumont successfully persuaded his followers to make a stand was known to the Métis as Tourond's Coulee. (Middleton's soldiers, unaware of its name, would call it Fish Creek.) The farm of the Tourond family on which the coulee was located was the farthest one south in the South Branch settlement. For the Métis, this was the boundary of their community, which an invader would approach at his peril. The incident which set off the 1869 resistance in which the surveyors were turned back from André Nault's farm is an exact parallel. As Middleton was about to discover, the fighting qualities of the Métis when defending their home territory were formidable.

The few days spent at Clarke's Crossing had removed whatever doubts had caused Middleton to turn aside from the direct route to Batoche.[10] His chief of staff, the dashing young Lord Melgund (who years later, as the Earl of Minto, would be Governor General of Canada), captured three Sioux scouts on April 18. The Indians claimed they had been coerced into acting on the rebel side and estimated Riel's numbers at only two hundred and fifty. This information fitted Middleton's preconceptions perfectly and he now began to fear that the rebels would refuse to put up even a token resistance. He decided therefore to split his force into two more or less equal parts, one for each side of the river, to enhance the chances of encountering the enemy. To divide one's force was contrary to one of the most fundamental tactical doctrines and Middleton did it over protests from Melgund, but he believed that either half of his army would be more than adequate. The cable ferry from Clarke's Crossing would be taken along to transfer the troops over when and if contact was made. The left bank column, consisting of the Grenadiers, French's Scouts, and the Winnipeg Field Battery, was put under the command of Lieutenant Colonel Charles Montizambert with Melgund as his chief of staff. On April 23 the split force marched out of Clarke's Crossing and at the end of the day made camp a few kilometres short of Tourond's Coulee.

That day there was intense debate in the Métis council at Batoche. The council was well aware of Middleton's intentions.[11] Their scouts, including one who was a teamster with the government force, reported regularly and if that was

Lord Melgund with French's scouts capturing Indian scouts, including Chief White Cap's son Blackbird, before the battle of Fish Creek. This sketch by Capt. H. de H. Haig, of the British Royal Engineers and attached to Middleton's column, first appeared in the *Illustrated London News* on May 23, 1885. [Glenbow-Alberta Institute]

not enough, they had up-to-date newspapers obtained from Qu'Appelle in which Middleton announced his plans in detail. Even so the argument over just where to meet the enemy continued until two o'clock, when a scout rushed into camp to announce that the soldiers were on the march. This news tipped the balance in favour of Dumont and about two hundred men set off for the south under his leadership, leaving only a handful to guard Batoche. They stopped to eat at the farm of Roger Goulet near Tourond's Coulee. Here Riel tried to reopen the question of where to fight, claiming that he had had a vision which indicated that the stand should be made at Batoche. At about eight o'clock, while the discussion was going on, a messenger rode in from Batoche with a report, which later proved false, that the Mounted Police were advancing from Prince Albert. Most of the men wanted to return but Dumont allotted only fifty to Riel for the trip back and pressed on with the rest. The plan seems to have been to launch an attack on Middleton's camp under cover of darkness. As it turned out, Dumont and his men were unable to find the camp until dawn was beginning to break. Dumont wisely concluded that surprise would now be impossible and pulled his men back to the coulee where they could have breakfast and get ready to fight.[12]

The position the rebels occupied was small in extent but quite complex. The stream, which is the only sizeable tributary between Clarke's Crossing and Prince Albert, had cut its way below the prairie level more or less at right angles to the Saskatchewan. About five hundred metres short of the main river the stream makes an abrupt ninety-degree bend to the right, straightens out for a short distance, then bends to the left before resuming its course to the river. This creates a wide spot in the ravine bottom at this point and the trail to Batoche, which in 1885 followed the bank of the Saskatchewan quite close to the river, swung inland to find an easier crossing of the ravine and the stream. The rectangle created by the meander of the stream was choked with dense willow brush and effectively divided the scene of battle into an upper and a lower area with the stream itself as the only link between them. Dumont stationed the bulk of his force in the upper position, where the trail crossed the ravine. A smaller group consisting mainly of Sioux and Cree allies were sent to the lower part of the ravine to prevent the attackers from crossing there. As the trail approached the ravine from the south it passed through open fields for the most part, but on both sides of the road there were isolated outlying poplar bluffs.

Dumont's fighting spirit was thoroughly aroused by the time he had made his dispositions, so much so that he could not wait for the enemy to move. About four o'clock he and Napoleon Nault rode to Middleton's camp and tried to attract the attention of some of the outlying sentries in the hope of luring them into an ambush. There is no indication from the government side that the two Métis were noticed. Dumont then went back to the coulee and had breakfast with his men. About seven o'clock scouts reported that Middleton was breaking camp and advancing. Dumont took twenty horsemen and waited in one of the poplar bluffs between the trail and the river. His plan was to wait until the advance guard had made its way past his position and down into the coulee. He would then attack it from the rear. The still-leafless poplars did not provide sufficient cover, however, and one of Boulton's Scouts spotted the horsemen waiting among the trees. The man turned and fled and Dumont spurred after him, intending, as he said later, to club him from the saddle to avoid wasting ammunition. He could not catch up and fired two shots at the retreating scout without hitting him. Dumont's men immediately opened fire, wounding two of Boulton's Scouts and forcing the others out of their saddles to the comparative safety of the ground. The battle of Fish Creek had begun.

As the 90th Rifles advanced, the Métis opened up a brisk fire but soon slowed down as they realized the battle was going to continue for some time. Ammunition was always short on the rebel side, some of the Métis soldiers having started the battle with only twenty rounds of ammunition. After the initial flurry they fired only when they could see a promising target. Often the less experienced gave their ammunition to those who were acknowledged to be better shots.[13] The Métis and Indians down in the ravine were not in much danger of being hit in spite of the tremendous volume of fire from Middleton's troops. Branches rained down constantly on the heads of the rebels and many small trees were completely severed by the storm of bullets.[14] The artillery, which should have given the government troops the advantage over opponents firing from cover, experienced great difficulties at Fish Creek. After firing off the few rounds of case shot available for ready use, the gunners had to go through the cumbersome process of filling shrapnel shells with powder and cutting fuses. The screwdriver used to open the powder barrels could not be found in the confusion and even a funnel to pour in the powder had to be improvised.[15]

Once these difficulties had been overcome, the nine-pounders opened fire at the only obvious targets, the farm buildings on the opposite side of the ravine. The noise of the artillery shells exploding and the destruction of the buildings was sufficiently frightening to cause substantial numbers of Dumont's men to desert, especially from the group in the lower part of the ravine closest to the river. Those who stayed quickly discovered that the artillery, although noisy, posed no greater threat than the rifle bullets, which went harmlessly overhead. The guns' trajectory was too flat to drop their shells into the ravine. In desperation the gunners tried pushing their weapons to the edge of the coulee so they could be pointed down at the enemy. This manoeuvre silhouetted them against the sky, making them ideal targets and resulting in heavy casualties. The effort was soon abandoned. Later in the day Middleton's troops managed to cross the lower part of the ravine and were able to position a gun on the other side so that it could fire up the axis of the ravine. This too proved a failure because the fuses for the shells could not be cut short enough to allow them to explode in the Métis' position.

Dumont spent the early part of the battle doing what he did best—encouraging his men by the example of his own fearlessness. He moved back and forth between his two groups of soldiers attempting to prevent desertions. Within the first hour of the battle he realized that there was a serious danger that Middleton would send a detachment inland and outflank the Métis position, so he took a few men, moved up the ravine, and set fire to the prairie to the east of the government position, hoping that the flames would spread toward the troops and panic them. But the soldiers were able to put out the fire, aided by the rain which began about ten o'clock and continued for the rest of the day. Dumont's movements over the next few hours are mysterious. He seems to have worked his way back to the north side of the coulee in an effort to rejoin the main body of his men. In his report to the Métis council the following day he said that he found his soldiers surrounded and could not get through to them.[16]

After some skirmishing with the troops who were protecting the gun that had been positioned on the Métis side of the ravine, Dumont headed off in the direction of Batoche. He soon encountered his brother Edouard at the head of a group of fifty or sixty men on their way from Batoche to the scene of the fighting. An argument ensued between Gabriel, who wanted to wait until nightfall to go to the rescue of the men trapped in the coulee, and Edouard, who wanted to go immediately. Gabriel was finally persuaded by the words of an Indian named Yellow Blanket, who said: "Uncle, when one wants to go and rescue his friends,

The battle of Fish Creek, behind the Métis defences in the coulee. [*The Montreal Daily Star*, 1885]

he does not wait for the next day."[17] The Métis rescue party arrived at the coulee just as Middleton's men were withdrawing. The Métis naturally believed that their arrival had driven off the enemy but it seems clear that the order to pull back had been given before the Métis reinforcements arrived.

The Métis in the upper part of the ravine had spent a long, exhausting day without any food. They sang the old songs of Pierre Falcon to keep up their spirits when they believed themselves to be cut off and they smoked their pipes to stave off hunger pangs. In the intervals between assaults on their position they prayed, led by Maxime Lépine, who had brought along a crucifix. The Métis had abandoned all offensive movements by noon and only fired to repel attacks on their position. They knew they were virtually surrounded and believed also that most of the others who had begun the battle with them were dead or captured. The best they expected was to be able to hold out until nightfall and make their way to freedom under cover of darkness. Late in the afternoon Middleton seems to have suspected the weakness of the Métis position and sent his interpreter, Tom Hourie, to try to assess the situation. Hourie got close enough to start a conversation with the Métis in the ravine but they cut him off abruptly when they realized he was trying to discover how many were left and to induce them to surrender.[18]

Those in the ravine were astonished when the troops opposing them began to withdraw as evening approached. They welcomed those who had come to rescue them with joy and relief, not unmixed with resentment against Gabriel Dumont, who they believed had abandoned them to their fate. Their mood is nicely illustrated in a story Isidore Dumas told. Dumas and Gilbert Breland, after leaving the scene of the battle, did not go directly back to Batoche with the

232

others but spent the night at the Dumas farm. On their way into Batoche the next morning they encountered Riel and Dumont. When they caught sight of them, Breland loaded his gun and, according to Dumas, the following exchange took place: "Gabriel addresses him: 'Why didn't you come last night?' G. Breland, pointing his gun in the direction of his chest, answers: 'And you, why did you run away?'"[19] Riel quickly intervened and the ugly moment passed. It was difficult to sustain bad feelings with the realization that a substantial victory had been won at the cost of only four killed on the rebel side.

There was little such satisfaction on the other side. The troops had started off in the morning in high spirits which matched the sunny April skies. Paymaster Sergeant Walter Nursey of the 90th Winnipeg Rifles reported in a letter to his wife that nearly the entire battalion was whistling as they marched (singing being forbidden) and bets were being offered on all sides "that the troops would return to Winnipeg without discharging a rifle save peradventure at a gopher or a goose."[20] There were not many takers. When the bullets did start flying, there was some initial reluctance on the part of the troops to move forward. The Métis could hear the officers urging their men on, "with many Goddamns." The example of their officers and of the regulars of the Artillery and the Infantry School soon brought them around. Middleton considered it particularly important that he set an example by ignoring enemy fire. He had his fur hat removed by a bullet and both his aides were wounded standing beside him but he remained calmly in control of himself and the battle. At the other end of the scale, the youngest soldier present, Bugler Billy Buchanan, aged fifteen, of the 90th Winnipeg Rifles, one of several boys who lied about their ages in order to be taken along, also served as an example of coolness under fire, cheerfully carrying ammunition to the troops in the front line.

The half of Middleton's force on the left bank of the river broke camp somewhat later than the other group. They were waiting for supplies to arrive from upriver. When the noise of firing was heard, Trooper Harold Rusden of French's Scouts was sent forward to investigate. He quickly discovered that a full-scale action was under way.

> I immediately dashed back to camp to give the news to Lord Melgund, but on the way nearly came to grief. I was carrying a Snider rifle and being both long and heavy it was very much in the way galloping through the timber. While passing between some trees the great cannon of a thing swung, caught a branch, swung round off the pommel and caught me a crack on the leg that nearly broke it, so I pitched the thing off and continued more comfortably without it.[21]

By the time Rusden returned with his report, the troops were ready to move and marched rapidly downstream to a point opposite the fighting. Here makeshift oars had to be fashioned to row the ferry scow across the river so that the cable could be attached and the ferry put into operation. All this took until noon. The artillery was shipped over first, followed by the Grenadiers. By three o'clock the new arrivals were in place, eager to try their hand at storming the remaining rebel position. To their chagrin, Middleton refused to let them attack. Middleton had already seen how the dense bush in the ravine prevented a successful charge. Casualties had been heavy and another attack would certainly have meant many more dead and wounded.

About four hundred men on the government side were actually engaged in the fighting and of those, fifty, one in eight, were casualties. Ten died. Proportionately, "A" Battery with fourteen casualties out of 110 men suffered the most heavily, although the 90th Winnipeg Rifles had more killed and wounded in total. It was assumed at first that the rebels had suffered comparable losses; many dead horses were found in the ravine after the battle and Middleton assumed that each horse represented an enemy casualty. For this reason and because the rebels abandoned their position at the end of the day, Middleton claimed a victory. Most of the journalists present loyally followed his example or simply evaded the issue and wrote long accounts describing the bravery of the troops and the fierce resistance of the strongly-entrenched enemy. The trenches and rifle pits so widely reported at Fish Creek were a collective illusion. The rebels had neither the time nor the tools to dig pits and trenches, but the story helped account for the inability of the militia to take the position. The Winnipeg *Times*, alone among Canadian newspapers, accurately assessed the battle. "A DEFEAT" ran its headline, "Little Doubt that Yesterday's Battle was a Reverse for Middleton."[22] The columns of the paper were bordered with heavy black lines.

Although he publicly denied it, Middleton's actions reveal that he, too, believed his first encounter with the Métis had been a defeat. From ebullient optimism, his mood switched abruptly to cautious pessimism. More troops and supplies were ordered out and from this point on in the campaign, no moves would be made without the most elaborate preparations.

More bad news followed quickly on the heels of Fish Creek. On April 26 emissaries from Big Bear's band arrived at Lac La Biche, north of Edmonton. They announced that Riel and Big Bear wanted the local Cree and Métis to take over the Hudson's Bay Company post. The Oblate priest at Lac La Biche, Father Henri Faraud, believed that the local people would have done nothing had they not been intimidated by the messengers. Once the looting began, however, they participated enthusiastically.

Men, women and children poured into the store, and into the house. In less than a quarter of an hour there wasn't a pin, a bit of merchandise, comestible of any sort, or fur left—everything had disappeared. Then, like all revolutionaries, they broke the windows, the doors, the tables, the window frames were chopped up with axes, books of every sort were torn into a thousand pieces and blown away by the wind; the women were having fun tearing lengths of cloth and dividing among themselves.[23]

The same day, farther to the east, a potentially more serious raid occurred. Green Lake, a hundred and fifty kilometres northeast of Battleford, was a major depot and trans-shipment point for the Hudson's Bay Company. Almost all the goods necessary to supply the posts of the Athabaska and Mackenzie districts, a territory stretching all the way to the Arctic Ocean, went through Green Lake. In April 1885 the Green Lake depot bulged with nearly a hundred thousand kilograms of supplies waiting for the spring breakup to go north. Included among the goods were two hundred guns and large quantities of ammunition. Lawrence Clarke tried to convince Commissioner Irvine to send a contingent from Prince Albert to protect the stores. Irvine, desperately worried about the possibility of an attack on the town, refused. Clarke organized a party of twenty Hudson's Bay Company employees, but they were not allowed to take any government guns or ammunition with them.

By the time the reinforcements were sent to Green Lake, it was too late. The Indians had already been there. Thanks to the energy and foresight of James Sinclair, the Hudson's Bay Company man in charge at Green Lake, the raiders got relatively little of value. On April 15 an Oblate priest had brought word of the Duck Lake fight. Sinclair immediately began emptying the warehouse and caching the contents at various places along the banks of the Beaver River. When the Indians, apparently a mixed group of Plains and Woods Cree, arrived on April 26, Sinclair pacified them with food from his remaining stocks. He claimed not to have any arms or ammunition and they left without troubling the settlement further.[24]

No one was killed or injured in the Lac La Biche and Green Lake raids, and in retrospect they seem rather minor and isolated incidents. But coming as they did so soon after the setback at Fish Creek, they appeared much more serious than they were. It looked like the rebellion was spreading rapidly and the first real effort to stop it had failed.

CHAPTER THIRTEEN

Cutknife: Otter's Reprieve

William Dillon Otter was an extreme rarity for his day, a professional soldier who had never served outside Canada. Professional soldiers of any kind were an almost invisible occupational group because of the small size of the permanent force. Chances of joining this select company were best if one happened to be British. Next best was to be a Canadian who had served in the British army. Since the only Canadian military force before the 1880s was the volunteer militia, a Canadian professional soldier was almost a contradiction in terms. Otter achieved the nearly-impossible by a combination of organizational skill, hard work, and intense desire. From the moment he enlisted as a private in the Queen's Own Rifles, the military was the centre of his life, whatever he might have had to do to make a living. As he put it himself in later years: "On the first day of my enrolment in this corps, I became imbued with an ardent desire and love for the order, system and discipline pertaining to and necessary in a military organization and as I advanced in experience, rank and service, the advantages of such grew on me."[1]

Otter needed every ounce of enthusiasm because he had few of the advantages that normally accompanied promotion in the militia. His family was neither wealthy nor politically influential, he had not attended university, and he was not a successful businessman or a rising young professional. His father, a clerk for the Canada Company, obtained a clerkship for his son after he left school. It was a steady but poorly-paid job offering no prospect for advancement. Perhaps because of the stultifying nature of his employment, Otter excelled in the militia. He took every available course and rose rapidly through the ranks, becoming a lieutenant in 1864 and adjutant of the battalion the following year at the age of twenty-one. In June 1866, Otter saw his first fighting at the Battle of Ridgeway, when the Queen's Own was called out to meet a Fenian invasion from the United States. Ridgeway turned out to be a near disaster. Inexperience and confusion on the part of the command resulted in the Queen's Own fleeing in panic from the battlefield. The rout burned in Otter's memory for the rest of his life.

Although Otter was painfully embarrassed by the flight of the Queen's Own at Ridgeway, it had few serious consequences. The Fenians were disorganized and pulled out the following day without attempting to follow up. On their return to Toronto, the battalion were greeted as heroes. Also on the positive side, Otter had discovered that flying bullets did not bother him. During the next

William Dillon Otter, one of
the first Canadian
professional soldiers.
[Montreal *Witness*, 1885]

decade and a half, Otter rose to the command of the Queen's Own, in the process making it into the most successful and best-trained unit in the country. In 1883, when the Infantry School opened in Toronto, Otter, who had been badgering the government for permanent military employment for several years, was given command with the rank of lieutenant colonel. The rebellion offered Otter the chance to put his years of peacetime soldiering into practice. Better still, it might bring an opportunity to wipe the shame of Ridgeway from the Queen's Own record.

On April 11, Otter got just what he wanted: a separate command. The panicky telegrams the residents of Battleford had been firing off to their political friends in the East, backed by numerous newspaper editorials demanding that the besieged settlers be rescued at once, had worked. One from *Saskatchewan Herald* editor P. G. Laurie to the Toronto *Mail* was more understated than many. "Country north of here burned for twenty miles along river by predatory bands and signal fires all around at night. Every house on north side raided & all cattle and horses driven off while for want of reinforcements Col. Morris unable to interfere.... Murderers of half a hundred men & women and destroyers of hundreds of homesteads Cannot be further pampered. Col. Morris has done everything possible to provide for safety & comfort but long waiting for help is moving them."[2]

Under the pressure, Middleton was forced to abandon his plan to lead one grand sweep through the rebel country. A separate column would have to be sent to Battleford. Middleton ordered Otter to get to Battleford as quick as possible. If the steamers are ready at Swift Current ferry within two days and can transport you, go by them to Clarks Crossing and proceed to Battleford using great caution especially on right flank and wait there. On arriving at Clarkes Crossing try and communicate with me to the right but go on if no chance of steamers starting by that time or [if they] cannot take your transport start at once by land. I have put Herchmer under your orders and you will find him invaluable. I have telegraphed for transport etc. Do not fear responsibility to carry out these directions.[3]

Otter would take those orders to mean that he had *carte blanche* in the method of relieving Battleford and in what to do when he reached the town. That was not what Middleton had intended, but his orders to Otter were typically vague. Middleton could claim credit if everything went well and avoid responsibility if anything went wrong.

Otter arrived at Swift Current early in the morning of April 12 with about fifty men of the Ottawa corps and a hundred artillerymen. The artillery had two nine-pounder field rifles and two Gatling guns. At Swift Current they met the two hundred and seventy men of the Queen's Own Rifles, fifty of the Toronto Infantry School and about fifty NWMP under Superintendent William Herchmer. The troops crowded around as Arthur "Gatling" Howard proudly demonstrated his weapons. "These curious implements of destruction we inspect with interest, and their trial is watched eagerly. A few rounds are fired at some duck on a distant pond—no execution is done apparently, but the rapidity of fire shows us how very deadly a weapon of this kind might be on proper occasions. We want now to see one tried on the Indians; from what we hear they seem to have definitely risen and we shall probably have some hard work before they are quieted again," Dick Cassels of the Queen's Own Rifles recorded.[4]

Early on the morning of April 14, the troops began the easy, forty-kilometre march to Saskatchewan Crossing, due north of Swift Current, which they reached that evening. Dick Cassels was not impressed with the countryside. "From Swift Current to the river we pass through a miserable dry sandy, literally, desert country, not a tree or bush to be seen: here there are a few withered poplar trees, but nothing to justify the oft heard appellation of 'well wooded' applied to the banks enclosing the 'fertile' valley of the Saskatchewan."[5]

It quickly became obvious that the river route would not do. The river was low, some of the steamers that were supposed to arrive from Medicine Hat were known to be stuck on sand bars, and others hadn't been heard from at all. Otter decided to make a dash straight north to Battleford, a distance of two hundred and twenty kilometres. Hampered by gale-force winds, the troops took more than three days to get themselves and their equipment ferried across the river but on April 18 they finally began their march, "and a disagreeable march it is: damp, dull, miserable day and the prairie a sea of mud. We see no vegetation at all and the country seems very wretched," Cassels wrote.[6]

Teamsters crossing the South Saskatchewan at Clarke's Crossing. The river proved hardest to cross at Saskatchewan Crossing when Otter's column encountered very bad weather. This sketch by Capt. H. de H. Haig first appeared in the *Illustrated London News* on May 23, 1885. [Glenbow-Alberta Institute]

The five hundred people in the Battleford fort were overjoyed to learn on April 14 that troops were on the way to rescue them. There were few Indians in the immediate vicinity of the town but prairie fires were raging. The Indians were setting fires to frighten the whites and the whites were setting fires to remove brush that would provide cover for attacking Indians. Indians had captured a courier sent from Prince Albert to Battleford and another one the Battleford residents had sent to Fort Pitt. The Indians were reported to have also captured one thousand cattle and six hundred horses. It was believed that Big Bear intended to move to Batoche and take Battleford on his way. One Battleford resident wrote: "Big Bear is on his way to join Riel and threatens to make things warm when he arrives. It is a race between him and the troops."[7] Indian scouts were busy trying, successfully, to scare the residents of the fort. Their war chief, Fine Day, instructed the small scouting parties he sent out to appear at various points where they could be seen from the fort. They were to keep moving and keep popping up to give an illusion of numbers.[8]

The long, cold, dreary march across the prairies was more than some of the troops had bargained for. The constant complaints about the food increased dramatically when they ran out of wood to cook with. Cassels recorded: "Owing to some mismanagement, no proper supply of wood has been brought with us, and there is none to be had tonight. Nothing in the shape of fuel is to be had for miles and miles and our poor fellows are obliged to content themselves after a hard day's work with [canned] beef, biscuit and cold water. We came to the conclusion that the biscuit at present being served out to us are some left behind by Sir Garnet after the Red River Expedition." The next day, there was still no wood and "great profanity is indulged in when it is found that again we have no means of doing any cooking. The men are rapidly becoming mutinous."[9]

On April 21, scouts from Battleford were surprised to find the police refugees from Fort Pitt on the river about seventy kilometres north of town. The residents of Battleford had believed they had all been killed when the fort was taken. NWMP Inspector Francis Dickens and his command reached the fort the next day. That evening, young Frank Smart, scouting with a companion about five kilometres south of the fort, was shot and killed by an Indian lying in ambush. His companion gave the alarm and a strong force of volunteers retrieved the body. "We will not attempt to describe the pain and grief that found expression in the camp when the remains of the young hero were brought in; nor the depth of the vows of vengeance that were recorded," P. G. Laurie wrote.[10]

Smart was buried the next afternoon and, as his employer, merchant James Clinkskill, described it:

> Just as we were returning from the grave a horseman was seen coming down the hill leading to the crossing on the Battle River. He was waving his arms in an endeavor to draw our attention. On some of our men going out to meet him, the horseman proved to be Charlie Ross, an old time member of the police. He was advance scout from Herchomer's [sic] force, informed us a relieving force was only a few miles away. It is impossible for me to describe the joy with which this news was received. Women were crying and embracing each other, men went about with a brisk jaunty air, every eye was brightened, the long suspense was broken at last.[11]

That same day, the troops of Otter's column encountered their first hostile Indians. South of the Eagle Hills, police scouts in advance of the main column surprised a few Indians butchering a cow. As one of the scouts approached to talk to them, the Indians fired a few shots, then quickly retreated north. The scouts captured some ponies and a wagon and apparently wounded one of the fleeing Indians.

A short time later, the troops came within sight of Battleford but, much to the chagrin of Cassels and his comrades, they camped for the night instead of moving on to the town. "We can see Battleford when about eight miles away from a height of land and are disgusted to notice clouds of smoke rising from the settlement. We are ordered to camp, however, much as we should like to press on and render help if help be needed. It is not considered advisable to advance when night is approaching."[12]

The smoke the troops saw was the result of the Indians' last defiant act at Battleford, the burning of Judge Rouleau's substantial home. Earlier in the day, they had burned the Hudson's Bay Company warehouse on the flats beside the river across from the fort, making, Clinkskill recalled, a great spectacle. "We could see it and the Indians dancing around it in fiendish glee. Suddenly a great flame arose in the air shortly after, a noise like a sharp peel of thunder rent the air and we could feel the tremor of the earth. The building had blown up, whether it was from gunpowder or coal oil which had been stored in the cellar, we can never know."[13]

The next morning, April 24, as the troops set up camp at the old government house (soon be be fortified and named Fort Otter), their commander went across the river to receive an enthusiastic greeting from the Battleford settlers. The troops, Cassels wrote, were impressed by the destruction in the neighbourhood of their camp. "On this side of the river there were originally some dozen houses and two or three stores forming what is called the Old Town. Four or five of these houses have been burned, the others dismantled and pillaged, and the stores completely gutted. Scarcely anything has escaped: what could not be taken has been destroyed. About us we see scattered in dismal confusion feathers, photos, books, tins, furniture, and desolation reigns supreme."[14]

Otter had lifted the siege of Battleford without a battle. But he, his troops, and the angry settlers were not content to let matters rest. The settlers wanted swift and harsh retribution. Pent up for so long, feeling helpless as they watched their property destroyed, and daily fearing an attack that would surely result in their deaths, they were eager to reassert the white man's authority. The troops were anxious for a fight, jealous of their comrades in Middleton's column who, they quickly learned, had had a brush with the enemy at Fish Creek. The day before the troops actually arrived, P. G. Laurie reported plans to march on Poundmaker's reserve immediately.[15] On April 25, rumours were current among the troops that they were about to be sent to fight the Indians. Queen's Own Rifles Lieutenant Harry Brock didn't understand the geography but he recorded the feeling in the camp. "We await orders at present having accomplished what we were sent to do, namely relieve Battleford. We expect to be sent to Fort Pitt about ninety miles up the river to punish Poundmaker, the chief of the Crees and his band, but know nothing definitely."[16]

Divinity student E. C. Acheson, a Queen's Own private, wrote that the feeling in camp was actually mixed, as were the rumours of what was to be done next, but "no man touched with human sympathy could look upon the desolate houses and ruined homesteads without registering a vow in heaven of eternal vengeance. Feather beds ripped up, pictures smashed, pianos in little bits, photographs with spear cuts on the faces and things done that only fiendish ingenuity could think of, and then the poor murdered men and women, and the fort crowded (564 people) with men, women and children, homeless and penniless. Sad, heartrending indeed is the sight, so do not wonder if our men if called to action prove harsh and unrelenting."[17]

The troops' eagerness increased on April 25 with the news of Middleton's fight and the recovery of James Payne's body and as the troops had more opportunity to view the destruction. Otter sympathized with the militant feelings of the Battleford settlers and his own soldiers. He also was keenly ambitious. Defeating rebel Indians in battle and breaking the back of the Indian resistance was just the kind of thing that would promote his career, but he had no direct orders from Middleton to take the fight to the Indians. If they had attacked him during the march or if he had found them in sufficient numbers at Battleford when he arrived, his duty would have been clear. Taking the offensive was a major decision. Hudson's Bay Company Commissioner Joseph Wrigley was pressuring Otter to move up to Fort Pitt and rescue the company's employees held captive by Big Bear's band.[18] That was clearly out of the question, especially as General T. B. Strange had already been assigned to do it. Otter had no orders to move away from the Battleford area, but he had not been specifically ordered to avoid advancing against the local Indians.

As soon as he arrived at the besieged town, Otter had telegraphed Middleton for instructions. "Act for defence of Battleford on your own judgement. You have sole command," the general replied.[19] Middleton thought that was sufficiently clear at least in one respect: Otter's responsibility was to the town. He had no mandate to complicate matters by widening the war. Otter was told at Battleford that the Indians could muster an army of no more than two hundred men and that, if the troops advanced on them, they would as likely flee as fight. There was the distinct possibility that Otter could score a substantial victory relatively easily and perhaps bloodlessly. Cassels recorded Otter's attitude: "It is not thought that there will be any fighting to do and if there is, Poundmaker has, we hear, only two hundred men and ought not to be able to do very much. The brigadier and staff evidently think that Poundmaker will surrender if we get near him at all."[20]

Otter decided to attack the Indians at Poundmaker's reserve. All he needed were orders to do it. Middleton had not specifically prohibited such an action, but he had not endorsed it either. So Otter avoided the general for the moment. On April 26, he sent a message to Lieutenant Governor Dewdney, the head of Indians Affairs in the North-West, because he was planning to attack an Indian reserve. "I would propose taking part of my force at once to punish Poundmaker leaving 100 men to garrison Battleford. Great depredations committed. Immediate decisive action necessary. Do you approve?"[21] Dewdney, unaware of Middleton's orders and as anxious as anyone to settle up with the Indians, quickly gave Otter exactly what he wanted. "Think you cannot act too energetically or Indians will collect in large numbers. Herchmer knows country to Poundmaker's reserve. Sand hills most dangerous ground to march through. Be sure to secure good reliable scouts."[22]

That same day, Middleton again telegraphed Otter, making his original instructions only a little clearer. "You had better remain at Battleford until you ascertain more about Poundmaker's force and the kind of country he is in."[23] Otter chose to interpret that not as a veto of aggressive action but as a sensible suggestion that he do a bit of scouting. The troops quickly learned that an expedition was planned. Cassels, anxious to fight, got himself attached to the Toronto Infantry School, for some of his own regiment, the Queen's Own, were to be left behind. Acheson got himself a job as chaplain to one of the companies

242

scheduled to go. "We don't quite know the nature of our work except that Poundmaker and his crew are to be put under, the reserve pillaged," Acheson wrote.[24]

Otter was trying to keep his specific plans as quiet as possible, nervous because he still didn't have the support of his commander. He was careful to tell some of those who asked, particularly newspaper reporters, that he did not plan to fight but that he would like to capture some of the cattle the Indians had taken from the white farmers. Having done the scouting required by his self-serving interpretation of Middleton's orders, Otter was all set to march on April 30. He sent another message to the general. "Am I to attack? Please give me definite instructions."[25] Middleton was not known for the precision of the orders he gave his subordinates. He still could not bring himself to give Otter a direct answer. "Fighting these men entails heavy responsibility. Six men judiciously placed would shoot down half your force. Had better for the present content yourself with holding Battleford and patrolling about the country."[26]

Otter again interpreted the order before obeying it. The troops he led to Poundmaker's reserve, three hundred men, two cannon and a Gatling gun, would be a "reconnaissance in force," patrolling the country. If they happened to run into an Indian army and someone started shooting, they would have to fight.

On May 1, Otter sent Middleton one last message. "Poundmaker hesitating between peace and war—am going to-day to try and settle matters with him."[27] If Otter found the general's instructions too vague, by this time Middleton was perplexed by Otter's messages. The little game of semantics the two of them were playing, each wanting to put the responsibility for a final decision on the other, was becoming hopelessly confusing. Perhaps, Middleton thought, Otter planned to try to talk with Poundmaker, an exercise that would be even worse than trying to do battle with him. The general replied: "Don't understand your telegram about Poundmaker. Hope you have not gone with small force. He must be punished, not treated with. You had better confine yourself to reconnoitring for the present."[28]

When Middleton's telegram arrived at Battleford, Otter had already left. Late in the afternoon of May 1, the march the troops had been so anxious to make began. Cassels recorded:

We have some fifty waggons and push on rapidly till night fall then make a laager [enclosed camp] and prepare to rest quietly till the moon rises. In the meantime we have something to eat and sit down quietly and discuss the prospects of the morrow. Poundmaker is supposed to be some thirty-five miles off and we hope to reach his camp by dawn. There is, of course, no chance of surprising him. His scouts have probably long ere this noticed our advance for signal fires have been burning all afternoon on the distant hills, but we want to reach him before he has time to move off.[29]

One of the very few accurate representations of the battle of Cutknife Creek. Capt. R.W. Rutherford made this sketch from a hill on the east side of the creek from which the gun he commanded covered Otter's retreat. The dots on the triangular field in the middle of the picture represent the positions of the troops during the battle. The hill at the extreme left is the one from which Fine Day directed the Indian fighters. [Toronto *Globe*, May 23, 1885]

Otter was wrong about the Indians' willingness to fight if they were attacked but he was right in thinking they were vacillating between peace and war. Poundmaker thought the Battleford Indians had done their part by besieging the town. It was up to the Métis army, which Riel had led him to believe was far stronger than it really was, to secure its territory. But since the battle of Duck Lake, messengers from Batoche had been arriving at Poundmaker's camp pleading for his military support. One such message read: "Rise; face the enemy, and if you can do so, take Battleford—destroy it—save all the goods and provisions, and come to us."[30] Poundmaker didn't know quite what to make of such messages. They made him uneasy. The Métis had always said they would come to the Indians' aid, not the other way around. The chief and captive Farm Instructor Robert Jefferson discussed one of the Métis letters one night.

He asked me what I thought of it. I said it read as though the Duck Lake people wanted help. Poundmaker made no remark but I could see that the idea was not all to his fancy. The first messengers had conveyed the impression that Riel and his Duck Lake following were going to carry all before them, and that the Indians' part was to sit quietly by, and yet participate in the benefits to result. Also, nothing had been heard from the other parts of the country—and much had been expected—from the west, from the north and from the Blackfeet. The worst was to be anticipated from this ominous silence.[31]

With a substantial white man's army close at hand, the Battleford warriors met on April 29 to consider their position. They had sent a messenger to Big Bear asking for reinforcements and now they wanted news and help from Riel. They sent him a letter. "We have here guns and rifles of all sorts, but ammunition for them is short. If it be possible we want you to send us ammunition of various kinds. We are weak only for the want of that. You sent word that you would come to Battleford when you had finished your work at Duck Lake. We wait still for you, as we are unable to take the fort without help."

They feared the troops would move from Battleford to attack them, the letter said, and the Indians needed the support of Métis fighters.[32]

But both Big Bear and Riel had their own problems. Big Bear's band was in much the same position as the Battleford Indians. They had done their part and were uncertain whether to take the offensive or wait for Métis successes. At Batoche, Riel was preparing defences against Middleton's advance. There could be no reinforcements for the Battleford Indians.

By 7 P.M. on May 1, Otter's column had covered almost thirty kilometres, about half the distance to Poundmaker's reserve. They stopped to rest, have dinner, and wait for the moon to rise to give them light to resume the march. Otter planned to try to surprise the Indians by attacking them at dawn. They moved on shortly before midnight and just after first light at about 4 A.M., Toronto *Mail* reporter "Eskimo" Billy Fox wrote, in the usual newspaperman's rhetoric of the time:

> all was quiet, bright and beautiful. The wild fowl, frightened from their quiet morning nap, flew screeching across the prairie towards some quiet resting place. There was not the first sign of Indians. As we rounded a small bluff on the trail we came upon their deserted camp. The marks of a couple of hundred teepees could be seen on one side. They appeared to have been hastily deserted, as many of the poles still stood as they had first been placed. We hurried on. The Indians were no doubt ignorant of our approach and did not expect us until the afternoon. To get as close to them as possible without being discovered was our aim. Everyone was anxious for the fray.[33]

Others in the column thought that the Indians, aware of the approach of the troops, were in the midst of fleeing. It did not occur to anyone that the Indians had merely moved their camp a very short distance.

The troops were on the steep banks of Cutknife Creek, named for a Sarcee warrior who had died near there in battle with the Cree some years before. Directly across the creek to the west was a long, steep hill with a large field enclosed by wooded ravines on the north and south. After not finding the Indians where he had hoped to, Otter had to change his plans. As Cassels recorded it: "It was decided to cross the creek, climb the hill, and have breakfast and rest the horses before pushing on. The stream proved to be rather hard to cross. After crossing it we had some five hundred yards of scrubby marshy lands to go through and then we began to climb the hill."[34] As the troops crossed the shallow creek in single-file and climbed its western bank, they saw some cattle grazing on a hill to the south. These, they supposed, were some of the cattle the Indians had taken but they still didn't know where the Indians themselves were.

From the field on the side of the hill, where the troops were headed, an impressive prairie panorama stretches east for about twenty-five kilometres. When the winds are light, it is a pretty setting for a picnic. On May 2, 1885, the

246

most accident-prone military commander could not have picked a worse place to have breakfast.

Cassels was in front of the main party of troops, a short distance behind the NWMP scouts and the artillery. It was 5:15 A.M. "Suddenly, just as the scouts reached the top of the first steep ascent, I heard a rattle of rifles ahead and then in a minute or two saw the police and some artillery lying down firing briskly over the crest of the hill and the guns and Gatling also working for all they were worth. At the same time bullets began to fly around us and puffs of smoke floated from the bushes on the right and left, showing us where they came from. Evidently we were in a trap."[35]

The entire Indian camp was just over the brow of the hill, in a huge semicircle facing the troops, undetected by Otter's scouts. From where Cassels stood, it was easy to believe they had fallen into a carefully-laid trap, but in fact the Indians' scouts were even more negligent than Otter's. Although they feared an attack, the Indian camp, with one exception, was sound asleep as the troops approached. An old man named Jacob had been in the habit of getting up before anyone else. As he reached the crest of the hill in front of the Indian camp on his morning ride he heard wagons, dozens of them, struggling to get across the creek. He wakened the camp and a small group of Stonies rushed off to check the approaching enemy as the Indians organized themselves for battle.[36]

The Stoney warriors reached the ravine on the south side of the hill at almost the same time as Otter's advance guard neared its crest, and the two groups began exchanging rifle fire. As the main body of militia ran up the hill to offer support, the artillery quickly brought its two field guns to bear on the Indian camp, lobbing shells towards the tents whose tops they could then see. Robert Jefferson was one of those awakened by the sound of gunfire and shells shrieking overhead. "I dressed hastily and hurried outside. All was confusion, as people poured forth from their tents, but it was the confusion of everyone attending to his or her own business and that business was to reach some place of safety from the coming onslaught. The deep voices of the men, the sharper tones of the women and the crying of children, all mingled as the crowd filed off behind the tents towards the south."[37]

Toronto *Globe* reporter William Baillie wrote that "the first three shells were put into the teepees on the hill to the right front. They were admirably aimed, and created consternation. The teepees were ripped over and the people scattered in every direction."[38] Jefferson ran to Poundmaker's tent, where he found the chief calmly dressing himself.

He donned the fur cap that he always wore and proceeded to invest himself in what looked like a patchwork quilt. In my ignorance, I ventured to ask him what it was, and my excuse for such an inopportune question is, that the garment—if it can be called a garment—had such a paltry, ordinary look, that I never connected it with the grave panoply of war. All the war-bonnets that I had seen might be tawdry, but they were barbaric, and essentially Indian. Poundmaker's expression, however, at once made me realise how flippant and hasty was my question. With great dignity he informed me that it was his war-cloak; that it rendered its wearer invisible to an enemy. Then he got up and stalked out of the tent without another word.[39]

The Indians' first thought was to protect their families. Otter and his men had the advantage of surprise, although they didn't realize that at the time and didn't even know how close they were to the main Indian camp. Had they followed it up instead of stopping at the crest of the hill to engage the few Stonies who came to meet them, the battle might have been a short one. Jefferson thought that if Otter had charged initially

there is little doubt that he would have attained his object, as, in order to protect the women and children, the Indians would have surrendered. They might even have given in if a flag of truce had been sent forward instead of a Gatling gun. If the Indians had elected to fight, he could have dispersed them by charges of horse. The weak point of the Indians' case was their anxiety to keep the fighting as far as possible from their women and children. Otter allowed them to fight on their chosen ground.[40]

Jefferson was probably correct but he was observing from the Indian side of the lines and he did not know that Otter had no cavalry with which to make a charge.

The Stoney warriors on the front line realized the damage the field guns would do if they found the range of the camp before the women and children had fled to safety. A small group of them made a brave charge in a desperate attempt to silence the guns or at least distract them for the moment. "They came on with war whoops and jumping up and tossing their blankets up above them and to right and left of them so as to misdirect our aim, then fell on the ground and fired at us. So sudden was the charge which was made evidently with a view to capturing our guns and the Gatling that the men were surprised and began to fall back," recorded artillery Captain Robert Rutherford.[41] The artillery commander, Major Charles Short, rallied his men, who rushed the Stonies and drove them back into the ravine at the south side of the field. Two Indians were killed, one of them a Nez Percé refugee from Chief Joseph's band. As they hurried back to their positions, the veteran policeman Corporal Ralph Sleigh, who had headed the small detachment at Frog Lake, became the first of Otter's force to die. Three of his comrades were wounded. In the confusion of the first few minutes, the militia, most of whom had never been under fire before, behaved remarkably efficiently. The artillery and police held the front, the Toronto Infantry School Corps lined themselves up to the right facing the ravine on the north, the Queen's Own Rifles and the Governor General's Foot Guards went to the edge of the ravine on the left where most of the Indians' firing seemed to be coming from, and the company of Battleford volunteers guarded the rear, facing the creek. The horses and wagons were corralled in a small depression near the centre of the field. Reporter Billy Fox described the scene:

Our musketry fire was at first wild, but the men soon got down to actual work. The Indians succeeded for a time in practising one of their old dodges. A blanket rolled about a stick, or a hat raised upon one would be cautiously lifted above the brush. Our men, mistaking it for a man, would rise and fire and as they did so they made excellent targets for the Indians, who were not slow to avail themselves of this opportunity to pick off a soldier. But the boys soon saw through the ruse, and after one or two had been struck very few shots were fired at dummies.[42]

War Chief Fine Day, young and inexperienced though he was, quickly recovered from the initial surprise. He organized his warriors into groups of four and five and sent them to move along the ravines to the north and south of the field the soldiers occupied. At any one time there were only about fifty Indians actually fighting the troops. The rest of the Indian fighters were in the rear, protecting the families in case Otter's force managed to get off the field and renew the attack.[43]

Having such an extraordinary advantage of terrain, the Indians needed only a few warriors to pin down Otter's force. Cassels described the battle site:

Roughly speaking we occupied a triangular inclined plane—the apex resting on the creek and the base running along the crest of the hill. In front of the hill and parallel to the crest was a ravine, about two hundred yards distant, and running down from this ravine on each side of us and in a direction nearly parallel to the sides of the triangle was another ravine. On the far side of the ravine on the right there was open ground, but on the left for a long distance the whole country was rolling and bushy, and it was from this side that the heaviest fire seemed to come.... The bullets came flying about us in a not over pleasant manner. We were exposed to fire from three sides and had to grin and bear it.[44]

When the troops concentrated their efforts in one area, the Indian warriors would simply move back through the ravine towards the crest of the hill and bring reinforcements to an area where the troops' fire had slackened. The troops would find fire coming very hotly from their right for a few minutes but when they moved on the Indians there the fire would suddenly stop, only to be compensated by a volley coming from the left. The Indians kept moving, confusing the troops not only about their numbers but about the direction of their attack. South of the field on top of a hill from which he could see the entire battlefield, Fine Day directed his warriors, aided by a small mirror which he used to signal their movements.

Four hours after the battle began, one of the two old seven-pounder field guns Otter had borrowed from the NWMP was disabled. Its rotten carriage had

Queen's Own Rifles privates, and chaplains, G.E. Lloyd (left and inset) and E.C. Acheson, recover the body of Private Dobbs of the Battleford Rifles during the battle of Cutknife Creek. [*The Canadian Pictorial and Illustrated War News*]

fallen apart. The other gun carriage was badly cracked, its gun lashed and wedged to it. "Every time the gun was discharged it jumped out of the trunnion holes. In fact it was a race between the gun and the gunners. The former jumped back every time it was discharged, and the latter had to follow it and carry it back to its place again," Fox wrote.[45]

A short time later, when there were few shots coming from in front of the troops, the Indians began peppering them from the left and almost behind them. The Battleford Rifles and a few men from the other corps advanced to try to dislodge the enemy there. Captain Rutherford turned his field gun around to give them support but in the process almost shelled his own troops. In that charge into the thick of the enemy fire, one soldier was killed and four wounded, including Queen's Own Private George Watts. "The bullets were humming and whistling around us. You could hear nothing but bullets whistling and rifles cracking all over the place. The brush in front and in the rear of us was fairly ablaze with rifles not 100 yards away, and on the right the Indians were firing from the top of the hill at us. It was a miracle that all of us were not killed," Watts wrote.[46] He and his comrades succeeded in gaining a new ravine on the troops' left, south of the main battlefield, but it was not possible for reinforcements to reach them, so they had to move back to their original lines.

Fine Day's warriors had virtually surrounded the troops by occupying the ravines to the north and south of the field and gradually working themselves into the gully through which the creek ran. For Otter's force, things were looking not only bleak; it seemed as if history might repeat itself. Watts watched the rest of the battle with the other wounded in the corral in the middle of the field, where he had time to reflect on the history that was in many minds that day. "Our fellows were as cool and steady as if on parade, and in fact so was all the brigade. They attribute the fact that we were not all killed, the same as Custer's outfit, to the steadiness and pluck of the boys."[47]

At about 11 A.M. the Indian fire on the front lines of the troops had slackened to such an extent that Captain Patrick Hughes, commanding the Queen's Own men closest to the artillery,

> felt like having a smoke and took out my pipe, but found I had no tobacco. I turned to the man next to me, poor Rogers, of the Guards, and asked him for some. He did not quite hear me, and said, "What, sir?" and then, like a flash, a bullet came from the left, hitting him on the left side of the head, and killing him instantly. Poor fellow, he never knew what struck him. I was terribly shocked, and jumped to him. He was only two feet from me. I held up his head, but he was stone dead, without even a move, his feet crossed and lying on his chest in the same position as the rest of us. Had I not been talking to him I might not have noticed his death for several minutes.[48]

By that time Otter had realized his position was hopeless. If it was impossible to advance against the enemy, withdrawing from the field seemed almost as dangerous. Staying on the field simply meant giving the Indians more time to leisurely pick off his exposed troops. "The Indians were making a great fight of it, and when chased out of one position resumed fire in another. Their tenacity is perhaps unexampled in Indian fighting. Their losses must have been severe. They looked as if they intended keeping it up all day, and it would have been certain disaster to our force to have been left at nightfall in the position into which we had been entrapped, without the assistance of the guns, one of which was now perfectly useless and the other almost so," the Toronto *Globe*'s Baillie reported.[49] Shortly after 11 A.M., Otter began to organize a withdrawal. He ordered the militia troops to the lines at the front and along the ravines to prevent a charge by the enemy while the Battleford Rifles began to try to clear the Indians from the bush to the rear. Captain Rutherford moved his field gun down the hill.

The scouts, Battleford Rifles, and artillery cleared a path for themselves to the rear and crossed Cutknife Creek. There they took up positions on hills that commanded the line of retreat across the creek. The teams and wagons moved down and across the creek as the main body of troops held the hill. Once the teams were safely across, the troops backed cautiously down the hill from the battlefield towards the creek and the apex of the triangle in Cassels' description.

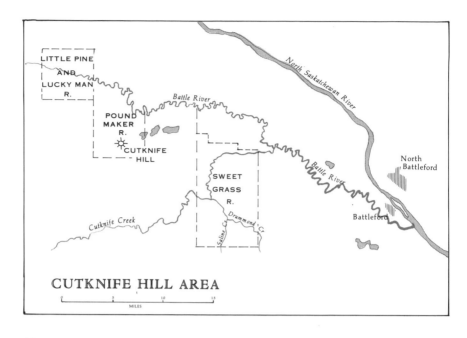

CUTKNIFE HILL AREA

"It was a moment of supreme danger. A large body of Indians poured down into the gully a considerable distance up, with the object no doubt of coming up with our men as they were crossing the gully and cutting them off from the teams and the party on the other side. If this could have been done, the chances would have been in favor of the whole brigade being slaughtered," Baillie wrote.[50]

The troops got across the creek far more easily than they had expected to. They did not know then why they had been so lucky, for Baillie's report was correct. The troops should have suffered enormous casualties trying to file through the gully and across the creek.

But the Indian warriors stopped firing and let the troops withdraw unmolested. Poundmaker had taken no part in the actual fighting. Only after the Indian victory was assured and the opportunity to massacre the fleeing troops presented itself did the chief step in, Jefferson recorded. "A number of Indians had mounted and were about to start after the retreating soldiers, but Poundmaker would not permit it. He said that to defend themselves and their wives and children was good, but that he did not approve of taking the offensive. They had beaten their enemy off; let that content them. So there was no pursuit."[51] In Plains Indian tradition, a political chief has no authority in war. The conduct of war is left entirely to the war chief and the members of the soldiers' lodge. The ability of Poundmaker to call off the warriors is a measure of the considerable stature he had gained among the Battleford bands. Had they known about it, the troops would have been thankful that Poundmaker had been so successful as a

252

politician. Jefferson wrote: "It is said that Otter had been forbidden to make any offensive movement, so he called this a reconnaissance in force. Had it proved a success, it would likely have received another name. But for the grace of God and the complaisance of Otter's Indian opponent, it would have been left to strangers to name it, for there would have been no survivors."[52]

At 12:15 P.M., the last shot was fired in the battle of Cutknife Creek. An hour later, the troops had their wagons loaded and began their march back to Battleford. As they left they started a prairie fire that in the brisk wind quickly spread to the woods lining the creek. Many of them had changed their minds about war; they had seen enough of actual shooting. Cassels wrote his brother:

> One's sensations under fire are certainly peculiar. I never felt afraid, but quite made up my mind I was to be hit and often wished myself back in Toronto. As one of the fellows said "I made up my mind to quietly leave the Regiment as soon as I get back to Toronto." It was very strange to have all this wretched work going on when everything was bright and fresh about us. A lovely Spring morning, birds singing near us, all should have been peaceful instead of the rattle of Gatling and rifle; and the sight of dead and wounded men made us realize only too well that not peace but war was there.[53]

Cassels had also gained a new respect for Indians. "They fought in a way that surprised the police, who have been accustomed to look upon them as arrant cowards. They are the beau ideal of skirmishers, expose themselves but little and move with marvellous quickness."[54]

On the way home and when they got to Battleford about 10 o'clock that night, the soldiers' tried to put the day's events in the best possible light. They had been forced to retreat with eight killed and about fourteen wounded. They had left large quantities of ammunition on the field, just what the Indians needed. However, they thought they had been met by a much superior enemy, numbering at least six hundred warriors. A horse that was believed to belong to Chief Little Poplar had been captured, leading to the rumour that he and Big Bear had moved down from Fort Pitt to join the Battleford bands. Many believed that, and they thought they must have inflicted terrible casualties. The cannon must have done much damage shelling the tents and ravines. The Gatling was seen to mow down whole groups of Indians at a time. Many of the individual soldiers could count the number of times they had killed an Indian and each had seen many fall from the shots of others. One newspaper reporter wrote that the troops had actually counted twenty-six Indian bodies on the field. Most of the soldiers thought at least one hundred Indians died and some estimates ranged much higher.

In fact, there had been six Indians killed and three wounded, Robert Jefferson wrote.

Otter at first argued that his object had been accomplished because he had forced Poundmaker to declare himself. Big Bear's band, if not the chief himself, had been fighting at Cutknife, the colonel reported. Later, when it became clear that Big Bear's band was nowhere near Battleford, Otter argued that his action had inflicted a severe check on Poundmaker, one that prevented him from moving north to join Big Bear. "The Victory! How Poundmaker Was Whipped," read headlines in the Toronto *World*. But that headline was an exception. Commentators treated the battle cautiously and most newspapers put noncommittal headlines on their stories.

Most newspapers, especially those in Toronto, did their patriotic duty and supported Otter editorially, although the support was often noticeably luke-warm. "The Battleford fight was no more decisive than the Fish Creek fight; but it has accomplished two things very satisfactorily. It has given Col. Otter's men an opportunity of testing themselves in an actual engagement with a strong force of skilful rebels; and it has taught the Indians that, even in ambushes and with two to one on their side, they cannot face the regular troops," said the Conservative Toronto *Mail*.[55]

But the *Saskatchewan Herald* exceeded the most optimistic opinion among the troops.

> The work of the Battleford Column under Col. Otter on the 2nd of May, in travelling forty miles to Poundmaker's camp, fighting six and a half hours with a force nearly three times their own, and returning in triumph to their camp inside of thirty hours, is one that will live in history. Tradition, too, will carry it down, for it struck such a blow at the central army of the Indians, entrenched in what they deemed an impregnable position, that it will be whispered at the camp fire while their language lasts. The rapidity and force of the blow was one they never deemed possible.[56]

In their own accounts, the soldiers concentrated on the coolness and bravery of their fellows and the efficiency of Colonel Otter, undeniable factors in the battle. But very few would comment on the final result. It soon became apparent that it was the Indians who were celebrating victory, despite the brave face the whites tried to put on. A week after the battle, the *Globe*'s Baillie wrote:

> Every day that passes is increasing the confidence, if not the numbers, of the Indians in their stronghold at the reserve, and as their confidence and numbers are increased the difficulties, of course, of our final dislodgement of them, will be correspondingly increased. There can be no doubt that they received a pretty severe scorching from us a week ago. But they were not routed. They held their ground, and to the Indian mind this meant the most signal victory. The precious lives we have lost, the sufferings of our wounded, go for nothing. All the heroism displayed on that day has but made our foe the bolder, the chances of an early settlement of this bloody rising of the Indians the less probable.[57]

Two old hands in the west, Roman Catholic archbishop Alexandre-Antoine Taché and former NWMP Superintendent James Walsh, were highly critical of Otter's activities. Newspapers reported that "both Archbishop Taché and Major Walsh think that the result of Col. Otter's engagement with Poundmaker will be to increase the Indian alarm. Col. Otter, they agree, should not have risked an engagement until he was strong enough to fight a battle and stay on the ground until he had dictated terms and compelled the chiefs to acknowledge submission."[58] Indian Agent John Rae, who had fled to safer ground in Winnipeg, was even more pessimistic than usual. Rae told reporters he "predicts a general uprising of all the Indians, and thinks a bloody war in inevitable. He says the Indians are well armed and trained. The government, he says, entirely underrate the strength of the Indians and the seriousness of the situation. The Indians with bows and arrows will fight as well as our troops. He thinks the whole country will be aroused in no time and all the tribes will be on the warpath."[59]

On May 7, scouts Otter sent to Poundmaker's reserve were chased and one was wounded by the Indians. The colonel still wanted to settle the Indian matter once and for all but he was belatedly willing to take the advice Walsh, Taché, and even Middleton offered. He would not take the offensive again until reinforcements arrived.

At the Indian camp feelings were mixed. They all believed they had won a great victory but they were uncertain about what to do next. Robert Jefferson described the argument.

> They could not hold their present position indefinitely; they would be starved out, if not conquered. (That they could be beaten fighting, they found hard to believe.) They must move in some direction. Here division came in. The body of the people now only wanted to get out of the mess in the easiest way possible. Others, including Poundmaker and some other prominent men, held that the proper course was to make for the hilly country round Devil's Lake and, if pressed too hard, take refuge with the Blackfeet where Poundmaker was sure of sanctuary.[60]

As Poundmaker and part of the Indian camp prepared to set out for the southwest, the warriors stopped them. The warriors wanted, Jefferson said, "to have the whole business settled one way or the other in the shortest possible time."[61] When they encountered Otter's scouts on May 7, the warriors were leading the entire camp east to join Riel at Batoche. From Middleton's point of view, it was the worst possible outcome of Otter's attack.

CHAPTER FOURTEEN

Decision at Batoche

The rain that began on the morning of the Fish Creek battle became sleet, then snow as the temperature fell that night, and before morning had developed into a major spring storm. Whether it was because of this weather or his newly-acquired respect for the enemy, General Middleton sent out only scouting patrols the next day and made no effort to occupy the position that his troops had expended so much blood to take. Nor was it until two days after the battle that the last two bodies were recovered from the ravine where they had fallen. The general state of nerves can be gauged from an incident on the night of April 26, when sentries opened fire on some teamsters who were arriving at the camp, setting off a general fusillade that woke everyone up. The next day the burials began and continued until April 30, when the last seriously wounded man, Lieutenant Charles Swinford of the 90th Winnipeg Rifles, died. Middleton planned to put the surviving wounded on one of the steamboats that were expected to arrive at any moment.

In his first telegram to Ottawa after the battle, Middleton clung to his original plan and informed Minister of Militia and Defence Caron that he would continue the march on Batoche at once.[1] Later the same day he changed his mind and announced that he would bypass the rebel headquarters and march directly to Prince Albert, where he could add a hundred Mounted Policemen to his force. This plan, too, was abandoned. The chief difficulty was the supply situation. The steamboats had not yet arrived and the long line of wagons stretching back to the railhead were subject to numerous interruptions. Some days the expected quota of supplies arrived, other days they did not. The soldiers' diaries from this point in the campaign are full of grumbles about inadequate food and occasionally meals missed altogether. Apart from the risk that a severe spring storm might lead to starvation, sending the seriously wounded that distance in jolting wagons would have drastically increased the number of deaths.

The steamer *Northcote* so anxiously awaited at the Fish Creek camp had left Swift Current April 23 accompanied by two barges. The whole entourage was loaded down with soldiers, supplies, medical personnel, and a Gatling gun. The river was still quite low but it was rising rapidly and it was expected that the *Northcote* would catch up to General Middleton in five days. There were rumours that the enemy planned to ambush the boat at a point known as the

Elbow, where the river turned northward, so the newly-arrived Surveyor's Intelligence Corps was sent to scout the area. No sign of Métis or Indian activity was found, and the surveyors waited with scant patience while the *Northcote* worked her way painfully downriver.[2]

A man was stationed on the bow of the boat constantly measuring the depth of the water with a long pole but his warnings to the bridge frequently came too late. As many as half a dozen times a day the steamer would ground on a sand bar. As one of the Midland Battalion who was aboard recalled it:

> Now a scraping, grating sound of the boat's keel upon the sand and she was fast. Then the spars would be set to work to try and push and raise her off. The engines were put back and the steamer throbbed from stem to stern, the steam hissed and roared in the escape pipe, the sand was stirred up from the bottom of the river until the water grew thick and yellow, and if she was not very hard aground, after a few minutes of this kind of thing she was loose but if unfortunately, as in the great majority of cases we were up high and almost dry on a bar, the tow line was thrown out and the services of the Midland were called into requisition when they generally made short work of it.[3]

On at least one occasion, no amount of pulling and hauling would budge the *Northcote*. Both steamer and barges had to be completely unloaded before they could be refloated, then laboriously reloaded again, a process that took a full twenty-four hours. The five day journey stretched out to two weeks but at last on May 5 the boat pulled into camp at Fish Creek.

The steamer *North West* loading wood for fuel at Prince Albert in the 1880s. The *North West* was a sister ship to the *Northcote*. [Glenbow-Alberta Institute]

In the interim the wounded had been moved back upriver to the tiny settlement at Saskatoon, which had been founded a few years previously by an Ontario temperance group. The inhabitants of the town had volunteered to care for the wounded. This eased one of Middleton's problems but the supply difficulties remained until the arrival of the *Northcote*. The delay in resuming the march against the rebels aroused increasing scorn and irritation on the part of many of the soldiers, who resented Middleton's apparent distrust of Canadians. Middleton's inability to move, whatever the reason for it, created a leadership vacuum which many of the younger Canadian officers were eager to fill. On May 2 word arrived of Otter's battle at Cutknife. It was not known at first just how close to disaster Otter had come in this adventure, and to the troops at Fish Creek it looked as if Otter was taking the initiative in the campaign away from an excessively timid Middleton. The growing discontent in Middleton's column found a focus in the commanding officer of the Midland Battalion, Lieutenant Colonel Arthur Williams.

Arthur Trefusis Heneage Williams was born to the life he led and that he aspired to. His father, John Williams, was a British navy veteran who fought with Nelson at Trafalgar and came to Canada towards the end of the War of 1812 to serve with Sir James Yeo, the British naval commander on Lake Ontario. For his service in the Canadian war, John Williams received a grant of land at what became Port Hope, Ontario, where he became the town's first mayor. He quickly parlayed his grant into substantial land holdings throughout the province. Arthur followed his father in a business and political career. After a stint in the provincial legislature, he was elected to the House of Commons in 1878. There his loyalty to John A. Macdonald was soon rewarded with the position of Conservative party whip. There was even talk that he was cabinet minister material. Williams did not speak often in the House, but he was well-liked by both his constituents and his colleagues, although the latter sometimes called him "the dandy of the House" for his playing the part of an English gentleman. Like his father, Arthur Williams enjoyed being called the "Squire of Penyrn," the name of the large family estate at Port Hope.

Williams wanted to be wealthy, proper, and popular, the epitome of the doctrine of noblesse oblige. Above all, he wanted to make his mark on history, as his war-hero father claimed to have done. But Arthur had not inherited his father's business acumen. He founded a small bank and became involved in one of Ontario's many railway companies, one that was known for its derailments and for missing its schedule. He sold off much of the family's Ontario land holdings and invested the money in land schemes in the North-West, in a colonization company, in coal lands, and in a residential suburb. The western investments proved only to be a drain on his resources and when Williams visited the North-West in 1883, it was becoming clear that he was in over his head, progressing steadily to financial ruin.

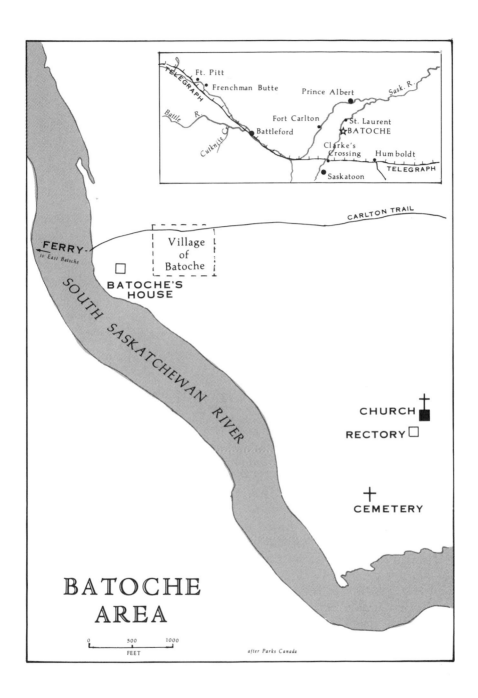

TELEGRAPH

Ft. Pitt
Frenchman Butte
Prince Albert
Sask. R.

Battle R.
Fort Carlton
St. Laurent
Cutknife C.
Battleford
BATOCHE
Clarke's
Crossing
Humboldt
TELEGRAPH
Saskatoon

CARLTON TRAIL

FERRY
to East Batoche

Village
of
Batoche

BATOCHE'S
HOUSE

SOUTH SASKATCHEWAN RIVER

CHURCH †
RECTORY □

† CEMETERY

BATOCHE
AREA

0   500   1000
FEET

after Parks Canada

Also in 1883, Williams became involved in his celebrated dispute with Major General Luard who, at his annual inspection, loudly criticized Williams' country troops then added a derisive comment about the marksmanship of "parliamentary colonels." Williams, fiercely loyal to his own men and even more defensive of his own status, accused Luard of insulting parliament and after the ensuing debate in the House of Commons, Luard, who was not very popular anyway, was dismissed, paving the way for Middleton's appointment. But his petulant and insistent manner during the Luard dispute did not do Williams' reputation much good either.

Williams was anxious to prove himself in battle. Early in 1885 he offered to raise a contingent for Imperial service in the Sudan, but was rebuffed by the British. By that time his financial future was looking rosier. His wife had died in a gruesome carriage accident in 1883 and he became engaged to the daughter of Minister of the Interior Sir David Macpherson, one of Canada's richest men. When the rebellion broke out, Arthur Williams was most anxious to achieve his most important ambition. The Squire of Penryn wanted to be a war hero.

For the Métis, Fish Creek had been a vindication of their traditional way of making war. Once again they had brought a greatly superior enemy to a standstill. But in the past this kind of victory had always led to the departure of the losers, leaving the victorious Métis in sole possession of the field, if not permanently, then at least for a season. This time was different. It quickly became apparent that the Canadian army had every intention of pursuing the fight, whatever weaknesses had been revealed at Fish Creek. The Métis response to this novel situation was to plan for a larger and better version of Fish Creek. The defences of Batoche would be carefully prepared, there would be more of them, and perhaps most important of all, they would be in the same psychological situation as if they had been defending their encampment against the Sioux far out on the prairie during a buffalo hunt. Retreat was possible from Fish Creek; there would be none from Batoche. Historians, even those most sympathetic to the Métis, have unanimously condemned this strategy, but in fact there was no other realistic option apart from surrender. The Métis were less mobile than ever because of the large number of horses lost at Fish Creek, and few of the Indian reinforcements they had hoped for showed up. Dumont directed the construction of trenches and rifle pits around the settlement, a work which was completed by May 5. Scouting was stepped up with even Riel as an occasional participant. A list of standing orders (*Règlements que les Soldats doivent observer à la lettre*) was issued to tighten up discipline.[4] The men were also specifically prohibited by order-in-council from tilling the earth, in case they might be tempted to abandon their military duties in favour of planting their crops.[5]

As he waited for the steamboats to arrive, Middleton was increasingly aware of the precariousness of his position. There had been two encounters in rapid succession that, however brave a face he put on the situation in public, he knew

Lord Melgund, later Governor General of Canada as Lord Minto, was Middleton's second-in-command at Fish Creek. [Montreal *Witness*, 1885]

would be interpreted as defeats of his forces by the Indian population. In fact, just at this time, there were incidents which revealed an increasing restlessness and defiance of authority on the part of previously quiet bands. There were the ominous incidents at Lac La Biche and Green Lake. The Cree at File Hills, uncomfortably close to the main line of communication with Qu'Appelle, left their reserve and stole some horses. Poundmaker was reported to be sending reinforcements to Riel. A proclamation issued on April 30 calling on the rebels to surrender brought no response. Within the government force, Melgund had been critical of his decision to split the column before Fish Creek and the junior officers were more and more restless. The need to make a move was becoming imperative.

On May 5 Middleton took most of his mounted troops and rode off toward Batoche. They encountered no enemy but came upon one house that had obviously been abandoned at short notice. The kettle was boiling on the stove and a hot meal was sitting on the table. The General, who was very partial to the pleasures of the table, sat down and made ready to eat. Before he could begin, however, his orderly casually mentioned that the Métis were very fond of horse meat. Middleton hastily abandoned the repast and a group of French's Scouts, who had planted the story, enjoyed the meal in his place.[6] The scouting party proceeded to within a few kilometres of Batoche and Middleton returned, reassured that no potential ambush sites along the lines of Fish Creek existed between his camp and the enemy location. On May 7 the troops left the Fish Creek camp and marched as far as Gabriel's Crossing, where Dumont had maintained his ferry. Dumont's house was substantial by the standards of the North-West and its furnishings even included a billiard table, Gabriel's most prized possession. The premises were thoroughly looted by the troops, as indeed every Métis farm had been along the way. The farms of white settlers did not escape the attentions of the soldiers either, unless the farmer was sufficiently alert to hide his livestock until the army passed.

Dumont's buildings were razed to the ground and some of the lumber was used to board up the main deck of the *Northcote*, which Middleton intended to use as a makeshift gunboat in the coming battle. A detachment of Infantry School men were assigned to the boat to provide fire power. Armour of three layers of three-inch planks backed by feed sacks proved impervious to rifle bullets. With rifles as its only armament, the *Northcote* could not do a great deal of damage to the enemy but it could provide a useful diversion if it was properly coordinated with the main attack. With all his force now on the east side of the river, strengthened by the addition of two companies of the Midland Battalion and the Gatling gun, Middleton felt reasonably confident of the outcome. On the May 8 the force left the riverbank trail and marched inland a few miles before turning north for Batoche. This way they avoided approaching the enemy stronghold through heavy bush. They camped that evening a few kilometres southeast of the settlement, knowing that battle was certain the next day.

Middleton's plan was to attack from the south at eight o'clock, just as the *Northcote* appeared opposite the settlement. With this simple plan he hoped to keep his inexperienced men and headstrong officers under control and over-whelm the enemy with superior fire power. Surprise was not an element in the tactical plans of either side. Middleton knew where his enemy was and, with the experience of Fish Creek, knew the Métis would fight stubbornly from well-concealed positions. The Métis knew exactly when Middleton would attack and were prepared to meet an assault from any direction. They also had plans for dealing with the *Northcote*. Their scouts had reported the modifications to the boat and they could easily have read about Middleton's plans in the newspapers as they had earlier. Dumont ordered his men to be ready to lower the ferry cable sufficiently to stop the boat as it came downriver. Once it was trapped by the cable it could be captured or destroyed at leisure.[7]

About a kilometre and a half south of Batoche the river bends westward quite abruptly. After flowing west for a kilometre it turns north for two kilometres before bending east then resuming its northward course. These bends in the Saskatchewan enclose on three sides a rough quadrilateral approximately one kilometre by two kilometres. Within this area the land slopes gradually from the prevailing prairie level fifty metres or so above the river to a relatively low ten-metre bank. This feature makes it a natural crossing point, and the tiny settlement owed its existence to the fact that the Carlton Trail crossed the river here. Batoche in 1885 consisted of a few stores and houses clustered on both sides of the trail just before it dropped down the steep bank to the river bottom. At the southwestern corner of the rectangle, just where the land began to drop off toward the crossing, was the church and rectory of St. Antoine de Padoue, with a small cemetery about two hundred and fifty metres from the buildings. The trail from the south split at this point with the right fork continuing to the St. Laurent settlement and eventually to Prince Albert. The left fork led through the churchyard and down the hill to the crossing. The area around the church was heavily wooded and split by a shallow ravine between the church and the cemetery. It was altogether an ideal position for the Métis style of warfare and Dumont, who had believed all along that the main attack would come from this direction, had filled the bush on both sides of the trail with rifle pits. These were dugouts a metre or so deep, faced with heavy logs which were loopholed for firing at the enemy. The pits held two or three men each and were secure against anything but a direct artillery hit.

In Middleton's camp on the morning of Saturday, May 9, the troops were awakened at four o'clock and were ready to march by 5:30. The camp was about nine kilometres from Batoche, a distance that Middleton estimated would be covered by 8:00 A.M., so the *Northcote* was instructed to try to be opposite the village at that time. Middleton's estimate turned out to be too optimistic. At eight o'clock the troops were still well short of the church and several kilometres from the settlement itself. The *Northcote*, on the other hand, having been consistently late so far in the campaign, was right on time. Ironically Middleton's plan to use it as a diversion from his main attack worked perfectly, only the timing was off. The boat was an irresistible target and large numbers of Métis

A Métis rifle pit at Batoche, part of the elaborate defences Gabriel Dumont created for the village. This sketch by Capt. H. de H. Haig first appeared in the *Illustrated London News* on June 27, 1885.

The fortified *Northcote*, travelling north on the South Saskatchewan River, runs the gauntlet of rebel gunfire at Batoche just before running into the ferry cable. This sketch appeared in the *Canadian Pictorial and Illustrated War News.*

and Indians left their positions and rushed to the riverbank to have a shot at her. A hail of lead converged on the *Northcote* but did no damage to the soldiers on board or to the boilers and engines, which were well protected by the improvised armour. It was quite another matter for the captain, a former Mississippi pilot by the name of James Sheets, whose wheelhouse was located, unprotected and unmistakable, on the upper deck. With bullets zinging through the flimsy boards of the wheelhouse, Sheets quickly decided that the safest place was on the floor. Out of control, the *Northcote* drifted helplessly down toward the ferry cable.

Fortunately for those on board Isidore Dumas, who had been ordered by Dumont to lower the cable, decided it was low enough and left it where it was. The cable caught the tall smokestacks, the mast and the long spars used to get the boat off sandbars, pulling them down in a tangle of wreckage. The rest of the boat was undamaged and clear of the cable. It drifted down past the settlement for about four kilometres before grounding. Major H. R. Smith, the officer in command of the soldiers on board, finding that the damage was light, wanted to return upriver at once, but Captain Sheets and his civilian crew had had their fill of acting as moving targets for the rebels. Nothing the furious Major Smith could say would budge them and the *Northcote* proceeded instead downriver to Prince Albert, her days of glory as a warship over. In retrospect it seems probable that the Métis were fortunate that the cable did not stop the boat.

Capturing or sinking the *Northcote* would have made no difference to the outcome of the battle since the boat was hardly in a position to inflict any damage on the rebels. On the other hand the struggle would undoubtedly have absorbed their attention until Middleton was in a position to begin his attack. As it worked out, the Métis were able to return to their positions just in time to meet the assault.

The column advancing toward Batoche made contact with the Métis just about the time that bursts of firing and the shrieking of the steamer's whistle told them that the *Northcote* had begun the fight. Just south of the church were a couple of houses occupied by a few Métis who opened fire on Boulton's Scouts at the head of the column. The nine-pounders were brought up and began to shell the houses, setting one on fire and driving out the Métis, who retreated up the trail in the direction of the settlement. The advance continued a little more cautiously until the church came into sight. The Gatling gun fired a few rounds into the rectory before the troops noticed a white flag flying from an upper window. The church was occupied by Father Moulin, several other priests, some nuns, and several families of refugees. None were hurt and General Middleton assured them of his good will. The troops continued to advance past the church for about half a kilometre until they came under fire from the bush on both sides of the road. From this location the buildings of Batoche could be seen clearly, along with the many tents that housed the Métis and Indian families camped there for the duration of the crisis. The guns were unlimbered and began to shell the rebel headquarters, causing large numbers of women and children to flee in terror from the tents.

Middleton had ordered Boulton's advance guard to halt and await further orders as soon as they came under fire.[8] Boulton's men and French's Scouts had dismounted after they passed the church and were on the right of the column. The heaviest rebel fire came from the rifle pits on that side of the trail. Middleton then deployed the 10th Royals in the centre and the 90th Winnipeg Rifles along with the Gatling on the left to protect the artillery. The two companies of the Midland remained in reserve near the church, which was taken over by the medical staff as a hospital. Once the troops were in position and somewhat less exposed, there was a lull in the firing which led some of the men to believe that they had driven off the rebels. While attention was concentrated on the right of the trail, however, a group of Métis had moved up through the bush on the left close to the guns. Suddenly they burst out of the trees in an effort to overrun and capture the guns. Only the quick reaction of Captain Howard in directing a stream of fire toward them from the Gatling saved the situation and drove them back into the trees. This was the only occasion until the final few minutes of the battle three days later that the militia had a clear view of their enemy, a situation they found intensely frustrating. Trooper Harold Rusden of French's Scouts wrote:

It began to get dreadfully monotonous, being down some distance apart from each other, firing at nothing, making guess shots and hearing the rebel bullets zipp, zipp all round you, and the everlasting clack as the bullets struck the trees. It was not the sort of fighting we expected at all. This sort of fighting is very bad for a young soldier. There is no excitement or rush to keep him up, his blood gets cold knowing that he is fighting at a disadvantage, that the enemy knows his position and he does not know how they are situated.[9]

After the attack was beaten off, the guns were prudently pulled back a couple of hundred metres closer to the church and the rest of the troops followed suit. The initiative remained with the rebels despite the failure of the attack. The Métis pulled most of the men who had taken part in the rush out of their rifle pits on the left and shifted them around to the right in an effort to outflank Middleton's position and cut off his line of communication with his camp. The fighting on the right was hot and heavy for a time and the rebel attack was not finally driven off until Captain Howard and his Gatling gun were shifted to that side to assist. It was now approaching noon and once again there was a lull in the battle. Early in the afternoon the guns were pushed forward, this time in an effort to bombard the rifle pits on both sides of the trail. Since they were firing blindly into the bush, their shells had no effect at all on the defenders. The guns were again in a very exposed position and Gunner William Phillips of "A" Battery was hit and severely wounded. He fell and rolled down the slope into the gully on the left of the trail.

The two Midland companies, who had been waiting impatiently in reserve, were ordered into the ravine to distract the enemy's attention so that Phillips could be rescued. Captain James Peters of the artillery and Dr. Alfred Todd, the regimental surgeon of the 90th Winnipeg Rifles, along with some volunteers, managed to get a stretcher down into the ravine. They found Phillips already dead but brought his body back. As soon as they were back within the lines the Midlanders were halted, much to their disgust. They were relatively fresh and eager to get to grips with the enemy. Resistance on the left of the trail had seemed light and most of them believed that they could have broken through with just a little extra effort. Middleton, however, was determined to keep the battle under strict control. A deserter from the Métis side had informed him that his opponents were desperately short of ammunition. He hoped to minimize casualties by forcing the rebels to exhaust their ammunition before letting his troops attack.

About three o'clock the Métis set fire to the prairie northeast of the church in a final effort to drive Middleton's men from their position. As it had been at Fish Creek, the effort was a failure. The wind shifted and the militia had no difficulty controlling it by lighting a backfire. Middleton had already concluded that the rebels were not going to break that day and the immediate question became one

Lieut. A.L. Howard, technical advisor on the Gatling Gun, was popular with the Canadian Troops. [Montreal *Witness*, 1885]

of breaking off the engagement in the least damaging way. Some of the staff argued in favour of withdrawing all the way back to the previous night's camp nine kilometres away. The situation certainly seemed anything but encouraging. Two men were dead and nine wounded by this time, and there was even less indication than at Fish Creek that the enemy had been touched. Rusden found the scene at the church in mid-afternoon gloomy and dramatic.

About the door of the church the ambulance waggons stood, here and there a stretcher with its sickening blotches of red, telling a tale of pain and suffering. Inside the church the wounded stretched out in a row and the busy doctors doing their best to alleviate the pain of dangerous wounds. In front of the church the Midland Regiment lying down taking cover, while the smoke of a prairie fire the breeds had attempted to light gave the picture a weird and warlike appearance.[9]

After consulting his staff, Middleton decided that a retreat all the way back to the camp with the enemy in pursuit would be too hazardous. The mounted troops were withdrawn from the line and sent back to bring up the transport and supplies to a new location about a kilometre south of the church. In this hastily chosen spot, a new fortified camp with trenches and wagons around the perimeter was set up. This "zareba" turned out to have nothing to recommend it except its proximity to the field of battle. It was on a ploughed field, in a slight depression, and was surrounded by bush. When the wagons arrived from the

267

south and were in position, Middleton pulled his troops out slowly and moved them back into the zareba. They had no sooner arrived than the rebels opened fire from the bush near the riverbank, wounding one man and killing two horses inside the zareba. The Midlanders were sent out to drive them off, which they were able to do although firing continued on and off until midnight. The rest of the troops, after eating for the first time since early that morning, were put to work digging trenches. By midnight these were finally completed to the point where the zareba was reasonably secure against attack. For the militia the long, exhausting, and frustrating day was finally over.

Late in the afternoon of the first day of the battle of Batoche, Middleton sent Lord Melgund off to Ottawa. The abrupt departure of the chief of staff at this crucial point in the campaign was a sensational and mysterious event. The general gave no reasons for the action at the time and speculation was rampant, not least because, unlike his chief, Melgund was enormously popular with the Canadian militia, officers and men alike. The most widely-accepted theory among the troops was that Middleton, after failing to take Batoche on the first day of the battle, now feared losing the whole campaign and was sending Melgund back to Ottawa in case it became necessary to organize a relief expedition using British regular troops. The newspapers allowed their imaginations even freer rein. The "Melgund Mission," as the press called it, came at exactly the right time since there was no direct telegraphic communication with Batoche and hard news was temporarily difficult to come by. In reality the departure of the chief of staff had nothing to do with the military situation. Melgund's wife had just discovered that she was pregnant and had made it clear to her husband that she did not intend to raise a child made fatherless in some obscure colonial scuffle. Melgund dutifully returned to Ottawa, but Victorian proprieties ruled out the public mention of so delicate a matter.

If Middleton was not panic-stricken by the possibility of losing to the rebels, neither was he very sure about what to do next. Sunday, May 10, was spent resting the troops from their exhausting ordeal of the previous day and improving the defences of the zareba, and not coincidentally this allowed Middleton to ponder courses of action. Sunday was one of those rare perfect spring days on the prairies, warm, sunny, and windless. Private Charles Clapp of the Midland Battalion wrote, "A heavy dew had fallen during the night but a more charming morning than the 10th of May never dawned." As if in keeping with the unaccustomed softness of the weather, military activity was much less strenuous than on the previous day. Early in the morning the Grenadiers and both batteries of field guns were sent off in the direction of the church. They quickly found that the rebels had established themselves in new positions in the bush to the south of the church and the cemetery. The advance halted without making any effort to drive the Métis from these positions. The guns were brought into action, firing mainly at the village but also at some houses that were visible on the other side of the river. Apart from keeping the gunners occupied, this does not seem to have accomplished much.

The Midlanders went out to the area between the zareba and the river. Here they spent the day digging rifle pits, the better to hold the area after sundown and prevent the rebels from using it to fire down into the zareba. Occasional shots from the rebel lines added spice to the enterprise. Private Clapp recorded, "With pickaxes and shovels we began our work but we were not allowed to proceed unmolested as we would frequently receive a heavy volley from the front and sometimes from our right flank which rendered it necessary for us to abandon for a time our implements and resort to our firearms; when we would drop down beside our half-constructed entrenchments and direct a heavy fire against the desperate and defiant rebels."[10]

The men of the 90th Winnipeg Rifles remained in camp and along with the two hundred or so teamsters who were there spent the day elaborating the trench system around the zareba. The trenches were dug about a metre deep with the earth thrown up in front to form a parapet. On top of the parapet was a log with another log placed a little above it to form a firing slit. Transverse walls were constructed every few metres to prevent an attacking enemy from enfilading the whole trench. The troops were sufficiently proud of their handiwork that sections of the trench were even given names.

That afternoon the Surveyor's Intelligence Corps arrived in camp. Among their ranks was Lewis Redman Ord, who was to write the most acid and entertaining account of the rebellion, published in 1886 as *Reminiscences of a Bungle, by One of the Bunglers*. After supper Ord and a friend went out to visit the Midlanders in their rifle pits to get an idea of how things were going.

The sun was setting and the firing of musketry had almost ceased so we did not lie very close; Wheeler and a redcoat were sitting in the pit and the third man was lying behind it, and all chatting comfortably when there came a sharp "pat" and "b-z-z-zng," a bullet flew past my ear and the crack of a rifle rang out. "Gad" said Wheeler coolly, "there's a hit anyway" and turning around showed where the bullet had punched a hole through the muscles of his arm near the shoulder, fortunately not touching the bone; an excellent shot, too, for the marksman must have been full five hundred yards distant.[11]

The mounted men of Boulton's and French's Scouts were sent out on a wide sweep to the right before heading back to approach Batoche from the east. There had been reports that a large open area existed to the east of the village which the Métis called "la Belle Prairie." Middleton wanted to find out if this offered a better chance to approach Batoche without the dangers of being fired upon from the bush. The reconnaissance confirmed the reports and the scouts returned in time to help with the trench construction. In the evening the infantry were pulled back in, having suffered one killed and five wounded with even less

The Gatling Gun was hastily purchased from the Americans at the outbreak of hostilities in 1885. This primitive machine gun gave the Canadian forces more firepower and boosted morale. [Montreal *Witness*, 1885]

visible result than the previous day. The day's defensive preparations had their effect, however, and the night passed without interruption from snipers.

On Monday, May 11, Middleton decided to explore further the possibility of attacking from the east. Boulton's Scouts, the Surveyors, and the Gatling made their way carefully to the open prairie discovered by the previous day's reconnaissance. The troops were waiting somewhat nervously at the edge of the trees, knowing from bitter experience that the tree line on the other side of the open area probably concealed enemy marksmen, when the general appeared and irritably ordered them forward to the top of a small ridge that ran through the middle of the clearing. Before they could respond, one of Boulton's Scouts, who had been sent back to bring up the ammunition wagon for the Gatling, galloped into the open. The Métis opened fire and Middleton's men followed suit. A brief but vigorous fire fight developed but did no damage to either side. Middleton then broke off the engagement and took his force back to camp in time for lunch. Later, in his official report, Middleton claimed that this movement was designed to draw the enemy away from their positions in front of the church so that the infantry could break through to Batoche, but his actions in the afternoon make this claim improbable.[12]

Had Middleton intended to take advantage of the diversion he had created, he would surely have rushed back to camp and pressed the attack vigorously. Instead the mounted contingent pursued a leisurely course back from their morning's work, pausing on the way to round up some stray cattle before eating a quiet lunch. Nor is there any evidence that the infantry had been told of the alleged plan. Colonel van Straubenzie, in charge of the foot soldiers, had been instructed only to occupy the previous day's positions and await further instructions. Ord's description of the scene that afternoon gives no indication that an attack was under way. After they finished lunch, Ord and several others sauntered out to watch the artillery at work. They were firing at houses on the other side of the river without causing any visible damage.

After whiling away the afternoon in this fashion for some time the keen sight of the decorated warriors descried a number of waggons moving up the trail from the ferry west of the river, and a shell was fired in that direction. I won't say that it was fired at them, for it hardly went into the same township and as our field glasses showed the fugitives to be cattle quietly grazing up the slope, it is well the shot went wide. . . . The General, who swaggered about showing his rotund and rather corpulent figure was quite indifferent whether they pinked him or not; but a number of the officers endeavoured to reconcile the dignity of rank with a wholesale amount of discretion, and it was rather ludicrous to see them standing in line, one behind the other, sheltered by a couple of small poplars rather thicker than a man's arm. Determined to give us precept as well as moral courage, our Commander nerves himself for the occasion and shouts, "Don't look at the gun, men—watch the road; d___n it men! don't look at the gun," rather unnecessarily, and rifles began to crack from our comrades in quite an alarming fashion, had their accuracy been reliable or the enemy in sight.[13]

Middleton later claimed that he used May 10 and 11 at Batoche to settle the troops down and accustom them to being under fire.[14] This was not how most of the soldiers saw it. Trooper Harold Rusden's comment was typical.

General Middleton made a mistake when he thought that the men were settling down to their work and getting steadier. On the contrary they were getting exasperated at the check and were getting dissatisfied and restless at this cold-blooded sort of fighting. They had no proof that they had killed a single rebel and a soldier likes to see the fruits of his work the same as any other man. They wanted to charge and being young and inexperienced soldiers could not understand why they should not charge, but generals usually know more about the whys and wherefores than privates, so the charge was kept back.[15]

Middleton clearly planned a leisurely siege of Batoche but his army was daily less willing to go along with him.

In the late afternoon of May 11, Colonel Williams and the Midland companies, tired of inaction and sensing that the enemy resistance in front of them was less than it had been, decided to test the rebel position. The

Midlanders were on the extreme left of the line facing the cemetery. Private Charles Clapp recorded the action in his diary.

> Colonel Williams with a portion of our detachment was in possession of a bluff overlooking the river in rear of the cemetery and taking advantage of the General's feint on the enemy's left, dashed down beyond the cemetery, drove the Indians who had been left to hold the rifle pits on the right out of them, captured and brought back to camp amidst the cheering of those who were left there pick-axes, shovels, pots, kettles, blankets—and a dummy which had been used to draw our fire, and which had been riddled with bullets. We had now regained all our lost ground but as it was getting dark we had to return to the zareba which we did in good order and were not pursued at all, neither was there any firing after we had retired.[16]

Williams was by this time in a semi-mutinous frame of mind and was quite ready to take matters into his own hands if the chance came. He was not even averse to trying to arrange the proper opportunity himself. He had defied Middleton's predecessor in time of peace and had emerged victorious; why should he not do so now when the chances for glory were infinitely greater?

Middleton seems to have sensed this mood among his subordinates. On May 12 he came up with a firm plan of action for the first time since the opening day of the battle. The mounted troops, the Gatling, and a field gun would attack from the east once again. The infantry would head for the church as before and would press their attack as soon as they heard Middleton's nine-pounder open fire. Middleton had no great faith that the plan would succeed. The previous day he had telegraphed Minister of Militia and Defence Caron, "Am in rather ticklish position. Force can succeed holding but no more—want more troops."[17] Some action was essential, however, and his plan seemed to offer as much hope as any other. The mounted troops took the now familiar path to "La Belle Prairie," where they dismounted and spread out in skirmishing order to protect the field gun. As soon as the gun opened fire, the Métis replied. They had obviously been expecting the attack and succeeded in killing one of the Surveyors almost immediately.

Lewis Redman Ord was part of a small group of Surveyors who were walking up a cut line through the bush to get into position when a volley of shots exploded from the bush. The troops reacted instinctively.

> Perhaps there is some sort of electrical connection between a fellow's ear and the muscles of his knees, causing them to contract, for down I went at once, and then began crawling up the slope when "Celluloid" called out "R_____! Kippen is gone!" "Badly hurt?" I asked, for I had not seen him fall. "I don't know, he is right behind you." I crawled back at once and though the veriest tyro a single glance told me that all medical skill was useless here; our poor comrade was lying in the old survey line on his right

side, one hand grasped the rifle he was about to use, his broad hat was still jauntily cocked on one side of his head, and so calm was his face that had it not been for the thin stream of blood flowing from his upper lip, one would have thought him asleep; the bullet had struck him just below the nose and passed directly through the brain producing instant death, so sudden in fact that he was dead before he fell, and suffered no pain whatever.[18]

Alex Kippen was a popular young man from Ottawa who had considerable experience surveying in the North-West. His friends called him "The Historian" and expected him to write an account of the rebellion when the fighting was over. With his death it was left to his friend Ord to record the experiences of the Surveyor's Corps. Kippen's death soured what had been a light-hearted adventure for Ord and helps to account for the bitter tone of his book.

After the firing had gone on for an hour or so, a horseman holding a white flag emerged from the trees in front of the rebel lines. It was one of the Métis' prisoners, surveyor John Astley, bearing a message for Middleton. It read, "If you massacre our families, I shall massacre the prisoners." Middleton assumed that the note referred to the shelling and wrote back that if the women and children were placed in a clearly marked house, they would not be fired on. While Middleton and Astley were conferring a second messenger, Thomas Eastwood Jackson, arrived on foot with an identical note. Astley agreed to return with Middleton's reply but Jackson refused to go back.

Middleton may well have misconstrued Riel's intentions in sending the message. It looks very much like an effort on Riel's part to open negotiations for a surrender, using the prisoners as leverage. The idea of using hostages to force the government to negotiate had been in his mind since the beginning of the rebellion. As many as four field guns had been firing at Batoche for the previous three days without injuring any of the women and children or apparently causing concern. Why should the firing of a single gun on the May 12 have produced this reaction? In the afternoon Riel sent Astley back with another note thanking Middleton for his humanitarian reaction. On the envelope Riel wrote another combination of threat and hint that negotiations were possible. "I do not like war and if you do not retreat and refuse an interview, the question remains the same concerning the prisoners."[19] Whether or not Middleton understood Riel's message is impossible to determine, but even had he interpreted the note as an offer to negotiate, it was too late. By the time the second message arrived, events were no longer under the general's control.

After the mounted troops left in the morning, the Midland companies and the Grenadiers were sent out to take up the previous day's positions and wait for the sound of Middleton's field gun to begin their attack. The wind was blowing very strongly away from the infantry and directly toward Middleton's position. Faint sounds of firing could be heard but nobody was quite sure if Middleton had opened fire as planned. The stolid van Straubenzie, who had been left in command of the infantry, was not a man to err on the side of initiative. Middleton had shown little aggressive intent on the previous days of the battle and van Straubenzie not unnaturally opted for caution. Part of the difficulty was that Middleton never discussed his plans with subordinates. Major Boulton, one of his warmest supporters, wrote of him, "I never met a man who was so thoroughly able to keep his own counsel, no one knowing until orders were issued what his projects were."[20] The infantry remained in their positions until noon, when the general and his contingent returned. Middleton made no effort to hide his fury at their lack of action and stalked off to lunch after reprimanding the colonels.

This criticism for not attacking was the opening that Colonel Williams, and to a lesser extent Grasett of the Grenadiers and Mackeand of the 90th Winnipeg Rifles, had been waiting for. The evening before they appear to have discussed the possibility of undertaking a charge if their orders could be stretched to cover such an action. Now Middleton could hardly criticize them for being too aggressive. The tongue-lashing Middleton administered to van Straubenzie made him more receptive to the Colonels' aggressive plans. Staff-Sergeant Walter F. Stewart recorded Williams' instructions to his men on the morning of May 12. His remarks make no sense except in the context of a determination on the part of the battalion commanders to charge the enemy in spite of their superior's caution. "On arriving there [the position near the cemetery] Col. Williams formed the companies into a square and addressed us in words scarcely above a whisper as follows: 'I have not received any orders to do what I am going to do. Batoche can be taken and will be taken today. We will advance through and along this ravine. I only ask you to follow me and we will go as far as we can. We will then be supported by the Royal Grenadiers and the 90th Rifles.'"

The charge worked almost exactly as planned. Williams and the Midlanders led off and the Grenadiers joined in. Only the 90th were a little slow to respond, presumably because Colonel Mackeand had put himself out of action that morning by spraining an ankle and command of his unit had passed to a subordinate who was not in on the unofficial plan. The best description of the action comes from Sergeant Stewart's diary.

> The forward movement through bush and ravines then began cautiously and without any firing, merely feeling out the hidden enemy.
>
> Ten minutes passed. Then suddenly a scattered firing came from across the river on our left. We pushed on then more rapidly and were presently met by a volley of shots on our front. Every man dropped to cover and returned the fire. We had at last located the enemy. Col. Williams cautioned us to take cover and lie low. "We will hold this ground until the Grenadiers and the 90th come up on our right." We could see nothing but banks and bush on our right. All the rifle pits of the enemy were still ahead of us and we knew a hot reception awaited us. A few of our men fell and there were many who had narrow escapes.

274

The firing now became heavier from both sides. Then the reinforcements arrived and our whole line was extended a full mile east. The advance all along the line then began in earnest, firing as we went in rushes, then taking what cover we could. There was no volley firing. Every man regulated his own shooting. Then a small fenced-in cemetery was reached. Here our men passed around either side then doubled up to re-form a line beyond. At this point the Indians and half-breeds put up their real fighting. Running from rifle-pit to rifle-pit, firing as they went they fell back, stubbornly contesting every foot of ground.

Snipers from across the river, 200 yards away on our left, kept up a steady firing that worried our flank men. Very heavy firing could be heard on our extreme right where we knew the 90th were having a hot time. All the mounted men, including Boulton's and French's Scouts and the Surveyors' Corps, leaving their horses behind, joined the infantry and further extended the right flank of the 90th. Everything was done to prevent the Indians from getting around to attack us in the rear. Suddenly when rounding a bend at the foot of a rise, the village of Batoche came in full view.[21]

Things were not quite as neatly arranged on the right as Stewart assumed. Captain French was so anxious not to miss the battle that he rushed out of the zareba by himself when the firing started. His men were not allowed to follow him because they had no leader. In the general confusion most of them were able to sneak away individually and join the fighting. General Middleton heard the noise and left his lunch to find out what was happening. By that time the battle was at its most intense and before he could attempt to exert any kind of control, the troops broke through the line of rifle pits at the top of the hill, drove out or killed their occupants, and ran in an increasingly mixed-up crowd down the hill and into the village. There they headed for the two largest buildings: the store where the prisoners were being held and Batoche's house. The momentum of the charge carried the troops into the buildings where they released the prisoners.

The battle was not yet over. Those Métis and Indians who had been drawn away to the east of the settlement by Middleton's morning operation now made their way to some rifle pits in a patch of bush near the village and opened fire on the buildings now occupied by the militia. Almost at once Captain French, who was firing from an upstairs window in Batoche's house, was hit in the chest and killed. For a moment it looked almost as if the rebels might rally and pin their opponents down in the village. Harold Rusden, who had managed to extricate himself from the zareba to join the battle, wrote:

The troops took cover behind the houses, stables and outbuildings and here for the first time the column seemed to manifest a desire to stay where it was. When a man gets behind cover and gets cooled down, it requires something to rouse him again, however a few fiendish yells set the ball rolling again and merciless showers of lead were again poured into the rebels. The Gatling gun came up and the nine-pounders got into position and midst the rattle and crash of the infantry, the incessant rattle of the Gatling gun and the whizzing and shrieking of the shells, the rebels abandoned their last stand and fled for their lives.[22]

The battle of Batoche was over. It was the only clear-cut defeat the rebels suffered but it was enough. They scattered, never again to reassemble as an army.

Those of the Métis who were not killed or wounded were disarmed and allowed to go home to their farms, unless they were immediately identified as members of Riel's council. Conspicuously absent from the list of dead, wounded, and prisoners were Gabriel Dumont and Louis Riel. Middleton and others worried that the two leaders might rally their followers and indeed there were some vague plans for those who escaped to meet at a secret place in the hills, but nothing came of them. The Métis wanted no more fighting. After waiting in hiding for a day or two to see what would develop, Dumont left for the United States. Riel surrendered on May 15 without making any effort to get away.

The Battle of Batoche broke the back of the Métis resistance but the rebellion was not over. At the Eagle Hills on May 14, warriors of the Battleford bands captured 21 teamsters and their wagon train which was carrying supplies for Colonel Otter's column. But after learning of the Métis defeat, the Battleford Indians stopped their movement towards Batoche. For the next few weeks, they would stay in the Battleford area and worry about the conditions the white man's army would likely impose on the Cree and Stonies when it came their turn to surrender.

By mid-May, the government had only one major worry left in the North-West: the Frog Lake Indians still apparently in rebellion north of Fort Pitt.

CHAPTER FIFTEEN

Frenchman Butte:
The Odyssey of General Strange

When General Middleton was at Qu'Appelle making his initial dispositions, his instinct was to keep his force concentrated, but a variety of circumstances prevented him from doing so, especially the intense public pressure to provide garrisons for the major towns. This had been the reason for dispatching Otter to relieve Battleford. The pressure was no less intense in the District of Alberta, the westernmost part of the North-West Territories. Residents of Calgary and Edmonton were bombarding Ottawa with panic-stricken telegrams demanding arms, ammunition, and troops. At first little could be done except to promise arms as soon as they became available and to authorize the formation of local volunteer units. Then a telegram arrived which promised to solve most of Middleton's problems in Alberta. Minister of Militia and Defence Adolphe Caron had been in touch with a recently retired British army officer, Thomas Bland Strange, who was ranching near Calgary. Strange had offered his services. Middleton was pleased. He and Strange had served together many years before in India and although Middleton considered Strange an eccentric, he was confident that Strange, as a former regular army man, could be relied on to follow orders, unlike the impetuous Canadian militia officers.

Thomas Bland Strange was one of the more colourful figures associated with the rebellion. He was a man who genuinely and fervently believed that Englishmen were innately superior to all other members of the human species. He never hesitated to make his opinions known but his prejudices were so open and generally good-natured that it was hard to dislike him. Strange was born in India in 1831, the son of a colonel in the British Army. When his father's regiment was transferred home he attended the Edinburgh Academy. From there he went to the Royal Military Academy, Woolwich, where aspiring artillery officers were trained. Upon graduation Strange served in the usual round of outposts of empire: Gibraltar, Jamaica, India, and various parts of Africa. He fought in the Indian Mutiny but to his great regret just missed the Crimean War. In 1871 Strange was appointed Inspector of Artillery for Canada, an appointment which in addition to overall responsibility for all artillery in the country, entailed direct command of "B" Battery and the Citadel at Quebec.

The appointment was one that Strange relished, partly because he was fluent in French and liked the French Canadians, partly because the job was sufficiently varied and challenging to absorb his truly amazing energies. (It did not

Major General Thomas Bland Strange, "Gunner Jingo," photographed in 1871 when he commanded the artillery at Quebec. Some thought he was none of what his middle name represented and everything his surname implied. [Glenbow-Alberta Institute]

astonish anyone who knew Strange that on the death of his first wife when he was eighty-seven, he immediately remarried. He lived to be ninety-four.) At Quebec Strange organized the garrison artillery, gave instruction to the militia gunners through "B" Battery, oversaw the other gunnery school at Kingston, and frequently led his men out on riot control duty in the city. He conducted experiments in moving and firing field guns in the winter on carriages with sleigh runners and lobbied the Canadian government vigorously for more and better equipment. In his off-duty moments he was an enthusiastic participant in the more strenuous winter sports, especially snow-shoeing and tobogganing.

In 1881 Strange was fifty. He was at the peak of his professional competence and had the vitality of most men half his age. It came as a bitter blow that year when he discovered that the army's new regulations required that he resign at once or forfeit his pension. His promotion to Major General from Colonel on his retirement softened the blow a little but could not compensate for the loss of power. In his autobiography, *Gunner Jingo's Jubilee*, he wrote, "A soldier of 40 is considered too old to lead 100 men, but an octogenarian is not too old to run or ruin an empire." Having discovered there was nothing he could do to change or evade the regulations, he immediately began making plans for a second career. In 1880 Strange had travelled to the west coast on an inspection tour and had been impressed by the possibilities of the ranching country of southern Alberta, where the government was granting large grazing leases.

After considering and rejecting sheep and cattle ranching, Strange finally decided to raise horses. They could be sold locally and eventually, he hoped, to the British Army. Strange formed the Military Colonization Ranch Company, obtained a large grazing lease southeast of Calgary, and launched himself on the enterprise with his usual vigour. He liked the life well enough. The ranch was staffed by his two sons and a number of former soldiers who had served with him at various times. After the ranch was established, Strange began to advertise it in English periodicals as a training school for young men of means and good family who wished to learn the business. To accommodate them he built an imposing ten-room house with attached schoolroom and dining hall.

The only thing that marred Strange's satisfaction with his second career was his neighbours. The Military Colonization Ranch was next door to the Blackfoot Reserve. Strange was not blindly prejudiced against all Indians; some he respected a good deal, especially Crowfoot, of whom he wrote, "Crowfoot, their chief, was like a dark Duke of Wellington in feature, and he had some of the level-headedness and shrewdness of the Iron Warrior." But in the early 1880s, alongside the Blackfoot Reserve was not the ideal location for a horse ranch. The horse occupied a very special place in Blackfoot culture. It was the single most important measure of wealth and status. A young warrior proved himself by stealing enemy horses and could do so in no other way. Of course the Mounted Police had been trying to introduce the notion that horse stealing was illegal but they had had only half a dozen years to alter a deeply-ingrained cultural pattern. When some of Strange's horses disappeared he fumed at the inability of the police and the judiciary to prevent the thefts and longed for "the short and decisive way they manage it over the border."[1]

The Military Colonization Ranch may or may not have been making money by 1885 (Strange claims it was), but certainly the owner did not hesitate for a moment when Caron sent him a telegram from Ottawa on March 29 asking him to raise a volunteer corps, even though he feared, correctly as it turned out, that service might jeopardize his pension. The eagle-eyed clerks in the War Office in London stopped Strange's pension and it took him years after the rebellion to get it reinstated. Strange had little time to worry about his pension in early April, however, because the situation in Alberta was changing from day to day. First he was authorized to organize a volunteer home defence corps but before he could complete that task he was given command of the whole district.[2] The original orders called for Strange to take his volunteers to Qu'Appelle to join Middleton's main column. Strange disliked the idea of taking away all the armed men and leaving Alberta defenceless and he wrote to Middleton to recommend that they stay. Middleton was inclined to agree and on April 6 he replied to Strange, "The fact is that everybody is scared and is losing their senses. I do not believe I shall fire a shot, though I intend being cautious."[3] Middleton was not displeased to have an opportunity to keep the opinionated Strange at a distance. Furthermore with Strange far from the scene of the trouble he could send him any militia units he considered unsuitable for his own use. These included all French Canadian units. Middleton distrusted their training and, less reasonably, feared they would be reluctant to fight the French Catholic Métis, so the 65th Mount Royal Rifles and the 9th Voltigeurs from Quebec City were ordered to Calgary.

Middleton also passed along the Winnipeg Light Infantry, a unit hastily thrown together after the outbreak of the rebellion. These three battalions together with the Rocky Mountain Rangers and the Alberta Mounted Rifles, the local volunteer groups, gave Strange an unexpectedly large force which changed the strategic outlook in Alberta. Strange began to think about the possibility of taking the offensive, leaving the mounted volunteers to patrol Blackfoot country and the border, and a few infantry to garrison the larger towns. Inspector Sam Steele, the most formidable of the early officers of the NWMP, was called back from keeping order on the CPR line construction in the Rockies to lead the scouts for the Alberta Field Force which was taking shape. Another police officer, Inspector A. Bowen Perry, brought one of the old Mounted Police field guns up from Fort Macleod. With the news of the Frog Lake killings and the accompanying pleas for help from Edmonton and Red Deer, Middleton ordered Strange to move north as soon as his troops arrived.

While he was waiting, Strange found much to occupy him. In addition to the apprehended threat from the Indians, a group of settlers south of Calgary were making threatening noises. In the years before 1885 a good many people had ignored the classification of the area as grazing land not open to homestead and had squatted on grazing leases in defiance of the large ranchers. When the ranchers had used the law and the NWMP to evict squatters, there had been much bitterness with occasional arson and cattle killing. Now the squatters saw in the uprising their first opportunity to put pressure on a government that had always sided with their enemies. On April 5 at the farm of John Glenn there was a noisy meeting that drew up a bill of rights calling for justice for the settlers. Sam Livingstone, the chairman of the meeting, went so far as to claim that the settler was "worse off than a wild animal, as a wild animal had a closed season in which he could not be hunted, but a settler was chased at all seasons of the year."[4] Several at the meeting reportedly advocated armed defiance if the government did not meet their demands. Strange, the habits and attitudes of command fast returning, asked for a declaration of martial law so that he could deal summarily with dubious characters, red or white. Fortunately he was turned down.

The Blackfoot were undoubtedly excited by the news of the rebellion, but whatever Strange may have feared, there was little possibility of their joining the Cree. The Cree sent emissaries with presents of tobacco to urge the Blackfoot to take part, but instead they offered their services to the government against the traditional Cree enemy. This was an idea that appealed greatly to John A. Macdonald, presumably because the government would not have to pay the Indians as much as the militia, and the prime minister kept badgering General Middleton and Lieutenant Governor Dewdney about it for most of April.[5] Neither one liked the idea at all and Strange found it unthinkable. Macdonald's queries were evaded until he finally dropped the plan.

Middleton apologized about sending the two French Canadian battalions to Calgary but Strange was delighted to have them. Even if they were untrained, he was confident of his ability to make them into competent soldiers in short order. When the 65th Mount Royal Rifles arrived in Calgary on April 12, their commanding officer, Lieutenant Colonel J. Aldéric Ouimet, MP, was in a highly agitated state. He had serious stomach problems, he told Strange. He had left some baggage in Winnipeg and should go back for it. If he went all the way to Ottawa it would be even better because he could personally expedite the shipping of supplies to the battalion. In Britain it was customary to give soldier Members of Parliament leave to attend sittings of the House while it was in session. Should not the same rules apply to him? The baffled Strange was happy to send Ouimet back East and turn the battalion over to his second in command. The hostile Ontario press immediately noted Ouimet's absence and held it up as an example of French Canadian cowardice. After flurries of telegrams between Caron and Middleton and Middleton and Strange, the unfortunate Ouimet was ordered back West. He spent some time under a doctor's care in Calgary before catching up with the battalion at Edmonton, where Strange left him in command of local defence.

By April 20 sufficient ammunition and food had arrived and enough transport had been assembled to allow Strange to begin the journey north, even though the Winnipeg Light Infantry had not yet arrived. On that day Strange left Calgary with half of the 65th Mount Royal Rifles, Steele's Scouts, and the Alberta Mounted Rifles. Both mounted units were composed mainly of ranchers and cowboys from southern Alberta. As soon as transport was available a second contingent consisting of the rest of the 65th, twenty Mounted Police, and the field gun would follow under the command of Inspector A. Bowen Perry. When the Winnipeg Light Infantry reached Calgary they would follow at once. The trip to Edmonton, although it was only three hundred and twenty kilometres, was not an easy walk. Calgary was a recent creation of the Mounted Police and the railway and there had been little travel between the two centres before 1885. The route had none of even the modest amenities of the Carlton Trail, such as ferries, trading posts, and stopping places. Several sizeable rivers had to be crossed and in the second half of the journey the trail often led through heavy bush and swamp, a difficult journey for the 175 wagons that made up the column's transport. No opposition was encountered along the way and at the Battle River the Cree chiefs Bobtail and Ermineskin appeared to proclaim their loyalty. Strange, putting on his best white-man's-burden manner, refused to shake hands with them but said he would do so on his return if they behaved themselves in the meantime. On May 1 the column reached Edmonton and camped on the north bank of the Saskatchewan under the walls of the Hudson's Bay Company fort.

The population of Edmonton received the column with relief which quickly turned to consternation when they discovered that the general intended to leave only one company of the 65th Mount Royal Rifles as a garrison. Consternation deepened when Colonel Ouimet organized and armed a group of Métis volunteers from nearby St. Albert. The Edmontonians had disbanded their Home Guard when Strange arrived but now hastily reformed it. To placate them the general promised them Snider rifles from the next shipment to arrive. When he left Calgary, Strange had sent the Methodist missionary John McDougall ahead to announce his coming and to order the construction of boats to carry his men downriver. The boats were of Strange's own design and he was mightily pleased to find them nearly completed by the Hudson's Bay Company's experienced boat builders when he arrived. There were five large, flat-bottomed scows with the cargo ingeniously arranged around the outside to act as protection for the troops in the middle. Another barge was fitted with a platform to mount the nine-pounder so that it could be fired from the water. Still another was strengthened to carry the horses with hay bales around the outside for protection. Strange also purchased and took along a ferry and cable.

The General's boats did not inspire confidence in all who were supposed to ride in them. The commanding officer of the Winnipeg Light Infantry, Lieutenant Colonel Osborne Smith, went so far as to express his misgivings in the form of an official letter of protest. Strange was far too experienced a soldier to be bothered by this kind of opposition. "The protests were met by ordering a Board of Officers, (selected on the principle of a jury to convict an Irish murderer,) to take the evidence of experienced H.B. navigators and the boat-builders themselves," he wrote.[6] No further protests were heard but the doubters had the dubious satisfaction of seeing some of their fears proved correct. The boats leaked so badly that the soldiers on board spent as much time bailing as they did at the oars. The horse boat made it only as far as Fort Saskatchewan, thirty kilometres downstream from Edmonton, before sinking.

On May 15 the force left Edmonton and as the movement downriver proceeded the expedition sorted itself into a more or less regular pattern. The mounted scouts travelled on the north bank of the river and the two infantry battalions took turns marching and rowing the boats. Three days' journey downstream brought the force to the Hudson's Bay post at Fort Victoria, where Strange halted for two days to await the arrival of Cree chief Pakan, who was believed to be loyal, in hopes of obtaining some of his people to act as guides. None was willing to go so Strange took the mounted troops, the pioneer detachment of the 65th Mount Royal Rifles, the field gun, and the Winnipeg Light Infantry and marched north away from the river to investigate the situation at Frog Lake. On May 23 the column reached the scene of the massacre. No one had visited the site since the killings and the scene was shocking even for Strange, who was a veteran of the Indian Mutiny. All the buildings of the settlement were burned to the ground and some of the decaying, headless bodies were unburied. The soldiers wasted no time in burying the bodies and leaving the scene. The same day they got back to the river at Fort Pitt, where they rejoined the 65th Mount Royal Rifles and the boats. Strange sent off a messenger to announce his arrival to Middleton and set his men to rebuilding the fort as much as possible so that it could be used as a headquarters during the search for Big Bear and his prisoners.

Strange had temporarily outrun his supply train by the time he reached Fort Pitt. Ammunition was still plentiful because no fighting had been done but food was short and the men were down to three-quarters of their normal rations. Not knowing how close Middleton was, Strange decided not to wait for him before going after Big Bear, since there were strong indications that he was still in the vicinity. After they had taken Fort Pitt the Indians had gone back to Frog Lake for a time and then returned to the neighbourhood of the fort. There were serious differences of opinion between the Plains Cree, most of whom wanted to go south and join Riel or Poundmaker, and the Woods Cree, who wanted a more passive role. On May 4 the Indians got some rather vague reports of the battle of

Cutknife indicating that Poundmaker had been defeated and was retreating. This news had two contradictory effects. Big Bear was so depressed by it that he gave up his leadership of the band. On the other hand the news strengthened the determination of the Woods Cree to stay out of any further fighting and to continue their protection of the captives. The Indians decided to hold a Thirst Dance to try to bridge the differences between the two factions while messengers went to find more definite news about Riel and Poundmaker.

It did not take Strange's men long to discover the Indians' trail, which led off to the northeast from Fort Pitt. This was no great feat of woodcraft since the passage of nearly a thousand people left a very noticeable track. Lewis Redman Ord, who was in on the later stages of the pursuit, described the process.

> I suppose the idea of waggons following an Indian trail through thickly wooded country is rather startling in civilized people, whose acquaintance with the noble red man is derived chiefly from the works of Fenimore Cooper or Parkman, but the Indian has sadly degenerated since the days of Pontiac and the trail left by Big Bear was no faint and indistinct track made by men with moccasined feet in single file or any such absurdity, it was a broad road cut through the woods, better than many a Canadian bush road, beaten by the feet of some hundreds of men and horses and the wheels of nearly a hundred carts.[7]

Steele's Scouts followed the trail a few miles from Fort Pitt and on the afternoon of May 27 had a brief skirmish with a Cree war party, killing one. They discovered a recent encampment in which they counted 187 teepee rings. Strange quickly brought up the Winnipeg Light Infantry and the field gun and set off after the retreating Indians. After marching several miles past the scene of the first encounter, the Indians were again sighted on the top of a ridge. The field gun was unlimbered and fired a few shots, driving the Indians off the top of the hill. The troops quickly moved to the crest and into the heavy bush on the other side. Strange decided not to push on at this point. It was getting dark and the 65th Mount Royal Rifles had not yet caught up. Camp was made and the soldiers settled down to a hungry night. The 65th had left all their food at the boats in their hurry to reach the sound of the fighting, and the other troops had to share their already reduced rations with them.

In the morning Strange's force pushed on, passing through another large campsite just before the trail dropped into a steep valley. The valley bottom was covered thickly with small poplar and willow bush. A small stream wound along the valley floor and much of it turned out to be marshy. On the other side of the valley was a steep, bare hill with trees along the crest. A bolt of calico cloth had been draped among the trees to the right as if signalling the column in that direction. Strange halted his force at the top of the bank and carefully examined the hill opposite with his field glasses. He could see fresh earth thrown up from

The Battle of Frenchman Butte. Capt. R.W. Rutherford made this sketch after visiting the scene of the fight. The Cree rifle pits were just at the crest of the hills in the background. The nine-pounder gun in the foreground is likely the one now at Fort Edmonton park in Edmonton. [Glenbow-Alberta Institute]

the construction of rifle pits just inside the tree line and decided that the Indians had prepared a trap for him. The troops were ordered down into the valley and the field gun opened up from the top of the hill. The soldiers quickly discovered that the valley bottom was an unpromising route. Men and horses sank deeply into the swamp and the troops fired blindly up the hill at the concealed enemy. There was a brisk exchange of fire but the two sides were far enough apart that few casualties resulted.

Strange correctly concluded that a charge up the bare, steep hillside against a well-dug-in enemy would be suicidal. A movement down the valley to the right would be almost as bad since the Cree positions overlooked the trail. Steele was sent to investigate the possibility of moving around to the left but reported that the whole area was covered by dense bush. To outflank the Indians on the left would have meant abandoning, at least temporarily, the horses and wagons, which Strange was not prepared to do. After a discussion with his officers he decided to break off the engagement and await supplies and reinforcements before resuming the pursuit. Unknown to Strange, the Cree were also preparing to retire, having been unsettled by the shells from the field gun which had caused a number of casualties. In the afternoon both sides retreated in opposite directions; the Cree travelled north into the bush and Strange moved his force

Sam Steele in 1883, probably the best-known of the early Mounties. He commanded a group of scouts and cowboys in General Strange's column. [Glenbow-Alberta Institute]

back to Fort Pitt. The hill where the Cree were entrenched was incorrectly identified by both Steele and Strange (and by a number of historians since) as Frenchman's Butte, and the battle took its name from that non-existent feature. A few miles to the south there is a large hill called Frenchman Butte, named for a Métis free trader who maintained a trading post there in the 1870s. From the accounts of both Steele and Strange it seems likely that this was the ridge the Indian war party was driven off by the field gun on the night before the battle.

After a shipment of supplies reached Fort Pitt from Edmonton, the column moved off once again, this time encountering no Indians at the scene of the fight. The trenches and rifle pits that the Indians had constructed were carefully examined and the soldiers found a note that the prisoners managed to leave among the debris that the departing Indians abandoned. While they were so occupied, word arrived that General Middleton had at last reached Fort Pitt with reinforcements. Strange decided to wait for him but sent Steele off with the mounted men, about seventy in all, to keep in contact with the Indians. Steele's men found the trail of a smaller group diverging from the main body a few kilometres from the battle site. This turned out to be a small group of Woods Cree with half a dozen of the prisoners, who waited for the scouts to catch up and surrendered. Steele's little force pushed on for two days and on June 3 caught up with the Cree where they had camped on the shores of Loon Lake. Steele's men caught the camp by surprise and their sudden attack forced the Indians to break camp hurriedly and retreat across a fordable narrows that connected two parts of the lake. Several Indians and one of the McLean sisters were wounded and a

Woods Cree chief, Cut Arm, was killed instantly as he stepped out of his teepee.

By this time three of Steele's men had been seriously wounded and the rest were down to fifteen rounds of ammunition per man. He pulled back several kilometres and camped, leaving a few men to watch the trail in case the Indians tried to follow. The sentries fired several volleys at what they took to be Indian scouts approaching their position.[8] In fact, the Indians had sent Hudson's Bay Company Factor William McLean and one of the other prisoners to try to negotiate a surrender but they were unable to get close enough to contact Steele's men. Their failure tipped the balance in the Indian camp back in favour of the war party. The Woods Cree were angry because of the death of Cut Arm, but fortunately for the prisoners his place was taken by another well-disposed leader, Louison Mongrain. Once again both sides retreated in opposite directions and the soldiers were condemned to another month in the wilderness.

With Riel defeated and Poundmaker under arrest, Middleton set about organizing the pursuit of Big Bear in a remarkably ponderous fashion. Strange, with the 65th Mount Royal Rifles and the Winnipeg Light Infantry, was ordered north west to Frog Lake, then north to the Roman Catholic mission at Beaver River, in case the Cree should decide to escape to the west. Otter was given "A" Battery, the Infantry School Corps, the Governor General's Foot Guard, and the Queen's Own Rifles, and was sent north from Battleford to Jack Fish Lake. Commissioner Irvine, with 130 Mounted Police, left Prince Albert, crossed the river at Fort Carlton, and patrolled north in the direction of Green Lake. Middleton himself assembled a force consisting of all the available mounted units: Boulton's Scouts, the Surveyors, French's Scouts, and a few Mounted Police under Superintendent Billy Herchmer, a Gatling gun, and 150 infantry from the 90th Winnipeg Rifles, the Grenadiers, and the Midland Battalion. He set off from Fort Pitt to take over from Steele the direct pursuit of the Indians. The four columns moving north roughly parallel to one another were designed to catch the Cree whichever way they turned and prevent them from breaking through to the south.

Strange's men were not in good shape by the time they were ordered to Beaver River. Many of them had completely worn out their boots and were reduced to marching with their feet bound in rags. All of them were tattered, dirty, and exhausted. Very warm weather had set in and the mosquitoes and other biting insects were out in force. Nevertheless the men slogged loyally on, dragging their field gun through swamps and reaching Beaver River on June 7. There Strange interrogated a group of Chipewyans who informed him that the Woods Cree would probably try to cross the Beaver River and head for Lac des Isles or Cold Lake. Strange had his men repair a few boats they found and sent a party of men down river to try to pick up the trail of the Woods Cree. They were unsuccessful, although the Chipewyans had been correct. The Woods Cree had broken away from the Plains Cree after the Loon Lake fight and had taken the

"On Big Bear's Trail—The Artillery Mess. 'A dashing young Officer' tossing a flapjack. The other Officer is sitting in the smoke, trying to keep the mosquitos off" in this sketch by artillery captain R.W. Rutherford. [Glenbow-Alberta Institute]

prisoners with them. They took the prisoners north across the Beaver River and remained there for some days before Factor W. J. McLean persuaded them to let the prisoners go. On June 19 the captives made their way to Loon Lake, where they were picked up and escorted to Fort Pitt.

Middleton's column proceeded north from Fort Pitt on June 3 for about sixteen kilometres, then halted. It was early in the day and the troops were mystified by the order to make camp. Just about this point the country changes quite abruptly from rolling parkland with numerous open stretches to solid, gloomy boreal forest. Middleton seems to have been concerned by the change and worried about the effect it might have on his supplies if the already narrow trail deteriorated too much to allow his wagons through. Some hastily-constructed pack saddles were tried out but proved useless as a replacement for the wagons so Middleton ordered the troops to construct Indian-style travois. They did so but when the travois were completed, they turned out to be able to carry even less than the pack saddles. Surveyor Ord, an old hand at travelling in the west if not at soldiering, could scarcely believe what was happening.

And what is done? The camp is turned into a factory for "travails," as if the idiocy of the pack-saddles were not enough and from about ten A.M. on Thursday until Friday night, nearly two days, we are in camp pottering over these primitive conveyances. What is a "travail"? As many people have never seen a "travail" or "travois" I will try to describe one. Suppose a couple of long poles between which a horse is harnessed as between the shafts of a cart, the rear ends of the poles trail on the ground and the load is carried on a frame-work of cross-bars just clear of the horse's hind legs and you have a travail; but do not think you can imagine how small a load can be carried on one, or what antics a horse accustomed to the civilized harness of a double team would perform when he found himself saddled with this primitive style of go-cart. On Friday night the infantry were sent back to Fort Pitt, and next morning, after this very necessary halt in our rapid forced march (?), we moved forward again, mounted men, Gatlings, waggons—oh, yes! waggons—and the travails? Packed on top of the waggons.[9]

Two days' march brought the force, which had picked up Steele's Scouts along the way, back to Loon Lake. The Indians had long since departed, leaving only the bodies of those killed in the fight with Steele and one Indian woman who had hanged herself, apparently because her husband had been killed. The next day the force went several kilometres beyond the lake before Middleton decided it was too swampy to continue. After returning to camp and discussing the situation with his staff, he confirmed the decision and issued orders to return to Fort Pitt. Most of the soldiers were eager to push on after Big Bear, even if it meant abandoning the supply wagons, and there was much grumbling even by such loyal and obedient souls as Trooper Rusden. The trip back was quickly accomplished and when he arrived at Fort Pitt Middleton found a message from Strange that he had discovered a large cache of flour at Beaver River. The Indians were known to be short of food, so Middleton decided that this must be where they were headed. The column set off for Beaver River at once. By the time Middleton arrived, there was still no sign of Big Bear's Indians. The general undertook a reconnaissance of his own to Cold Lake but had no better luck than Strange's men, so he consoled himself by spending a day fishing in the lake. He had scarcely returned to Beaver River when word arrived from some of Strange's Indian scouts that the Woods Cree were releasing the prisoners near Loon Lake. Middleton hurried back to Fort Pitt to meet them with the troops following at a more leisurely pace.

The other columns had no better luck than Strange and Middleton. Otter's force marched north from Battleford to Jack Fish Lake, then proceeded to carry out patrols in a rather aimless manner. The only consistent feature of their marches seemed to be that they managed to find a good lake to swim in at the end of each day. There was little anxiety about the possibility of meeting the enemy and the militia enjoyed these sightseeing tours through the countryside. Orders finally arrived June 29 and the column marched for Fort Pitt on June 30, quite happy to abandon the swimming tournament that had been organized for that day in favour of the prospect of getting home.[10]

When the Plains Cree and the Woods Cree split up at Loon Lake, Big Bear's band set off with the intention of going to Batoche to join Riel. The band began to break up almost immediately. Ayimāsis and Dressy Man left the first day and rejoined the Woods Cree before escaping to the United States. Big Bear pushed on, now apparently with the intention of surrendering. He passed close to the easternmost government force which was looking for him, the Mounted Police contingent under Commissioner Irvine that was heading north to Green Lake. The police missed him, however, and had the same frustrating experience as the other columns. The forced marches through the bush quickly reduced them to a dirty and bedraggled collection of scarecrows. Many were wearing flour sacks for shirts by the time the hunt ended. The warm weather and the necessity to examine abandoned Indian campsites brought to the men's clothing unwelcome guests that had to be disposed of in any way possible. One of the militia officers who accompanied Irvine's column actually found his men spreading their shirts over ant hills so that the ants could clean out the lice.

On July 2 Big Bear, now accompanied only by his youngest son, Horse Child, appeared at Fort Carlton and surrendered to the four-man Mounted Police detachment that had been left there to watch the ford when Irvine went north. As one of his pursuers remarked rather sourly, Big Bear surrendered to the only four men in the North-West Territories who weren't looking for him. The surrender was a symbolic end to the rebellion.

By the time the old chief gave himself up, the militia were lined up on the river bank at Battleford waiting for the steamers to arrive to take them on the first leg of the journey home. Their jubilant mood was dampened when Colonel Arthur Williams, "the Squire of Penryn," always the most popular officer not only with his own men of the Midland Battalion but with all the soldiers who came in contact with him, suddenly fell ill and died on July 4 of what was officially described as "brain fever." His death shocked and saddened the militia, who were increasingly disenchanted with Middleton. Williams' death played no small part in the growth of the belief that he was the real hero of Batoche.

All the militia engaged in the operations in the north against Big Bear were loaded onto steamboats and shipped down the Saskatchewan to Lake Winnipeg. Here they transferred to other boats for the journey to Winnipeg. The line of communication troops to the south went back via the CPR. Middleton planned a mass parade of all the troops through the streets of Winnipeg on July 16 but torrential rain drowned out the plan. The homesick militia were by now thoroughly sick of military life and in no mood to wait around for the weather to improve so they could stage a spectacle for the general's benefit. When this mood communicated itself to the staff, the troops were hastily loaded on trains and sent to the Lakehead, where they boarded lake steamers for home. Every city and town that had sent a unit greeted their return with ecstatic crowds, and an orgy of banquets, church services, speeches, and plans for memorials followed. By the end of July all the troops were home and the last military operation in which Canadians shot and killed each other was over.

PART THREE

Stamping Out the Embers

CHAPTER SIXTEEN

The Trial of Louis Riel

Long before the soldiers were sent home the government began making plans for Riel's trial. Ottawa would not have been displeased if Riel had been a casualty of the battle of Batoche. The government would, in all probability, even have preferred to see Riel escape to the United States rather than try him. After his capture, opposition newspapers openly predicted that the government would arrange an "escape." They continued to do so until the trial was actually under way. Left with no alternative, the government made their preparations with great care to ensure that Riel received the maximum penalty. The trial was in one sense a straightforward, open-and-shut case, there being no possible doubt that Riel had led an armed rebellion against the legally constituted government.[1] The events of 1885 included none of the legal ambiguities that the transfer of the Hudson's Bay Company territories to Canada had created in 1869. Because the North-West Territories were still not fully integrated into the Canadian legal system by 1885, however, there were a number of highly complex legal issues involved. The intricacies of the case were such that they were not fully grasped by any of the lawyers on either side although they included some of the best legal minds of that era.

The core of the government's prosecution team consisted of three lawyers who were among the most highly respected members of their profession. Christopher Robinson of Toronto was the son of John Beverly Robinson, a man who had done more than any other single individual to form the Upper Canadian legal system in the half century between 1812 and 1862. Christopher Robinson was as talented as his father and had represented the Canadian government in such important and complex international cases as the Bering Sea arbitration. There was no more smooth and polished courtroom performer in the country. The second member of the team was B. B. Osler, by far the best known Canadian criminal lawyer of his day. The fact that Osler was a Liberal helped offset the appearance of political bias on the part of the prosecution. The Deputy Minister of Justice, George Burbidge, was the third pillar of the prosecution. A few years after his involvement in the Riel trial, Burbidge would be the architect of the Canadian Criminal Code, the first comprehensive codification of the criminal law in the British Empire. For essentially symbolic reasons a French Canadian lawyer, T. C. Casgrain of Montreal, and a westerner, D. L. Scott of Regina, were also added.

The strain of the rebellion shows clearly in this sketch of Louis Riel drawn by Capt. H. de H. Haig at the time of the rebel leader's surrender. The sketch first appeared in the *Illustrated London News* on June 27, 1885. [Glenbow-Alberta Institute]

Riel was penniless when he surrendered and was thus unable to provide himself with defence counsel, but his supporters in Quebec collected money for a defence fund and were able to come up with an impressive array of legal talent. The two principal defenders were François-Xavier Lemieux, the leading French Canadian criminal lawyer of the time and future Chief Justice of Quebec, and Charles Fitzpatrick, later Minister of Justice in Laurier's cabinet and Chief Justice of the Supreme Court. Two junior counsel, James Greenshields of Montreal and T. C. Johnstone of Winnipeg, rounded out the defence.

The government very nearly prejudiced its case on a technicality at the outset. When Riel was captured, Minister of Militia and Defence Caron ordered him taken to Winnipeg. The Minister did not elaborate in his brief telegram to Middleton, but the reasons appear to have been that it would be easier there to guard against attempts to free Riel and that Caron assumed that Winnipeg was where the trial would take place. Five years earlier he would have been correct. Before 1880 the Territorial courts were not empowered to try capital cases and had to send them to Manitoba or British Columbia. Many historians have tried to manufacture a plot out of Caron's change of instructions, sent on May 21, a

The Regina courthouse where Riel and most of the other rebels were tried. [Glenbow-Alberta Institute]

week after the initial telegram, ordering Riel to Regina instead of Winnipeg. The theory is that the government wanted to deny Riel the half French-speaking jury that would have been his right in Manitoba. The difficulty with this interpretation is that there is not a shred of direct evidence to support it. Caron's original order was clearly due to an oversight, corrected by the Minister of Justice, who pointed out that Riel could not legally be tried in Manitoba. Once this difficulty had been sorted out, Riel was taken to Regina and turned over to the keeping of NWMP Inspector R. Burton Deane, an ex-Royal Marine who had recently joined the police.

With the question of the venue settled, the next important matter was the nature of the charge. By raising a rebellion and making war on the representatives of the Queen's government, Riel had committed treason. The question was, what was the law of treason in the North-West Territories in 1885? Like any other former British colony, the North-West Territories had acquired the full range of British law in effect at the time the British took over from the aboriginal inhabitants. In this case the date was that of the royal charter granting the territory to the Hudson's Bay Company, May 1, 1670. After that date laws passed by the British parliament and interpretations of those laws by British courts ceased to apply unless they were specifically adopted by the local legislature. When the North-West Territories became part of Canada in 1870, therefore, its law consisted of British law as of 1670 modified by local legislation passed by the Council of Assiniboia during the two centuries of Hudson's Bay Company rule. The Council of Assiniboia was much closer to a municipal council than a colonial legislature and had never bothered to address itself to such majestic offences as treason. It tended to be more concerned with such matters as the penalties for allowing pigs to run loose. Thus in 1870, treason in the North-West Territories was exactly what it had been two centuries earlier. The Statute of Treasons, passed by the British parliament in 1352 during the reign of Edward III, was the law under which Riel was charged.

Some writers have portrayed the government lawyers as having dredged up an obscure medieval law in an effort to avoid having to try Riel under more modern and humane legislation. In fact, had Riel carried out his rebellion in Ontario or in England, the legal situation would have been the same. The statute of 1352, modified and interpreted by centuries of judicial decisions and learned commentary, was still the basic law of treason in Britain and throughout the Empire. The Statute of Treasons, as with most medieval law, was ferocious in its penalties. The judge who found someone guilty of treason had no option but to order him hanged, drawn, and quartered, and to have all his possessions confiscated by the Crown. Over the years, the confiscation and mutilation had been dropped, but the courts could still not assign any penalty short of death.

In a more humane age than that of Edward III, the mandatory death penalty was awkward because juries would sometimes refuse to convict in treason cases when the involvement of the accused was relatively minor. In the nineteenth century, therefore, the British government had introduced by statute a new offence known as treason-felony, which allowed the courts to award any penalty from a few days imprisonment to life. The British statute was copied by the Canadian parliament in 1868 when it passed "An Act for the Better Security of the Crown and of the Government." In 1873 this act, along with most of the rest of Canadian criminal law, was extended to the North-West Territories. Technically the government had the option of charging Riel with either treason or treason-felony and, in fact, the other leading rebels were charged with treason-

Louis Riel addressing the jury at the end of his trial. [Glenbow-Alberta Institute]

felony and given fairly short jail sentences. But in the circumstances of 1885, when dozens had died because of Riel's actions, it would have been inconceivable to charge Riel with any offence that did not carry the death penalty. To do so, however, left the court with no flexibility.

The fact that Riel was an American citizen introduced an additional complication. A foreigner cannot, of course, break the law and expect to escape punishment. Treason, even though it is a rather special kind of criminal offence involving a violation of the duty of obedience owed to the sovereign, is in the eyes of the law no different in principle from theft or murder. The situation of a foreigner committing the offence of treason is covered under an ancient and well-recognized principle of law known as the doctrine of local allegiance. Since the visitor to a country in theory accepts the protection of his person and property by the host government, he in turn owes that government obedience, even though he is not a citizen. The difficulty in Riel's case arose from the fact that British law of the period held that a person born a British subject could not lose that status later through naturalization in another country. To satisfy Canadian law Riel had to be charged as a British subject, but the United States had always strenuously objected to this doctrine and the two countries had actually gone to war over the issue in 1812, when the British persisted in impressing American seamen into the Royal Navy on the grounds that they were British subjects. To avoid diplomatic complications, the charge against Riel consisted of two sets of three identical counts, one of which named Riel as a subject of Her Majesty, the other simply as "living within the Dominion of Canada and under the protection of our Sovereign Lady the Queen."[2]

The information and complaint against Riel charging him with taking up arms at Duck Lake, Fish Creek, and Batoche was sworn by Alexander David Stewart, Chief of Police of Hamilton, Ontario. Stewart was generally considered to be Canada's most progressive and efficient police chief. He had reformed and rebuilt the Hamilton police force of the 1880s into one of the best in the country and was a natural choice as the government's chief investigator to put together the cases against Riel and the other rebels. Stewart was of Scottish ancestry but was born in Italy, where his father was employed as a Presbyterian chaplain. As a young man in Toronto he first made a name for himself through his prowess in sport, at one time being considered the outstanding all-round amateur athlete in Canada. In 1878 he married Emily Otter, youngest sister of Lieutenant Colonel William Otter. Stewart was a great favourite of the press because of his penchant for uttering highly quotable and frequently controversial remarks. Passing through Winnipeg on his way west, the "genial and handsome chief" had time for a brief interview with a reporter for the Winnipeg *Sun*, and got off a typical sally. "He intended to get all the evidence he could against Riel and by any means, for, said the chief, with a sly laugh, 'I guess the idea is to hang him.'"[3] In addition to his role as chief investigator, Stewart as signer of the complaint had

O.B. Buell took this photograph at the time of the 1885 trials. *Back row, left to right*: NWMP Constable Blache, Father Louis Cochin, NWMP Superintendent Burton Deane, Father Alexis André, prosecutor Christopher Robinson. *Front row, left to right*: Horse Child, Big Bear, Hamilton police chief Alex Stewart, Poundmaker. [Glenbow-Alberta Institute]

some political value. He was a well known Liberal so his signature helped establish the non-partisan character of the government's case.

The trial began at eleven o'clock on July 20 in the small courtroom which was one of the prefabricated frame buildings that had been erected in Regina a few years previously to house the government and the NWMP. Riel's lawyers opened by objecting to the venue and arguing that a capital case should not be tried before a stipendiary magistrate and the six-man jury provided for under the North-West Territories Act. After a brief adjournment, the first objection was dropped and the attorneys for both sides spent the afternoon arguing the competence of the court. This was an issue that had been decided the previous month when an appeal court had upheld the right of the Territorial courts to try capital offenses in the case of a murderer named Connor, who had been sentenced to death in Regina. The judge, Hugh Richardson, after hearing the arguments, which were lengthy and learned, rejected the plea. Riel's lawyers then entered a rather half-hearted objection to the double set of charges, which was again promptly turned down by Richardson, who seems to have been as well prepared as any of the participants.

The following day Riel's lawyers asked for an adjournment of a month to allow them to bring in a number of witnesses they held to be essential to their defence. These included Gabriel Dumont, Michel Dumas, and Napoleon Nault, now in the United States, and three medical men from Eastern Canada. Richardson granted a week's adjournment but refused to consider immunity for the witnesses who were fugitives across the border. Riel personally signed the affidavit requesting Dumont, Dumas, and Nault. His lawyers signed a separate one requesting the medical witnesses. The two separate affidavits made it clear

Witnesses at the Riel trial. *Back row, left to right*: William Tompkins, Harold Ross, Peter Tompkins, Eastwood Jackson. *Front row, left to right*: George Ness, Charles Nolin, John Astley, Thomas Sanderson. [Glenbow-Alberta Institute]

that Riel and his counsel had different views on how the defence should be conducted.

When the court reconvened on July 28, the prosecution began by introducing Riel's letter to NWMP Superintendent Crozier at Fort Carlton calling on him to surrender. With the first witness, Dr. John Willoughby of Saskatoon, the strategy of both sides became clear. Robinson led off the examination for the Crown by trying to demonstrate that Riel both intended to raise a rebellion and actually took up arms to do so. In his cross-examination Fitzpatrick made no effort to disprove Riel's connection with the uprising but tried instead to draw out the witness on the more extreme elements of Riel's plans for future of the North-West and the church. Most of the rest of the witnesses on the first day had been Riel's prisoners at Batoche and the pattern of questioning continued in exactly the same manner on both sides.

On the morning of July 29 the prosecution finished with Riel's captives and began calling some of the soldiers who had been involved, starting with General Middleton and ending with Superintendent Crozier. Riel sat quietly through the first day and a half of testimony, but when Charles Nolin came to the stand his attitude changed abruptly. Nolin was Riel's cousin, but he had never fully accepted Riel's leadership in 1870 and he had similar doubts in 1885. Nolin had been among those who arranged for Riel to return from the United States in 1884 but later abandoned his support for Riel when rebellion became a possibility. Riel regarded Nolin as a traitor and found his testimony more than he could bear. As Lemieux was completing the cross-examination, Riel became agitated and broke in on the questioning to demand a chance to refute Nolin. This incident brought the conflict between Riel and his lawyers out in the open.

The prosecutors immediately said that they were willing to let Riel ask questions. Judge Richardson would have gone along but Fitzpatrick and Lemieux were adamant. Until the time came for his closing statement, Riel could speak only through his lawyers. Riel could see by this time that sole strategy of his defenders was to prove his insanity and he objected strenuously to their approach on two grounds. In the first place he did not believe he was insane. In the second, a trial which concentrated on his mental state would do nothing to bring before the world the Métis grievances, the crimes of the government, and his own plans to solve the problems of the region. Riel's lawyers acted out of a genuine concern for the best interests of their client. They knew that the only possible way of winning an acquittal was to convince the jury of Riel's insanity. The law recognized no justification for rebellion. The strategy of the defence was an issue on which there could be no compromise and after his lawyers threatened to quit if he persisted, Riel agreed to remain silent.

When the court opened on July 30 it was the turn of the defence to call their first witness, Father André. It was at this point that they made their first and only effort to argue justification for the rebellion. Father André was questioned extensively about the efforts to get action from the government and the lack of response until the rebellion was imminent. Perhaps this was done deliberately to show Riel the futility of such an approach because of his outburst the previous day. Lawyers of Lemieux's and Fitzpatrick's experience cannot have had any illusions about how far they would get with this approach. As soon as Lemieux's line of questioning became clear, the prosecution objected and Judge Richardson, as he was bound to do, upheld them.

The defence returned to a discussion of Riel's mental state. Father André believed very strongly that Riel was insane but he proved ultimately to be a damaging witness for the defence case. On cross-examination the prosecution skilfully drew out the story of the bribe in such a way as to make it appear that Riel had bargained very rationally for personal gain. The next two defence witnesses, Philippe Garnot and Father Fourmond, were not much better. Garnot, the reluctant secretary of the Métis council, was concerned mainly with establishing his own innocence and was exceedingly cautious in his answers, almost monosyllabic. Father Fourmond believed Riel to be insane but his reasons were based on the prisoner's heretical religious notions. Father Fourmond's lengthy theological discussion, sufficiently abstruse that a more sophisticated interpreter had to be found half way through, did not mean a great deal to the Protestant jury.

The next morning saw the introduction of the first expert medical witness, Dr. François Roy, Superintendent of the Beauport Asylum near Quebec City. With Roy's testimony, as with that of all the medical witnesses and most of the others, the defence was attempting to prove Riel's insanity. In 1885 in Canada and Britain (and any other English-speaking country for that matter) there was no legislated definition of what constituted insanity. The defence of not guilty by reason of insanity was part of the common law and had been very largely established as a result of two famous nineteenth century cases. Before 1800 the law had been quite simple, allowing for acquittal on grounds of insanity if the accused was, as a British judge put it in 1724, "totally deprived of his understanding and memory, and doth not know what he is doing, no more than an infant, than a brute or wild beast."[4] This so-called "wild beast test" was easily administered in the courts because any layman could make a considered judgement about whether or not an accused was totally deprived of reason.

In 1800, a former English soldier named Hadfield attempted to assassinate King George III. Hadfield, who had been invalided out of the army because of severe sabre wound to the head suffered while fighting the French, was charged with treason. During his trial he explained very lucidly that God had told him that he must die for the good of mankind. Being a devout man, Hadfield found himself in a dilemma. God wanted him to die but as a good Christian he could not commit suicide, which was against the teachings of the church, nor could he commit a capital crime which harmed someone else. After much thought he had come up with his ingenious scheme to take a shot at the King but deliberately fire wide. In this way no one would be hurt but the authorities would be obliged by the letter of the law to execute him.

It was obvious to everyone concerned that Hadfield was insane and yet he could not be considered so under the wild beast test. He was quiet, had an excellent memory, and clearly had the ability to reason. The court solved the problem by acquitting Hadfield on the grounds of "partial insanity." This verdict effectively scrapped the wild beast test as the sole criterion for insanity and introduced the concept of what psychiatrists of the day called "monomania" to the law. This was the idea that an individual might be perfectly normal in every area of life except one. After Hadfield's case it was much more difficult to determine who was insane and who was not, so the second important effect of the case was to make the expert witness an essential part of any trial involving insanity. While the ordinary layman might not be able to detect monomania, the expert, because of his special knowledge and training in systematic observation, could. Trials in which the sanity of the accused was an issue could be won by the side which could assemble the most convincing panel of expert witnesses.

This was demonstrated most vividly in 1843 during the trial of Daniel McNaghten. The accused in this case was labouring under the delusion that the Prime Minister, Sir Robert Peel, was persecuting him. McNaghten shot Peel's secretary, Edward Drummond, in the mistaken belief that he was shooting Peel. McNaghten's lawyer collected an impressive array of expert witnesses and moulded their testimony into such a convincing argument that he was able to convince the jury his client was a victim of monomania and he was found not guilty. The acquittal caused such intense public indignation that the government took the extraordinary step of asking the common-law judges to answer a series of five questions which would clarify the law concerning the insanity defence. The judges' answers to these questions are known as the McNaghten Rules and have constituted the basic law governing insanity defences in most common law countries ever since.

At the risk of oversimplifying, it can be stated that the McNaghten Rules established two major principles. The first was that the insanity of the accused, partial or total, must be such that he was unable to comprehend the illegality of his act. The judges rejected the idea that an individual could be acquitted if he knew his action to wrong yet was unable to resist the impulse to do it because of the nature of his delusion. The second principle was an attempt to restrict the scope of expert testimony. Unless the doctor was actually treating the accused at the time of the offence, he could not give a direct opinion about his sanity. Under the McNaghten Rules, lawyers were only supposed to ask hypothetical questions of the experts, whether, for example, a particular type of behaviour could be considered to constitute insanity.

Riel's trial was conducted under the assumption by all parties that the McNaghten Rules applied, but one of the stranger aspects of the case is that they probably should not have. The Rules were a part of British common law that had developed after 1670 and which therefore should not have applied in the courts of the North-West Territories. Some time after the trial the Canadian government seems to have belatedly realized the situation, because less than a year later parliament passed legislation specifically extending the common law as of 1870 to the North-West Territories, thus retroactively legitimizing the trial. If Riel's lawyers saw the oversight they certainly took care not to raise the issue, since the error worked in their client's favour.[4]

Because Dr. Roy had actually treated Riel for mental illness at the Beauport Asylum near Quebec City in the 1870s, he was potentially the most damaging expert witness for the prosecution. Their cross-examination concentrated on the lapse of time since Riel had been confined at Beauport and the large number of inmates who went through the gates of the asylum each year. The second medical witness, the Superintendent of the Toronto Lunatic Asylum, Dr. Daniel Clark, had had no previous contact with Riel. Considering this, the court allowed the defence a great deal of latitude in examining Dr. Clark. Fitzpatrick asked him directly if, on the basis of the testimony he had heard, he considered Riel to be insane. Clark replied that he did. The Crown did not object to this line of questioning, presumably because they felt confident of being able to counter it. Prosecution lawyer Osler's cross-examination went directly and unerringly to the heart of the matter. First he got Clark to admit that Riel knew the nature and quality of his actions and that the actions were illegal. Second he got an admission that Riel's actions could be accounted for by clever malingering as well as by insanity and that only months of direct observation would permit

Clark to tell the difference for certain. The prosecution under the McNaghten Rules had the great advantage that the burden of proof was on the defence. Osler was skilfully planting seeds of doubt in the minds of the jury.

The prosecution strengthened its case against Riel's insanity by calling some expert witnesses of its own. Dr. James Wallace, Superintendent of the Hamilton Asylum for the Insane, testified bluntly and unequivocally that he believed Riel to be completely sane. Nothing the defence attempted could shake his testimony. Dr. Augustus Jukes, the NWMP surgeon who had visited Riel daily since his capture, claimed no special expertise in the area of mental illness but testified that he had seen no indication of insanity in his extensive conversations with the prisoner. The most the defence could get Jukes to admit was that he had never raised the subject of religion with Riel. The prosecution also recalled a number of lay witnesses, including General Middleton and NWMP Superintendent Deane, all of whom testified that Riel had been entirely rational in his dealings with them.

A modern observer of Riel's trial might wonder why his attorneys, if they were intent on proving his insanity, did not put him on the stand and question him directly on his religious beliefs and political ideas, subjects which almost invariably provoked violent reactions. The answer is that the law did not allow them to. One of the more curious features of the Canadian criminal justice system in 1885 was that the defendant in a criminal trial could not testify as a witness for either the defence or the prosecution (except in cases of common assault). The accused was allowed his closing statement after the defence had completed its case but no questions were permitted.

Riel took full advantage of his opportunity when it came. There can be few longer or more eloquent such statements in Canadian legal history. Riel spent part of his time justifying his actions by discussing the grievances of the Métis and the unresponsiveness of the government. Most of his speech, however, dealt with the question of his own sanity. He thanked his lawyers for doing their best to get him off and he thanked Dr. Roy for his good intentions. Then he proceeded to demolish, point by point, the arguments for his insanity. It was a remarkable performance, and if the defence had any hopes of acquittal before Riel began speaking, they can have had none by the time he finished. After Riel's speech, Robinson's summation for the Crown and Judge Richardson's charge to the jury were anticlimactic. It took the jury only thirty minutes to return a verdict of guilty, but they accompanied their decision with a recommendation for mercy. After another lengthy and this time considerably more rambling speech by Riel, Judge Richardson sentenced him to hang at Regina on September 18.

Riel's lawyers immediately launched an appeal to the Manitoba Court of Queen's Bench, which was the appeal court for the North-West Territories. The principal basis for the appeal was the question of the validity of the six-man jury,

The trial of Louis Riel. *Left to right*: Charles Nolin (barely visible), interpreter (standing), prosecutor Christopher Robinson (in robes), Judge Richardson and Magistrate Lejeune (on bench), Riel, prosecutor B.B. Osler (in robes), NWMP Superintendent Burton Deane (seated at right). [Glenbow-Alberta Institute]

although the insanity question was raised as well. The appeal court, in a unanimous decision, rejected the arguments of the defence. The six-man jury, they admitted, was something of an oddity in a common-law jurisdiction, but the undoubted right of parliament at Ottawa to create such a jury overrode the matter of its size. The judges were even firmer in their rejection of the appeal against the lower court's finding that Riel was not insane. After the Manitoba court handed down its judgement, there was a final appeal to the highest tribunal in the empire, the Judicial Committee of the Privy Council. The execution had to be postponed first to October 22, then to November 10, to allow the appeals to be heard. The Judicial Committee listened to Riel's lawyers present their case but ruled that no grounds for an appeal existed.

As soon as Riel was sentenced on August 1 the public, which had been following the trial via the verbatim reports that appeared daily in the newspapers, began to express opinions. On the whole, the reaction of the English-speaking population was predictable. The Tory press and its readers were rather smugly satisfied that justice had been done. The Liberal newspapers could not have been more pleased if they had written the jury's response themselves. During the fighting they had been in the rather awkward position of trying to combine condemnation of the government with support for the suppression of the rebellion. Now they could have it both ways because the jury had condemned Riel to death, which they thought he deserved, but had also recommended mercy, which they could and did interpret as an implied criticism of the government neglect that had caused the rebellion. The only fear that the opposition press had was that Riel might escape and let the government off the hook. The Toronto *Globe* and other Liberal papers were full of speculation that the government, having ostentatiously convicted Riel, would now arrange his escape to avoid the political consequences of hanging him, or at least look the other way while Riel's friends rescued him.

These rumours of a rescue plan seem to have been not entirely without foundation. A plan of sorts to release Riel and smuggle him across the border seems to have been made by Pascal Bonneau, a French Canadian businessman living in Regina. Before coming to Regina, Bonneau had been a rancher and horse trader in the Wood Mountain area between Regina and the border, where there was a sizeable Métis community. If anybody could arrange to rescue Riel, Bonneau was the man to do it. He had the horses, he had the contacts in the area, and he knew the country. Late in his life, Bonneau told his daughter and son-in-law, who was an amateur historian and indefatigable collector of material relating to the rebellion, that Lieutenant Governor Dewdney had approached him after the trial to set up an escape for Riel. According to Bonneau's story he was to set up relays of fast horses every sixteen kilometres between Regina and the border. Riel's guards would be taken care of in some unspecified manner and he would be whisked across the border to the United States. The scheme fell through, however, when one of the Wood Mountain Métis revealed details of the scheme to Charles Nolin on the mistaken assumption that Nolin knew what was going on. Nolin, who had been the chief witness against Riel at his trial, naturally told the authorities, who doubled the guard, and the rescue had to be abandoned.[5]

The story sounds plausible on the surface and Bonneau would not appear to have any motive to lie to his daughter, but there are difficulties in accepting it. The Wood Mountain Métis, who were an essential part of the scheme, had remained loyal to the government during the rebellion and had, in fact, formed a group of scouts to assist the NWMP in patrolling the border. Independent evidence corroborating the story is almost entirely absent. Regina was certainly alive with rumours about an escape plan in the fall of 1885 and there is a newspaper report that Bonneau had gone to the United States and returned with a large number of fast horses. That is all. Nothing in the Mounted Police Reports or the diaries and reminiscences of those involved indicates that extra guards were assigned or that the police had heard any reports of an escape attempt. It seems likely that Bonneau and his friends may have talked about plans among themselves and may even have taken some steps to set up the escape route. The rest is surely an old man's embroidery of the past.

From the outbreak of the rebellion to the end of the military campaign, the French Canadian press had followed the same pattern as that in English Canada:

Conservative newspapers had condemned the rebels and praised the government; opposition journals had criticized government handling of the unrest but had enthusiastically cheered on the militia. With Riel's conviction there was a fundamental and highly significant change. After the finding of insanity in Jackson's case, held during the recess in Riel's trial, the French Canadian press confidently expected that the insanity verdict would be repeated. To the French Canadian population, steeped in Catholicism, Riel's heresies were much more real and jarring than they were for the English Protestant majority. No one in Quebec had the slightest doubt that Riel was of unsound mind.

When the jury brought in its verdict of guilty, the shock in French Canada was profound and crossed even the most deeply ingrained party lines. Suddenly the French newspapers were full of references to another famous trial that had taken place in the United States a few years earlier. In 1880, Charles Guiteau had assassinated the American President, James Garfield, acting under the delusion that in doing so he was obeying the will of God. The trial at which Guiteau was eventually convicted was one of the most notorious in nineteenth century American legal history. The jury chose to ignore much evidence and expert testimony that Guiteau was insane. Guiteau was scarcely cold in his grave before public opinion, which had supported his conviction, began to shift. Within a year the trial was universally considered a miscarriage of justice. As far as the French Canadian press was concerned, Riel's trial was an exact parallel. The rumblings from the Quebec press were dismissed by Prime Minister John A. Macdonald, whose Conservatives had dominated the province's politics for a generation, as a temporary aberration. It was to prove the worst miscalculation of Macdonald's political career.

CHAPTER SEVENTEEN

The Other Trials:
Justice Unbalanced

During Riel's trial, the jails at Regina and Battleford were filled with a cast of supporting characters. The entire Métis council, except those in the United States, were waiting for the government to decide what charges to lay against them. Will Jackson was charged with treason-felony. His case seemed easiest to handle. Chiefs Poundmaker, Big Bear, One Arrow, and White Cap were all charged with treason-felony, as was Tom Scott, the white leader of the English half-breeds. Some of those responsible for the Frog Lake murders and the killing of Payne and Tremont near Battleford were awaiting trial on murder charges along with three Frog Lake Indians charged in the killing of the wehtikow. Four Sky Thunder, of Big Bear's band, was charged with setting fire to the Frog Lake church. Dozens of other Indians were charged with offences that ranged from treason-felony to theft and possession of stolen goods. Not including most of the Indians, the government prosecutors had a list of 202 people they had charged or were considering charging as a result of the rebellion. Some of the Métis and a large number of the Indians involved in the outbreak had fled to the United States, among them Gabriel Dumont, Michel Dumas, Fine Day, Ayimāsis, Chief Little Poplar, and some of those involved in the Frog Lake killings.

To the prosecutors, the government at Ottawa, his family, his lawyer, and most of the Canadian public, the case of Will Jackson seemed simple enough. Here was a man brought up in a strict Methodist environment who had not only converted to Catholicism but had embraced Riel's peculiar version of that religion. Here was a white man, not long in the North-West, who not only wholeheartedly supported the Métis and the Indians but clung to odd ideas that the natives somehow lived a more moral life than the whites. His behaviour since his arrest was additional proof that William Henry Jackson was insane.

Jackson was one of the two dozen prisoners escorted from Prince Albert to Regina near the end of June 20. He was shackled in the back of the wagon to Chief One Arrow and he was guarded by Hugh Nelson, a Prince Albert volunteer and veteran of the Battle of Duck Lake, who later wrote about the trip. Jackson made every effort to be uncooperative. At times he refused food. He refused to be led around. He even refused to relieve himself. Nelson and Jackson had a particular dislike for each other and Nelson's description of the trip is obviously highly coloured. "Jackson had not shaved or cut his hair for possibly the 3 or 4 months and was playing crazy. He would not keep quiet, so we separated him from the Indian [One Arrow] and hobbled him, but he kept rolling around sometimes quite a distance."[1] When night came, Nelson was exasperated with Jackson and probably more than a little vindictive towards him. He staked him to the ground spreadeagled and threw a blanket over him.

When they reached Humboldt, the dispute between Jackson and his captors reached an extreme. In Nelson's words:

All the rest of the prisoners would go quietly to ease themselves, but Jackson made both dung and water in his underwear. Would not do it when taken out of the wagon. He got so filthy that even the other prisoners objected, and Inspector [G. E. Sanders] told us we would have to give him a bath at the next water. We camped at a slough and Geo. [Cockrill] and I took him out and over [to] the edge of the water, and stripped him, tore some of his clothes off, and then we had to push him into the water. He walked out till the water was up to his arm pits, and would make faces and duck under, then bob up, but he would not come out, and the Inspector thought he might drown himself. Walters and Baker, General store in P.A. [Prince Albert] had got a stock of underwear in the fall of 1884, colored strips round the legs of drawers, in Yellow Blue and red like some hockey suits, and Jackson was wearing a suit of them. The piss had run the dye and his legs were stripped like the underwear, and the Indians said he had his war paint on. Finally the Inspector sent two horsemen in on the opposite side to drive him out. The wagons had been drawn up alongside the slough, and when he came out he ducked around the end of the wagon and off across the prairie as hard as he could go and being naked he outdistanced the others but was run down by a man on horse, and brought back. That was the last time he was unshackled from the Indian.[2]

When he came to trial on July 24 at Regina, during the adjournment of the Riel trial, Will Jackson was as recalcitrant as ever. He refused to answer to his name but after the charge was read, he interjected: "As far as responsibility of mine about what you call rebellion, I have always declared myself perfectly responsible, that is to say, as Riel's secretary, and I wish to share his fate whatever that may be."[3] This implied desire to be hanged was just an additional grounds for the plea his lawyer entered and with which everyone in the court agreed: not guilty by reason of insanity.

As legal formality required, a jury was empanelled and B. B. Osler announced the Crown would not contest the defence plea. Eastwood Jackson related for the court some of the events of the rebellion, coupled with his highly biased opinion that his brother was not in his right senses. There was little evidence that any crime had been committed but the defence called two doctors, neither of whom had any expertise in insanity and both of whom testified that if

Jackson were insane at the time of the trial, it was only a mild form of insanity. NWMP physician Augustus Jukes testified: "I have never seen anything about him to give me the impression that his actions were uncontrollable, it is rather his mental hallucinations, his ideas. He holds peculiar ideas on religious matters in connection with this trouble, and in connection with the new religion of which he thinks Riel is the founder, and which he thinks it is his duty to sustain."

By the time the jury returned the verdict that everyone except Jackson wanted, the charade had taken about thirty minutes. Will Jackson was sent to the lunatic asylum in Manitoba.

As soon as the Riel trial finished, the prosecutors turned their attention to the Métis council, trying to coerce guilty pleas and save the time and expense of trials. The prisoners' advisors told them, Philippe Garnot recalled: "They have decided to convict you and we see no means of saving you because you can not be certain of a fair trial. The Crown has offered that if you plead guilty, you will be charged with treason-felony. But, if you refuse, you will be charged with high treason and several of you will be executed."[4]

The lawyers for the Métis believed the Crown had enough evidence for high treason convictions and they were worried about the feelings of Regina juries. On August 3, lawyer Daniel Carey wrote to Archbishop Taché, who had hired him to help with the Métis' defence. "The Crown had decided to indict them all for High Treason, and the proof in every case being complete, and the Regina juries being very hostile, we had no doubt that sentences of death would be recorded against them all."[5] But the evidence in at least some of the cases was not as strong as Carey believed and the Crown had in fact already decided to charge the councillors with treason-felony. In the middle of July, chief prosecutor George Burbidge telegraphed Minister of Justice Alexander Campbell that despite the strength of the evidence against the councillors, their "execution, if convicted, would not be thought of because they were not leaders or were compelled to take first steps by more or less force."[6] The prosecutors had, therefore, decided that treason-felony charges would be the wisest course, Burbidge said.

All the councillors and other Métis prisoners at Regina except Garnot and Moïse Ouellette accepted the bargain. "Father André then had the goodness to tell me that I would be hanged. I told them that I did not consider myself guilty and I could not conscientiously plead guilty and that, if I was hanged, it would be more as a victim of the hatred for my nationality," Garnot wrote.[7] More pressure followed and the two balky councillors held out only for an extra day before they also agreed to plead guilty to treason-felony.

The only thing the defence lawyers believed they could do was present evidence to mitigate the sentences. In this effort, they had lots of help. Most of the white prisoners the Métis had held wrote affidavits attesting to the kind treatment they had received from various of the accused. Charles Nolin wrote a strong appeal for his friends. As usual, and with a fair bit of exaggeration, he blamed everything on Riel. Surveyor John Astley, who had been a prisoner of the Métis, went even farther than Nolin in condemning Riel, conjuring up unlikely conversations with the Métis leader to show that most of the Métis were innocent victims. Father Fourmond and Father André let their rhetoric soar, portraying the Métis as poor, uneducated, ignorant dupes and Riel as a diabolical snake, a would-be Pope, and a venal opportunist. The gist of most of the affidavits was that the Métis were forced into rebellion either directly by Riel or indirectly by the force of circumstances.[8]

On August 14, eleven prominent Métis, including Garnot, Albert Monkman, Maxime Lepine, and seventy-two-year-old Pierre Parenteau, were sentenced to seven years in jail. Three, including Moïse Ouellette and Alex Fisher, were sentenced to three years, and four got one year. Seven Métis, including Emmanuel Champagne, schoolteacher Octave Regnier, and eighty-two-year-old Alexis Labombarde, were conditionally discharged. The Crown decided not to proceed against four of the accused, including Charles Nolin's son, André, and Daniel Parenteau, whom the prosecutors believed to be insane. There were still a few Métis in jail awaiting trial but with the exception of Riel and Magnus Burston, a very minor figure in the rebellion, no other half-breed would ever actually be tried. After a rebellion that was supposed to have resulted from Métis agitation and to have been led by Métis, the legal system put most of its effort into prosecuting Indians. There would be no plea-bargaining with the Indian accused. The government was determined to put them all on trial and find them all guilty.

The day before the Métis councillors were sentenced, One Arrow, chief of the Cree reserve on the eastern edge of the Batoche settlement, was tried before Judge Hugh Richardson and a six-man jury after pleading not guilty to treason-felony. The trial did not begin well for One Arrow. The indictment read in part that One Arrow "together with divers other evil-disposed persons to the said Alexander David Stewart unknown, armed and arrayed in a warlike manner, that is to say with guns, rifles, pistols, bayonets and other weapons, being then wickedly and feloniously assembled and gathered together against our said Lady the Queen, most wickedly and feloniously did levy and make war against our said Lady the Queen . . . and against the peace of our said Lady the Queen, her Crown and dignity."[9]

In translation to the Cree idiom, the indictment came out as an accusation of knocking off the Queen's bonnet and stabbing her in the behind with a sword. One Arrow had not even met the Queen let alone subjected her person to any such indignities. "Are you drunk?" he asked the interpreter. The chief wanted to know to whom the indictment referred. When he was told the government was accusing him of those deeds, One Arrow lost his patience. "No! Wait! Wait! I will speak!"[10] But under the rules of the day, the chief could not give evidence. He had to trust his white lawyer to do the talking for him.

In opening the Crown's case, Thomas-Chase Casgrain told the jury that One Arrow could have been charged with high treason but because the Indians "have an indefinite notion of the allegiance which they owe to their Sovereign, it was thought proper to bring this man before you on an accusation for a crime of lesser degree." One Arrow willingly joined the rebels and fought with them at Duck Lake and Batoche, Casgrain said.[11]

Surveyor John Astley was the Crown's star witness but all that he could swear to was that One Arrow had been at Batoche. He apparently saw One Arrow armed, but that was not unusual among the Indians and he could not say that the chief had ever fired his gun. When he took a message from Riel to Middleton on the last day of the Battle of Batoche, Astley saw One Arrow near the rifle pits but he could not say for certain what he was doing there. He heard One Arrow talking with Riel and with members of his band but Astley did not understand Cree and so could not say what was being said.

The Toronto *Mail*'s correspondent said that One Arrow was, with the exception of Poundmaker, the most intelligent Indian in the Regina jails. But under cross-examination by defence lawyer Beverly Robertson, Astley said One Arrow was often described as "a worthless hound." The courtroom broke into laughter. Robertson, the aggressive lawyer the government had hired to defend the Indians at Regina, was not amused. Astley had heard that said about many other Indians, the lawyer suggested. A few, Astley replied. That was, in fact, Astley's opinion of most Indians, Robertson suggested. No, the witness replied. Who, specifically, had called One Arrow a "worthless hound"? Almost everybody who knew him, Astley said, and Robertson kept pressing, trying to attack Astley's credibility on the basis of his prejudice against Indians.

The Crown's two other witnesses, Indian Agent John Lash and Deputy Sheriff Harold Ross, who had both been rebel prisoners, were even less specific than Astley about acts of rebellion One Arrow might have committed. Defence lawyer Robertson hardly bothered to cross-examine Lash, only trying to bait him about the notion that One Arrow was a "worthless hound." He asked no questions at all of Ross.

Unlike most of the other treason trials he conducted in 1885, Judge Richardson took no notes of the evidence in the One Arrow case. Lawyer Robertson thought there was none worth noting. He told the judge: "Not a tittle of evidence has been given here to show that this man at all participated in the purpose for which this rising was made. The most that is shown is that he was present when fighting was going on, but he himself doing nothing. It seems to me that that is the gist of the whole evidence. It amounts to nothing more than that." Robertson asked Judge Richardson to direct the jury to bring in a not-guilty verdict.

The defence lawyer argued that it was not enough for the Crown to show merely that an accused was present during rebellion. They had to also show that he participated in it or at least knew what was happening. From what the Crown had presented against One Arrow, it was not even clear that the chief knew that a rebellion was occurring, he argued.

But B. B. Osler argued that the Crown had shown that there was a rebellion and the onus was on the accused to show that he may have been at the scene innocently. What the Crown and defence lawyers discussed at One Arrow's trial was a fine legal point, but for One Arrow and many other Indians charged with treason-felony it was critical. Was a person's mere presence among rebels in 1885 sufficient proof of treason? Neither defence lawyer Robertson nor prosecutor Osler believed that it was. But they argued about the nature of the evidence that must, by law, be brought to show that a person's actions while among rebels amounts to treason. If Judge Richardson understood the argument, he did not make it clear to the jury. On the other hand, though they both tried, Robertson and Osler did not explain the complicated law very well. The six laymen who formed the jury must have found it highly confusing. What Robertson needed more than anything was for Judge Richardson to tell the jury clearly that the law required something more than a person's mere presence to constitute treason. But if he didn't get that, if Judge Richardson badly or incorrectly explained the law to the jury, Robertson had absolutely no recourse. Unlike most other jurisdictions, in the North-West in 1885 there could be no appeal from the judge's charge to the jury, a situation Robertson pointedly noted during the One Arrow trial.

Defence lawyer Robertson realized that he was not only dealing with difficult law and questionable evidence but that there was an element of racism, a feeling that no doubt had been heightened by Astley's "worthless hound" testimony. He pleaded with the jury to take into account One Arrow's background as a member of a race and culture alien to theirs. The fact that One Arrow was an Indian might in itself be enough to explain why he was at Batoche during the rebellion, Robertson told the jury. "We know that an Indian, when any excitement is going on, is very apt to go where the excitement is in the hope that he might get something to eat. Now, that is not treasonable felony. It is not treasonable felony even for a band of Indians to go and rob a store to feed themselves, by any means. It is not treasonable felony for a band of Indians to go to try and release one of their own number that is in prison." One Arrow's presence might also be explained by what was known about Riel's activities, Robertson said. "Riel carried on the whole of this scoundrelly business by means of all kinds of intimidation, and falsehood and imposture. We know that, and my explanation to you is that these people were frightened and imposed upon by him, just as it was proved at his trial that he imposed upon hundreds."

To be found guilty, in law One Arrow had to have had an intent to aid the rebellion, an understanding of what was happening, his lawyer said. "Unless, for instance, he understood what Mr. Riel was after, unless he understood his scheme, and that he wanted to depose the Queen, to drive her out of these territories, and establish a new republic of his own, unless he understood all that, and did it for that purpose, and was there encouraging and aiding in that, he is not guilty of this offence."

Osler's address for the prosecution was much shorter than Robertson's defence statement. He told the jury that One Arrow's actions at Batoche could not be construed as consistent with innocence. As soon as Osler finished, Robertson began a new argument on the nature of the evidence necessary to prove treason. The defence lawyer thought the prosecutor's address to the jury had been inncorrect on the law of treason. The rebellion of 1885 fit the legal definition of a "constructive levying of war" not a "direct levying of war," Robertson said. It was an important distinction. In a case of a direct levying of war, such as an invasion, an accused person's mere presence among the rebels is enough for a treason conviction even if that person did not know what was being done. But in constructive levying of war, the Crown must prove that the accused helped the rebels. "I want the jury to understand it must be shown that the prisoner actually aided and assisted in the acts of violence that constituted the constructive levying of war," Robertson said, paraphrasing the standard legal authority of the time. Osler at first demurred, then bowed to Robertson's interpretation. But the prosecutor said that the Crown had proved One Arrow had acted with and aided the rebels. Judge Richardson seemed confused.

In his short charge to the jury, Judge Richardson entirely ignored the law that the defence and prosecution had spent so much time trying to define. But he was careful to instruct the jury about circumstantial evidence, as Robertson had asked him to do. Circumstantial evidence, as Astley's was, could not convict a person unless it was well corroborated by other witnesses.

Despite the complex law, Robertson's aggressive defence, and the amount of circumstantial evidence, the jury returned a guilty verdict after deliberating only ten minutes. One Arrow then addressed the court and said that he had never intended to harm anyone, that he was at Batoche under compulsion. "Gabriel took me prisoner. He asked the whole of us to go down to the place. I now beg your Honors and all you learned people here to—I know I have done nothing wrong, I can't see where I have done anything wrong against anybody so I beg of you to let me go, to let me go free."

In passing sentence, Judge Richardson told One Arrow:

Old as you are, and gray-haired as you are, you knew you were doing wrong, you knew you had no right to leave your reserve where you had promised to live, and, much as I dislike to punish an Indian, or to punish anybody, much as I dislike to pass sentence on anyone, I shall be as wanting in my duty to the public and to the Crown as you were if I did not place such a punishment upon you as would make you feel it, as also make the other Indians of the country know what would become of them if they followed your bad example. If my memory does not fail me, I recollect giving you personally some words of good advice three or four years ago at Prince Albert, and if you had followed them you would not be here.

Richardson sentenced One Arrow to three years in penitentiary.

Father Louis Cochin, who attended the trial, was disgusted. He wrote Archbishop Taché that the jury "without a doubt, have no schooling, and understood nothing of the lawyers' speeches, for or against. However nothing can be proven against this poor man."[12]

Poundmaker's trial, which began on August 17 before Judge Richardson, was regarded as second in importance only to the Riel trial. At Poundmaker's two-day trial, there were no arguments about the meaning of the law or the nature of the evidence required to prove a charge of treason-felony. It was clear that Poundmaker was the chief of a band of Indians who apparently rose in rebellion. The Crown tried to show that Poundmaker had a hand in the rebellion by directing and encouraging the Indian effort. The defence tried to show that Poundmaker had lost control of his band and that what authority he exercised was limited to trying to stop the violence. The cornerstone of the Crown's case was the letter written at Cutknife on April 29 and sent to Louis Riel, signed, apparently, by Poundmaker and four other Indians. The Crown argued that Poundmaker had dictated part of the letter and had directed Farm Instructor Robert Jefferson, who had the job of writing it down, to sign his name to it. The defence argued that there was no evidence that Poundmaker had composed any of the letter, nor was there any clear evidence to show that the chief had agreed to have his name appear on it.[13]

The letter itself was proof enough of a rebellious intent. It bragged about the success of Big Bear's band at Fort Pitt and mentioned that the Battleford Indians had killed a number of whites. The letter told Riel that, in essence, Battleford was under siege. The letter asked for news and ammunition. The Crown wanted to prove that Poundmaker intended to levy war against the government as evidenced not only by the letter by but his actions during the so-called siege of Battleford, the Battle of Cutknife Creek, and during the seizing of the transport team and taking of prisoners on May 14.

Farm Instructor Robert Jefferson, Poundmaker's brother-in-law and the Crown's star witness, testified at length about his own actions during the rebellion and about the conversations he had with Poundmaker while he was held captive by the Indians. But the most important part of his evidence concerned the April 29 letter. Jefferson was nervous in the witness box and his answers often appeared confused and imprecise. Asked by whose authority he signed Poundmaker's name to the letter, he first answered: "By the authority of the men that told me to write the letter." At this point, it was not clear exactly who had told Jefferson to write the letter, except that Poundmaker was present in the tent when the letter was composed. Prosecutor David Scott asked Jefferson if he had any authority from Poundmaker to sign Poundmaker's name. He replied: "Well, I consider I had. I would not have written it if I had not had authority, that is very certain." Poundmaker at least knew his name had been signed, Jefferson testified after a further question. How did he know, Scott asked, and Jefferson gave a confusing answer.

> Well, when they were finished, you see one said one thing and another another, and it was very difficult to do anything at all, and I began to get puzzled, and I did not know who was the man that was running the business at all, and Oopinowwaywin was sitting here, and I believe he dictated the latter part of the letter, and when it was done I said whose name am I going to put here? Oopinowwaywin said this man, pointing to Poundmaker, as if it was very silly to ask such a thing, and I looked at Poundmaker and said is that so? Yes, he said, and the other fellow said, put all our names down, so I put them all down.

Defence lawyer Robertson, who had taken a dislike to Jefferson, made a sharp attack on his credibility with abrupt questions during his cross-examination. Jefferson was not nearly as precise about details when Robertson asked him the questions as when the Crown had asked him. During the long cross-examination, Jefferson's testimony became increasingly confused on most points. But he stuck to one vital point, although he could not be too specific about it: Poundmaker had agreed that his name should be signed to the letter.

Robertson hoped to establish that once a soldiers' tent was erected in an Indian camp the political chief no longer had any power, at least in matters of war. But Jefferson, although he later wrote that was his belief, had only seen a soldiers' tent erected once, during the 1885 troubles, and said at the trial he couldn't testify very well as to its meaning. Robertson had a bit better luck in his cross-examination of another Crown witness, Peter Ballendine, who testified that Poundmaker took no direct part in the sacking of Battleford. But the defence lawyer did not ask Ballendine about the significance of a soldiers' tent, something the experienced trader and Dewdney's "secret agent" among the Indians might have been able to testify about. Hudson's Bay factor William McKay's evidence was similar to Ballendine's. Some of the captured teamsters testified that as far they knew, Poundmaker had no part in the attack on their wagon train.

Joseph McKay, the farm instructor on Strike-Him-on-the-Back's reserve, testified for the defence that when a soldiers' tent was erected the political chief lost his power to control his band and remained unshaken in his testimony despite vigorous cross-examination by B. B. Osler. The most unlikely witness in the trial was John Craig, the farming instructor on Little Pine's reserve and the victim of the assault that had nearly started a war a year before. He testified in Poundmaker's defence that the chief had apparently no violent intentions when they met as the Indians were on their way to Battleford at the end of March. Robertson also called a Cree Indian, Grey Eyes, to testify about the meaning of a soldiers' tent and reinforce the defence position. Grey Eyes said that the soldiers' tent in Poundmaker's camp during the rebellion had been erected by the Stonies, but once it was erected the warriors were in control of the camp. "The chief has no control over anyone when that soldiers' tent is up," Grey Eyes said. Robertson also called Father Louis Cochin to testify to Poundmaker's good character and to say that during the time he spent as a prisoner in the Cree camp Poundmaker was responsible for his safety. Unfortunately for Robertson, the Crown used Father Cochin's testimony to try to show that Poundmaker did indeed exercise influence in the camp because he had been in a position to protect Father Cochin.

Robertson's and Osler's statements to the jury were both less than thirty minutes long. They addressed the prime point of evidence: whether Poundmaker had control of his band during the uprising and had signed his own name to the letter.

In his charge to the jury, Judge Richardson bolstered Jefferson's credibility. "Do you believe—to begin with Jefferson; do you think he is an honest man? Mind you, he has not been contradicted. He has not been contradicted by any witness in the facts that he has sworn to, nor has any witness been brought before us, nor have we heard that he is unreliable, that he is not to be believed as a witness. You must bear that in mind. Do you believe him? If you do believe him then he says he would not, to use the strongest expression, have put his [Poundmaker's] name to that letter if he hadn't been authorized by him." He did not directly instruct the jury about the law of treason.

The jury returned in half an hour with a guilty verdict. Poundmaker addressed the court with an uncharacteristicly short speech, one that lost a good deal in the translation. One thing that everyone in the courtroom undoubtedly understood, although it was not brought out at all in evidence, was Poundmaker's allusion to stopping the fight at Cutknife Creek and saving the lives of many of Otter's soldiers.

Judge Richardson, although he said he had known and liked Poundmaker for a number of years, sentenced the chief to three years in penitentiary. "I would rather prefer to be hung than to be in that place," Poundmaker said when sentence was passed.

Father André, after watching the trials, was bitter towards the government and its legal system. He wrote Archbishop Taché that the North-West was in the grip of despotism. He especially criticized the Regina juries. "The jurymen are all Protestants, enemies of the Métis and the Indians, against whom they maintain bitter prejudices. Before such a jury you cannot expect an impartial judgement, as we have seen in the case of One Arrow and Poundmaker. If there were two innocent people in the world, it was assuredly these Indians against whom nothing has been proved if not that they had always been well-disposed towards the whites."[14]

On September 8, Louis Goulet appeared in court charged with treason-felony arising from the Frog Lake massacre. The same day, five Breysalor half-breeds appeared on similiar charges arising from their activities in Pound-maker's camp. Yellow Mud Blanket, Poundmaker's brother, and Lean Man were charged with the half-breeds. The Crown had worked hard to gather evidence in these cases, particularly against trader Charles Bremner and his Breysalor companions, among whom after the rebellion they had found some clothing and a rifle belonging to the troops. But there was not enough evidence to even warrant a trial. After paying $400, the half-breeds were released from jail on a promise to appear if they were called for trial. No money was required from the Indians.[15]

Except for Will Jackson, Tom Scott was the only white man charged with an offence arising from the rebellion, and even he was more clearly associated with the English half-breeds than with his own race. In the summer of 1885, that became a bit of an embarrassment to the government. Eastern newspapers were full of vague allusions to stalwart citizens of Prince Albert who had aided and abetted Riel. In Quebec, people wondered aloud why it seemed French Catholics were jailed and sentenced to hang when everyone knew that the rebellion was more an expression of general dissatisfaction with the government, dissatisfaction that included many white, English-speaking Protestants. Goaded by the newspapers, the government directed its prosecutors at Regina to make out as strong as possible a case against Scott and to try to find other whites who could be charged with treason.

That was easier said than done. The prosecutors' own legal advisor said the case against Scott was too weak to guarantee a conviction and, try as they might, the prosecutors could not gather any worthwhile evidence against any other whites. The government had been particularly stung by a series of articles in the Toronto *Mail*, the leading Conservative newspaper in the country, about the "Prince Albert White Rebels." The government demanded to know who had written the stories. The *Mail* refused to tell. In desperation, B. B. Osler wrote a not-so-polite letter to *Mail* manager Christopher Bunting, warning that the newspaper might be held to be an accomplice to treason. The Crown might start proceedings against the *Mail* in the North-West or it might even have a treason trial in Toronto, Osler wrote. "Do not take it as a threat. It is intended as a friendly warning."[16] The *Mail* still refused but after further pressure referred the prosecutors to its general rebellion reporter, George Ham, in Winnipeg. Ham had not written the "white rebels" stories and no record survives of what he told the prosecutors, if anything. In any case, there would be no prosecutions of whites other than Tom Scott and Will Jackson.

The prosecutors had sent their Scott file to Stephen Brewster, an English lawyer living at Prince Albert, for an outside opinion. Brewster's reply was discouraging. "The case against Scott seems to be founded as far as I can judge on suspicion with perhaps a little ill feeling combined."[17] Scott's only crime, Brewster wrote, was that he spoke a little louder than his neighbours in trying to get redress of grievances. He recommended that the prosecution be dropped unless the Crown found stronger evidence. But there were good political reasons to continue with the case and to make the best of it, so the government hired Brewster to assist the Crown in the Scott trial.

Scott's case, like Poundmaker's, hinged on a letter, the one Scott had written in hasty optimism after the March 23 meeting at the Lindsay School House when he told the Métis that "the voice of every man was with you."

After a lengthy and futile objection on jurisdictional grounds by Scott's lawyer, prosecutor B. B. Osler opened his case on September 9 with a lengthy statement. Scott's responsibility for his acts might be considered greater than a half-breed's or an Indian's responsibility, Osler said, because he had had a better opportunity for understanding that rebellion was wrong. Scott had, of course, not taken up arms himself and there was even some evidence he tried to stop the fighting, Osler admitted.[18]

> The evidence will show that as far as he was concerned, he was not one of those who desired to fight. He was one of those however who sought to bring constraint upon the Government, who aided and comforted those taking arms, although perhaps it will be made to appear that when the resort to arms took place, he did perhaps what he could to prevent immediate bloodshed. Just as a man who starts a conflagration by his carelessness or his act and is frightened at the result and seeks to put an end to it, so we say this man by his aid and by his comfort and his assistance up to a certain point helped in rebellion and was one of the causes leading to rebellion.

Scott's lawyer, Henry Clarke, would not even admit that his client had signed the controversial letter. He forced the Crown to spend much of its time in the courtroom trying to get witnesses to identify Scott's handwriting over constant objections by Henry Clarke about their line and method of questioning. Even if Scott had signed the letter, the defence position was that it was in an effort to stop rebellion, not incite it. Despite the Crown's best efforts, the prosecution's case was as weak as Brewster had first feared it would be, especially when it was subjected to Clarke's vigorous cross-examination and legal objections.

When the Crown closed its case, Clarke asked Judge Richardson to direct the jury to bring in a not-guilty verdict. When Scott was alleged to have committed treasonable acts, there was not even any evidence to show a state of rebellion existed, he argued. Richardson refused to direct the jury, as he had refused when Beverly Robertson made a similar request at the One Arrow trial. At the very least, there was evidence of a rebellion, Judge Richardson said, and that was enough to send the case to the jury. Anyway, the judge did not believe he had the power to direct a verdict.

Henry J. Clarke was no ordinary lawyer. An Irish Catholic fluent in English, French, and Spanish, he had been a prospector during the California gold rush and a journalist before establishing a considerable reputation as a criminal lawyer in Montreal. He had fought with the militia in the Fenian raids of 1866 and had written a biography of his friend, Thomas D'Arcy McGee. He had moved west in 1870 to help establish the first government of the province of Manitoba and became its first attorney general. Clarke became the political spokesmen for the moderate Manitoba Métis and, in 1872, when he failed to persuade Louis Riel not to run for parliament, the attorney general entered the election against him. The confrontation between Clarke and Riel became so violent that at one point Clarke challenged Riel to a duel, before both men withdrew to make way for George Cartier. Clarke vigorously denied rumours that he had engineered the arrest of Ambroise Lepine on a charge of murdering Thomas Scott, but he successfully prosecuted Lepine on the charge. Clarke was a political opportunist whose brash manner offended many.

Henry Clarke knew the North-West and its people intimately. He used his knowledge and his flair for public speaking to good advantage in his political life and he intended to use it to get Tom Scott off the treason charge. He had several witnesses to call, but he opened the defence case with an impassioned address to the jury, probably one of the most bombastic speeches ever heard in a Canadian courtroom. Clarke's performance delighted spectators at the trial. The *Manitoba Free Press* reported:

> The Scott trial will probably be the most memorable of the state trials; at all events it is proving the most interesting to spectators. There were several scenes in the court to-day between Messrs. Clarke, Q.C., and Osler, Q.C., and altogether it was the most stormy session witnessed since the commencement of the trials. Objections were taken time and again by the defense and all the rulings were against the Crown. As the case stands at present Scott is virtually acquitted, and to-morrow will probably see the end of the case. Clarke spoke for three hours, and his is considered the greatest speech of the whole trials. It was a strong indictment against the Dominion Government.[19]

The newspaper reporter did not exaggerate. Clarke made a wonderful speech. In law, justification is no defence to a charge of treason. But Clarke knew that a good political speech might move a jury. And he knew his audience. He knew that Scott's alleged treason was the outcome of a widespread and deeply-rooted sense of alienation from Ottawa. He knew that his client was a prosperous and respected member of the same community to which the jurymen belonged. He might have suspected even that one or two on the six-man jury harboured a secret wish that they had had the courage to do what Scott had done.

Clarke didn't confine his discourse on politics and history to the North-West. He began with the Romans and worked his way through the Magna Carta, discussing the morality of rebellion against oppression. From the events of 1869, Clarke passionately traced the history of the North-West grievances in detail. The people of the North-West had been petitioning and protesting for many years, he said.

> Their petitions have gone to Ottawa, their resolutions passed at their meetings have have been sent there, no return has been heard, it was worse than a refusal, they were treated with that contempt that galls a man far worse than a direct and positive refusal.... That is the way they were treated. Petition after petition went—the thing is notorious, they have appeared in the press, their petitions have been spoken of in the House, on the floor of the House;...they asked for their rights and why were they not accorded to them? Why were they not accorded to them?... Is it because these people are weak? Is it because they had no representatives in Parliament, that their rights should be trampled upon, and that they should be treated worse than the Government dared treat the Indians, because there was sufficient in them of their Scotch and French forefathers that they did for years patiently but complainingly bear up against the injustice that was being done them? Patiently but complainingly they bore it all. They bore it from day to day, and from week to week, and from month to month, until fifteen years had rolled around, and still they were as far from a settlement as they were fifteen years ago.

His client was not one to take injustice without complaining, Clarke told the jury, but he did not oppose the government by rebellion nor did he encourage anyone else to rebel. His client was no criminal; he was an honest, loyal man who had the temerity to demand his rights.

> Now, the object in this prosecution is to try and identify Scott with this rebellion.... It is nothing of the sort. That is not it at all. It is this, the French half-breeds, a number of them have been arrested, and a number of them have been convicted. A number of Indians have been arrested, and some of them have been convicted. Now, to please the Province of Quebec, we must convict a white man or we are gone at the next elections. Gentlemen, this is not a criminal prosecution. It is neither more nor less than a political persecution.... I defy the Crown to find that man guilty of any act that is

illegal and against the British constitution. On the contrary, he stands there to-day before you as loyal a man as sits in the [jury] box, and as loyal a man as sits on the bench, and as loyal a man as sits at the counsels' table, the only misfortune is that he happened to have the impudence to go to public meetings to demand the rights of himself and his family, and to give that demand in unmistakable language, such as an honest man need never fear to utter.

The agitation for the redress of grievances was legal and justified, Clarke said. He tried to give the impression that the rebellion itself might be justifiable, though his client, of course, took no part in it. But Clarke drew the line at excusing his old rival.

Louis Riel was sent for. Louis Riel came, unfortunately for Canada, unfortunately for this country. Louis Riel came back, but was he the same Louis Riel of 1869 and 1870? No; with all the outward form of the same man, the man was not there. The man of 1869 and 1870 was as intellectual a man probably as you could meet, of his age, on the continent of America, a man of sound mind and sound judgment; but the life that he led during the five or six years was enough to drive any man crazy, and he became crazy, a dangerous lunatic, a very dangerous lunatic, as dangerous in a community as a rabid dog.

Clarke wound up his address with a plea for some of the Indians and half-breeds charged with treason-felony, particularly Big Bear, who was awaiting trial and who was credited with protecting Teresa Gowanlock and Teresa Delaney after the Frog Lake killings. He pointedly noted that the Frog Lake murderers had not yet been tried but many people had been jailed for treason on what Clarke regarded as weak evidence.

With the exception of one or two Indians that are to be tried, and probably another farce or two with some of the unfortunate half-breeds that have been locked up four or five months because they did not participate in any row or rascality, that this [the Scott trial] is about the closing trial of this series. I suppose it is. They have locked up that unfortunate man Poundmaker, and Big Bear is to be tried, and we have no doubt he will be punished. Punished for what? It is necessary to make a victim.... Why is it that the poor old man [Big Bear], who at the risk of his own life, defended the honor and lives of British matrons when they were in the hands of his young men, and their lives—worse than their lives, more sacred, their honor, was in the keeping of these poor unfortunate wild men? Why do they keep that old man locked up? And why do they allow hundreds of ruffians who imbrued their hands in blood to be to-day free?... But, meantime, just give us one white victim so as to counterbalance any offence that we may offer to the Province of Quebec, and we will thank you for it, we will make a victim of that victim, we will make it a cry at the next elections, and we will carry it out at the polls, and we will secure another lease of our political existence that should have ceased with the first gun that was fired by the people that were seeking their rights.

The speech probably guaranteed acquittal. Added to the weak evidence, the jury must have been thoroughly frightened of bringing the wrath of Henry J. Clarke down on their heads if they dared return a guilty verdict. But Clarke wasn't finished. He led a number of defence witnesses, including Anglican minister Edward Matheson, Charles Nolin, and Father André, through lengthy testimony on Scott's good reputation and his apparently innocent actions before and during the rebellion. One witness even testified that when the fighting broke out Scott had offered to raise a company of English half-breeds to fight for the government. Clarke's final address to the jury the next day, September 10, lasted less than an hour, during which he heaped more scorn on the Crown's inability to muster any convincing evidence of treason.

Clarke's was a tough act to follow and in his address to the jury B. B. Osler took the defence lawyer to task for seeming to condone rebellion. But Osler's was a calm, straightforward synopsis of the evidence and the law. Osler relied primarily on the evidence that Scott had written the letter. Even if the letter were written in an effort to avoid bloodshed, it still may have given aid and comfort to the rebels, and that was enough to prove treason, Osler told the jury. Osler realized that the letter was the only real scrap of evidence he had and he spent very little time going over other testimony. Richardson addressed the jury at much greater length than he had during other trials but he, too, dwelt on the question of the authenticity of the letter. The jury took twenty minutes to acquit Scott. The spectators cheered.

Big Bear's case was a relatively simple one. When he came to trial on September 11, the day after Scott was acquitted, the Crown attempted to show that Big Bear had promoted rebellion on April 2, the day of the Frog Lake killings, in mid-April when Fort Pitt was seized and sacked, towards the end of the month when a letter was apparently written from Big Bear's camp to the Whitefish Lake Indians, and on May 28, the day of the battle of Frenchman Butte. As well, Big Bear had aided rebellion simply because he was the chief of a rebellious band, the same general circumstance the Crown had used in the Poundmaker case.

Beverly Robertson thought he had a particularly good chance of winning Big Bear's freedom. The Scott case proved victory was possible and Robertson had lined up an impressive array of witnesses to testify that Big Bear had lost control of the band and that he used all his energy trying to save white lives and trying to stop the violence.

To a remarkable degree, the Crown's own witnesses made out the defence contention, assisted by prosecutor David Scott's clumsy questioning and lack of appreciation of the rules of evidence. Most of the Crown witnesses had been prisoners of the Big Bear band during the rebellion and they testified that the chief had apparently lost control and that he had on several occasions tried to stop the violence. Evidence of a letter Big Bear allegedly wrote asking the Whitefish Lake Indians to join him was not very damaging. The Crown could not produce the actual letter and Judge Richardson quickly put a stop to hearsay evidence about its contents.[20]

Hudson's Bay Company trader Jim Simpson said that when he saw Big Bear shortly after the Frog Lake killings, the chief said, "It is not my doings. I said, now this affair will all be in your name, not your young men. He says, it is not my doings, and the young men won't listen, and I am very sorry for what has been done." Stanley Simpson, the Hudson's Bay Company clerk at Fort Pitt, put a much different colour on Big Bear's thoughts. He testified he overheard the chief urging his band to kill whites and saying that he wanted the head of the whites' military commander. During the battle of Frenchman Butte, Simpson said he overheard Big Bear congratulate his men for killing so many soldiers. But Simpson did not stand up well under Beverly Robertson's cross-examination. It turned out that his memory was hazier than he had first admitted and his knowledge of the Cree language was questionable. Simpson couldn't repeat in Cree what Big Bear had said, though he claimed to understand it far better than he could speak it. As Robertson pressed the witness on his knowledge of the Cree language, prosecutor Scott had his worst idea of the day. He suggested that Peter Hourie, the court interpreter, put a question in Cree to the witness. Simpson failed the little test miserably.

When the Crown closed its case, Robertson asked Judge Richardson to direct the jury to find Big Bear not guilty, a request the judge refused as he had at the other trials.

The defence witnesses, all prisoners of Big Bear's band, gave much the same evidence as the Crown witnesses. When Frog Lake trader Bill Cameron testified about what he had heard Big Bear say, Scott tried to pay the defence back for its questioning of Simpson's linguistic competence. Scott asked Cameron to repeat the exact words in Cree. To the prosecutor's chagrin and the defence lawyer's delight, Cameron, whose memory matched his capacity for language, did it.

Robertson was so confident that he decided not to call all the witnesses he had ready to testify. In Robertson's view, the evidence showed the government ought to be thanking Big Bear for his efforts during the rebellion, not prosecuting him. This time, even the Crown witnesses had been on Robertson's side, with one exception and he had made that exception look pretty foolish. The evidence was so consistent and so much in Big Bear's favour that it would be risking boring the jury to call any more witnesses, Robertson decided. He may also have been wary that the Crown might be able to turn the evidence of some defence witnesses around against Big Bear, as had happened with Father

Cochin, the last witness in the Poundmaker case. He may have thought it best to quit while he was ahead.

In his address to the jury, Robertson dwelt on one factor that he hadn't brought out very well during the testimony: the position and responsibility of a chief of an Indian band.

> The Indian looks to his own little band; apart from them he can do nothing; apart from them he cannot live; he must remain with his band; he cannot get away from them; he is not free if he sees mischief being done, he is not free to say, I will move away from here, I will go among other people who won't do these things; he cannot do that, and what else has my learned friend, Mr. Scott, to rest upon here in making a case against Big Bear, except that he was with his band?

Robertson still was not explaining it very well. An ordinary Indian could, of course, move off if he didn't like what was taking place. But a chief, even a chief who had lost his power and was being abused, could not. By custom, a chief could not just resign as a white politician might resign in difficult circumstances. The duty of a chief is not so much to lead as to support his band, to guide them and help them as best he can even if they do not take his advice.

Robertson also realized he would have to counter the bad publicity Big Bear had been receiving. The chief's name was virtually permanently set in headline type and in every fresh Indian outrage, real or imagined, during the rebellion, Big Bear would figure prominently in the newspapers. Robertson told the jury, "You must know, as I know, the outrageous reports we have heard about this old man Big Bear. All the sins of his tribe, and a great many sins they never committed, were laid upon his shoulders, in the public print."

Robertson had not thought it necessary to address the legal question of whether a person's mere presence among a band of rebels is proof of treason. But in his speech to the jury, prosecutor Scott mentioned it, though he probably extended the principle far enough to satisfy Robertson. Scott argued that though evidence showed Big Bear had tried to save prisoners' lives, there was no evidence to show that he resisted other efforts of the rebels. To that extent, his continued presence with his band was treason, Scott thought. Robertson's argument against that was simply on the evidence, not on the legal question. He believed there was ample evidence to show that Big Bear had resisted the rebels throughout the rebellion.

It was when Judge Richardson addressed the jury that the legal question blew up.

> If the evidence is to be believed, . . . a state of rebellion existed prior to the 2nd April, and the prisoner knew it. Now, if he knew it, what was his duty? What was his first duty, and in what way could he relieve himself of that

duty? His first duty was the same as yours and mine would be, not to be found in the rebel camp, but to be found where law and order prevailed. That was his first duty, and if that was his first and main duty, what excuse could there be, what excuse is there why he was not? Well, the only excuse which the law recognizes is this—taking the words themselves of the authorities "the fear of present death is the only excuse. Suffering, or any other mischief not endangering his person, or the apprehension of personal injury less than would deprive of life, is not a justification of a traitorous act."

Robertson was appalled. It was the constructive versus direct levying of war argument he had had in the One Arrow case, a legal technicality that was crucial to the Indians charged with treason. In the One Arrow case, B. B. Osler had quickly come around to Robertson's interpretation but Judge Richardson apparently still didn't understand. Robertson believed, probably correctly, that the rebellion of 1885 was a "constructive levying of war" in legal terminology, or at least that was all the Crown was making it out to be. The passage Richardson quoted referring to fear of death as the only excuse for a person's presence among rebels was applicable only to the direct levying of war. The same authority Richardson quoted said: "In the case of a constructive levying of war, those only of the rabble who actually aid and assist in doing those acts of violence which form the constructive treason, are traitors, the rest are merely rioters."[21] Richardson was not likely deliberately distorting the law of treason but it is highly probable he didn't understand it.

When Big Bear's jury retired, Robertson asked Judge Richardson to bring them back to correct the mistaken impression the judge had given them about the law. "Will your Honor tell the jury now that if they are satisfied upon the evidence that, although he was there, he was not aiding and abetting them, then he ought to be acquitted?" Richardson finally agreed to bring the jury back for further instructions. The judge asked the jury to consider

> whether a sufficient explanation has been given for his presence in the place where he is described to have be been; that you should consider whether he was there compulsorily—I think I have got that right now to suit Mr. Robertson—or whether he was there against his will, and acting solely in the interests of peace.
>
> Robertson—If they think, though he was there, he was not actually aiding and abetting them, if they are satisfied on that, then they ought to acquit him.
>
> Richardson—And that if he was there against his will and giving no assistance whatever, then he would be entitled to an acquittal.

The judge still had it wrong. In law, the Crown had to show that the accused had been aiding and abetting the rebels, as defence lawyer Robertson pointed out. But if Judge Richardson had left it there, Robertson probably would have been pleased. Unfortunately, the judge kept talking. He quoted a precedent out

324

of context and almost brought the argument back to where it began.

> If a number of men band themselves together for an unlawful purpose, and in pursuit of their object commit murder, it is right that the court should pointedly refuse to accept the proposition that a full share of responsibility for their acts does not extend to the surgeon who accompanied them to dress their wounds, to the clergyman who attends to offer spiritual consolation, or to the reporter who volunteers to record their achievements; the presence of anyone in any character aiding and abetting or encouraging the prosecution of those unlawful designs must involve a share of the common guilt.

That passage did mention aiding and abetting, as Robertson quickly pointed out when Judge Richardson read it, but the impression it leaves is that mere presence among rebels constitutes treason. Judge Richardson did not tell the jury that the precedent he quoted involved a direct levying of war, the 1866 Fenian raids, and was not applicable to the Big Bear case. Nor did he explain that evidence at the Fenian trials showed that the newspaper reporter referred to was more likely a colonel in the Fenian army who had been seen giving directions to the troops and that the clergyman-surgeon were one and the same person, an Irish Catholic priest who had been seen armed with a revolver directing and encouraging Fenian soldiers.[22]

If the Big Bear jury was not totally misled on the law of treason, it must have been at least extraordinarily confused. The jury deliberated for fifteen minutes before finding Big Bear guilty. The jurymen made a strong recommendation to mercy, a small consolation for Robertson, who had just had by far the most discouraging day since he began defending the 1885 Indian rebels.

On September 25, just before Judge Richardson sentenced him to three years in the penitentiary, Big Bear addressed the court for two hours. No one recorded much of the speech. One newspaper reporter described it as "more or less laughable"[23] but another found it an eloquent address, a denial of any guilt in connection with the rebellion, a statement that the Indians were the real owners of the North-West and "in conclusion he made a powerful appeal for the children and helpless of his tribe."[24]

Robertson was back in court on September 16 defending nine Cree who were charged with treason-felony resulting from the Frog Lake killings, the sacking of Fort Pitt, and the Battle of Frenchman Butte. These nine fell into the grey area of the law far more than anyone else Beverly Robertson defended.

Even the Crown admitted the case was weak. In his opening statement, prosecutor David Scott told the jury: "Although, perhaps, we cannot prove any particular acts or outrages on the part of any of these prisoners, we can show that they were present with that (Frog Lake) band.... Although they may not have committed those outrages themselves they were combining with others who did commit them." Scott had trouble proving even the Indians' mere presence among the rebels. In the confusion of identifying the nine men in the dock, it is probable that at least one was not identified at all as being even at the scene of any rebellious acts.[25]

The Crown's star witness was Frog Lake trader Bill Cameron but he only managed to show that at least a few of the accused were among the Frog Lake Indians and that all of them had good credit ratings with the Hudson's Bay Company. There was absolutely no evidence that any of them had taken any part in any councils or in any fighting or in any taking of prisoners or in any pillaging. There was some indication that some of the accused might have helped dig rifle pits at Frenchman Butte, but the evidence was confusing and the evidence also showed that some of the white prisoners of the Frog Lake Indians helped dig rifle pits. At one point, defence lawyer Robertson interrupted his cross-examination to say: "As to these Indians, I am just in this position, that I can find nothing against them except that they are members of the band." Later, during one of his many interruptions of Scott's questioning, he said: "The mere fact of their being Indians of the same band does not make evidence against these prisoners. Let him show they were conspirators."

The evidence was even weaker than prosecutor Scott had anticipated. In his closing address, the prosecutor said:

> As I said in my opening address I doubted whether we could from any of the evidence that we have collected in this case, bring home to any one of these prisoners any glaring outrage in connection with the rebellion, and as it turns out, the evidence has not disclosed anything of that kind. It has disclosed this much, however, that these men were present in the camp of Big Bear and other bands who were associated with him, and that those bands were in open rebellion against the Government. That rebellion commenced the 2nd April at Frog Lake, at which the settlement there was taken possession of by Indians—perhaps by these. It is not shown conclusively that these Indians took any part in that outrage, but it is shown that it was taken by Indians with whom they were living and acting.

After Scott did such a nice job of pointing out the glaring weakness of the Crown's case, defence lawyer Robertson declined to make a closing address. Richardson again quoted the Fenian precedent to the jury, probably leaving them with the impression that a person's mere presence among rebels is proof enough of treason. Robertson might have thought that the case against these Frog Lake Indians was so obviously weak that even an improperly instructed jury could not, in good conscience, find them guilty. And the jury did take a decent interval, an hour, for their deliberations. But they found all nine accused guilty as charged. Five of the six jurymen recommended mercy. Richardson sentenced them all to two years in penitentiary.

The next day, September 17, Beverly Robertson defended four Sioux and one Cree charged as a result of the Battles of Duck Lake and Batoche. Things were getting stranger. The Crown appeared to have a stronger case than they had had against the Frog Lake Indians for there was some indication the five accused were actually involved in the fighting. But Scott put up a much less vigorous prosecution. He called only two witnesses, compared with the six in the Frog Lake case. The witnesses had seen the Indians armed at Batoche. They could not say they had seen any of them actually fire his gun but they all seemed to be moving with the rebel army. Scott gave only a short opening address and didn't bother to sum up the case for the jury.[26]

When it was defence lawyer Robertson's turn to sum up, he simply said: "I am not going to address the jury, and I leave it for your honor." This time, Judge Richardson accommodated the defence lawyer. He seemed annoyed the Crown had not tried very hard and he was perhaps disappointed, as Robertson was, with the performance of the juries in the previous cases. He pointedly reminded the jury that they had only two witnesses on which to base their judgement, that only one of the defendants had been anywhere near Duck Lake on the day of the battle, and he reminded the jury strongly that an accused is entitled to the benefits of the doctrine of reasonable doubt. "They are entitled to the same consideration as any white man, or any person who is under the protection of the British Crown, and they ought not to be convicted, no conviction ought to take place unless a jury is convinced, conclusively, and as a result from considering, undoubtedly in their minds, that they were implicated." He did not tell the jury his interpretation of the treason law. Despite Richardson's careful directions, the jury took only thirty minutes to find all the accused guilty. The judge sentenced four of them to three years in penitentiary. Red Eagle, Chief White Cap's son-in-law who had been wounded in the fighting, got six months in jail.

When Sioux chief White Cap came to trial on September 18, Beverly Robertson was in a fighting mood. He was angry with Richardson for his misinterpretation of the treason law. He was angry with the juries which seemed to base their quick decisions more on his clients' race than on the evidence. He was angry with the Crown for bringing some of the cases to trial at all. He was angry with surveyor John Astley, who seemed to pop up as the Crown's star witness in nearly every case and whose memory seemed to be full of vague impressions and prejudice.

White Cap was charged with treason-felony on the grounds that he had apparently led his band from their reserve near Saskatoon to join the rebels and had assisted in the Battles of Fish Creek and Batoche. The Crown witnesses testified that the chief had been at Batoche during the rebellion but only Astley's testimony connected him directly with the fighting. Astley testified that he saw White Cap in the rifle pits as he carried the message from Riel to Middleton on May 12, a contention the chief, through his lawyer, specifically denied.[27]

As usual, Astley did not bear up well to defence lawyer Robertson's vigorous and sarcastic cross-examination. He was certain the chief had been there even though he could not remember what he was wearing at the time. There had been a lot of other Indians in the area and Astley was running a gauntlet of heavy gunfire. Robertson's asked him:

> You were so cool that although there were a lot of other old men out of about 150 Indians that you had been in the habit of seeing, in the excitement of that moment, when you were not thinking about anyone in particular, but you were going in hope of saving the threatened lives of the prisoners, your fellow-prisoners, with a fire going on all around you, a rifle fire, although you tell us you did [not] notice even what head dress the old man had on, yet you are prepared to swear you recognised his face so distinctly that you can distinguish it from those other old men that you saw among the Indians those different times?

Astley replied that he knew White Cap's face as he knew his own, but Robertson's persistent questioning must have had its effect. And Astley's evidence was not all negative. He testified, probably to Robertson's surprise, that he regarded the Sioux chief as having a good reputation.

Philippe Garnot testified that White Cap had been made a member of the rebel council but that, as far as he knew, the chief did not understand either Cree or French, the two languages the council used in its deliberations. Robertson used his cross-examination of Garnot to try to establish the legal point he and Judge Richardson had grappled with in previous trials, and which he intended to use in his address to the jury. He got Garnot, as secretary of the Métis council, to say several times that he understood the Métis to be in rebellion to force the government to grant them rights to land. In legal terms, that could be construed as a constructive levying of war rather than a direct levying of war, as a deliberate attempt to actually overthrow the government might be considered. In a constructive levying of war, a person's mere presence among rebels was not enough for a treason conviction; an accused had to be shown aiding and abetting the rebellion.

Robertson had only one witness to call for the defence, but he intended to make the most of him. Gerald Willoughby, a Saskatoon trader who spoke Sioux and who knew White Cap well, gave the chief a glowing character reference. In a long examination by Robertson, Willoughby described meeting and talking with the chief as he and his band moved towards Batoche in April. White Cap had no intention of joining the rebellion but the Métis were more or less forcing him to go to Batoche, Willoughby testified. Robertson spent most of his address to the jury, a better address than he had delivered in the other cases, going over Willoughby's testimony in detail.

Robertson had not succeeded in previous trials by trying to persuade the Regina jurymen of the justice and logic of his position, so he began his address to the White Cap jury by insulting them:

Since the conviction of Big Bear, I have felt that it is almost a hopeless task to attempt to obtain from a jury in Regina a fair consideration of the case of an Indian. It has seemed to me that it is only necessary to say in this town to a jury, there is an Indian, and we will put him in the dock to convict him. But perhaps in feeling that, I did an injustice to the jurymen of Regina. I hope I did. Nothing but such a conviction as that of Big Bear could have brought me to think so, and I try to believe again this morning that I was mistaken in the estimate I formed in consequence of that verdict. I am going to appeal to you now as if you were perfectly fair-minded, as I hope that you are. I am going to ask you, notwithstanding what I have seen in this court already in these Indian cases, I am going to make one more appeal in the hope that this time I have before me men who will regard the evidence against an Indian, and scrutinize it with a desire to do him justice, and not to press unduly upon him, just as fairly as if it were a white man they were dealing with; and I am going to ask you to acquit White Cap and I ask it with perfect confidence in the result, provided only I can get you to consider the evidence fairly and without prejudice.

By this time, Robertson had realized that Judge Richardson's directions to the juries on the law of treason were not merely confusing but that the judge himself did not understand the law. He proceeded to lecture the judge, through the jury.

His Honor has told juries before in these cases that the mere presence of the prisoner in the camp was sufficient to convict him, unless it was conclusively proved to you that he was prevented from leaving it by the instant fear of death and nothing short of that would excuse it. I have submitted to his Honor with all deference, of course, and I am bound, in the discharge of the duty cast upon me here, not as the hired advocate of the prisoner, for I am not, but because the Government has sent me here to see that if I can, that he gets fair play. I am bound to dissent from that ruling and to protest against it, and I do so. I say that that is not the law. I say that in a case of this kind, while it is competent to a jury to infer, if they think the circumstances warrant it, to infer from the presence of the accused in a rebel camp, that he is there aiding and abetting, the question is not whether he was there, but the question is whether he was aiding and abetting and encouraging them, and the jury is not bound to infer at all that because he was there, he was aiding them. His being there is not a crime, otherwise the man who was there, if such there were, doing his utmost to defeat the aims of the rebels, would be a guilty man.

Robertson was ready for Judge Richardson to disagree and he appealed directly to the jury. "I ask you, whatever his Honor may tell you, and I appeal to you as six men of sound common sense, whatever his Honor tells you is the law, to do moral justice to that poor old man, and, if necessary, over-ride the law as you have a right to do in these cases. . . . The evidence is not such as would justify you in condemning a dog to be hanged, and I ask you to say, whatever His Honor may tell you, that that old man should not be punished for anything he has done in this matter."

Robertson's comments stung the judge. In his short address to the jury, Richardson took the defence lawyer to task, but slightly apologetically.

What may have transpired, or what may have occurred, what wrong I may have done in the opinion of any young gentlemen has nothing whatever to do with this case. . . . Speaking generally of the law, rebellion is wrong, and not only is rebellion wrong, but the presence of anyone in any character aiding and abetting or encouraging rebellion or the prosecution of the unlawful design must involve a share of the common guilt.

With the emphasis on aiding and abetting, Judge Richardson had finally put the treason law in a light that was favourable to the defence.

Robertson won. It was his only victory but it was a decisive one. The jury took just fifteen minutes to acquit White Cap. The newspapers said the verdict was "generally approved." White Cap shook hands with the jurors as they left the courthouse.[28]

With the White Cap verdict, the operations of the legal system at Regina had only a few loose ends to tie up. During September and October, several Frog Lake and Batoche Indians were discharged on condition they appear for trials which would never be held. André Nault and Abraham Montour, the Métis emissaries who had accompanied and assisted the Frog Lake Indians, escaped trial by the purest chance. They appeared for trial in Judge Richardson's court on October 5 but their lawyer said that one of his witnesses was unavoidably absent and the judge granted a delay. Before the trial could be resumed, the Minister of Justice directed the prosecutors to abandon the case, for reasons that are no longer clear.[29]

On October 10, Magnus Burston, an English half-breed, came to trial on a charge of treason-felony. He was the only half-breed other than Riel actually tried on charges resulting from the rebellion and he was the only one of the Regina defendants to chose trial without a jury. Hillyard Mitchell had left Burston in charge of his store at Duck Lake shortly before the battle there. There was little indication Burston had actually joined the rebellion but some evidence at his trial indicated he may have had a hand in setting fire to Mitchell's house and may have helped appropriate goods from the store. But the evidence was not strong enough for Judge Richardson and he acquitted Burston.[30]

The Indians charged in the Frog Lake murders and the councillors who, with Poundmaker, had signed the letter to Riel were all in jail in Battleford in September awaiting trial. Despite his disgust with the Regina guilty verdicts,

Father André thought most of the Indians and Métis could count themselves lucky they had not been tried at Battleford before Judge Charles Rouleau. "Judge Richardson is certainly a just and impartial man and I bear him witness that I would much rather see our people judged by him than by Judge Rouleau who is a vindictive man and a servile instrument in the hands of the government," Father André wrote Archbishop Taché.[31]

Father André wasn't the only person who believed that the outcomes of trials of rebels before Rouleau were a foregone conclusion. Assistant Indian Affairs Commissioner Hayter Reed was delighted with the judge's attitude and was looking forward to lots of hangings witnessed by lots of Indians. He wrote Lieutenant Governor Dewdney about the advantages of public hangings. "I am desirous of having the Indians witness it—No sound threshing having been given them I think a sight of this sort will cause them to meditate for many a day."[32]

In June and July, Rouleau had tried the very first cases resulting from the rebellion, dispensing his peculiar brand of justice to Indians charged with theft and possession of stolen goods. The Indian Department had provided the Indians who appeared before Judge Richardson with the services of Beverly Robertson. But there was no such consideration extended to those at Battleford, even for those charged with murder. Despite that, many of the accused had the presence of mind to plead not guilty. And, although the Indians had a very slight understanding of the white man's adversary legal system, many of them cross-examined witnesses and in a couple of cases, the accused elected trial by jury. A few won acquittal and the Crown declined to proceed against some others. Most of the Indians who appeared before Judge Rouleau were charged with relatively minor offenses, many of them with simple possession of small amounts of rebellion plunder. But those found guilty of theft and possession of stolen goods usually received from Rouleau far stiffer sentences than Richardson was handing out for treason-felony. The standard sentence in Rouleau's court in a clear but non-violent case was six years in penitentiary, whether it was theft of a $50 watch or a herd of thirty-five horses. Some Indians against whom there was relatively weaker evidence, but who were nonetheless found guilty, received proportionally lighter sentences. Rouleau's theft and related cases dragged on until the end of October. By that time he had tried more than thirty men in the minor cases, acquitting about six of them and giving about nine others six-year sentences. Rouleau's sentences were a bit high and he seemed quicker to convict than other judges in the North-West at the time but a six-year sentence for theft was not out of line.[33]

Near the end of September, when the charred remains of Rouleau's substantial home at Battleford were hardly cold, the judge tried a number of cases resulting from the burning of the buildings in the Frog Lake community after the killings. Two Frog Lake Indians pleaded guilty to arson and received ten years in penitentiary. Four Sky Thunder's crime was slightly greater. Rouleau sentenced him to fourteen years for the arson of the Frog Lake church.[34]

Judge Rouleau tried four Indians on charges of treason-felony. Three of them had apparently signed the letter that had been so damaging in Poundmaker's case and the evidence at their trial was similar, though much shorter, than the evidence presented against the chief. One of the councillors of Big Bear's band, who had apparently taken an active part in the band's military activities, also appeared before Rouleau. The judge sentenced them all to six years in penitentiary.[35]

Some of those who had taken part in the Frog Lake killings had fled to the United States but some remained behind to face trial. Wandering Spirit was the only one of those accused of Frog Lake murders who pleaded guilty. On September 22, Judge Rouleau sentenced him to death for murdering Indian Agent Tom Quinn. Although the other five Indians charged with murder at Frog Lake pleaded not guilty, they were not inclined to do much cross-examination or call their own evidence for, the judge was told several times, the Crown witnesses had told the truth. After short trials, all five were sentenced to hang, Bad Arrow and Miserable Man for killing carpenter Charles Gouin, Walking the Sky for killing Father Léon-Adélard Fafard, and Little Bear and Iron Body for killing trader George Dill. Rouleau also passed the death sentence on the two Indians charged with the murders in the Battleford area. Itka pleaded guilty to murdering Farm Instructor James Payne and Man Without Blood to murdering farmer Barney Tremont. Louison Mongrain chose a jury trial but that, too, was a routine affair without the intervention of a defence lawyer and the Frog Lake Indian was sentenced to hang for killing NWMP Corporal David Cowan at Fort Pitt on April 15. The Crown decided not to proceed against Dressy Man on the same charge.[36]

A jury refused to bring in a guilty verdict in one of the murder cases. Frog Lake Indians Charlebois, Bright Eyes, and Dressy Man were charged with killing She Wins, the wehtikow, near Frog Lake on April 13. The jury found Charlebois and Dressy Man guilty of murder and Rouleau sentenced them to hang with the other murderers on November 27. But, presumably because he had used a gun instead of the more gruesome instruments, a sword and a club, the jury found Bright Eyes guilty only of manslaughter. Rouleau sentenced him to twenty years in penitentiary.[37]

The strangest trial resulting from the rebellion, and one of the most sensational, did not take place in the North-West at all. In September 1885, Montreal's attention was focused on the case against Edmund Sheppard, editor and proprietor of the Toronto *News*. It was a new *cause célèbre* for the French Canadians.

Sheppard's newspaper was vociferously pro-labour and violently anti-French Canadian. Back in April, the *News* published an interview with Sergeant

George Nelson of the Royal Grenadiers, who had been invalided home with rheumatism. Among his several controversial statements, Nelson had some choice words for Montreal's 65th Battalion. "They are the worst, most mutinous, reckless, disorderly gang I ever met in my life.... They could not have behaved worse. Colonel, majors, captains, lieutenants, non-commissioned officers and men were all drunk together." Eagerly pressed by the *News*, Nelson detailed the behaviour of the French Canadian battalion. They stole, fought among themselves, and refused to fight the rebels, he said. The *News* went on to speculate that Colonel Aldéric Ouimet, MP, had returned East not because of a sick wife, the usually-accepted excuse, but to ask the government to disband his worthless battalion.[38] Ouimet was incensed by the story. To protect the reputation of his battalion and the dignity of all French Canadians, he quickly announced he would launch suit against the *News* and claim $50,000 in damages for libel.

By the time the case came to the courts in September, the injured parties had taken the legal action a step farther. Ouimet's second-in-command, Major Aimé Dugas, a Montreal police magistrate, was charging Sheppard with criminal libel in a private prosecution. In court, the *News* tried to show that Sheppard had not been aware of the article before it appeared. In the Montreal courtroom, before a French Canadian jury, that hardly mattered because they knew too well of Sheppard's dislike of the French. In the witness box, Sergeant Nelson denied saying anything that was attributed to him in the interview. In a rambling address to the jury, which some spectators heckled and the judge and prosecutors interrupted, Sheppard said he never meant to insult French Canadians but he was unwavering in his view that English should be Canada's only official language. If duelling had not gone out of fashion, the dispute between him and Dugas would have been more easily solved, Sheppard told the jury.[39] Despite the animosity between Sheppard and the French Canadians, the jury was lenient. They returned a a special verdict that Sheppard was guilty of libel but that he had not known the facts in the Nelson interview were false. The judge imposed a light fine of $200.

The verdict and sentence didn't satisfy the spectators. On his way out of the courthouse, Sheppard found himself confronted by a howling mob and a lieutenant of the 65th Battalion who vowed to use his riding crop on the newspaperman. Sheppard warded off the blows with his umbrella and, as he prepared to draw his revolver, Major Dugas rushed to his defence. Sheppard got safely out of town and back to Toronto where he was greeted, the *News* reported, by a torchlight parade of four thousand cheering supporters.

CHAPTER EIGHTEEN

Dénouement

At first it seemed as if Macdonald had been right in his view that the political storm in Quebec would soon blow over. As the impact of the trial faded and the lengthy appeal process began, the initial excitement died down. Macdonald seems to have bought this temporary peace at the price of hinting to his key Quebec cabinet ministers that the government would extend clemency to Riel if the appeal failed. In October the newspaper *Le Nord* of St. Jérôme which was the voice of the powerful Secretary of State, J.-A. Chapleau, stated bluntly, "It is clear Riel will not be executed; that was decided some time ago by our government leaders, and we can now emphasize it . . . Riel will not be hanged."[1] Letters and petitions continued to pour in from all over the province and Quebec MPs felt the pressure.

By 1885 the Conservative party had controlled Quebec politics for a generation. This complete dominance of the province was, in turn, the cornerstone of the party's hold on national power. The Quebec Conservative party was a monolithic alliance between the big business in Montreal which controlled the economy of the province and indeed of much of Canada, and the church which controlled the hearts and minds of the voters, especially in the rural areas. The opposition Liberals were scarcely more than a fringe party with a few scattered seats and little prospect of winning more. The Liberals were the political heirs of the old Parti Rouge, which had been nationalist, anti-clerical, and opposed to confederation. The Liberals had inherited from the Rouges the unremitting hatred of the Church. Only eight years before, the Liberals had managed to persuade the Vatican to send a special envoy to Canada to investigate the political ties of the Quebec hierarchy. The envoy had announced that the Quebec Liberal party was not an organization that Catholics were forbidden to belong to and he warned the bishops that their priests should not tell their parishioners directly which candidates to vote for.

This prohibition was a technical victory for the Liberals, but it did not prevent the church from drawing up lists of political principles that made it unmistakably clear which party a good Catholic should vote for. After all, some priests were heard to say, hell was *rouge* but heaven was *bleu*. The really significant political division in Quebec in 1885 was between two factions of the Conservative party: the moderates led by J.-A. Chapleau and the extremist advocates of an almost theocratic domination of state by church who were

popularly known as the "Castors." Their spokesman in the federal cabinet was Sir Hector Langevin, the Minister of Public Works who had toured the West in 1884. The power struggle between the two factions within the Macdonald government was one reason the Old Chieftain was able to manipulate his French Canadian colleagues and ignore the popular discontent in Quebec.

The continued expression of popular concern did mean that Quebec Tories had to be given some additional support. In October, as the appeal process was grinding to its inevitable end, Macdonald agreed to the appointment of an informal medical commission to reconsider the question of Riel's sanity. This was purely a political gesture to the French Canadian wing of the party. If Riel was executed, and Macdonald was determined he would be, then the Quebec members could use the commission's findings as additional justification. Macdonald was certainly the country's leading expert at this kind of political manipulation and he did his best to determine the commission's findings in advance.

The first man named to the commission was Dr. Michael Lavell, a former professor of obstetrics at Queen's University who was now Warden of Kingston Penitentiary. Lavell was a staunch Tory from Macdonald's own constituency who could be counted on to do the right thing. Macdonald would have preferred to have a one-man commission but a French Canadian member was absolutely essential. After diligent searching, Macdonald came up with Dr. François-Xavier Valade, who appeared to have all the right qualifications: he had no special training or experience in cases of insanity; he was relatively young and could be expected to defer to the older Lavell; he was a protégé of Caron, Macdonald's most loyal Quebec cabinet minister; and, best of all, he was on the government payroll, making over $1000 a year testing food samples for the Inland Revenue Department. Physicians in the nineteenth century did not have the almost automatic prosperity of today's doctors. There were plenty of poor medical practitioners around and government appointments like Valade's were highly prized. This was not a man who would lightly go against the wishes of the government.

Riel's execution date was fast approaching by the time the commission was appointed. The two doctors rushed west by train in the first week in November and, without revealing their identities, interviewed Riel and the people who had been closest to him since the trial: Superintendent Deane, Father André, and NWMP Surgeon Jukes. Macdonald had asked Jukes also to do another report on Riel's sanity and, since he had been in daily contact with Riel for months, he was the first to reply. On November 6 he sent off a report which confirmed the position he had taken at the trial: that Riel was eccentric but legally sane. Three days later he had a sudden change of heart and wrote a long letter to Macdonald urging that Riel's writings be studied to help come to a conclusion about his sanity. It was evident that Lavell and Valade would not be able to complete their reports and get them to Ottawa before November 10, so the execution was postponed once more to November 16.

Lavell did what Macdonald expected him to do and reported that as far as he was concerned Riel was "an accountable being and knows right from wrong."[2] Valade unexpectedly refused to fulfill the role assigned to him of obedient junior colleague echoing Lavell's opinion. Valade spent a good deal of time with Father André, whose opinions had changed dramatically since the spring. During the rebellion and to some extent even during the trial, Father André had seen Riel as the evil genius who had tempted the Métis away from the path of righteousness for his own personal advancement. Since the trial Father André had visited Riel almost daily and had persuaded him to recant his heretical ideas. Father André knew, however, that Riel's obedience was only on the surface. In their conversations he kept returning to his obsessions and only the continual threat of deprivation of the sacraments made him pay lip service to orthodox religious ideas. At the end of August, Father André wrote to Father Albert Lacombe,

> I spend hours talking to him and I tell you that his conversation does not lack attraction but I am persuaded that it will be impossible for a long time to set this man free with the ideas that dominate him. With the confidence that the Indians and Métis of the North-West have in him it would be dangerous to liberate him. He would expose the public peace to great danger. But it would be an unpardonable crime and a dastardly blot on the history of Canada to execute him rather than shutting him up in an insane asylum where he will be well treated.[3]

Lavell realized that Father André, a very forceful personality, was influencing Valade, and he reported the development to Macdonald.

On November 9, both Lavell and Valade gave separate short reports to

Lieutenant Governor Dewdney, who telegraphed them to Ottawa. The operative portion of Valade's read as follows: "After having examined carefully Riel in private conversation with him and by testimony of persons who take care of him, I have come to the conclusion that he is not an accountable being, that he is unable to distinguish between right and wrong on political and religious subjects which I consider well marked typical forms of a kind of insanity under which he undoubtedly suffers, but on other points I believe him to be quite sensible and can distinguish right from wrong."[4] Dewdney accompanied the two reports with a covering opinion that, astoundingly, concluded that the two reports said essentially the same thing with only minor semantic differences. Armed with this and the telegraphed reports, Macdonald was able to convince his cabinet that the execution should go ahead as planned.

Riel spent most of the last week of his life in apparent calmness, performing his religious observances with his customary devotion. He had few possessions apart from the clothes on his back, but on November 6 he made a will which requested that he be buried in the cemetery at St. Boniface. Much of his time he spent writing a final statement about his activities in the North-West before the rebellion. On the evening of November 15 the official word came through from Ottawa that the execution would go ahead. Sheriff S. E. Chapleau set the time of the execution for eight o'clock in the morning. That night Riel wrote a final letter to his mother and spent the rest of his time in prayer. In the morning he went calmly to the scaffold, even comforting Father André, who could not stop himself from weeping. Precisely on time the hangman released the trap and Riel was pronounced dead two minutes later.

Eleven days later, eight Indians went to the scaffold at Battleford singing their war songs. Those convicted of murdering the wehtikow (cannibal) and

Louison Mongrain, who had killed NWMP Corporal David Cowan, had had their sentences commuted. A Regina *Leader* reporter commented from Battleford: "The carrying out of the sentences passed has been greated [sic] with great satisfaction by the white residents here, who have no sentimental sympathy for the red-skinns [sic] who did the plundering and murdering in this district and it is believed the executions will have a wholesome effect upon the Indian tribes and tend largely to the preservation of peace."[5] Wandering Spirit and his fellow convicted murderers were buried in an unmarked grave near the banks of the North Saskatchewan at Fort Battleford.

Riel's wife and children had gone to Manitoba to live with his mother after the Métis defeat at Batoche. Marguerite was pregnant at the time and in October, while Riel was awaiting execution, the child arrived prematurely and died within a few hours. Marguerite herself did not live much longer than her husband, dying in the early months of 1886 from tuberculosis. Riel's daughter, Angelique, did not survive childhood. His oldest son, Jean, was the beneficiary of a substantial trust fund collected mainly in Quebec. He was taken there after the death of his mother and raised by a French Canadian family. Jean married but had no children. He died in 1908 and there are no direct descendants of Louis Riel.

Gabriel Dumont was joined in Montana by the surviving members of his family in the summer of 1885. He may have tried to organize an escape for Riel but the only evidence for that consists of some vague stories collected by Joseph Kinsey Howard from elderly Métis in Montana in the 1940s. Dumont was offered a position as one of the feature attractions of Buffalo Bill's Wild West Show but turned it down. When his wife, Madeleine, died as the result of an accident in the spring of 1886, however, Dumont accepted the offer. His stardom was short-lived. The American public quickly forgot about the rebellion and within a year Dumont had dropped from top billing to anonymous extra. In the summer of 1886 a general amnesty was proclaimed for all who had taken part in the rebellion, but Dumont was far from ready to return. For the next two years he lived part of the time in Montana and part of the time he travelled with Buffalo Bill. Some time in this period he claims to have visited France, but this is unlikely.

Dumont continued to wander back and forth across North America until 1893, when he decided to return permanently to his old home. He moved back to his river lot on the Saskatchewan and set about applying for his land title under the homestead regulations, a procedure that had been interrupted by the rebellion. He also applied for and received the land scrip he was entitled to under the 1885 settlement with those Métis who had not been included in the Manitoba Act. Dumont's last years were tranquil. He hunted a little, farmed a little, and traded a little at Fort Carlton. In the spring of 1906, almost twenty-one years to the day after the battle of Batoche, he died of a heart attack, an

Stony Mountain Penitentiary, Winnipeg, 1886. *Standing, left to right*: Father Albert Lacombe, Big Bear, Warden Samuel Bedson, Father Clouthier. *Seated, left to right*: unidentified priest, Poundmaker. [Glenbow-Alberta Institute]

almost-forgotten figure in a west that was being inundated by hundreds of thousands of settlers each year.[6]

None of those who were convicted for participating in the rebellion served out their full prison sentences. Poundmaker, who had tried to lead his people peacefully into the new era and who had been attacked then jailed by the whites whose side he took, not surprisingly sickened rapidly in jail. After less than a year in Stony Mountain Penitentiary he was clearly dying and the authorities released him. Four months later, while visiting Crowfoot, his adoptive father, on the Blackfoot reserve, Poundmaker died on July 4, 1886. Big Bear lasted a little longer but he too was seriously ill by early 1887 and was released in March. He had never taken a reserve and now it was too late. His people were scattered across the North-West Territories and Montana. He spent the last few months of his life on Poundmaker's reserve, where he died on January 17, 1888. His grave is in an out-of-the-way spot near the boundary of the reserve.

Of all the survivors of the rebellion, William Henry Jackson's subsequent career was the longest and most colourful. After his escape from the Manitoba insane asylum shortly before Riel was hanged, he went on a speaking tour of several northern states. In 1886 he moved to Chicago, where he became a labour organizer, anarchist, and a member of the Baha'i faith. He had his name legally changed to Honoré Joseph Jaxon. For the next sixty years any radical cause that came to his notice could count on his support, the more unpopular the better. He had a contracting business from time to time but neglected it in favour of writing and speaking for everything from the Haymarket rioters of the 1890s to the Mexican Revolution of 1910 to public lotteries in the 1930s.

Jackson returned to western Canada in 1908 and ran in the federal election of that year in Prince Albert as an Independent Liberal. His former neighbours were not yet ready for a Liberal quite as independent as Will Jackson and he got only a handful of votes. He travelled around Alberta and Saskatchewan for the next year or so as a sort of free-lance labour organizer before returning to

Chicago once more. After the First World War Jackson moved to New York, where he remained for the last thirty years of his life. He still spoke out on controversial public issues at every opportunity but in the final stage of his life he concentrated his efforts on a new goal, collecting a library to be used for the education of the Indians of North America. By the 1940s he had accumulated tons of books and documents, which he kept in the basement of an apartment building where he worked as superintendent. Tragically in 1951, when Jackson was ninety, the owners of the building threw him and his library out into the street. The shock of seeing forty years of collecting carried off as trash was too much for the old man, who suffered a stroke and died within a few weeks.[7]

General Middleton emerged from the rebellion as a hero, if not in the minds of all those who served with him, then certainly for the public at large. The Canadian Parliament voted the victorious general a gift of $20,000 and recommended that he be knighted. Her Majesty was pleased to oblige and the General became Sir Frederick Middleton, KCMG. Within a very short time, however, a half-forgotten incident of the rebellion came back to haunt Middleton. At Battleford he and some of his officers had appropriated some furs belonging to a Métis prisoner named Charles Bremner. Ironically the furs were promptly stolen from Middleton by someone else and he forgot about them. Bremner did not forget. When his trial was over Bremner charged Middleton with taking his furs and the general denied it. Bremner was an extraordinarily persistent individual and kept on pushing until he managed to enlist the aid of the Liberal party. The Liberals were able to force a House of Commons investigation into the incident in 1890. The investigation vindicated Bremner and pronounced Middleton's actions to be illegal. The scandal ruined Middleton's reputation in Canada and he was forced to abandon plans to become president of an insurance company on his retirement. He returned to England, where there had been no unfortunate publicity, and in 1896 was given the sinecure of Keeper of the Crown Jewels at the Tower of London.

Lieutenant Colonel Otter returned to the obscurity of the Canadian Militia staff until the outbreak of the Boer War in South Africa in 1899. Otter was given command of the first Canadian contingent to go to South Africa, a hastily-assembled collection of militiamen known as the 2nd (Special Service) Battalion, Royal Canadian Regiment. It was like 1885 all over again, hastily preparing inexperienced and untrained troops for battle, this time against a much more formidable and better-armed enemy. The RCR fought creditably at the battle of Paardeberg under Otter's leadership. After South Africa Otter returned once again to the internal squabbles and conflicts of the militia staff. In 1912 he retired and became Sir William Otter in recognition of his long and distinguished service. When the First World War broke out Otter was called out of retirement to organize and run the Canadian government's alien internment camps. He died in 1929 at the age of eighty-five.[8]

General Strange went back to his ranch near Calgary and divided his time between harassing the local authorities about alleged Indian depredations and the War Office for the restoration of his pension. Not long after the rebellion he was kicked by a horse, shattering the bones below his knee. The break refused to respond to the treatments of Alberta doctors and Strange finally concluded that under the circumstances ranching was not a practical proposition any longer. He sold his ranch and returned to England, where his leg gradually recovered. In the 1890s he got a job as a salesman for the Maxim Machine Gun company and travelled as far as Australia and Hawaii in that capacity. Eventually he managed to get his pension restored but he remained convinced to the end of his life that his services in Canada entitled him to a knighthood at the very least.

Chief Stewart, after concluding his investigation in the fall of 1885, returned to Hamilton and immediately became involved in a nasty adultery scandal. He deserted his wife and family and fled to New York, where he spent two years working for the Pinkerton Detective Agency. In 1887 he returned to Hamilton and was reconciled with his wife. He became a successful businessman and civic politician, serving a term as mayor in the mid-1890s. When gold was discovered in the Klondike, Stewart's inherent instability came to the fore again. He and several companions tried the disastrous overland route to the Yukon through Edmonton. They failed to make it. In the winter of 1899 Stewart died on the Peel River of a combination of scurvy and starvation.

Most of the Mounted Police who took prominent parts in the rebellion did well in later years. Sam Steele was promoted to Superintendent a few months after the rebellion. He served in the South African War with Lord Strathcona's Horse, helped found the South African Constabulary, transferred to the British Army, and ended his life as Major General Sir Sam Steele. Inspector A. Bowen Perry, who commanded the artillery in Strange's column, rose to the rank of Commissioner and commanded the Mounted Police for over twenty years after 1900. Commissioner Irvine was the big loser in this group. His lack of aggressiveness with his force at Prince Albert finished his career in the NWMP. Irvine was forced to resign in 1886 and ended his career as Warden of Stony Mountain Penitentiary. The rebellion produced no dramatic changes in Western Canada. The North-West Territories did get representation in parliament but it could be argued that would have happened anyway. The issues that had created discontent among the settler population were not altered by the rebellion, and after the turn of the century farmers' protest groups reappeared in more sophisticated forms, culminating in the formation of the Progressive Party after the First World War. The Half Breed Commission continued its distribution of land scrip to the Métis and there was an additional scrip issue in 1900. As a people, however, the Métis continued to face the same bitter choice: assimilate to the dominant society or keep moving out to the fringes to eke out a marginal existence. The Indian Department took advantage of the large number of troops

Cartoonist J.W. Bengough presented the Liberal view of the rebellion in *Grip* magazine, September 12, 1885.

in the Territories to overawe the recalcitrants and settle the remaining holdout bands on reserves. After 1885 they even attempted to enforce a policy of not allowing Indians to leave their reserves without the Agent's permission. The death rate on the reserves climbed rapidly and the native population of western Canada declined until the 1940s.

The most significant long-term results of the rebellion occurred not in the North-West but in the Province of Quebec. When Riel was hung, a storm of outrage swept through French Canada uniting old enemies, dissolving political alliances, and creating new ones. On the November 23, 1885, a great protest meeting was held on the Champ de Mars in Montreal with speakers from every party and faction. One of the speakers who made a big impression on the crowd was Wilfrid Laurier, who had held a minor cabinet post in the Mackenzie government but had not attracted much attention before this meeting. Laurier's stirring speech at the Champ de Mars meeting was his first step toward the leadership of his party and the prime minister's office. For a brief time all options were open. The leader of the Parti National in Quebec, Honoré Mercier, offered to step down and let J.-A. Chapleau take over and lead a united front against the executioners of Riel. Chapleau found the offer tempting but realized that it would mean all-out conflict between French and English. He turned the offer down and along with the other French Canadian cabinet ministers closed ranks behind Macdonald. Mercier turned instead to the Liberals and found them more receptive.

Mercier was an unprincipled demagogue but in the Riel execution he had found an unbeatable issue. The Parti National, with support from the Liberals and some breakaway Conservatives, won the 1886 provincial election in Quebec by a narrow margin. Mercier's government survived only one term before collapsing in a welter of scandal but it had accomplished the impossible in breaking the Conservative hold on Quebec. Without control of patronage and with its factional divisions deeper than ever, the Conservative machine began to sputter. With almost glacial slowness the Quebec electorate began to shift its loyalty to the Liberal party. In the 1887 federal election the Conservatives still won a small majority of Quebec seats. In 1891 the Liberals won a small majority. In 1896 it was a Liberal landslide. This was arguably the most fundamental shift in Canadian politics between Confederation and the present. A virtually guaranteed majority in Quebec and with it the dominant position in national politics had passed into the hands of the Liberal party because of the events far away on the Saskatchewan River.

Notes

CSP—Canada Sessional Papers.

DIA black series—Department of Indian Affairs archives, black series.

Glenbow—Glenbow-Alberta Institute Archives.

HBC—Hudson's Bay Company Archives.

PAA—Provincial Archives of Alberta.

PAC—Public Archives of Canada.

PAM—Provincial Archives of Manitoba.

SAB—Saskatchewan Archives Board.

Chapter 1—The Métis and Red River

1. The best biography of Riel is G. F. G. Stanley, *Louis Riel* (Toronto, 1963). An essential supplement for anyone seriously interested in the subject is Thomas Flanagan, *Louis "David" Riel: Prophet of the New World* (Toronto, 1979).
2. Desmond Morton, *The Queen v. Louis Riel* (Toronto, 1974), p. 145.
3. Ibid., p. 76.
4. Alexander Ross, *The Red River Settlement, Its Rise, Progress and Present State* (London, 1856), p. 253.
5. William F. Butler, *The Great Lone Land: A Narrative of Travel and Adventure in the North-West of America* (London, 1872).
6. Ross, *Red River Settlement*, p. 252.
7. C. K. Sissons, *John Kerr* (Toronto, 1947), pp. 110-112.

Chapter 2—Settlers and Government

1. There is no biography of Dewdney. He left extensive collections of papers which are located at the Public Archives of Canada and the Glenbow-Alberta Institute.
2. *Manitoba Free Press*, April 4, 1883.
3. Ibid., December 20, 1883.

Chapter 3—Agitation: The Métis at the South Branch

1. C. K. Sissons, *John Kerr*. (Toronto, 1946), p. 88.
2. Glenbow, *Hardisty Papers*, item 143.
3. Ibid.
4. Ibid.
5. Ibid., item 154, Clarke to Smith, January 15, 1872.

6. Ibid., item 144, Clarke to Archibald, January 17, 1872.

7. Ibid., item 140, Archibald to Christie, January 11, 1872.

8. PAA and SAB, *Petite Chronique de St. Laurent, 1872-1885*. The words describing the north-south extent of the community are: "10 milles plus bas que le traverse et dix milles plus haut que le présent hivernement." There seems to be no doubt that the settlement is St. Laurent, putting the southern limit of the community at Gabriel's Crossing. However, the crossing could be Batoche's, which would put the northern limit at Garièpy's Crossing or, as the authors believe, Garièpy's, which would put the northern limit at St. Louis.

9. PAA and SAB, *Petite Chronique, 1872*.

10. Ibid.

11. *Manitoba Free Press*, July 21, 1875.

12. PAA and SAB, *Petite Chronique, 1875*.

13. *Saskatchewan Herald*, August 25, 1878.

14. CSP, 1886, #45a, and printed in *Epitome of Parliamentary Documents in Connection with the North-West Rebellion, 1885* (Ottawa, 1886), p. 291, pp. 292-3, pp. 298-9.

15. Ibid., #45b, and printed in *Epitome*, p. 317.

16. Ibid., #45a and 45b, three petitions, printed in *Epitome*.

17. 42 Vict., c.31, s.125(3).

18. *Saskatchewan Herald*, April 12, 1880.

19. CSP 1886, #45a, and printed in *Epitome*, pp. 311-314.

20. Ibid., #45b, and printed in *Epitome*, pp. 324-325.

Chapter 4—Indians and Treaties

1. Alexander Morris, *The Treaties of Canada with the Indians* (Toronto, 1880), p. 170.

2. Ibid.

3. William Butler, *The Great Lone Land* (Toronto, 1924), p. 385.

4. John McDougall, *On Western Trails in the Early Seventies* (Toronto, 1911), pp. 13-14.

5. Glenbow, *Hardisty Papers*, item 149, and Butler, *Great Lone Land*, p. 369.

6. The positions of Chiefs Big Bear and Sweetgrass are based on a camp drawing of circa 1870 by Chief Fine Day in David Mandelbaum's *The Plains Cree*, p. 371. Chiefs Big Bear and Little Pine and many of the Prairie People are often included in the River Cree division.

7. Butler, *Great Lone Land*, p. 358.

8. Ibid., p. 360.

9. Morris, *Treaties*, p. 106.

10. Ibid., pp. 173-174.

11. Peter Erasmus, *Buffalo Days and Nights* (Calgary, 1976), pp. 244-245.

12. Ibid., pp. 246-247.

13. Ibid., p. 249.

14. Morris, *Treaties*, pp. 210-211.

15. Erasmus, *Buffalo Days*, p. 251.

16. Ibid., pp. 251-252.

17. Morris, *Treaties*, p. 213.

18. Ibid., p. 354.

19. Ibid., pp. 219-220.

20. Ibid., p. 195.

21. *Opening Up the West, NWMP reports 1874-1881* (Toronto, 1973), Macleod 1878 report, pp. 20-1.

22. Ibid., p. 22.

23. *Saskatchewan Herald*, August 26, 1878.

24. Ibid., January 27, 1879.

25. Ibid., June 2, 1879.

26. Quoted in Hugh Dempsey, *Crowfoot* (Edmonton, 1972), p. 113

27. *Saskatchewan Herald*, June 30, 1879 and August 11, 1879.

28. Montreal *Gazette*, September 29, 1879.

29. Ibid.

30. *Saskatchewan Herald*, December 15, 1879, Dewdney speech at Battleford, November 27, 1879.

31. PAC, *Macdonald Papers*, Vol. 210, pp. 242-243, Dewdney to David Macpherson, August 4, 1881.

32. *Saskatchewan Herald*, February 9, 1880.

33. Ibid.

34. *Opening Up the West*, Crozier report, December 1880, pp. 30-31.

35. *Saskatchewan Herald*, April 26, 1880.

36. Ibid.

37. Ibid., July 5, 1880.

38. Ibid.

39. Ibid., August 2, 1880.

40. Ibid., August 16, 1880.

41. John McLean, *Canadian Savage Folk* (Toronto, 1896), p. 380.

42. Quoted in Hugh A. Dempsey, *Crowfoot*, p. 121.

43. PAC, DIA black series, file 34,527, L'Heureux to Dewdney, September 24, 1880.

44. *Saskatchewan Herald*, March 28, 1881.

45. Ibid.

46. Robert Jefferson, *Fifty Years on the Saskatchewan* (Battleford, 1929), p. 103.

47. Toronto *Mail*, August 24, 1885.

48. Jefferson, *Fifty Years*, p. 126.

49. W. B. Cameron, *Blood Red the Sun* (Edmonton, 1977), p. 56.

50. *Saskatchewan Herald*, January 21, 1882.

51. Ibid., September 30, 1882.

52. Edmonton *Bulletin*, February 3, 1883, Bobtail et al. to Macdonald, January 7, 1883.

53. *Manitoba Free Press*, February 23, 1883, Macdonald report excerpts.

54. *Saskatchewan Herald*, June 9, 1883.

55. Ibid., August 4, 1883.

56. Edmonton *Bulletin*, February 9, 1884.

Chapter 5—Confrontation 1884

1. SAB, R-17, Edwin to Nellie Brooks, February 26, 1884.

2. N. M. W. J. McKenzie, *Men of the Hudson' Bay Company* (Ft. William, 1921), p. 116.

3. PAC, DIA black series, file 10,181, Keith to Dewdney, February 19, 1884.

4. Ibid., Reed to Macdonald, February 27, 1884.

5. R. B. Deane, *Mounted Police Life in Canada* (London, 1916), p. 144.

6. Ibid., pp. 145-146.

7. Ibid., p. 147.

8. Ibid., p. 148.

9. PAC, DIA black series, file 10,181, Herchmer to NWMP comptroller Fred White, February 26, 1884.

10. Ibid., Reed to Macdonald, February 27, 1884.

11. Deane, *Mounted Police Life*, p. 149.

12. PAC, DIA black series, file 10,181, Reed to Macdonald, February 27, 1884.

13. Deane, *Mounted Police Life*, p. 149.

14. PAC, DIA black series, file 10,181, Reed to Macdonald, February 27, 1884.

15. *Saskatchewan Herald*, April 5, 1884.

16. PAC, DIA black series, file 12,667, Dewdney to Macdonald, April 28, 1884.

17. Ibid.

18. *Saskatchewan Herald*, May 31, 1884.

19. *Manitoba Free Press*, May 17, 1884.

20. PAC, DIA black series, file 29. 6506-4 part 1, Edwards to McDonald, May 13, 1884.

21. Ibid., Reed to Macdonald, May 20, 1884.

22. *Settlers and Rebels, NWMP Reports, 1882-1885* (Toronto, 1973), Irvine 1884 report, p. 8.

23. PAC, DIA black series, file 29. 6506-4 part 1, Irvine to Fred White, May 27, 1884. A similar account appears in *Settlers and Rebels*, Irvine report, 1884.

24. Ibid., McDonald to Dewdney, May 29, 1884.

25. Ibid., file 309A, Vankoughnet to Dewdney, February 5, 1884.

26. Ibid., Dewdney to Macdonald in reply to Vankoughnet letter, February 12, 1884.

27. *Saskatchewan Herald*, June 14, 1884.

28. Edmonton *Bulletin*, June 14, 1884.

29. Ibid.

30. Robert Jefferson, *Fifty Years on the Saskatchewan* (Battleford, 1929), p. 109.

31. PAC, DIA black series, file 309B, Rae to Dewdney, June 21, 1884.

32. Jefferson, *Fifty Years*, pp. 109-110. Jefferson is confused about the times of day of the various events. The times are detailed in the *Saskatchewan Herald* of June 25, 1884.

33. Jefferson, *Fifty Years*, p. 111.

34. PAC, DIA black series, file 390B, Crozier to Dewdney, June 22, 1884.

35. Ibid.

36. Ibid.

37. *Saskatchewan Herald*, June 25, 1884.

38. PAC, DIA black series, file 390B, Crozier to Dewdney, June 22, 1884.

39. Jefferson, *Fifty Years*, p. 116.

40. Ibid., pp. 116-117.

41. *Saskatchewan Herald*, July 12, 1884.

42. PAC, DIA black series, file 309B, Dewdney to Rae, July 4, 1884.

43. *Saskatchewan Herald*, July 12, 1884.

44. PAC, DIA black series, file 309B, Rae to Reed, June 23, 1884.

45. *Saskatchewan Herald*, June 28, 1884.

46. PAC, DIA black series, file 309B, Crozier to Dewdney, June 25, 1884.

47. Ibid.

48. Ibid., Dewdney to Macdonald, July 4, 1884.

49. Ibid., Vankoughnet to Dewdney, June 27, 1884.

Chapter 6—The Return of Riel

1. Guillaume Charette, *Vanishing Spaces, Memoirs of Louis Goulet* (Winnipeg, 1976), p. 110.

2. Ibid., p. 111.

3. Ibid.

4. Ibid., p. 113.

5. Ibid.

6. PAM, MG3 D2 #18, minutes of meeting, April 21, 1884.

7. Ibid., minutes of meeting, May 6, 1884.

8. PAC, Dewdney Papers, vol. 6, p. 2281-2284, M. C. W. to Riel, May 18, 1884. The authors have edited slightly the poor translation from the original French.

9. Ibid., p. 2284-2287, T. Z. to "Chère Ami," May 20, 1884.

10. PAA, Oblate Papers, Grandin circular letter June 10, 1884.
11. G. F. G. Stanley, ed., *The Collected Writings of Louis Riel* (Edmonton, in publication), #3-004.
12. Ibid.
13. Provincial Archives of British Columbia, F 5. 2/D51A/v. 2, Dewdney diary, June 6, 1884.
14. CSP 1886, #52c, printed in *Epitome of Parliamentary Documents in Connection with the North-West Rebellion, 1885* (Ottawa, 1886), p. 381.
15. *Sun River Sun*, June 12, 1884.
16. PAC, Dewdney Papers, vol. 6, pp. 2230-2232.
17. Ibid.
18. CSP 1886, #52c, printed in *Epitome*, p. 387.
19. *Le Manitoba*, July 24, 1884.
20. *Collected writings of Louis Riel*, #3-006.
21. *Le Manitoba*, July 24, 1884.
22. CSP 1886, #52c, printed in *Epitome*, pp. 383-384, André to Dewdney, July 7, 1884.
23. Ibid., pp. 388-389, André to Dewdney, July 21, 1884.
24. Prince Albert *Times*, July 18, 1884.
25. *Collected Writings of Louis Riel*, #3-007, Riel to "Gentlemen," July 18, 1884.
26. PAC, Dewdney Papers, vol. 6, p. 2226, André to Riel, n. d.
27. CSP 1886, #52c, printed in *Epitome*, pp. 388-389, André to Dewdney, July 21, 1884.
28. Prince Albert *Times*, July 25, 1884.
29. CSP, 1886, #52c, printed in *Epitome*, pp. 388-389, André to Dewdney, July 21, 1884.
30. *Collected Writings of Louis Riel*, #3-009, Riel to Joseph Riel and Louis Lavallée, July 25, 1884.
31. PAC, Dewdney Papers, vol. 4, pp. 1515-1516, Macrae to Dewdney, July 2, 1884.
32. *Manitoba Free Press*, July 7, 1884.
33. Glenbow, Dewdney Papers, pp. 505-506, Macdonald to Dewdney, July 10, 1884.
34. PAC, DIA black series, file 29,506-4 part 1, Vankoughnet to Macdonald, July 12, 1884.
35. Glenbow, Dewdney Papers, pp. 1493-1496, Crozier to Fred White, July 27, 1884.
36. Identified and quoted by G. F. G. Stanley, *Birth of Western Canada* (Toronto, 1961), p. 290.
37. PAC, DIA black series, file 15,423, Macrae to Dewdney, August 25, 1884.
38. PAC, Department of Justice records relating to the rebellion, p. 3661, Thomas Eastwood Jackson statement.
39. *Saskatchewan Herald*, Sept. 6, 1884.

40. Glenbow, Dewdney Papers, pp. 1402-1405, Rouleau to Dewdney, September 5, 1884.
41. *Collected Writings of Louis Riel*, #3-012, Address to the Minister of Public Works.
42. PAC, Dewdney Papers, vol. 2, pp. 612-625, Forget to Dewdney September 18, 1884.
43. Glenbow, Dewdney Papers, pp. 1402-1405, Rouleau to Dewdney, September 5, 1884.
44. Ibid.
45. Ibid., pp. 1398-1401, Reed to Dewdney, September 4, 1884.
46. PAC, DIA black series, file 949, Ballendine to Reed, November 8, 1884 and Ballendine to Dewdney, January 2, 1885. Other Ballendine reports in same file.
47. PAC, Dewdney Papers, vol. 1, pp. 320-321, Keenan to Crozier, September 25, 1884.
48. Ibid., pp. 318-319, Crozier to Dewdney, October 2, 1884.
49. Ibid., p. 325, Keenan to Crozier, October 4, 1884.
50. Glenbow, Dewdney Papers, pp. 797-798, Macdonald to Fred White, September 15, 1884.
51. PAC, Dewdney Papers, vol. 2, pp. 390-391, Dickens to Crozier, October 27, 1884.
52. Glenbow, Dewdney Papers, pp. 1104-1110, Vankoughnet to Dewdney, December 5, 1884.
53. Ibid., pp. 1111-1116, Dewdney to Vankoughnet, December 12, 1884.
54. *Collected Writings of Louis Riel*, #3-0014 and #3-016, Riel to Grandin, September 5 and September 7, 1884.
55. PAC, Dewdney Papers, vol. 2, pp. 612-625, Forget to Dewdney, September 18, 1884.
56. *Collected Writings of Louis Riel*, #3-017, Pétition à votre excellence en conseil, n. d. but presumably soon after September 7, 1884.
57. Ibid., #3-026, Petition "To his Excellency the Governor General, of Canada, in Council," December 16, 1884.
58. PAC, RG 15, Department of the Interior, Dominion Lands Branch, correspondence, file 83,808, Jackson to Chapleau, December 16, 1884.
59. PAA, Oblate Papers, André journal.
60. A. -H. de Tremaudan, *Histoire de la nation métisse dans L'Ouest canadiene* (Montreal, 1935), pp. 418-419.
61. PAC, Dewdney Papers, vol. 4, pp. 1329-1334, Macdowall to Dewdney, December 24, 1884.
62. Desmond Morton, ed., *The Queen v. Louis Riel*, p. 234, André testimony.
63. *Collected Writings of Louis Riel*, #3-023, Riel to Taylor, October 1, 1884.
64. PAC, Dewdney Papers, vol. 1, pp. 28-30, André to Dewdney, January 21, 1885.

65. Glenbow, Dewdney Papers, p. 545, Macdonald to Dewdney, February 20, 1885.

Chapter 7—The Eleventh Hour

1. *Manitoba Free Press*, April 15, 1885, interview with John Brown.
2. Quoted in Donald B. Smith, William Henry Jackson; Riel's Secretary, *The Beaver*, Spring 1981.
3. Thomas Flanagan, *The Diaries of Louis Riel* (Edmonton, 1976), p. 38.
4. SAB, D R298 #5, W. H. Jackson to Riel, September 22, 1884.
5. George Stanley, ed., *Collected Writings of Louis Riel* (in publication), #3-020, Riel to T. E. Jackson, September 29, 1884.
6. PAA, Garnot Mémoire.
7. *Collected Writings of Louis Riel*, Jackson to Riel, January 27, 1885, quoted in footnote to #3-026.
8. PAM, MG3 D2 #19, presentation to Riel, January 1, 1885.
9. PAC, Dewdney Papers, vol. 1, pp. 338-340, Crozier to Dewdney, February 2, 1885.
10. Ibid., pp. 36-40, André to Dewdney, February 6, 1885.
11. CSP, 1885, #116. Order-in-Council re Half-Breed Claims Commission.
12. Glenbow, Dewdney Papers, pp. 531-532, Dewdney to Macdonald, draft, February 4, 1885.
13. Ibid.
14. PAA and SAB, *Petite Chronique de St.-Laurent*, 1885.
15. Desmond Morton, *Queen v. Louis Riel*, p. 358, Riel speech.
16. Toronto *Globe*, July 2, 1885, extracts of February 2, 1885, letter, W. H. Jackson to Albert Monkman, contained in T. E. Jackson letter to *Globe*.
17. Quoted in Thomas Flanagan, *Riel and the Rebellion: 1885 Reconsidered*, pp. 96-97.
18. Toronto *Globe*, July 2, 1885, letter from T. E. Jackson.
19. PAA, Garnot Mémoire.
20. Morton, *Queen v. Louis Riel*, p. 198, Nolin testimony.
21. Ibid.
22. Flanagan, *Riel Diaries*, p. 54.
23. *Manitoba Free Press*, August 29, 1885, letter from T. Gething Jackson.
24. Flanagan, *Riel Diaries*, p. 54.
25. Morton, *Queen v. Louis Riel*, p. 198, Nolin testimony.
26. Toronto *Mail*, April 13, 1885. Other sources mention a remarkably similar meeting that was supposed to have taken place a week earlier, March 1. However, it seems clear from the *Saskatchewan Herald* of March 13 that the meeting referred to here was on March 8.
27. Ibid. The Métis destroyed the original of the 1885 bill of rights after the battle of Duck Lake and no copy is thought to exist. The one quoted here,

supplied by an anonymous correspondent to the *Mail*, seems to be an accurate version, although the demands it contains are milder than might have been expected.

28. PAC, Dewdney Papers, vol. 1, p. 41, Dewdney to André, March 4, 1885.
29. *Saskatchewan Herald*, March 13, 1885.
30. PAC, Dewdney Papers, vol. 1, pp. 348-351, Crozier to Dewdney, February 27, 1885.
31. Ibid., p. 316, Crozier to Dewdney, March 13, 1885.
32. Ibid., p. 353, Dewdney to Crozier, March 13, 1885.
33. Toronto *World*, March 13, 1885.
34. PAC, Dewdney Papers, vol. 1, pp. 192-194, Clarke to Dewdney, March 14, 1885, two telegrams.
35. *Saskatchewan Herald*, March 20, 1885.
36. PAA and SAB, *Petite Chronique de St. Laurent*, 1885.
37. Quoted in George F. G. Stanley, *Louis Riel* (Toronto, 1963), p. 222.
38. Montreal *Gazette*, May 26, 1885.
39. PAA and SAB, *Petite Chronique de St. Laurent*, 1885.
40. PAC, Dewdney Papers, vol. 7, p. 2686, Crozier to Dewdney, March 17, contained in Dewdney to White, March 18, 1885.
41. Glenbow, Dewdney Papers, pp. 1671-1672, Dewdney to Wrigley, March 18, 1885.
42. Ibid., p. 1428, Crozier to Dewdney, March 18, 1885.
43. PAC, Dewdney Papers, vol. 1, p. 360, Crozier to Dewdney, March 18, 1885.
44. Morton, *Queen v Louis Riel*, p. 144, Ness testimony.
45. Toronto *Mail*, April 24, 1885, Willoughby letter to parents, April 8, 1885. Willoughby's account in this letter is remarkably similar to the statements he gave to Department of Justice investigators and to his testimony at Riel's trial.
46. Ibid.
47. PAC, Department of Justice records relating to the rebellion, pp. 3575-3578, Willoughby statement.
48. Toronto *Mail*, April 24, 1885. Willoughby letter.
49. Morton, *Queen v Louis Riel*, p. 137, Lash testimony.
50. Ibid, p. 159, Walters evidence.
51. PAC, Department of Justice records relating to the rebellion, pp. 2787-2790, Louis Marion statement.
52. PAM, MG3 C20-1 #4, W. H. Jackson to "My Dear Family," September 19, 1885.
53. Ibid.
54. PAA, Garnot Mémoire.
55. Morton, *Queen v Louis Riel*, p. 164, Mitchell testimony.
56. Ibid., pp. 86-87, McKay testimony.

57. Ibid., p. 88, McKay testimony.
58. Ibid., pp. 69-70.
59. CSP, 1886, #52, Queen vs. Scott and PAC Department of Justice documents in connection with the rebellion, Scott trial.
60. *Collected Writings of Louis Riel*, #3-031.
61. PAC, Department of Justice records, note following p. 3472 and various statements re Scott case, particularly Craig statement.
62. SAB, Matheson Papers, A. M421.
63. Ibid., Buck Papers, IV-9, Ruth Buck paper, *White Rebels of 1885 in Saskatchewan*, p. 7, based on Matheson documents.
64. Ibid., Buck Papers, II-15 (original) and Matheson Papers A. M421 (copy).
65. CSP, 1886, #52, Queen vs. Scott, indictment.
66. Morton, *Queen v Louis Riel*, pp. 378-379, trial exhibit #14. Craig copy quoted in Ruth Buck, *White Rebels*, has signatures of all Métis council, but lacks postscript.
67. PAM, MG3 C20-1 #4, W. H. Jackson to "My Dear Family," September 19, 1885.
68. Ibid.

Chapter 8—The Fighting Begins: Duck Lake

1. PAM, MG10 F1, Récit Gabriel Dumont.
2. PAA, Garnot Mémoire.
3. G. F. G. Stanley, trans., "Dumont's Account of the North-West Rebellion," *Canadian Historical Review*, XXX, 3, September 1949.
4. PAM, Récit Dumont. Récit Patrice Fleury. Stanley, "Dumont's Account."
5. Winnipeg *Sun*, June 2, 1885, George Flinn interview with volunteers.
6. Montreal *Gazette*, May 12, 1885, Alex Stewart account.
7. Winnipeg *Sun*, May 8, 1885.
8. PAC, Department of Justice records relating to the rebellion, various statements of Duck Lake battle participants.
9. Stanley, "Dumont Account."
10. Montreal *Gazette*, May 12, 1885, Stewart account.
11. Stanley, "Dumont Account."
12. Ibid.
13. Ibid.
14. PAM, Récit Patrice Fleury et al., Isidore Dumas account.
15. HBC, E. 9/28a, p. 260-263, Diehl statement re Carlton claims.
16. PAC, Dewdney Papers, vol. 2, p. 822, Irvine to Dewdney, March 27, 1885.
17. Ibid., vol. 3, p. 1136, Dewdney to Macdonald, March 27, 1885.
18. Ibid., vol. 5, pp. 1988-1989, Reed to Dewdney, March 27, 1885.
19. PAA, André Journal.

20. Ibid.

21. Ibid.

22. Glenbow, Faithful Companions of Jesus, March 28, 1885.

23. Ibid.

24. PAA, André Journal.

25. *Family Herald and Weekly Star*, December 29, 1955, "The Night of the Alarm."

26. Ibid.

27. PAM, MG3 C20-1 #4, W. H. Jackson to "My Dear Family," September 19, 1885.

28. PAC, Department of Justice documents, pp. 3661-3669, T. E. Jackson statement.

29. *Collected Writings of Louis Riel*, #3-047, Riel to People of Prince Albert.

30. PAM, MG3 C20-1 #4, W. H. Jackson to "My Dear Family," September 19, 1885.

Chapter 9—Mobilization

1. Rebellion headlines, see for example, Winnipeg *Times*, March 23, 1885, and Toronto *World*, March 23, 1885.

2. New York *Herald*, March 24, 1885.

3. J. S. Willison, *Reminiscences, Political and Personal* (Toronto, 1919).

4. D. Morton, *Ministers and Generals: Politics and the Canadian Militia* (Toronto, 1970)

5. PAC, Caron Papers, Caron to Middleton, March 28, 1885.

6. Diary of R. S. Cassels, March 30, 1885, in R. C. Macleod, ed., *Reminiscences of a Bungle* (Edmonton, 1983), pp. 105-107. Copies of the Cassels diary are in PAC and Glenbow.

7. Toronto *World*, March 28, 1885.

8. Toronto *News*, April 6, 1885.

9. PAC, Reminiscences of Joseph Crowe.

10. Port Hope *Guide*, April 10, 1885.

11. PAC, Crowe Reminiscences.

12. Cassels Diary, April 3, 1885, in Macleod, *Bungle*, pp. 112-114.

13. PAC, Caron Papers, Middleton to Caron, April 1, 1885.

14. Ibid., Middleton to Caron, April 11, 1885.

Chapter 10—Battleford and Frog Lake: A Spring of Blood

1. Saskatoon *Star-Phoenix*, June 17, 1932, W. B. Cameron interview with William McKay.

2. SAB, Reminiscences of James Clinkskill, p. 3.

3. PAC, Dewdney Papers, vol. 4, p. 1489-1490, Ansdell Macrae to Dewdney, March 27, 1885.

4. Ibid., vol. 7, p. 2422, Dewdney to Rouleau, March 27, 1885.

5. Toronto *World*, October 6, 1885, Diary of James Payne, March 28, 1885.

6. Glenbow, M4432, partial transcript of Rae report, July 20, 1885.

7. Toronto *Mail*, May 15, 1885, interview with Miss Taylor.

8. SAB, Clinkskill, p. 3.

9. Saskatchewan *Herald*, October 12, 1885.

10. Ibid.

11. Manitoba *Free Press*, March 31, 1885.

12. Robert Jefferson, *Fifty Years on the Saskatchewan* (Battleford, 1927), pp. 125-126.

13. PAC, Dewdney Papers, vol. 5, pp. 1872-5, Rae to Dewdney, March 30, 1885.

14. Saskatoon *Star-Phoenix*, June 17, 1932, Cameron interview with McKay.

15. PAC, Dewdney Papers, vol. 5, pp. 1879-1880, Rae to Dewdney, March 30, 1885.

16. Ibid., p. 1881, Dewdney to Rae, March 30, 1885.

17. Ibid., vol. 4, p. 1543, Dewdney to Middleton, March 30, 1885.

18. *Manitoba Free Press*, March 31, 1885.

19. *Saskatchewan Herald*, April 23, 1885.

Chapter 10—Battleford and Frog Lake: A Spring of Blood

1. Saskatoon *Star-Phoenix*, June 17, 1932, W. B. Cameron interview with William McKay.

2. SAB, Reminiscences of James Clinkskill, p. 3.

3. PAC, Dewdney Papers, vol. 4, p. 1489-1490, Ansdell Macrae to Dewdney, March 27, 1885.

4. Ibid., vol. 7, p. 2422, Dewdney to Rouleau, March 27, 1885.

5. Toronto *World*, October 6, 1885, Diary of James Payne, March 28, 1885.

6. Glenbow, M4432, partial transcript of Rae report, July 20, 1885.

7. Toronto *Mail*, May 15, 1885, interview with Miss Taylor.

8. SAB, Clinkskill, p. 3.

9. Saskatchewan *Herald*, October 12, 1885.

10. Ibid.

11. Manitoba *Free Press*, March 31, 1885.

12. Robert Jefferson, *Fifty Years on the Saskatchewan* (Battleford, 1927), pp. 125-126.

13. PAC, Dewdney Papers, vol. 5, pp. 1872-5, Rae to Dewdney, March 30, 1885.

14. Saskatoon *Star-Phoenix*, June 17, 1932, Cameron interview with McKay.

15. PAC, Dewdney Papers, vol. 5, pp. 1879-1880, Rae to Dewdney, March 30, 1885.
16. Ibid., p. 1881, Dewdney to Rae, March 30, 1885.
17. Ibid., vol. 4, p. 1543, Dewdney to Middleton, March 30, 1885.
18. *Manitoba Free Press*, March 31, 1885.
19. *Saskatchewan Herald*, April 23, 1885.
20. SAB, Clinkskill, pp. 6-7.
21. G. H. Needler, ed., *Suppression of the Rebellion in the North-West Territories of Canada*, 1885 (Toronto, 1948), p. 19.
22. *Manitoba Free Press*, April 2, 1885.
23. Winnipeg *Daily Sun*, May 8, 1885, letter, Dickens to Rae, March 30, 1885.
24. W. B. Cameron, *Blood Red the Sun* (Edmonton, 1977), pp. 28-29.
25. Guillaume Charette, *Vanishing Spaces, Memoirs of Louis Goulet* (Winnipeg, 1980), pp. 158-159.
26. Glenbow, M539, Box 3, W. B. Cameron, The Story of the Three Scouts.
27. Cameron, *Blood Red the Sun*, p. 30.
28. Ibid., p. 31.
29. Ibid., p. 33.
30. Ibid., pp. 33-34.
31. Ibid., pp. 35.
32. Sluman, Norma and Jean Goodwill, *John Tootoosis: Biography of a Cree Leader* (Ottawa, Golden Dog Press, 1982), p. 62.
33. Ibid., p. 63.
34. Cameron, *Blood Red the Sun*, p. 36.
35. Ibid.
36. Ibid., pp. 41-42.
37. Charette, *Vanishing Spaces*, pp. 120-121.
38. Cameron, *Blood Red the Sun*, pp. 42-43.
39. Ibid., p. 46-47.
40. Charette, *Vanishing Spaces*, p. 122.
41. Cameron, *Blood Red the Sun*, p. 48.
42. Charette, *Vanishing Spaces*, p. 123.
43. Cameron, *Blood Red the Sun*, p. 48.
44. Charette, *Vanishing Spaces*, pp. 123-124.
45. Toronto *Mail*, June 10, 1885, interview with W. B. Cameron, and Sluman and Goodwill, *John Tootoosis*, p. 71.
46. *Saskatchewan Herald*, October 5, 1885, trial transcript.
47. Cameron, *Blood Red the Sun*, p. 51.
48. Ibid.
49. PAA, Judge Charles Rouleau trial notes, Queen vs. Miserable Man, October 3, 1885.

50. Toronto *Globe*, June 23, 1885, interview with Teresa Gowanlock.
51. *Saskatchewan Herald*, October 19, 1885, trial transcript.
52. Ibid.
53. CSP, 1886, #52a, Queen vs. Papuh-make-sick, printed in *Epitome of Parliamentary Documents in Connection with the North-West Rebellion, 1885.* (Ottawa, 1886), p. 358. Walking the Sky was often referred to as Round the Sky.
54. *Saskatchewan Herald*, October 19, 1885, trial transcript.
55. Charette, *Vanishing Spaces*, p. 126.
56. Hughes, Stuart, ed., *The Frog Lake "Massacre"* (Toronto, 1976), p. 161.
57. Ibid., pp. 162-164.
58. Ibid., pp. 164-165.
59. Ibid., 165.
60. Charette, *Vanishing Spaces*, pp. 127-128.
61. Glenbow, M539, Box 3, The Narrow Escape of the Mann Family.
62. Winnipeg *Daily Sun*, June 27, 1885, interview with William McLean.
63. *Manitoba Free Press*, June 23, 1885, Quinney diary.
64. Toronto *Mail*, June 11, 1885. Missionary John McDougall heard this story from the Frog Lake Cree and told it to reporter George Ham.

Chapter 11—The Fall of Fort Pitt

1. SAB, Reminiscence of James Clinkskill, pp. 9-10, p. 7.
2. Ibid., p. 10.
3. *Saskatchewan Herald*, April 23, 1885.
4. SAB, Clinkskill, p. 18.
5. Robert Jefferson, *Fifty Years on the Saskatchewan* (Battleford, 1929), p. 140.
6. PAC, Dewdney Papers, Vol. 3, pp. 1165-1170, Hardisty to Wrigley, in Dewdney to Macdonald, April 4, 1885.
7. Edmonton *Bulletin*, April 11, 1885.
8. PAC, Dewdney Papers, vol. 3, p. 910, ? to Langevin, April 7, 1885.
9. PAC, MG29 E40, McDougall et al to Strange, April 7, 1885.
10. Glenbow, M4343, Scollen to "Dear and Reverend Father," April 20, 1885. A copy of this letter is in PAA, Oblate Papers.
11. Ibid.
12. Ibid.
13. Ibid.
14. Ibid.
15. Edmonton *Bulletin*, April 18, 1885.
16. Glenbow, Scollen to "Dear and Reverend Father," April 20, 1885.
17. PAC, DIA black series, file 19,550-2, Lucas to Dewdney April 15, 1885.
18. Guillaume Charette, *Vanishing Spaces: Memoir's of Louis Goulet* (Winnipeg, 1980), pp. 135-138.

19. W. B. Cameron, *Blood Red the Sun* (Edmonton, 1977), pp. 88-89.
20. Ibid., p.90
21. Toronto *Globe*, July 17, 1885, interview with William McLean.
22. Cameron, *Blood Red the Sun*, pp. 93-94, Big Bear to Martin, April 14, 1885. The letter appears to have been mis-dated. It was probably written in the morning of April 15.
23. HBC, E. 9/29, pp. 128-131, McLean statement re Pitt claims.
24. Cameron, *Blood Red the Sun*, p. 103.
25. Ibid., pp. 103-106.
26. CSP, 1886, #52a, Queen vs. Mongrain, printed in *Epitome of Parliamentary Documents in Connection with the North-West Rebellion, 1885* (Ottawa, 1886), pp. 362-364.
27. Cameron, *Blood Red the Sun*, p. 95, W. J. McLean to wife, April 15, 1885. The letter was widely reprinted in newspapers in May and June, 1885, and was a topic of considerable discussion.
28. Cameron, *Blood Red the Sun*, pp. 100-101.
29. Ibid., p. 107.
30. *Weekend Magazine*, No. 32, 1968, Duncan McLean story.

Chapter 12—Standoff at Fish Creek

1. R. C. Macleod, ed., *Reminiscences of a Bungle, by One of the Bunglers* (Edmonton, 1984), p. 19.
2. PAC, Harold Penryn Rusden, Notes on the Suppression of the North West Insurrection, in Macleod, *Bungle*, p. 247.
3. SAB, Diary of R. K. Allan, April 13, 1885.
4. PAA, André Journal.
5. Ibid., Garnot Mémoire.
6. PAM, Récit Gabriel Dumont.
7. PAC, Dewdney Papers, vol. 6, p. 2371, Métis Council Minutes, March 31, 1885. Among the PAC Dewdney papers there are two copies of the large number of rebel documents captured at Batoche, including the council minutes and numerous scouting reports. Another copy of the Batoche papers in the Department of Justice records relating to the rebellion. Some were published in the Sessional Papers in 1886.
8. PAA, Garnot Mémoire.
9. PAC, Dewdney Papers, vol. 6, pp. 2255-2256, p. 2260, p. 2273, Métis Council Minutes, April 17, 1885.
10. PAC, Caron Papers, Middleton to Caron, April 20, 1885.
11. Ibid., Dewdney Papers, vol. 6, pp. 2316-2318, scouting reports, April 23, 1885.
12. PAM, Récit Gabriel Dumont.
13. PAM, Récit Patrice Fleury et al., J. Caron's Account.

14. Ibid., Elie Dumont's Account.
15. G. W. L. Nicholson, *The Gunners of Canada* (Toronto, 1967), p. 120.
16. PAC, Dewdney Papers, vol. 6, pp. 2340-2353, various Métis reports of the Battle of Fish Creek.
17. PAM Fleury, Yellow Blanket quote, Edouard Dumont's Account.
18. The Métis singing and the conversation with Hourie are reported in most Métis accounts of the battle. The Hourie incident is also recorded in the Regina *Leader*, May 12, 1885, and other newspapers.
19. PAM, Fleury, Account of Isidore Dumas.
20. Regina *Leader*, May 12, 1885.
21. PAC, Rusden, in Macleod, *Bungle*, p. 259.
22. Winnipeg *Times*, April 25, 1885.
23. Fr. Henri Faraud to Fr. Joseph Fabré, in Stuart Hughes, ed., *The Frog Lake "Massacre": Personal Perspectives on Ethnic Conflict* (Toronto, 1976), pp. 331-332.
24. HBC, Statements re Green Lake claims.

Chapter 13—Cutknife: Otter's Reprieve

1. Quoted in Desmond Morton, *The Canadian General: Sir William Otter* (Hakkert, Toronto, 1974), p. 17
2. Glenbow, Coleman collection of telegrams relating to rebellion, #700, Laurie to Toronto *Mail*, April 14, 1885.
3. PAC, MG30 G 14, corres. vol. 1, file 3, Otter papers, Middleton to Otter, April 11, 1885.
4. PAC, Cassels diary, April 12, 1885, in R. C. Macleod, ed., *Reminiscences of a Bungle* (Edmonton, 1983), p. 126.
5. Ibid., April 14, 1885, p. 130.
6. Ibid., April 18, 1885, p. 133.
7. Toronto *World*, April 15, 1885.
8. Robert Jefferson, *Fifty Years on the Saskatchewan* (Battleford, 1929), p. 139.
9. Cassels diary, April 19 and April 20, 1885, and Macleod, *Bungle*, pp. 134-135.
10. *Saskatchewan Herald*, April 23, 1885.
11. SAB, Reminiscences of James Clinskill, p. 28.
12. Cassels diary, April 23, 1885, in Macleod, *Bungle*, p. 138.
13. SAB, Clinskill, pp. 28-29.
14. Cassels diary, April 24, 1885, in Macleod, *Bungle*, p. 140.
15. *Saskatchewan Herald*, April 23, 1885.
16. Glenbow, M136, Brock to parents, April 25, 1885.
17. Toronto *World*, May 18, 1885, Acheson to "Will," April 28, 1885.

18. Winnipeg *Sun*, April 27, 1885.
19. PAC, Otter Papers, Middleton to Otter, April 25, 1885.
20. Cassels diary, May 1, in Macleod, *Bungle*, p. 149.
21. PAC, Dewdney Papers, vol. 5, p. 1806, Otter to Dewdney, April 26, 1885.
22. Ibid., p. 1807, Dewdney to Otter, April 26, 1885.
23. PAC, Otter Papers, Middleton to Otter, April 26, 1885.
24. Toronto *World*, May 18, 1885, Acheson to "Will," April 28, 1885.
25. PAC, Otter Papers, Otter to Middleton, April 30, 1885.
26. Ibid., Middleton to Otter, April 30, 1885.
27. Ibid., Otter to Middleton, May 1, 1885.
28. Ibid., Middleton to Otter, May 1, 1885.
29. Cassels diary, May 1, 1885, in Macleod, *Bungle*, p. 150.
30. Morton, Desmond, ed., *The Queen v Louis Riel* (Toronto, 1974), p. 376,
    Riel trial exhibit #9. Riel transcript also printed in *Epitome of
    Parliamentary Documents in Connection with the North-West Rebellion, 1885*
    (Ottawa, 1886).
31. Jefferson, *Fifty Years*, pp. 137-138.
32. CSP, 1886, #52b, Queen vs. Mus-sin-ass et al., and #52, Queen vs.
    Poundmaker.
33. Toronto *Mail*, May 19, 1885.
34. Cassels diary, May 2, 1885, in Macleod, *Bungle*, pp. 151-152.
35. Ibid., p. 152.
36. Jefferson, *Fifty Years*, p. 144.
37. Ibid., p. 144.
38. Toronto *Globe*, May 21, 1885.
39. Jefferson, *Fifty Years*, p. 144.
40. Ibid., p. 143.
41. Glenbow, Diary of Captain R. W. Rutherford, May 2, 1885.
42. Toronto *Mail*, May 19, 1885.
43. Fine Day's activities are partly, and sometimes not very accurately,
    described in an interview with Father Louis Cochin in the *Manitoba Free
    Press*, July 25, 1885 and in an interview with Louis Chapalet in the
    Montreal *Witness*, reprinted in the Toronto *News*, June 4, 1885.
44. Cassels diary, May 2, 1885, in Macleod, *Bungle*, p. 152.
45. Toronto *Mail*, May 19, 1885.
46. Toronto *News*, May 22, 1885, letter from George Watts, May 7, 1885.
47. Ibid.
48. Toronto *Mail*, May 23, 1885, Patrick Hughes to father, May 4, 1885.
49. Toronto *Globe*, May 21, 1885.
50. Ibid.
51. Jefferson, *Fifty Years*, p. 143.
52. Ibid.

53. *The Family of Cassels*, privately printed, Dick to Hamilton Cassels, May 6, 1885.
54. Cassels diary, May 2, 1885, in Macleod, *Bungle*, p. 157.
55. Toronto *Mail*, May 8, 1885.
56. *Saskatchewan Herald*, May 4, 1885.
57. Toronto *Globe*, May 22, 1885.
58. Toronto *World*, May 9, 1885.
59. Toronto *Globe*, May 9, 1885.
60. Jefferson, *Fifty Years*, p. 147.
61. Ibid., pp. 147-148.

Chapter 14—Decision at Batoche

1. PAC, Caron Papers, Middleton to Caron, April 25, 1885.
2. R. C. Macleod, ed., *Reminiscences of a Bungle* (Edmonton 1983), pp. 12-13.
3. PAC, Diary of Charles S. Clapp.
4. PAM, MG3 C19, Règlements, May 2, 1885.
5. PAC, Dewdney Papers, vol. 6, p. 2385.
6. PAC, Rusden, and Macleod, *Bungle*, p. 268.
7. PAM, Récit Gabriel Dumont.
8. C. A. Boulton, *Reminiscences of the North-West Rebellions* (Toronto, 1886), p. 260.
9. PAC, Rusden, and Macleod, *Bungle*, pp. 275-276.
10. PAC, Diary of Charles S. Clapp.
11. Macleod, *Bungle*, p. 27.
12. G. H. Needler, ed., *Suppression of the Rebellion in the North-West Territories of Canada, 1885* (Toronto, 1948), pp. 49-50.
13. Macleod, *Bungle*, pp. 31-32.
14. Needler, *Suppression*, p. 50.
15. PAC, Rusden, and Macleod, *Bungle*, pp. 283-284.
16. PAC, Clapp Diary.
17. PAC, Caron Papers, Middleton to Caron, May 11, 1885.
18. Macleod, *Bungle*, pp. 35-36.
19. G. F. G. Stanley, ed., *Collected Writings of Louis Riel* (Edmonton, in publication), #3-053 and #3-055, Riel's messages to Middleton.
20. Boulton, *Reminiscences*.
21. Metropolitan Toronto Library, Diary of Staff-Sergeant Walter Stewart.
22. PAC, Rusden, and Macleod, *Bungle*, p. 289.

Chapter 15—Frenchman Butte: The Odyssey of General Strange

1. T. B. Strange, *Gunner Jingo's Jubilee* (London, 1893).
2. PAC, Caron Papers, Caron to Strange, March 29, 1885.
3. Strange, *Gunner Jingo*, p. 406.

4. Calgary *Herald*, April 6, 1885 and *Manitoba Free Press*, April 7, 1885.
5. PAC, Dewdney Papers, vol. 3, p. 1187, Macdonald to Dewdney, April 10, 1885 and vol. 3, p. 1199, Macdonald to Dewdney April 12, 1885, and others.
6. Strange, *Gunner Jingo*, p. 454.
7. Macleod, *Bungle*, p. 65.
8. S. B. Steele, *Forty Years in Canada* (London, 1916), pp. 224-227.
9. Macleod, *Bungle*, p. 67.
10. Cassels Diary, June 30, 1885, in Macleod, *Bungle*, pp. 211-212.

Chapter 16—The Trial of Louis Riel

1. D. H. Brown, "The Meaning of Treason in 1885," *Saskatchewan History*, 1975.
2. Desmond Morton, *The Queen v. Louis Riel*, pp. 3-7.
3. Winnipeg *Sun*, June 29, 1885.
4. R. V. Arnold (1724), quoted in Simon Verdun-Jones and Russell Smandych, "Catch-22 in the Nineteenth Century: The Evolution of Therapeutic Confinement for the Criminally Insane in Canada, 1840-1900," *Criminal Justice History: An International Annual*, 1981, p. 88. Another article by Professor Verdun-Jones, "'Not Guilty by Reason of Insanity': The Canadian Roots of the Insanity Defence, 1843-1920" in L. A. Knafla, ed., *Crime and Criminal Justice in Europe and Canada* (Waterloo, Ontario, 1981), is very useful for understanding the law as it related to insanity in Canada in 1885. McNaghten's name is often spelled M'Naghten.
5. SAB, SHS 56, file 3.

Chapter 17—The Other Trials: Justice Unbalanced

1. SAB, SHS 29, Nelson to "Jack," April 29, 1944.
2. Ibid. A similar account appears in Hugh Nelson's pamphlet *Four Months Under Arms* in SAB.
3. All trial material from *Queen vs. Jackson, Sessional Papers 1886, #52*.
4. PAA, Garnot Mémoire.
5. SAB, Taché Papers, Carey to Taché, August 3, 1885.
6. PAC, Department of Justice papers relating to the Rebellion, letterbook, p. 142, Burbidge to Campbell, July 18, 1885.
7. PAA, Garnot Mémoire.
8. All affidavits and sentences in *Queen vs. various Métis* CSP *1886, #52*.
9. Queen vs. Kah-pah-yak-as-to-cum, CSP 1886, #52, standard treason-felony indictment.
10. SAB, Taché Papers, Cochin to Taché, August 14, 1885. There is some evidence of a remarkably similar incident during Big Bear's trial.

11. All trial material from Queen vs. Kah-pah-yak-as-to-cum, CSP 1886, #52.

12. SAB, Taché Papers, Cochin to Taché, August 14, 1885.

13. All trial material from Queen vs. Poundmaker, CSP 1886, #52.

14. SAB, Taché Papers, André to Taché, August 20, 1885.

15. PAM, Judge Hugh Richardson trial notes (copy in SAB) and Regina *Leader*, September 10, 1885.

16. PAC, Department of Justice papers relating to the North-West Rebellion, letterbook, pp. 229-231, Osler to Bunting, August 3, 1885.

17. PAC, Department of Justice papers, pp. 2535-2537, Brewster opinion, n. d.

18. All trial material from Queen vs. Scott, CSP 1886, #52.

19. *Manitoba Free Press*, September 10,1885.

20. All trial material from Queen vs. Big Bear, CSP 1886, #52.

21. Archbold's Pleading, Evidence and Practice in Criminal Cases, 1938 edition, p. 1088. This edition appears to contain the same wording as the one the 1885 lawyers used.

22. Upper Canada Court of Queen's Bench, 1866, Regina vs. McMahon and Regina vs. Lynch.

23. *Manitoba Free Press*, September 26, 1885.

24. Toronto *Mail*, October 5, 1885.

25. All trial material from Queen vs. Big Bear's band, Nan-e-sue et al., CSP 1886, #52.

26. All trial material from Queen vs. Oka-doka et al., CSP, 1886, #52.

27. All trial material from Queen vs. White Cap, CSP, 1886, #52.

28. *Manitoba Free Press*, September 19, 1885.

29. Queen vs. Abraham Montour and André Nault, CSP, 1886, #52.

30. Queen vs. Magnus Burston, CSP, 1886, #52.

31. SAB, Taché Papers, André to Taché, August 20, 1885.

32. Glenbow, Dewdney Papers, pp. 1240-1249, Reed to Dewdney, September 6, 1885.

33. PAA, Judge Rouleau trial notes, various cases.

34. PAA, Rouleau notes, Queen vs. Four Sky Thunder and other cases.

35. CSP 1886, #52b, Queen vs. Mus-sin-ass et al., printed in *Epitome of Parliamentary Documents in Connection with the North West Rebellion, 1885* (Ottawa, 1886).

36. CSP *1886, #52a*, various cases, printed in *Epitome*.

37. Ibid., Queen vs. Charles Ducharmes et al. The jury verdict is incorrect as printed in the *Epitome*. The verdict is correctly described in Judge Rouleau's notes, PAA, case number 48.

38. Toronto *News*, April 21, 1885.

39. Montreal *Gazette*, September 23, 1885.

Chapter 18—Dénouement

1. *Le Nord*, early October 1885, quoted in H. Blair Neatby, *Laurier and a Liberal Quebec: A Study in Political Management* (Toronto, 1973), p. 28.
2. Thomas Flanagan, *Riel and the Rebellion: 1885 Reconsidered* (Saskatoon, 1983), p. 139.
3. PAA, Oblate Papers, André to Lacombe, August 31, 1885.
4. Flanagan, p. 139.
5. Regina *Leader* supplement, December 3, 1885.
6. George Woodcock, *Gabriel Dumont* (Edmonton, 1975).
7. Donald B. Smith, "William Henry Jackson: Riel's Secretary," *The Beaver*, 1981, pp. 10-19 and "Honoré Joseph Jaxon: A Man who Lived for Others," *Saskatchewan History*, 1981, pp. 81-101.
8. Desmond Morton, *The Canadian General: Sir William Otter* (Toronto, 1974).

Bibliography

I. Unpublished Sources

Archives of Ontario
    Diary of J. M. Delamere (Mu 840)
    Diary of J. T. Symons (Mu 844)
    Letter and Sketch by Col. H. J. Grassett (Mu 2121)
    Williams Family Papers (Mu 3217 to 3222 and Mu 3384)

Glenbow-Alberta Institute
    Coleman Telegram Collection (BN .C692)
    Dewdney Papers (M320)
    Diary of R. K. Allan (M12)
    Diary of R. S. Cassels (BG.3 .Q3)
    Diary of Staff-Sergeant C. H. Connon (A 5215)
    Diary of Captain R. W. Rutherford (M 4924)
    Diary of G. E. Sanders (A 5215 f.1)
    Faithful Companions of Jesus Annuals (M135 f.4 and M1395 f.5)
    Hardisty Papers (M477)
    Hougham Papers (M539)
    Jukes Papers (M607 and M609)
    Letters of Henry Brock (M136)
    Reminiscences of Joseph Hicks (M515)

Hudson's Bay Company Archives
    Statements Re Property Destroyed During the Rebellion (E9/28)
        Carlton
        Battleford
        Pitt
        Lac La Biche
        Battle River
        Green Lake

Metropolitan Toronto Library
    Diary of Staff-Sergeant Walter F. Stewart
    Recollections of an Eventful Life, Newton A. Myer

Montana Historical Society
    Joseph Kinsey Howard Papers
    The Story of Harry Cash

Oregon Province Archives, Society of Jesus
    Letters of Eberschweiler

Provincial Archives of Alberta
    Diary of A. W. Kippen (70.174)
    Diary of James Henry Long (70.377/1)
    North-West Rebellion of 1885, Medical and Surgical History (74.1/326)
    Oblate Papers: Files re rebellion (71.220)
                    Lettre du P. André à Mgr. Grandin (André Journal)
                    Mémoire de Ph. Garnot (in 71.220)
                    Petite Chronique de St. Laurent
    Judge Charles B. Rouleau Trial Notes

Provincial Archives of British Columbia
    Diary of Edgar Dewdney (F 5.2/D5 1A/v.2)

Provincial Archives of Manitoba
    Diary and memoirs of George A. Flinn (MG3, C13)
    Diary of A. N. Mowat (MG3, C9)
    Diary of James E. Stodgell (MG3, C21)
    Journal of Peter N. Rolston (MG3, C10)
    Journal of W. J. Watts (MG3, C12)
    Mémoires dictés par Gabriel Dumont (MG10, F1)
    Mémoires de Louis Schmidt (MG9, A31)
    Récit Gabriel Dumont (MG10, F1)
    Récit Patrice Fleury, et al. (MG10, F1)
    Reports of Royal Commission on Rebellion Losses (MG3 C14)
    Riel Collection (MG3 D1 and MG3 D2)

Public Archives of Canada
    Caron Papers (MG27, I-D-3)
    Department of Indian Affairs (RG10), Black Series
    Department of Justice (RG13), Records Relating to Louis Riel and the
        North-West Rebellion, 1873-1886.
    Dewdney Papers (MG27, I-C-4)
    Diary of R. S. Cassels (MG 29, E43)
    Diary of J. A. Forin (MG29, E44)
    Diary of Lawrence Miller (MG29, E42)
    Diary of Thomas Sallans (MG 29, E99)
    Macdonald Papers (MG26A)
    Minto Papers (MG27, II-B-1)
    Otter Papers (MG30, G14, E242)
    Reminiscences of Charles S. Clapp (MG29, E103)
    Reminiscences of Joseph Crowe (MG29, E80)
    H. P. Rusden, "Notes on the Suppression of the North-West Insurrection"
        (MG29, E64)

T. B. Strange Papers (MG29, E40)
W. D. Mills Collection (MG29, E10)

Saskatchewan Archives Board
    Ruth Buck Papers (R20)
    Caswell Papers (C C308)
    Thomas Craigie's Story (SHS13)
    Diary of Lieutenant J. A. V. Preston (CP924)
    Edward Matheson Papers (A-M421)
    Angus McKay Papers (SHS 37, A M192)
    Hugh Nelson, "Four Months Under Arms" (SHS159)
    Petite Chronique de St. Laurent, 1872-1885, and various other parish
        records (R500)
    Prince Albert Old Timers' Reminiscences (North-West Rebellion
        pamphlet file)
    Reminiscences of James Clinkskill (Mfm. 2.304)
    Reminiscences of William Laurie (DL373)
    Taché Papers (AT20)

II. Newspapers

    Edmonton *Bulletin*
    Journal de Québec (Quebec City)
    La Patrie (Montreal)
    Le Manitoba
    London (England) *Standard*
    London (Ontario) *Free Press*
    Lindsay *Post*
    Manitoba Free Press (Winnipeg)
    Montreal *Gazette*
    Montreal *Star*
    Montreal *Witness*
    New York *Herald*
    Peterborough *Examiner*
    Port Hope *Guide*
    Prince Albert *Times*
    Quebec *Mercury*
    Regina *Leader*
    Saint Paul (Minnesota) *Pioneer-Press*
    Saskatchewan Herald (Battleford)
    Thunder Bay *Sentinel*
    Toronto *Globe*
    Toronto *Mail*
    Toronto *News*

Toronto *Telegram*
Toronto *World*
Winnipeg *Manitoban*
Winnipeg *Times*
Winnipeg *Sun*

III. Books and Printed Documents

Adam, G. Mercer. *The Canadian North-West*. Toronto, Rose Publishing Co., 1885.

Ahenakew, Edward. *Voices of the Plains Cree*. Toronto, McClelland and Stewart, 1973.

Anon. *The Story of Louis Riel the Rebel Chief*. Toronto, J. S. Robertson and Brothers, 1885.

Anon. *The True Inwardness of the Canadian Northwest Rebellion Exposed; or, Who is to Blame?* n.p., n.d.

Barnard, W. T. *The Queen's Own Rifles of Canada 1860-1960*. Toronto, Ontario Publishing Co., 1960.

Begg, Alexander. *History of the North-West*. 3 volumes. Toronto, Hunter, Rose and Company, 1894-5.

Boulton, C. A. *Reminiscences of the North-West Rebellions*. Toronto, Grip Printing and Publishing, 1886.

Bowsfield, Hartwell. *Louis Riel*. Toronto, Oxford University Press, 1970.

Butler, William F. *The Great Lone Land: A Narrative of Travel and Adventure in the North-West of America*. London, Sampson Low, Marston, Low and Searle, 1872. (Edition cited: Toronto, Musson, 1924.)

Cameron, W. B. *The War Trail of Big Bear*. Toronto, Ryerson, 1926. Re-published with additions as *Blood Red the Sun*. (Edition cited: Edmonton, Hurtig, 1977)

Canada, Parliament. Sessional Papers, 1885, 1886, and various.

Champion, T. E. *History of the 10th Royals*. Toronto, Hunter, Rose and Co., 1896.

Charette, G. *Vanishing Spaces: Memoirs of Louis Goulet*. Winnipeg, Editions Bois-Brûlés, 1976. Originally published as *L'Espace de Louis Goulet*.

Cochin, R. P. *Missionaires et sauvages pendant la guerre des Métis*. Paris, A. Hennuyer, 1894.

Daoust, Charles Roger. *Cent-vingt jours de service actif*. Montreal, E. Senecal et Fils, 1886.

Davidson, W. M. *The Life and Times of Louis Riel*. Calgary, Albertan Publishing, 1951.

Deane, R. Burton. *Mounted Police Life in Canada*. London, Cassel and Co., 1916. Facsimile edition: Toronto, Coles, 1973.

Dempsey, Hugh A. *Crowfoot: Chief of the Blackfeet*. Edmonton, Hurtig, 1972.

Denison, G. T. *Soldiering in Canada*. Toronto, George N. Morang and Co., 1901.

de Tremaudan, A. H. *Histoire de la nation Métisse dans l'ouest Canadien*. Montreal, Lévesque, 1935.

Epitome of Parliamentary Documents in Connection with the North-West Rebellion, 1885. Ottawa, Queen's Printer, 1886.

Erasmus, Peter. *Buffalo Days and Nights*. Calgary, Glenbow-Alberta Institute, 1976.

Flanagan, Thomas. *Louis "David" Riel: Prophet of the New World*. Toronto, University of Toronto Press, 1979.

————. *Riel and the Rebellion: 1885 Reconsidered*. Saskatoon, Western Producer Prairie Books, 1983.

————, ed. *The Diaries of Louis Riel*. Edmonton, Hurtig, 1976.

Giraud, Marcel. *Le Métis Canadien*. Paris, Institut d'Ethnologie, 1945.

Goodspeed, D. J. *Battle Royal, A History of the Royal Regiment of Canada*. Toronto, Royal Regiment of Canada Association, 1962.

Howard, Joseph Kinsey. *Strange Empire: A Narrative of the North-West*. New York, William Morrow and Company, 1952.

Hughes, Stuart. *The Frog Lake "Massacre": Personal Perspectives on Ethnic Conflict*. Toronto, McClelland and Stewart, 1976.

Jefferson, Robert. *Fifty Years on the Saskatchewan*. Battleford, Canadian North-West Historical Society, 1929.

Lamb, Robert E. *Thunder in the North*. New York, Pageant Press, 1957.

Le Chevalier, Jules. *Batoche: Les missionaires du Nord-Ouest pendant les troubles de 1885*. Montreal, l'Ouvre de Presse Dominicaine, 1941.

Maclean, John. *Canadian Savage Folk*. Toronto, William Briggs, 1896. Facsimile edition: *Native Tribes of Canada*. Toronto, Coles, 1980.

Macleod, R. C., ed. *Reminiscences of a Bungle, by One of the Bunglers, and Two Other Northwest Rebellion Diaries*. Edmonton, University of Alberta Press, 1984.

Mandelbaum, David G. *The Plains Cree*. Regina, Canadian Plains Research Centre, 1979.

McDougall, John. *Pathfinding on Plain and Prairie*. Toronto, William Briggs, 1898. Facsimile edition: Toronto, Coles, 1971.

————. *On Western Trails in the Early Seventies*. Toronto, William Briggs, 1911.

McKenzie, N. M. W. J. *The Men of the Hudson's Bay Company*. Ft. William, Times-Journal Press, 1921.

Morris, Alexander. *The Treaties of Canada with the Indians of Manitoba and the North-West Territories*. Toronto, Bedfords, Clarke and Co., 1880. Facsimile edition: Toronto, Coles, 1979.

Morton, Desmond. *Ministers and Generals: Politics and the Canadian Militia*. Toronto, University of Toronto Press, 1970.

————. *The Canadian General: Sir William Otter*. Toronto, Hakkert, 1974.

————. *The Last War Drum: The North-West Campaign of 1885*. Toronto, Hakkert, 1972.

————, ed. *The Queen v Louis Riel*. Toronto, University of Toronto Press, 1974.

Morton, Desmond and R. H. Roy, eds. *Telegrams of the North-West Campaign*. Toronto, Champlain Society, 1972.

Mulvaney, Charles Pelham. *The History of the North-West Rebellion of 1885*. Toronto, A. H. Hovey and Co., 1885.

Needler, G. H., ed. *Suppression of the Rebellion in the North-West Territories of Canada, 1885*. Toronto, University of Toronto Press, 1948.

Nicholson, G. W. L. *The Gunners of Canada*. Toronto, McClelland and Stewart, 1967.

Opening Up the West, North-West Mounted Police Reports, 1874-1881. Toronto, Coles Publishing Co., 1973.

Oppen, W. A. *The Riel Rebellions: A Cartographic History*. Toronto, University of Toronto Press, 1979.

Payment, Diane. *Batoche (1870-1910)*. St. Boniface, Les éditions blé, 1983.

Report Upon the Suppression of the Rebellion in the North-West Territories and Matters in Connection Therewith in 1885. Ottawa, Queen's Printer, 1886.

Settlers and Rebels, North-West Mounted Police Reports, 1882-1885. Toronto, Coles Publishing Co., 1973.

Sluman, Norma and Jean Goodwill. *John Tootoosis: Biography of a Cree Leader*. Ottawa, Golden Dog Press, 1982.

Sissons, C. K. *John Kerr*. Toronto, Oxford University Press, 1946.

Stanley, G. F. G. *Louis Riel*. Toronto, Ryerson Press, 1963.

————. *The Birth of Western Canada*. Toronto, Longman's, Green and Co., 1936.

————, ed. *Collected Writings of Louis Riel/Ecrits Complets de Louis Riel*. Edmonton, University of Alberta Press (1985—in publication).

Steele, S. B. *Forty Years in Canada*. London, H. Jenkins, 1915. Facsimile edition: Toronto, Coles, 1973.

Strange, T. B. *Gunner Jingo's Jubilee*. London, J. MacQueen, 1893.

Williams, W. H. *Manitoba and the North-West*. Toronto, Hunter, Rose and Co., 1882.

Woodcock, George. *Gabriel Dumont*. Edmonton, Hurtig, 1975.

Index

We include major variations of Indian names in brackets. Where possible, we have rendered historical attempts at writing Cree names into modern spellings in the y dialect and have included older versions where there are substantial differences. We have preferred English translations of the names of Cree individuals, but where we have used a Cree name in the text for a person who was also known in the historical literature by an English translation, we include the translation also in brackets.

For locations listed in this index, we use the modern provincial descriptions and not territorial district descriptions.

374

Halpin, Henry, 215–16.
Ham, George H., 316–17.
Hamilton, Ont., 296, 341.
Hamilton Asylum for the Insane, 302.
Hanifin, Joseph, 140, 141.
Hardisty, Factor Richard Charles, 208.
Haymarket riot, 339.
Henry, Pierre, 143.
Herchmer, Supt. William M. (Billy), 67,
  82–83, 84, 89, 178, 188, 238, 240, 242, 287.
High Treason – see Treason, High.
Hincks, Sir Francis, 159.
Hind, Henry Youle, 19.
Hoodoo, Sask., 144, 149.
Horse Child, 290; pictured, 190, 297.
Hourie, Peter, 322.
Hourie, Tom, 232.
Howard, "Capt." Arthur, 238, 266.
Howard, Joseph Kinsey, 338.
Hudson Bay railway, 34, 124.
Hudson's Bay Company, 14, 17, 18, 31, 33,
  39, 40, 41, 44, 54, 113, 119, 122, 138, 139,
  146, 149, 159, 160, 161, 166, 181, 186, 187,
  189, 192, 193, 195, 197, 201, 203, 206, 207,
  208, 209, 211, 212, 214, 216, 219, 234, 235,
  240, 242, 282, 283, 287, 292, 294, 314, 322,
  326; Rupert's Land sale, 19, 20, 30, 35,
  52–53; Red River resistance, 20, 22;
  relationship to Indians, 49–50, 72–73, 78,
  117; North-West rebellion supplies, 168,
  172, 177.
Hughes, Capt. Patrick, 251.
Humboldt, Sask., 144, 224, 307.
Hungry (begging) Dance, 91.

Imasees – see Ayimāsis.
Indian agents/instructors, attitudes of, 72, 74,
  75–76, 78–79, 83, 92–94, 95, 98, 120–21,
  179–81, 182–83, 191; confrontations with
  Indians, 68, 76, 77–78, 81–82, 83, 91,
  92–95, 97–98, 100, 115–16, 192–94;
  enforcing policy, 68, 75–76, 79–80, 81–82,
  91, 94, 100–01, 102, 115–16; North-West
  rebellion, 141, 179–81, 182–83, 186, 191,
  192–94, 196, 197, 198, 212.
Indian conditions, hunger, 49, 55, 63–64, 65,
  66–67, 68–69, 72, 73, 74–75, 81, 82, 84–85,
  88–89, 115, 120, 124, 184–85, 186, 216;
  sickness, 49, 50, 86, 88–89, 90, 184–85.
Indian grievances, 49, 52–53, 54, 55–57;
  agents/instructors, 72, 79–80, 86, 120, 186;
  fresh meat, 67, 68–69, 77–78, 79, 86, 88,
  90, 117, 191, 196; farming assistance,
  59–60, 72, 75, 79, 85; rations policy, 62–63,
  65, 66–67, 68–70, 72–73, 74–75, 78, 79,
  81–82, 83–85, 116, 120, 122, 124, 193, 194,
  216; reserve locations, 57, 88, 115, 116;
  treaty promises, 79, 86, 88, 92, 115, 116,
  184–85.
Indian Head, Sask., 76–77, 81, 88.
Indian Mutiny, 220, 277, 283.

Indian policy – see Canadian Indian policy.
Indian reserves (see also individual nations
  and treaties), 31, 42, 52, 53, 55, 59, 62, 64,
  65–66, 73, 75, 86, 88, 94, 115; contiguous
  reserves, 57, 65, 79.
Indian treaties, 61–62, 63–64, 65, 71–72, 73,
  74–75, 78, 92, 114, 116, 120; No. 4, 44,
  52–53, 55, 57, 59, 77, 79, 88, 90; No. 6,
  53–59, 61, 63, 68, 70, 71, 74, 78, 79, 137;
  No. 7, 44, 59; famine clause, 57, 72, 120.
Iron Body (Pēyopiskowēniw, often called
  Napese), 199, 332; pictured, 117.
Irvine, Commissioner Acheson Gosford, 76,
  89–90, 139, 144, 149, 153, 155, 160, 161,
  162, 163, 166, 224, 235, 287, 290, 341.
Isbister, James, 104, 106.
Itka, 183, 332.

Jack Fish Bay, Ont., 176, 177.
Jack Fish Lake, Sask., 287, 289.
Jackson, Cicely, 128.
Jackson, Elizabeth, 128, 166.
Jackson, Thomas Eastwood, 116, 129, 133,
  163–64, 165–67, 273, 307; pictured, 289.
Jackson, Thomas Gething, 128, 134.
Jackson, William Henry (later Honoré Jaxon),
  124–25, 128–30, 131, 132–33, 134–35, 141,
  148–49, 159, 164, 165–67, 306–08, 316,
  317, 339–40.
Jacob, 247.
Jasper, Alta., 59.
Jefferson, Robert, 70, 72, 92–95, 97–98,
  184–85, 206, 207, 244–45, 247–48, 252,
  253, 255, 313–14.
Jobin, Ambrose, 143.
Johnstone, Thomas Cooke, 293.
Joseph, Chief, 248.
Judith Basin, Mont., 68.
Jukes, Dr. Augustus, 302, 308, 336.

Kāwēchetwēmot (or Kamēchetwemot), 96,
  97, 98, 100, 117, 199.
Keenan, Sgt. Harry, 121.
Kelly's Saloon, 209.
Keith, Hilton, 81.
Kerr Brothers, 140, 141.
Kerr, George, 141.
Kerr, John (Batoche), 141.
Kerr, John (Ontarion), 18, 37.
King Bird, 197; pictured, 117.
Kingston, Ont., 169, 175, 279.
Kingston Penitentiary, 335.
Kippen, Alex, 272–73.
Klondike gold rush, 341.

Labombarde, Alexis, 309.
Lac des Isles, Sask., 287.
Lac La Biche, Alta., 234–35, 261.
Lacombe, Fr. Albert, 336; pictured, 339.
Lac Ste. Anne, Alta., 210, 212.